THE POISON IN THE GIFT

Ritual, Prestation, and the Dominant Caste in a North Indian Village

Gloria Goodwin Raheja

The University of Chicago Press

Chicago and London

Gloria Goodwin Raheja is an associate of the Committee on Southern Asian Studies at the University of Chicago.

The University of Chicago Press, Chicago 60637
The University of Chicago Press, Ltd., London

Printed in the United States of America

97 96 95 94 93 92 91 90 89 88 54321

Library of Congress Cataloging-in-Publication Data

Raheja, Gloria Goodwin, 1950–
The poison in the gift : ritual, prestation, and the dominant caste in a north Indian village / Gloria Goodwin Raheja.
p. cm.
Bibliography: p.
Includes index.
1. Ceremonial exchange—India—Pahansu. 2. Gujars—Rites and ceremonies. 3. Brahmans—Rites and ceremonies. 4. Kinship—India—Pahansu. 5. Caste—India—Pahansu. 6. Pahansu (India)—Social life and customs. I. Title.
GN635.I6R34 1988
392'.0954'2—dc19 87-28924
CIP

ISBN 0-226-70728-8 (cloth)
0-226-70729-6 (paper)

CONTENTS

FIGURES

Plates appear on pages 189–200

TABLES

PREFACE

This monograph is a study of the semiotic aspects of giving and receiving, *len-den* as it is called, in the Hindi-speaking region of northern India. It is based on eighteen months of fieldwork, carried out mostly in the village of Pahansu, from September 1977 to March 1979. More specifically, it is a study of the way in which three important aspects of intercaste and kinship relations—aspects that I have called centrality and mutuality, as well as hierarchy—are differentially foregrounded and implemented in the contexts of the giving and receiving of particular named prestations.

My inquiries in the field, in Pahansu, came to address what Trautmann has called "the central conundrum of Indian social ideology," what Heesterman has referred to as "the inner conflict" of Indian tradition, what Dumont has characterized in terms of a distinction between religious ideology and "temporal power," and what Marriott has analyzed in terms of the varying transactional strategies of *jāti*s and *varṇa*s engaged in givings and receivings that transform the natures of the participants. My fieldwork came to be focused largely upon the relationship between Ksatriya and Brahman or, in local terms, between the Gujar landholders and cultivators and the Gaur Brahmans of Pahansu. In this locally enacted relationship between the dominant caste on the one hand and the Brahman and service castes on the other, as well as in the textual discourses concerning king and Brahman upon which Trautmann and Heesterman relied, the giving and receiving of prestations is central. The most important of these prestations is *dān*.

That this is the first ethnographic study to report in detail on the significance of *dān* and to explore systematically the semiotic aspects of this giving and receiving in relation to kinship, caste, and ritual is surprising, if only for the reason that *dān* is given great importance in Hindu textual traditions. Gonda (1965) has remarked on the striking continuity, from the Vedic through the Puranic texts, in the social and ritual significance placed upon the giving and receiving of *dān*. In the *Laws of Manu*, for example, it is said that in the first age of the cycle of four *yuga*s, the chief duty is the performance of austerities, in the second it is knowledge, and in the third, sacrifice. But in the fourth age, in which all of history has in fact been played out, it is the giving of *dān* that is the central value. Immediately following this verse in Manu, a description of the "duties" of the four *varṇa*s is given, in which the giving and the receiving of *dān* are crucial in what Manu calls the "protection of the universe" (*sarvasyāsya tu sargasya guptyārth*) and in the differentiation of the *varṇa*s themselves (Manu 1:86–91).

Dān is crucial to the life of the village as well. Through analyses of the ritual and linguistic contexts of the giving and receiving of *dān*, the chapters of this study demonstrate that the centrality of the dominant Gujar landholders of Pahansu in the local configuration of castes, their role as *jajmān*s ("sacrificers") and givers of *dān* par excellence, is not simply an empirical fact of their landholding or their "temporal power" in the village and the region, or a matter of their hierarchical position. The Pahansu data indicate that the central conception of *dān* as a prestation that, when given in the proper ritual contexts and to the appropriate recipients, transfers inauspiciousness and brings about the auspiciousness, well-being, and protection of the person, the family, the house, and the village, is far more important than hierarchical considerations in structuring intercaste and kinship relations within the village. Gujars as well as the other castes of the village view this sacrificial function—the protection of the village through the giving of *dān*—as the ideological core of Gujar dominance in Pahansu. That this ritual significance of the giving and receiving of *dān* has hitherto been virtually ignored in the ethnography of caste and kinship has, I suggest, distorted our understanding of crucial aspects of village social life in Hindu South Asia, particularly insofar as the position of the dominant caste is concerned.

The fieldwork upon which this study is based was supported by grants from the Social Science Research Council/American Council of Learned Societies, and from the American Institute of Indian Studies. I am grateful to the Delhi School of Economics, University of Delhi, and to Veena Das in particular, for granting me affiliation during my research in India.

Fieldwork among the Gujars of Saharanpur District would never have been possible without the help of my friend Mahipal S. Tomar of Meerut University. It was Mahipal who first suggested to me that I study the Gujar community, after I had decided to focus my research on a dominant landholding caste, and he very generously gave of his time and energy in helping me to find a village in which to live and work. More recently, his comments on an earlier version of the manuscript have helped me avoid several errors of interpretation. I cannot even begin to thank him for the assistance he has given me, or for the gift of his friendship.

During its long gestation period, this study has benefited from the careful readings given it by numerous teachers, colleagues, and friends.

My greatest debts are to McKim Marriott and they are more numerous than I could acknowledge here. Though I may perhaps have stressed, in these pages, the points at which our interpretations of South Asian social life have differed, the extent to which my own work has been shaped by his seminal insights, particularly his 1976 paper, will be obvious.

Many of the interpretations in these chapters have built upon the analyses of North Indian kinship and gift-giving in the work of Sylvia Vatuk. Sylvia has been a source of sage advice, both theoretical and practical, ever since the inception of this project, and it was because of her comments and questions that several of the sections in chapter 5 were greatly expanded from an earlier version.

I wish also to thank Jane Bestor, Ronald Inden, Jonathan Parry, Lee Schlesinger, and Thomas Trautmann. I have benefited both from their encouragement and from their criticisms of the analyses presented in these pages.

I could never adequately thank the many people of Pahansu who took me into their homes and their lives as a "sister" and a "daughter" and who are responsible for whatever success attended the fieldwork. There are however several individuals and families who went above and beyond the already rigorous demands of Gujar hospitality and whom I must single out for special thanks.

For nearly eighteen months, I lived in the household of Telu Ram and Jabar Singh, and it is not an overstatement to say that had it not been for their generosity in allowing me to join their family, the research could never have been carried out. Telu Ram's knowledge of Pahansu history and his general perspicacity were invaluable to me. My daily conversations with him always seemed to bring order and coherence to my observations of village life. Asikaur, my Pahansu "mother," looked after me, concerning herself not only with my well-being as we might think of it, but with my well-being and auspiciousness in her sense of them as well; and so from her I learned much of what those concepts entail in Pahansu. The younger wives, the *bahūs* of the house, Rajavati, Simla, and Santroj, patiently bore my awkward attempts to "participate," and made me feel at home in Pahansu.

The intelligence and solicitude of Mangal Singh and Sukhbir Singh greatly facilitated my fieldwork. My countless conversations with the women of their house—Bugli, Atri, Kamalavati, and Sansar—illuminated for me many aspects of the Gujar way of life; their companionship and sense of humor often buoyed my spirits during the many long days of fieldwork.

I am also grateful to Buddhi Prakash Kaushik, "Buddhu Pandit," for guiding me through the intricacies of ritual and astrology with extraordinary patience and good humor. Illam Singh Nai and his family extended many kindnesses to me; I shall always be grateful to them for sharing their joys and their sorrows with me.

Raj Raheja has been an unfailing source of support and encouragement, despite the long separations imposed by my language study and fieldwork in India. His confidence in me, when my own was often lacking, has kept me on course since the very beginning of my work in anthropology. Both our children, Kevin and Lauren, were born while this book was in preparation. I thank them for the joy they have brought to my life, a joy that puts everything else into perspective.

CHAPTER ONE

Introduction: Toward a Redefinition of "Dominance" in North Indian Society

The Village and the Region in Historical Perspective

When two strangers meet on a bus, at a pilgrimage place, or at a market town in northwestern Uttar Pradesh, the question often asked first is *kaun sā gām hai terā* ("What is your village?") and the comment that will often follow, when the name of the village is given, is *jāṭõ kā gām hai* ("It's a village of Jats"), or *gūjarõ kā gām hai* ("It's a village of Gujars"), or perhaps *rājpūtõ kā gām hai* ("It's a village of Rajputs"). Even by Brahmans and people of lower castes, villages in this part of Uttar Pradesh are frequently identified with the locally dominant landholding caste in residence there. In this part of the Upper Doab, the region between the Ganges and the Yamuna rivers, only one such caste normally occupies a particular village,[1] and its members may comprise as much as two-thirds of the total village population.

In southwestern Saharanpur District, where my fieldwork was carried out, Gujars are the predominant landholding caste. Nineteenth-century British records tell us that a large part of Saharanpur District was called "Gujarat" because of Gujar preponderance—in both population and landholding—and as late as the early twentieth century, the *parganā*s of Gangoh, Nakur, and Rampur, as well as bordering areas of Muzaffarnagar District, were still identified by this term (see fig. 1). According to the Census of 1891 and the Census of 1931, the Gujar population of Saharanpur District exceeded that of any other district in Uttar Pradesh except Meerut; in terms of percentage of population, Gujar dominance is more decisive in Saharanpur District than anywhere else in U.P. (Schwartzberg 1968,90).

Gujar predominance in the area is long-standing. The *Ain-i-Akbari* of 1596 indicates that they were the principal landholders in a number of *parganā*s in the Upper Doab by the sixteenth century (Elliot 1869, 2: map facing p. 202). By the mid-eighteenth century, they had expanded their holdings and had acquired considerable political power, centered especially at Dadri in Bulandshahar District, at Paricchatgarh in Meerut District, and at Landhaura in eastern Saharanpur District. This regional dominance and the kingship (*rājya*) exercised by Gujar chiefs still figure

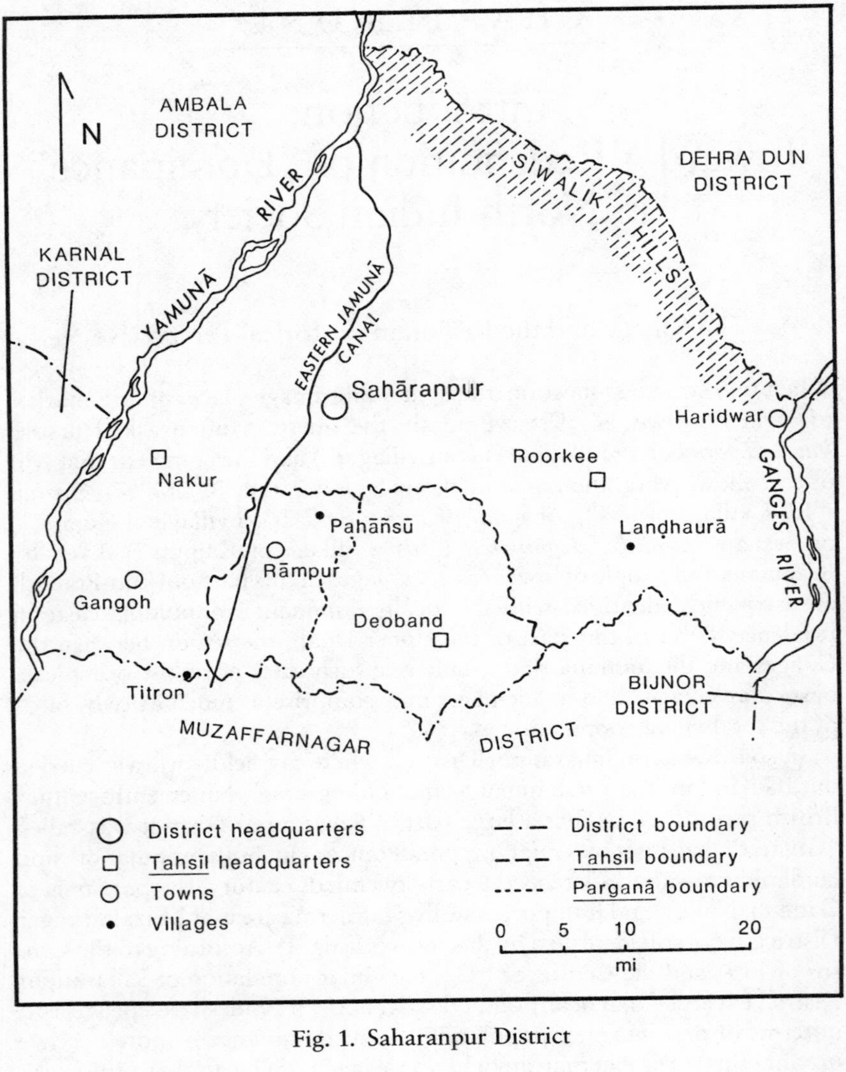

Fig. 1. Saharanpur District

prominently in oral traditions current among Saharanpur Gujars and in the depiction of their identity as Ksatriya "kings" in printed histories of the Gujar *jāti*. (See, for example, Varma 1971: 92–98.)

The Landhaura estate is particularly important in this respect. Gujars of the Khūbaṛ *got* (the clan still dominant in the village in which I worked) held more than 500 villages there, and that situation was confirmed in 1759 in a grant by a Rohilla governor of 505 villages and 31 hamlets to one Manohar Singh Gujar. By 1803 the Landhaura villages numbered 794 under Raja Ram Dayal Singh. These holdings, at least those in the original grant made by the Rohilla governor, were initially recognized by the British in land settlements concluded with Ram Dayal and his heirs. As the years passed, more and more settlements appear to have been made with the village communities, however, and by 1850 little remained of the once vast estate of the Landhaura Khūbaṛs (Atkinson 1875: 199–206). But Gujar women all over Saharanpur District still sing at weddings of the greatness of the *lanḍhaurevāle rājā*.

In the southwestern part of Saharanpur District, in "Gujarat," there were no such large estates, but there Gujar dominance, though less spectacular, has been marked by no such dramatic declines. Early British records report that Gujars were the chief landholders in the district as a whole, and particularly in "Gujarat," the three *parganā*s of Gangoh, Nakur, and Rampur. According to the 1870 Settlement Report, for example, Gujars held 20,070 acres of land in Rampur *parganā*, followed by Rajputs with 16,109 acres, Baniyas with 6,479 acres, Brahmans with 1,605 acres, and Jats with 1,419 acres. Though statistics on the current distribution of land by caste are unavailable, it would seem that the relative standings of Gujars, Rajputs, and Jats as landholders in the district have persisted.

The *parganā* of Rampur has long been a prosperous area, with its fertile clay and loam soils and canal irrigation.[2] The chief crop of the spring harvest (*rabī*) is wheat, and very fine rice is grown in the winter season (*kharīf*). Sugarcane, a ten-month crop, has been extensively cultivated for many years. The cultivation of sugarcane in the area was facilitated by the opening of the Eastern Jamuna Canal in 1830. The canal and its network of distributaries has had a profound impact in Rampur *parganā* and in the western part of Saharanpur District as a whole. By the latter part of the nineteenth century, 54.76 percent of the cultivated acreage in Rampur *parganā* was being irrigated by the canal; this figure was the highest of any *parganā* in the district.

While there have been some negative environmental effects of canal irrigation, particularly water-logging (Nevill 1921, 304) and salinization of the soil (Stone 1984, 134–44), and some agricultural diseconomies in comparison with well-irrigation (Whitcombe 1972, 61–119), the canal, on balance, has had a positive effect on the prosperity of the Upper Doab region. Canal irrigation allowed for a greater intensity of cultivation, that is, a greater percentage of *dofaslī* land, fields bearing two crops in the course of a year (Stone 1984, 111–13). This was particularly true in Rampur *parganā* (Nevill 1921, 305–6). Gujar cultivators largely abandoned the use of wells in many villages of southwestern Saharanpur District because canal irrigation required less labor and fewer bullocks, and thus it freed these resources for other productive uses that raised, overall, the yields of both irrigated and unirrigated fields in a holding (Stone 1984, 102–4). Canal irrigation may also have been adopted because it was not disruptive of, and may in fact have reinforced the characteristic landholding pattern of the Upper Doab, in which peasant cultivators rather than large *zamīndārs* more often held proprietary rights (ibid., 346).

H. Le Poer Wynne, an assistant settlement officer in Saharanpur District, assessed the three *tahsīls* of Deoband (in which the Rampur *parganā* is located), Nakur, and Roorkee in 1867, and was struck in particular by the prosperity and agricultural competence of the Gujars of Gangoh and Rampur *parganās*:

> I came continually upon villages in which the proprietors had been relieved from the heaviest embarrassments, and had been reclaimed from persistent habits of crime by the introduction of canal water. . . . They have been reclaimed from the improvident habits and the tendency to cattle-raiding which characterize their brethren. This happy result is due to the canal. The reward which the use of canal water held out to industry was so great, so immediate, and so certain, that all the traditions of the caste succumbed to the prospects of wealth, so that the Goojurs throughout the region watered by the canal are the most orderly, contented and well-to-do of men. (*Report of the Settlement of Saharunpore* 1870)

Similar observations concerning the "civilizing" effect of the canal on Gujar communities in the Upper Doab region were made in the nineteenth century by British settlement officers in Muzaffarnagar, Meerut, and Bulandshahar Districts as well (Whitcombe 1972, 84–85; Stone 1984, 109–10, 343–44).

Wynne and the other settlement officers may have overestimated what they called the "civilizing" effect of the Eastern Jamuna Canal in transforming the way of life of the Gujar communities in the Upper Doab. Nevertheless, the Gujars of these districts have long been considered quite different from their caste "brethern" in other parts of North India who make their living as wandering pastoralists, who occupy a low position in local caste hierarchies and a peripheral position in village social life, and who are often held in disrepute.

As the predominant landholders of southwestern Saharanpur District, Gujars prospered. The Settlement Reports indicate that most of the land was worked by village landholders, who in general were able to escape heavy indebtedness and the transferrence of their land to Baniya moneylenders. Stokes's analyses (1978) of Settlement Report figures show that in 1868 Baniyas held 10.4 percent of the cultivated land in Rampur *parganā,* a low percentage even in comparison with other areas of Saharanpur District, in which, as a whole, losses to Baniya moneylenders and others were lower than in the rest of Uttar Pradesh. Stokes's figures seem also to indicate that Gujars lost proportionately less land than the other agricultural castes—Rajputs, Jats, and various Muslim groups—of the district (ibid., 162).

In Pahansu, very little land appears to have been transferred from the Gujars of the Khūbaṛ *got* in the nineteenth century. One field of a Gujar farmer is nowadays called *baniyõ kā khet* because it had once been made over to a *mahājan,* a Baniya moneylender, but this loss persists in village memory as an exception. Villagers still talk about Pankī Sāhib (R. Spankie, the Saharanpur district magistrate in the 1850s) as being ultimately responsible for the transfers that did occur in somewhat greater numbers in some of the villages in the vicinity of Pahansu.[3] That the British district magistrate should, 120 years later, still be held responsible for the losses to Baniya moneylenders is not surprising; as Stokes (1978, 179) points out, most transfers of land to Baniyas stemmed from indebtedness prompted by the pressures of land revenue demands.[4] Within the purview of Pahansu residents, villages in which the *adhikār* ("entitlement," "responsibility") of much of the land was transferred to Baniyas or to large landholders (*jagīrdār*s) are still described as *kacce gām:* they are "uncooked," "incomplete," "imperfect," "incoherent," or "unripe" villages, in contrast to the *pakkā* ("cooked," "perfect," "coherent," "permanent") villages, like Pahansu, in which Gujar cultivators retained possession of their lands. Today this contrast appears to be associated with important differences in the characteristic form of local social relations among castes.

People in Pahansu point to Nainkhera and Landhauri, neighboring (*guwāṇḍ*) villages, as examples of the landholding configurations that persist as a result of the land transfers at the time of Pankī Sāhib (see fig. 2). In these villages, some land is held by people of most of the resident castes, but in Pahansu, where land transfers to Baniyas were very limited, virtually all of the land is still held by Gujar cultivators of the Khūbaṛ *got,* a monopoly that underscores their centrality in the social and ritual life of the village.

Several aspects of the social situation in nineteenth-century Saharanpur may shed some light on the differential rates of land transferral and the consequent differences in present-day landholding patterns. In *The Peas-*

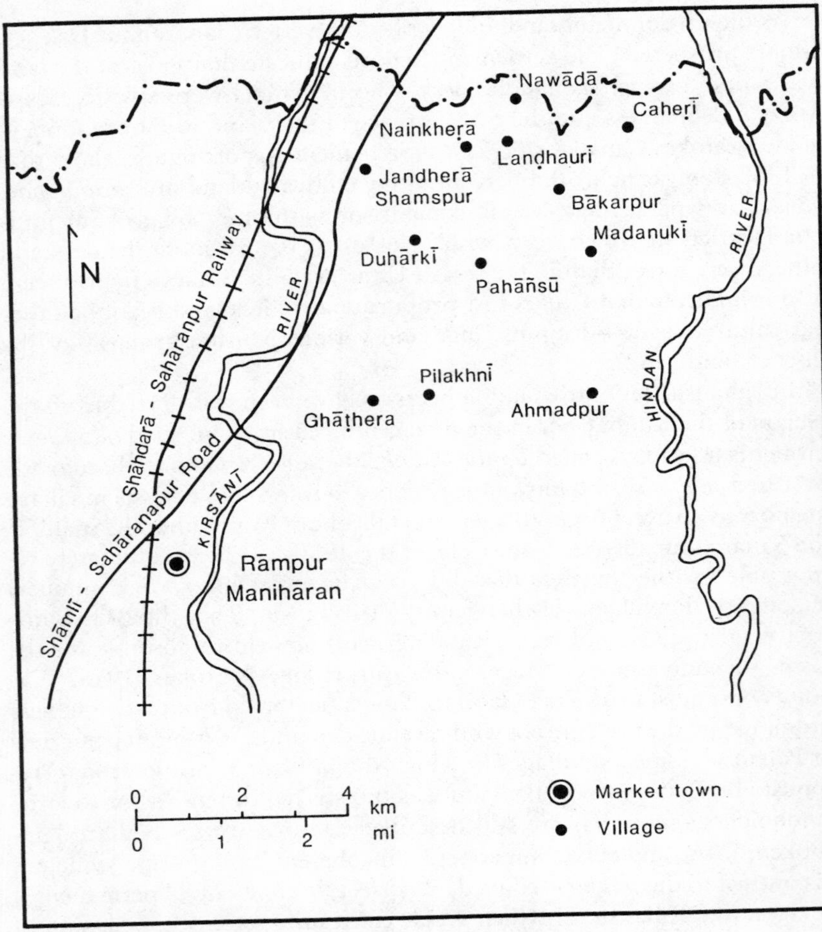

Fig. 2. Northern Rampur *parganā*

ant and the Raj, Stokes has indicated that in this part of Uttar Pradesh, certain factors seem to have been associated with a freer circulation of proprietary rights in the nineteenth century. First, where *zamīndārī* land tenures were prevalent, he points out, a market in land titles and the circulation of proprietary rights were more likely; in contrast, where cultivating "brotherhoods" held the land in *bhāīācārā* or *paṭṭīdārī* tenures (as was the case in Pahansu), land transfers to outsiders were much less likely to occur.[5]

Kessinger (1974, 69) has also pointed out that in nineteenth-century Vilyatpur, a Jat *bhāīācārā* village in the Panjab, although individual families held land that could be transmitted to descendants or leased to tenants, the tenurial pattern limited the right to dispose of the land through sale. Land in such villages could be sold to other Jats within the village, but not outside of this proprietary body. As is the case in Pahansu, the dominant caste in Vilyatpur still retains control of virtually all of the land.

The second factor that Stokes considers to be of importance in limiting land transfers in the nineteenth century is the supravillage organization of the clan area (the *khāp,* as it is called among the Muzaffarnagar Jats, or the *ilākā,* among the Saharanpur Gujars). Perhaps even more than the tenurial structure of the individual village, strong local clan organization seems to have been of crucial significance in minimizing, not only extra-caste transfers of land, but also transfers outside the locally dominant clan (*got*). Stokes gives as an illustration H. Le Poer Wynne's description, from the 1870 Settlement Report, of areas of the Gangoh *parganā* (in which Gujars of the Baṭār *got* were dominant) in southwest Saharanpur District:

> [These areas are] held and cultivated by utterly improvident Goojurs who form a compact mass, able and willing to keep any outsider from settling among them. A few wealthy bankers have ventured to purchase a whole village here and there, but as a rule all who have ventured to buy up the share of an impoverished coparcener have been unable to make their footing good in the new "purchase." The warning has been accepted by moneyed men in general, so that now a Goojur of these parts can get no credit whatever. (Stokes 1978, 169)

Clan territories, *ilākā,* have remained more or less intact at least since the mid-nineteenth century. British administrative officers, writing in the Settlement Reports and in the District Gazetteers, described groups of villages held by various *gots* in specific localities: the twelve villages held by the Chonkar (the *bārah chonkarõ*) in the area around Titron in the southern part of Gangoh parganā near the Muzaffarnagar border, the "fifty-two" villages (*bāonī*) of the Baṭār Gujars, and the "eighty-four" villages (*caurāsī*) of the Khūbaṛ *got* (including the village of Pahansu) in the Rampur *parganā*.[6] Although these numbers are conventional numerations not to be taken literally, large numbers of villages in these areas are still held by Gujars of these particular *got*s, and the "clan territories" and the solidarities they represent are still of major importance in elections, marriage negotiations, cooperative ventures in the marketing of sugar cane, and in the image Gujars have of themselves as prosperous and powerful men of the Ksatriya *varṇa*.

If, as Stokes suggests, the existence of these "clan territories" was an important factor in minimizing land loss and the dispersal of proprietary rights on the part of the dominant caste in the nineteenth century, it is significant that Pahansu, a village of Khūbaṛs in the Khūbaṛ *ilākā*, experienced relatively few land transferrals, while in neighboring villages not of the Khūbaṛ *got* (populated by Gujars more-or-less isolated from others of their own clan) land loss was much more common. It is these villages that Pahansu people describe as "incoherent" (*kaccā*).

Despite, then, the introduction of private proprietary rights in land and the idea of land as a commodity during colonial rule, and despite the sometimes disruptive effects of heavy revenue demands on indebtedness, the basic features of landholding in Pahansu, and in the surrounding villages held by Gujars of the Khūbaṛ *got*, seem to have remained virtually intact. Some resistance to the idea of land as simply an alienable, anonymous commodity, to be bought and sold on the market, is still very much in evidence in Pahansu. Something of the local oral history of Gujar landholding in the village may help us to understand this resistance.

According to materials provided by the Bhāṭ, the genealogist who serves the Khūbaṛ clan,[7] and oral accounts I heard in the village, Gujars have been the landholders in Pahansu for twelve generations, or about 250–300 years. Oral accounts assert that Hindu Gujars of the Khūbaṛ *got* were living in Islamnagar, a village said to be near the Yamuna River. Because of conflicts with Muslim landholders there, Khūbaṛs left that village and lived for a time in a village called Dhedpur.[8] From there some of the clan settled other villages in the *khadir* (low-lying land near the river), and others went to Pahansu and made their living, at first, by cattle-herding. Pahansu land was at that time, according to these oral accounts, held by Muslims of the Saini *jāti*, a caste of gardeners and cultivators now found principally in Bijnor, Muzaffarnagar, and Saharanpur districts. The Khūbaṛ Gujars, it is said, began to acquire land and to consolidate their position in the village. With the help of fellow Khūbaṛs from the *khadir*, they finally drove the Sainis from the village. Then they built their houses and forts and cultivated their fields as the sole landholders of Pahansu.[9]

The Khūbaṛ Gujars of Pahansu trace their ancestry to a man named

Phule Singh, whose seven sons (Dalpath, Galpath, Jhandu, Mathal, Tetha, Raya, and Ruda) are said to be the ancestors of all of the Khūbaṛs in the *caurāsī* ("eighty-four" villages) in Rampur *parganā* (fig. 3). Jhandu is the ancestor of the Pahansu Khūbaṛs, although many generations elapsed before his descendant Hetham actually settled in the village of Pahansu. Hetham had four sons. Munshi, the first, had no offspring, and the second, Hirdha, is said to have founded another village near Pahansu. Only one household today remains in Pahansu as the descendants of Birkhan, the third son. The rest of the Khūbaṛs are descended from Ramsa, the fourth son. Now Ramsa had three sons, only one of whom, Mohan, produced male offspring. Mohan himself had six sons, and it is from this generation (*pīṛhī*) that the major social divisions among Pahansu Khūbaṛs are traced.

The oldest and youngest of the six sons of Mohan had no sons of their own, but the descendants of the other four form distinct units in Pahansu social life today. The second son of Mohan, Jadho, is the progenitor of a "lineage" unit (*kunbā*) called nowadays the *ādhevālā* or *gaṭhvālā kunbā*. The *kunbā* called *banglevālā* traces its ancestry to the third son, Naina, and the *jhūnke kā kunbā* is said to be descended from the fourth son of Mohan, Naurang. Dayaram was the fifth son, and the offspring of four of his sons (his youngest son left no progeny) form four additional *kunbā*s in the village. There are seven households today in Pahansu who trace their ancestry to Mokam, the eldest son, and they form the Dholi *kunbā*. The largest and perhaps most prosperous *kunbā* in Pahansu, called Sadhu *heṛā,* is descended from Harkishan. The Gulab *kā kunbā* is descended from Ramkishan, the third son, and the Dharamsingh *kā kunbā* from Nichar, the fourth son of Dayaram.

When recounting this succession, then, villagers distinguish seven "lineages." In most contexts, however, it is said that there are four *kunbā*s. The *banglevālā* and *jhūnke kā kunbā* are counted in the *ādhevālā kunbā* because of the "mixture" (*mel-jul*) and "brother conduct" (*bhāīācārā*) that are said to exist among them. The seven households of the Dholi *kunbā* are said to be a part of the Sadhu *heṛā kunbā*. These four *kunbā*s—the *ādhevālā,* Sadhu *heṛā,* Gulab *kā,* and Dharamsingh *kā*—are thus foremost in everyday village life and thought.

During the colonial period, these four *kunbā*s were of importance as *paṭṭī*s, landholding units for the collection of revenue. A *lambardār,* who by hereditary right represented the *paṭṭī* and collected the land revenues from it, existed for each of the units; the title *lambardār* still exists in the village and is often used for senior descendants of these men.[10] The contemporary relevance of the four *kunbā*s has still to do largely with the land. While villagers speak of a *kunbā* as being united in nurturance—*dūdh hamārā ek hī hai,* "our milk is one"—as being the descendants of a

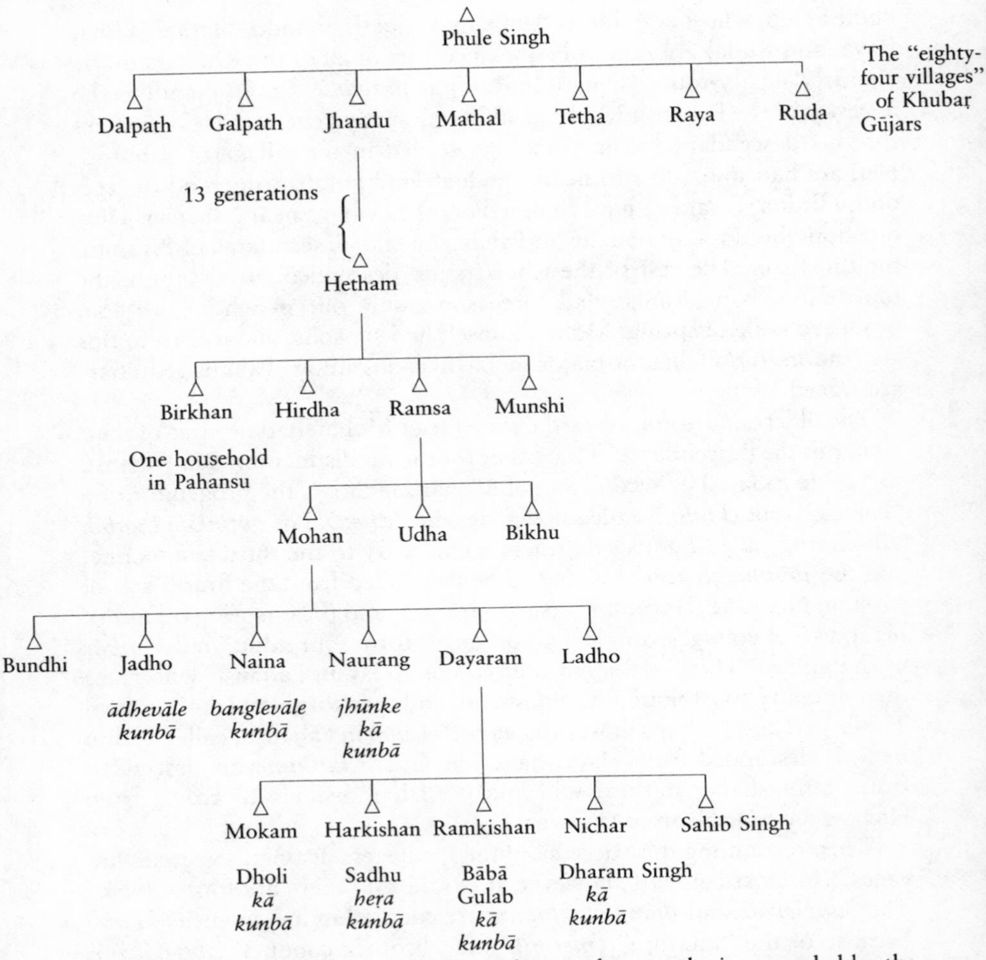

Fig. 3. Gujar *kunbā*s in Pahansu. According to the genealogies recorded by the Bhāṭ, between six and nine generations have passed since the generation in which "the four *kunbā*s divided," that is, the generation of Jadho, Naina, Naurang, and Dayaram.

single mother and father (*ek hī mā-bāp kī praṇālī hai*), and as united by a common place of origin (*paidāīś*), these meanings are of course contextually variable. Villagers may ascribe these qualities to one of the four *kunbā*s, but in other contexts, smaller units within the lineage group may also be termed *kunbā*s and then opposed to one another as having different "milk" and a different place of origin. (This "place of origin," *paidāīś*, refers to a particular house in the village or to a particular neighborhood in which the relevant ancestor is said to have been born.) There is a certain fixity, however, in the meaning and referent of the term *kunbā* insofar as landholding is concerned. It is a matter of great concern to Gujars in Pahansu that the land held by men of the *kunbā* remain within that *kunbā*. Here the referent of the term is invariable; in such contexts, a *kunbā* is one of the four major units that existed as *paṭṭīs* in the last century, and it is only within these units that land should be transferred.

It is also a matter of great importance that a landholder have sons to whom he can pass on the land he has inherited from his father, and a Gujar man who finds himself in a childless marriage will often take a second wife in the hope that she will provide him with a son. Occasionally, non-Khūbaṛ men who may be the husbands or sons of daughters of the village may come to work the Pahansu fields of a man who dies without a male heir, and these men are accepted in the village as long as they do not try to sell the land to someone outside the village or to someone outside the *kunbā* of the original owner.

Suresh, a man of the Kalśān *got* had, some years prior to my stay in Pahansu, come to the village to work the lands of his mother's father, a man of the Sadhu *heṛā kunbā*. He moved into his mother's father's house in *baṛvālā mohallā* ("banyan tree neighborhood," so named because of the large banyan tree that used to stand at the end of the street), one of the neighborhoods in which Sadhu *heṛā* families live. In 1978, Suresh decided that he wanted to sell his land and return to his own village in Muzaffarnagar District. He received an offer of Rs. 3,000 per *bīghā*, a total of Rs. 55,000, from a man of the *ādhevālā kunbā*. But Sadhu *heṛā* men were violently opposed to such a sale outside of the *kunbā* of the original owner. They said that Satave, a Sadhu *heṛā* man of banyan tree neighborhood, had the "right" (*hak*) to purchase the land because his father was the brother of Suresh's mother's father. Satave was willing to pay Rs. 2,000 per *bīghā*, but Suresh argued that this was not enough and insisted that he would sell the land to the man of the *ādhevālā kunbā*. The Sadhu *heṛā* men remained adamant, and a village *pancāyat* meeting was held to settle the dispute. The village council decided that Suresh was not obligated to sell the land specifically to Satave, as many of the men of banyan tree neighborhood were pressuring him to do, but that he could not sell the land to anyone outside of the Sadhu *heṛā kunbā*. Suresh then announced that he had decided to stay in Pahansu because he said that he wanted Rs. 3,000 per *bīghā* of land and none of the Sadhu *heṛā* men were willing to pay that much. Things remained like this for several weeks, but once again Suresh became determined to sell the land. After a number of moves and countermoves, the land was sold in various parcels at varying prices, but none of it was sold outside the Sadhu *heṛā kunbā*. Village opinion weighed too heavily for Suresh to be able to sell the land as if it were simply a matter of private property that could be bought and sold at will.

My data on land transfers within the village during the past century are at best anecdotal, but the circumstances surrounding one of the very few inter-*paṭṭī* transfers of land that I know about may be instructive.

Sometime around 1925, Rajaram, the eldest man of the only family in Pahansu descended from Birkhan (see fig. 3), mortgaged his land to one Dalechand, a Baniya moneylender from Deoband. The mortgage (*girvī*) was apparently defaulted upon, and Dalechand announced his intention to sell the land at auction. A *pancāyat* meeting was held in Pahansu, and a pledge was made (by dropping salt into a small pot of water, a powerful pledge even now) not to allow the land to be sold. But a long chain of surreptitious negotiations with the Baniya followed, and the land was finally purchased by a man of the Sadhu *heṛā kunbā,* whose grandson now calls the fields that were purchased the *tālevālī zamīn,* the land of Tala, the father of Rajaram. It may very well be the case that this inter-*paṭṭī* transfer of land was not successfully blocked because of the relatively peripheral position of the family of Rajaram, the lone descendants of Birkhan in the village, who are not considered to belong to any of the major *kunbā*s of Pahansu.

Around the same time, in 1928, a man of the Sadhu *heṛā kunbā* incurred a very large debt at the marriage of his daughter, and his land was held as security. When the payments could not be met, there was an attempt to sell the land. But three other landholders of the debtor's *kunbā* redeemed the land and returned it to the original landholder, because of their strong feeling that the land of the *kunbā* should not be alienated. As Telu Ram, the grandson of Goharu, one of the three landholders, said to me: "It was a matter of our prestige (*izzat*). Our noses would have been cut off [a great insult would have been suffered] if the land had gone away." In this second case, the transfer of land was prevented through the action of the men of the landholder's *paṭṭī.* But in the case of Rajaram, the transfer of land did occur, perhaps because he stood in some ways outside of this very strong *paṭṭī* organization.

In these relatively recent incidents, we have a glimpse of the sort of mechanism, the sort of attitudes about the alienability of land, that may have prevented wholesale loss of land in the nineteenth century. Of crucial significance in these land disputes was the very strong *kunbā* or *paṭṭī* organization, around which seems to have crystallized the idea of the unbreakable connection between land and its cultivator. At another level, a similar connection between the land and the *got* may have been operative when, as Stokes observes, land loss in the nineteenth century was kept to a minimum in areas of strong clan organization.

Historically, these aspects of landholding—the *bhāīācārā* and *paṭṭi-*

dārī tenures prevalent in the southwestern part of Saharanpur District, among Gujars in particular; the tenacity of the "clan area" in both landholding and kinship relationships; as well as the strong intravillage *paṭṭī* or *kunbā* organization that in Pahansu still prevents transfers of land outside of a relatively small kinship unit—have not only stabilized the distribution of proprietary rights, but also constituted meaningful centers in relation to which the giving and receiving of goods and services occur and are understood today.

The focus of this study is the analysis of the linguistic and ritual contexts of the prestations—the daily giving and receiving of many types of goods and services—that are crucial to the on-going social life of the village and in the constitution of Gujar dominance in Pahansu. Many such prestations have been partially described in the context of the so-called *jajmānī* system, the system of allotting customary shares of the harvest to members of various castes (Brahmans, Barbers, Washermen, Sweepers, Potters, Carpenters, and so on) tied to particular cultivators in hereditary service arrangements. In Pahansu, despite the introduction of cash-cropping and a great many other innovations in agricultural practice, such arrangements are still of great importance. Not only do many of the service castes derive most of their livelihood from these distributions at the harvests and at other times of the year, but Gujars, as well as people of the other castes, understand and construe their relatively central or peripheral positions in the local configuration of castes as being constituted in and through these arrangements and prestations. These prestations, I will argue in the following chapters, are not reducible to matters of hierarchy nor to what Dumont (1970) has termed the "temporal power" of the dominant caste and a "shame-faced Ksatriya model." Nor are they wholly reducible to the mutuality of which Wiser (1936) wrote.

In many parts of India, the economic and symbolic significance of such prestations has apparently declined or even disappeared. In his 1957 paper "Reciprocity and Redistribution in the Indian Village," Neale sketched the relationship between these customary arrangements, specifically, the distribution of shares of the harvest, and the precolonial situation in which a "profusion of overlapping claims" rather than "ownership," alienability, and market considerations characterized landholding within the village community and in the wider polity. The prestations made in the context of the *jajmānī* "system" are only understandable, and possible, in relation to a conception of land based at least partially on principles that are not of the market.

Now Stokes, as we have seen, has very neatly traced a situation in some areas of the Upper Doab (including the *parganā* of Rampur) in which factors such as the *bhāīācārā* and *paṭṭidari* tenures and the "clan areas" (and, as we have noted, the strong *kunbā* or *paṭṭī* organization) mitigated against the complete transformation of land into a commodity, and hence against the dispersal of land among different castes. I have tried to show that these factors are still relevant to an understanding of the position of Gujars in rural Saharanpur District today. I am also suggesting that their presence and their impact on ideas and practices connected with landholding may in some measure account for the surprising extent to which prestations of many kinds, some of which we associate with the *jajmānī* "system," have remained at the core of Pahansu social life and Gujar dominance there. I will return to this theme in the last section of this chapter.

What I will have to say in the following chapters about the semiotic of exchange concerns, then, the way of life and ways of thinking that I observed in a particular village situated in a very particular and complex set of historical and geographic circumstances. The prestation patterns that here structure so much of the intercaste and kinship relations are, in this part of northwestern Uttar Pradesh, particularly elaborate and pervasive. It is possible, though, that what I have to say of these prestations and this way of life, and of the cultural constructs that are implicated in them, may be of relevance for understanding gift-giving, ritual, and dominance in other parts of Hindu South Asia.

Pahansu Today

Pahansu is located in Deoband *tahsīl,* in the northwestern part of the *parganā* of Rampur, about eight kilometers from the small market town of Rampur.[11] To reach the village, one leaves the main Shamli-Saharanpur road at the village of Jandhera and travels on a *pakkā* road that winds through the fields of Duharki, Nainkhera, and Pahansu before reaching the Pahansu *abādī,* or habitation site (see figs. 4 and 5). Villagers frequently travel this road—on foot, on bicycles, or on carts pulled by water-buffaloes—to Rampur for the Thursday market, to the bus stop at Jandhera, or to Saharanpur, the district headquarters approximately fifteen kilometers north of the village. Narrower unpaved roads connect Pahansu with the surrounding villages, and these are traveled on foot and by water-buffalo cart by the Pahansu Washermen, Barbers, Potters, and Brahmans who serve several of the smaller nearby villages; by women who, accompanied by a husband or a husband's younger brother, may visit women of their natal village who are married in a *guwāṇḍ,* a neighboring village of Pahansu; and by the residents of nearby villages who come to the schools and the dispensary in Pahansu.

Pahansu villagers cultivate a total of 1,532 acres, nearly all of which is irrigated by a branch of the Eastern Jamuna Canal, and by supplementary

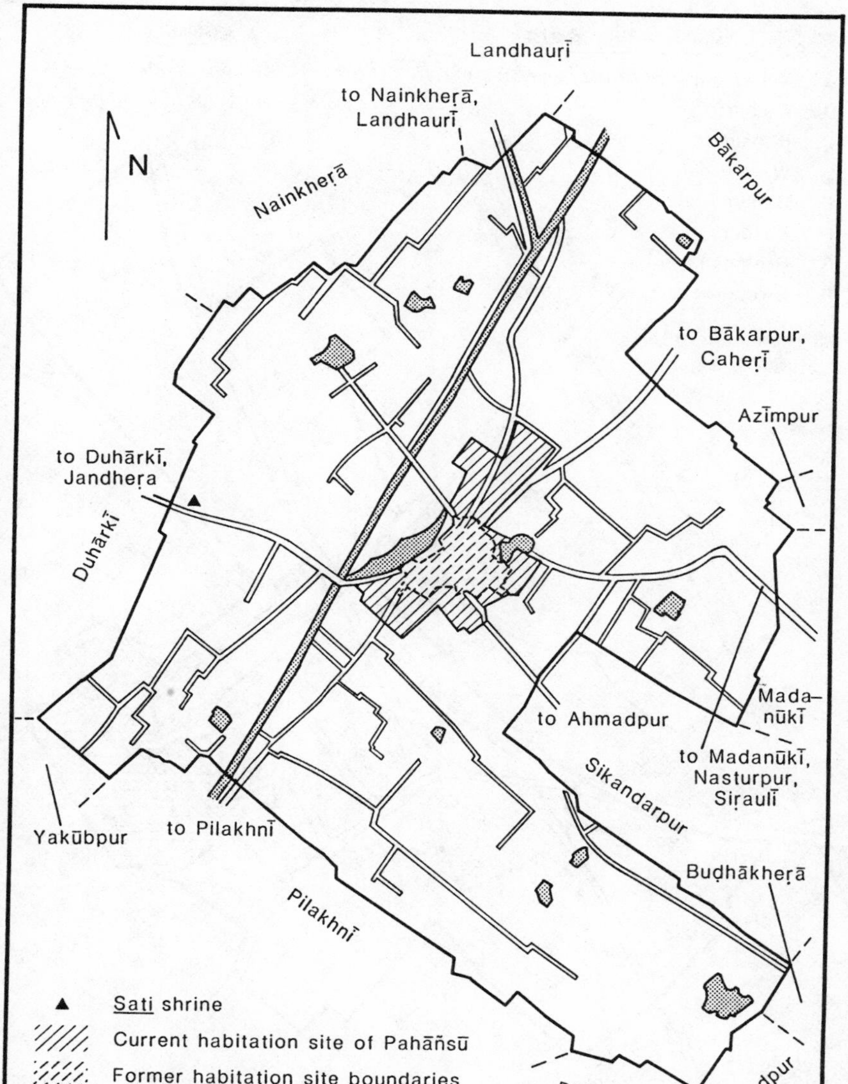

Fig. 4. Pahansu habitation site, fields, and surrounding villages

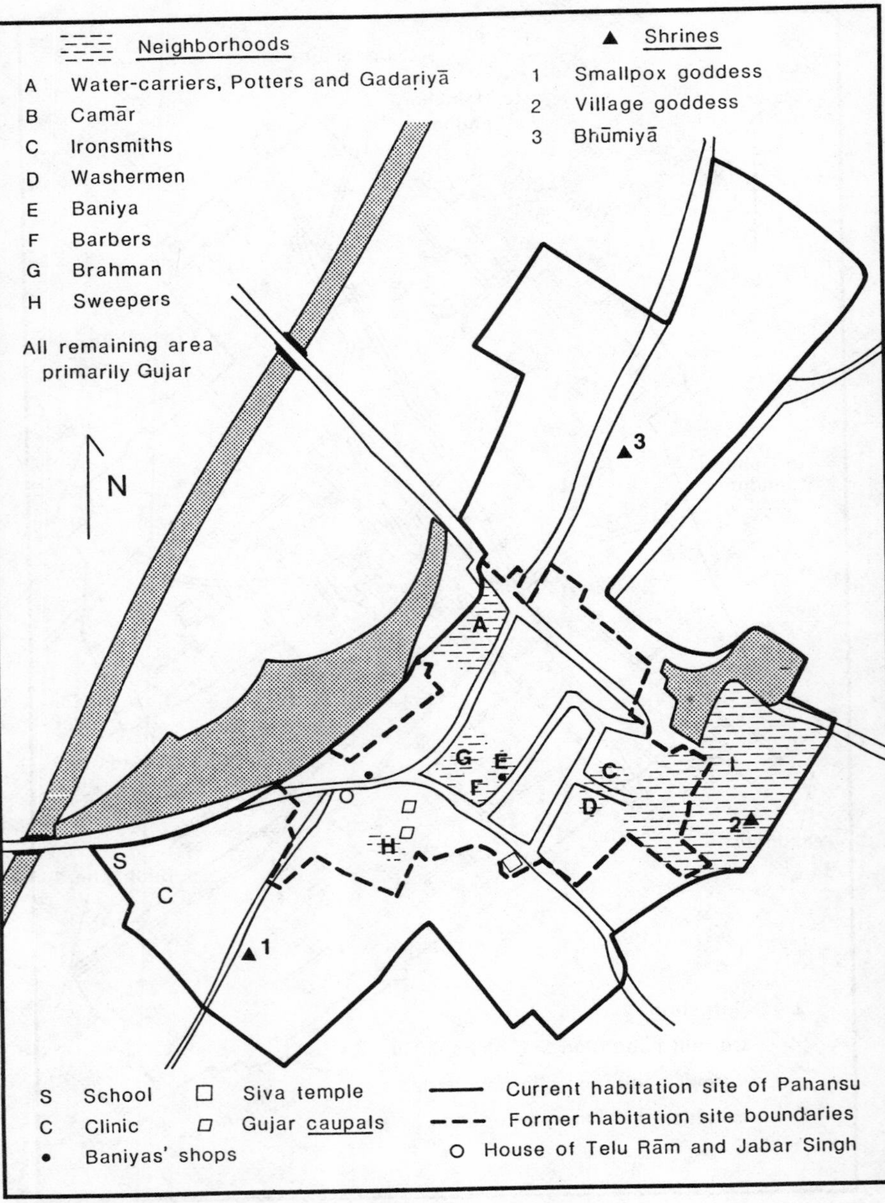

Fig. 5. Pahansu habitation site (*abādī*)

TABLE 1
Distribution of Landholdings in Pahansu (1978)

Size of Holding (acres)	Number of Landholding Families
<1	14
1–5	60
5–10	79
10–15	22
15–20	5
20–30	7
30 or more	4*

*These four holdings include one of 34 acres, one of 43 acres, one of 57 acres, and one of 60 acres.

tube wells. In all, 1,275 acres lie within the boundaries of Pahansu itself, and the remaining fields are in the tracts of the neighboring villages of Bakarpur, Sikandarpur, Pilakhni, Duharki, Nawada, and Cehari. All but 28.6 acres of this land is held by Gujar cultivators; four Brahman families hold a total of 20.5 acres (some of which was acquired at the time of the implementation of the Zamindari Abolition Act, and some was acquired as *dān* from Gujars) and twelve Leatherworkers hold a total of 8.55 acres. Wheat, rice, and sugarcane are, as in the Rampur *parganā* as a whole, the principal crops grown on this land. Some villagers also grow potatoes, pulses, *bathuā* (*Chenopodium album*), carrots, cauliflower, and mustard for home use. A few of the more prosperous farmers have very small mango orchards on their lands, and their wives may set aside small plots for the planting of cotton, processed at home for family use.

Pahansu irrigation records list a total of 191 landholdings; of these, about 25 have been subdivided recently into two or three separate holdings. The distribution of land, as recorded in the irrigation records, is shown in table 1.

The people of Pahansu, numbering approximately 2,500 in 1978, all live in a central habitation site surrounded by cultivated fields. The *abādī* includes not only the houses, the Gujar meeting places (*caupāl*), the three small shops run by Jain Baniyas, and the schools, but also the *gher*s of many of the Gujar agriculturalists. *Gher*s are walled enclosures for cows and water buffaloes that usually include a sitting place, where men gather at night to discuss politics and village affairs. Many new *gher*s have been built in recent years on the outskirts of the *abādī* in what were once cultivated fields. Electricity had, in 1979, not yet reached the village, but Pahansu was served by both junior and senior basic schools, a dispensary, a post office located in the house of the Barber postman, the three small shops selling matches, tea, sugar, kerosene, cooking oil, and other household sundries (payment for which is usually made in grain), and a tea-stall at the outskirts of the village. Three Gujar farmers and a Goldsmith operated presses for processing sugarcane into jaggery for village use.

People of fifteen castes (*jātis*) live in Pahansu. Gujars are the most numerous, comprising slightly more than one-half of the total population. Nearly all of the Gujars are of the Khūbaṛ *got*. The few Gujar men of other clans who now live in the village originally came there to work the lands of a wife's father or mother's father who had had no sons to inherit his land. There are two households of Gujars of the Barsohe *got* in Pahansu, a family of Kalśān Gujars, and one of the Baṭār *got*. Khūbaṛ identity looms large in the affairs of the village and of the region, and these Gujars of other clans are always regarded somewhat as outsiders in the village. The two families of the Barsohe *got,* for example, are always referred to by everyone, even people of other castes, as *barsohevāle* ("the Barsohe ones"). Their men take very limited roles in village affairs, even though one of the families settled in Pahansu about 150 years ago, and the other approximately 100 years ago.

The internal divisions of the Pahansu Khūbaṛs have been sketched in the previous section. The division into four *kunbā*s or *paṭṭī*s bears some relationship to residential patterns within the *abādī*. Families of the Sadhu *heṛā kunbā* reside mostly in the center of the village, just south of the main Brahman neighborhood, and in the southwestern part of the habitation site. Houses of the *ādhevāle kunbā* are clustered primarily in the northern part of the habitation site, while those of the Gulab *kā kunbā* and the *kunbā* of Dharam Singh are located primarily in the southeastern part of the village. *Paṭṭī* demarcations within the habitation site may at one time have been of greater salience than they are at the present time, particularly now that some of the more prosperous landholders have begun to build new, more substantial houses at the outskirts of the old *abādī* boundaries.

All but a very few of the Gujar families are landholders; those who are not work the land of other Gujars on a share-cropping (*baṭāī*) basis, or they work as agricultural laborers. The principal occupations of the other castes in Pahansu, together with the approximate number of households in the village, are given in table 2.

The structural position of Gujars in the caste configuration of the village and the region is dependent not only on their possession of the land, but also on the pattern of their relationships with the other castes in terms of the giving and receiving of specific named prestations, as the "protectors" and *jajmān*s ("sacrificers") of the village. Of the fourteen non-Gujar castes of Pahansu, six are involved in hereditary *jajmānī* relationships with Gujars and obtain their livelihood primarily through the acceptance of grain from Gujar *jajmān*s. In return for the performance of their spe-

TABLE 2

CASTE AND OCCUPATION IN PAHANSU

Caste Name	Traditional Occupation	Number of Households	Occupation in Pahansu
Gūjar	agriculturalist	210	owner cultivator
Brahman	priest	8	priest, postman
Baniyā	merchant	3	shopkeeper
Sunār	goldsmith	2	silversmith, sugarcane press operator
Dhīmān (Baṛhaī)	carpenter	1	carpenter
Kumhār	potter	3	potter, tailor
Nāī	barber	3	barber, postman
Dhobī	washerman	2	washerman
Gaḍariyā	shepherd	4	agricultural laborer, weaver
Jhī̃var	water-carrier	20	agricultural laborer, basket-weaver
Luhār	ironsmith	2	blacksmith
Telī	oil-presser	2	begging, cotton-carder, agricultural laborer
Manihāran	bangle-seller	1	bangle-seller
Camār	leatherworker	100	agricultural laborer
Bhangī	sweeper	17	sweeper, midwife[a]

[a] A number of Bhangī men are employed in Calcutta, but the small amounts of cash that they have been able to send to their wives and children in the village have not permitted the latter to abandon their traditional employments in Pahansu.

cific services, Barbers, Washermen, Sweepers, Carpenters, and Ironsmiths receive, as *kamīn*s of their Gujar *jajmān*s, payments of grain at the *sāvanī* harvest of rice in the month of Kārttik, and at the *sāṛhī* harvest of rice in the month of *baisākh*. *Phaslānā* (from *phasal,* "harvest"), as these prestations are called, is viewed as payment for the household and agricultural services rendered by members of these castes, who are said to be "attached" or "joined" (*lage hue* or *joṛe hue*) to their hereditary Gujar *jajmān*s, and therefore to have a "right" (*hak*) to a "share" (*hissā*) of the newly harvested grain from the fields of their *jajmān*s. Additional payments, also conceived of as shares, are given by Gujars to nearly all of the castes in the village (except Baniyas) for the performance of various ritual services, mostly on the occasions of festivals, marriages, births, and deaths.

Prestations construed as shares are not the only type given by Gujars to those castes attached to them in hereditary service relationships. Brahman *purohit*s (hereditary family priests) attached to Gujar families also receive portions of the two harvests. These portions constitute the bulk of their incomes, but they are not thought of as "shares" or as "payment," and they are not termed *phaslānā*. The Brahman's portion of the harvest, for which it is said that he has an "obligation" (*pharmāyā*) to accept rather than a "right" to claim, is called *dān*. Although the largest portions of the harvest given to other *kamīn* castes are not *dān*, people of these castes receive smaller *dān* prestations at the harvests, and they likewise have an "obligation" to accept *dān* from Gujars on very many occasions throughout the yearly cycle of seasons and festivals and throughout the life cycle. Gujars have a "right" to give *dān* to their *purohit* and their *kamīns*, and it is always given in the context of ritual actions that are said to promote the "well-being [achieved through] gift-giving" (*khair-khairāt*) and "auspiciousness" (*śubh*) of the Gujar donors through the transferral of inauspiciousness (*nāśubh*) to the recipients.

While it is the case that people of all *jātis* give *dān* at various times, either to specific kinsmen or to other castes, Gujars are the *jajmāns* and givers of *dān* par excellence in the village. It is they who fill this role at the ritual of Bhūmiyā, "the one of the land," the village deity in whose ritual nearly all of the castes participate, each *jāti* having a specific function to fulfill in relation to the whole. Gujars have the ritual performed for the "protection" and well-being of the village as a whole, they provide food for the feast that follows, and they give the *dān* to Brahmans at the conclusion of the day-long ritual in the month of Bhādwe. Brahmans officiate in their capacity as priests and cook the food that is to be offered to the deity and the food for the feast. It is also their "obligation" to accept the offerings to Bhūmiyā as the *pujāpā*, the *dān* of the ritual. Barbers make banana-leaf plates and clean the cooking vessels, Potters provide clay vessels, Sweepers beat on their drums, Water-carriers bring water for the ritual and for the feast (the only occasion on which this caste performs its traditional function), and so on. In the ritual for Bhūmiyā, Brahmans accept *dān* for the auspiciousness of the village as a whole, while the other castes are involved in duties of quite a different sort. But in many other contexts—the various calendrical rituals and the rituals of the life cycle—Brahmans and the other castes involved in *jajmānī* relationships with Gujars perform identical ritual functions as recipients of *dān*. Moreover, Gujars regard it as extremely significant that they never accept *dān* at all, except for the "gift of a virgin" (*kanyā-dān*) at the time of a marriage. Members of all other *jātis* frequently give *dān* to the husbands of their daughters and sisters (who are called *dhiyānā* in such contexts), but except for the actual wedding gifts, Gujars never do so, though on some occasions they do give *dān* to married daughters and sisters, their *dhiyānī*. The specific *dān* prestations that people of other castes (both Brahmans and *kamīns*) give to these male kinsmen are given by Gujars to Brahmans or to the *kamīn* castes, and this too is held, by both Gujars and the other castes, as a significant aspect of the position of Gujars in the local configuration of castes.

Gujars see themselves and are seen by all others as standing at the center of village life. They cultivate the land and through the many prestations that they, as *jajmāns*, give to other castes, they not only provide the grain for village sustenance but bring about the well-being and auspiciousness of the entire village. The way in which this is accomplished, the specific patterns of giving and receiving, and the linguistic and ritual contexts of the prestations will be the principal focus of the following chapters. The significance of the role of Gujars as *jajmāns*, as givers of *dān,* is rendered mythologically salient in that Gujars in Pahansu say that they are descended from King Harishcandra, who when pressed by the Brahman Vishvamitra to give everything he owned in *dān* gave even himself, his wife, and his son to be sold by the rapacious Brahman.[12] Not only are many Gujars in the village able to recite a version of this very old and widespread story, but it is also heard in the form of a song sung by Gujar women at the rituals of the sixth day (*chaṭṭhī*) after the birth of a son, as if to proclaim that the new member of the Gujar *jāti* should hold Harishcandra himself as a model for the conduct of his life in the village.

That it is the Gujar *jāti* in particular (or at any rate the Ksatriya *varṇa,* which Gujars alone are held to represent in Pahansu) that should take Harishcandra as a model for the giving of *dān* is suggested in the words of several of the verses of this song (*gīt*). The first verses describe Harishcandra's *dān,* the giving of his wealth and his kingdom, and of himself, his wife, and his son to the Brahman. The next verses describe the sale of Harishcandra and his family in Banaras.

[Refrain] Listen to the story of King Harishcandra:
The three creatures have gone to Kashi to be sold.

[1] Who will take the son?
Who will take the queen?
Who will take the wise King Harishcandra?

[2] A *seṭh* [Baniya merchant] is taking the son;
A Brahman is taking the queen;
A Bhangi is taking King Harishcandra.

[3] What does the son do?
What does the queen do?
What does King Harishcandra do?

[4] The son gathers flowers,
The queen makes breads;
King Harishcandra burns dead bodies.

The allusions in the fourth verse are to incidents in the story after the three have been sold. Harishcandra was sold to a low-caste person who worked at the cremation ground (in the song, a Bhangi, and in other versions, a *caṇḍāla*), and who forced the king to burn the bodies there. In a version of the story from Meerut District given in Temple (1884–1900, 3:53–88), the son is still sold to a *seṭh* and Harishcandra to a *caṇḍāla;* but the queen is sold, not to a Brahman, but to a prostitute. Just as the Meerut version stresses that the sale of the three was made without reference to clan (*got*) or relationships (*nātā*), the substitution in the Pahansu version of the Brahman for the prostitute emphasizes the caste identity of Harishcandra as Ksatriya. It opposes him to Brahman (both as recipient of the *dān* and as purchaser of the queen), to Baniya, and to Untouchable. Thus, just as their participation in the worship of Bhūmiyā marks, ritually, the role of Gujars as the foremost givers of *dān* among the castes in the village, the song of their forebear marks, mythologically, their distinctiveness.

When I first arrived in Pahansu and told Mangal Singh, a member of the Sadhu *heṛā kunbā,* that I had come to his village to learn about the Gujar *jāti* and the part they play in village life, his response was to tell me the story of Harishcandra, and then the story of Jagdev Singh Panwar, from whom the Khūbaṛ *got* is said to have descended.[13]

The following is Mangal Singh's story of his forefather (*pūrvaj*), as he puts it, which I have translated from his Hindi account.

> There was a king, Jaisal, who was the greatest king, and there were many smaller kings, and among them was Jagdev Panwar. Everyday, the wife of the Bhāṭ [genealogist] used to come to the court of the great king to accept *dān*. One day when she came to the court, Jagdev too was sitting there. The Bhāṭ woman looked at Jagdev and covered her head (*ghūngat nikāl liyā*) with her shawl. The great king then asked her why she did this: "Everyday you come here and you don't cover your head; why have you done so today?"
>
> The Bhāṭ woman said: "Today in your court sits the greatest giver of *dān*. For this reason I have covered my head. [Mangal Singh commented at this point that women cover their heads before *baṛe ādmī,* "big" or senior men.] That king replied: "Who is a greater giver of *dān* than I?" The Bhāṭ woman said: "He is Jagdev Panwar." The king said: "Tomorrow, you go to his house to accept *dān,* and then come back here. I will see what sort of *dān* he gives and I will give ten times that amount in *dān*."
>
> The Bhāṭ woman went away, and Jagdev went back to his house. At night Jagdev said to his queen: "Today we have been made equal to the king Jaisal. But Jaisal said that he would give ten times as much in *dān* as I give. So what *dān* should I give, so that he will not be able to surpass it?" The queen said to Jagdev: "You have done a very wrong thing. You are a very small king, and he is a very great king. We cannot do anything in comparison with him." Jagdev said: "We are of the

Panwar *got* [many Gujar *gots* have alternative names that are generally associated with Rajput clans, and the Khūbaṛ *got* is also known as Panwar], we can never be defeated; in place of wealth or pomp, we can give our lives (*śān ke badle mẽ prāṇ de dete haĩ*)." The queen then asked: "What *dān* will you give that Jaisal will not be able to surpass?" Jagdev said: "I will give my own head as *dān,* and then we will see how he will give ten times that."

Morning came. Jagdev took a bath and then cut off his head with his own hand, and the queen wrapped it in some cloth. Then the Bhāṭ woman came, and she said: "Jagdev said that he would give me *dān.* Yesterday in the court, the great king said that I should first accept *dān* from Jagdev's house, and then return to the court. And he said that he would give me ten times that amount in *dān.*" The queen then put Jagdev's head, still wrapped in the cloth, in the Bhāṭ woman's *jholī* [the end of her shawl, in which *dān* is often received], and said to her: "Take this *dān.*"

The Bhāṭ woman went away from there, and in the road she saw what she had been given in *dān.* She saw that it was the head of Jagdev. Then she went to the court of the great king. The king said: "Show me what *dān* you have brought from there. I will give ten times that in *dān.*" The Bhāṭ woman said: "You will never be able to give ten times this in *dān.* You have been defeated." The king said: "Show it to me." Then in front of the whole court, the Bhāṭ woman put Jagdev's head on a table. When the people in the court saw this they were very sorrowful. And the great king had to accept defeat. And he said: "A greater *dān* than this could never be given."

The Bhāṭ woman took the head back to Jagdev's house, and gave it to Jagdev's wife. The queen then joined it to Jagdev's body and prayed to Bhagvān: "Give my husband the gift of life." Then Bhagvān made him live, and everyone began saying: "Victory to Jagdev Panwar, the greatest giver of *dān.*"

And Mangal Singh added: "This story is about the power of giving *dān* (*dān kī vīrtā*). We too are such givers of *dān,* the Khūbaṛs of today." The relationship between the Pahansu Khūbaṛs and Jagdev Singh and the significance of their role as givers of *dān* are reenacted, as it were, for Gujars in the village when their own Bhāṭ comes to record births and marriages in his *pothī,* in which the supposed genealogical connection between the Khūbaṛs and Jagdev is recorded, and also when the Bhāṭ is asked to sing at weddings of the legend of Jagdev, the progenitor of the *got,* and then is given *dān.*

Stories of Jagdev's *dān kī vīrtā* are also told by Muslim Doms from the village of Nawada who consider Pahansu Khūbaṛs to be their *jajmāns.* They occasionally come to Pahansu to tell the story of Jagdev and the *dān* of 54 *karoṛ* (540 million) rupees he once gave, and to receive *dān* in the form of a few pounds of grain.

Theoretical and Ethnographic Perspectives

Caste

Prestations made in and through *jajmānī* relationships are, as I will argue, the principal way in which intercaste relationships and Gujar dominance are constituted in Pahansu.

The so-called *jajmānī* system has been a focus of a great deal of discussion, if not of sustained ethnographic investigation, in anthropological studies of village life in South Asia. Wiser's detailed description (1936) of prestations made in Karimpur, a village in southwestern Uttar Pradesh, provided both the impetus and much of the ethnographic data for the debates of the late 1950s, which centered largely on questions of whether the *jajmānī* system is "exploitative" and to what extent the system can be analyzed as simply an economic interdependence of the various castes in a village community (Beidelman 1959; Harper 1959; Orenstein 1962).

In these studies, as well as in more culturally sensitive studies that came later, ritual services were often considered along with those like barbering, ironsmithing, and pottery-making that seemed to have more pragmatic functions. Yet almost without exception, anthropologists have failed to examine the linguistic and ritual contexts in which the prestations are actually made, and the fact that the giving and receiving are themselves ritual acts has been overlooked. The most important consequence of this neglect has been that indigenous categories of prestations have seldom been elucidated with any care; whatever a *jajmān* has given his Barber or his Brahman, or any of the other servicing castes, has been seen as a "payment" by most observers (e.g., Wiser 1936; Kolenda 1963) or as an expression of certain complementary customary rights on the part of these castes, given in recognition of the performance of their caste-related occupations (Dumont 1970, 157–58; Fuller 1977, 101; Heesterman 1985, 191). The failure to distinguish prestations given as *dān* from those given as *phaslānā* "shares" has made it impossible to discern the ideological core of *jajmānī* relationships.[14]

Viewing all of these prestations simply as "payments" and the enduring relationships between patron and client simply as a "method of work allocation and accounting" (Commander 1983, 289) or as an "exchange of produce, goods and services within the Indian village community" (Fuller, n.d.) has led a number of observers to argue that the *jajmānī* "system" is an anthropological fiction (Good 1982; Commander 1983; Fuller, n.d.). In Fuller's view, the notion of a system should be abandoned because the distributions of grain on the threshing floor that are observable today are mere remnants of a wider pre-British system in which portions of the harvest were given to the ruler and a whole host of intermediary political chiefs, as well as to the Brahman priest and other village functionaries (1977, 100–101). Although he calls for a more precise typology of forms of exchange in India, his own failure to distinguish the various categories of prestations made by a *jajmān*, his predisposition to see everything in terms of "payments," has led him too quickly to dismiss the possibility that the ensemble of *jajmānī* relationships constitutes a culturally meaningful entity. In the chapters that follow, I will argue that the meaning of these relationships depends crucially on the giving of *dān* to people of many castes, and on the role of the dominant caste *jajmān* as "sacrificer" and protector of the village. I will also show that the *jajmānī* system is not only a matter of intercaste relationships and prestations; donors act as *jajmān*s and givers of *dān* to their married sisters, daughters, and father's sisters (the women they call *dhiyānī*) as well.[15] In their capacity as recipients of *dān* prestations, these women (and sometimes their husbands) have ritual roles that are analogous to those of the Brahmans and *kamīn*s who in Pahansu accept *dān* from their Gujar *jajmān*s.[16]

There has never been any doubt that *jajmānī* relationships within a village are organized around the dominant caste, the landholding caste residing in the village.[17] As early as 1938, Hocart, while insisting on the essentially "religious" character of caste systems as organizations for ritual, for the performance of sacrifice to procure "freedom from premature death and disease," nevertheless saw that castes are organized, for the performance of ritual, around the king or, at the village level, around the cultivator (Hocart 1950, 7).[18] In relation to the king or the cultivator, various caste groups such as Brahman priests, washermen, and drummers all perform similar ritual services: "Priest, washerman and drummer are treated alike, for they are all priests; only the brahman is a higher kind of priest and so more munificently rewarded" (ibid., 44). Hocart suggests that the "priestly" duties of these castes are similar; they involve the removal of disease and planetary afflictions, participation in *bali* offerings to gods and demons, and the performance of various aspects of the rituals of death. In these rituals, the king or the cultivator is the sacrificer, the "chief actor, [who] supplies the offerings, and bears the expense" (ibid., 35). For Hocart, it is this sacrificial basis of caste that is fundamental (ibid., 17–18).

Where Hocart saw a ritual organization centered on the king or cultivator, Beidelman, Harper, and Orenstein saw a purely economic interdependence focused on the dominant caste, a system in which the occupational specializations of the various castes were of paramount importance in relation to the economic dominance of the landholders. While suggesting that such craft specializations and ritual duties are not in fact strictly distinguishable, Hocart stresses that it is the ritual and priestly functions that loom large in the constitution of intercaste relationships (ibid., 16, 11).

Now Pocock and Dumont also recognize that *jajmānī* relationships are, as Pocock puts it, "organized around one institution, the dominant caste of a given area" (Pocock 1962, 79). They define this focus, not as a "principle informing a system," but as a "nonideological residuum" (Dumont 1970, 213). While commending Hocart for his insight that caste systems are fundamentally "religious" and organized with respect to ritual functions, both argue that the centrality of the landholder (or the king) is simply a function of the economic power of the dominant caste, and that it is fully encompassed within an ideology of hierarchy in which it is the Brahman priest, rather than the king or the cultivator, who is the ideological point of reference in the system. In giving priority to the ideology of hierarchy, particularly to the opposition of the pure and the impure, it is of course impossible for Dumont and Pocock to acknowledge that the ritual services performed by the "pure" Brahman and the "impure" Washermen and Barbers could in any way be religiously equivalent in relation to the king or cultivator. Thus the particular religious functions of the various castes that Hocart discussed (e.g., those involved with the acceptance of *bali* offerings) are totally ignored by Pocock and Dumont, in favor of ritual functions that are said to be directly involved with the opposition of the pure and the impure. Thus Pocock argues that the essential ritual functions of the various service castes have to do with the removal of impurities from their *jajmān*s, to whose "status" (hierarchical position with respect to the Brahman) they are essential. The Brahman is here perceived as the preeminently pure being who does not involve himself in the impurities of the body in which many of the service castes must, by virtue of their craft and ritual specializations, be concerned.

In order to maintain this view of *jajmānī* relationships as being concerned essentially with hierarchy and the separation of the pure and the impure, it is necessary to show that, despite the demonstrable centrality of the dominant caste, the position of the Brahman priest (*purohit*) and the service castes (*kamīn*s) with respect to the cultivating caste are radically different. Following Dumont and Pocock, for example, Parry goes to considerable lengths in his description of *jajmānī* relationships in a Kangra village to show that "a *purohit*'s services are simply not commensurate with the services of a *kamīn*" and that the prestations received by *purohit*s and *kamīn*s are fundamentally different (1979, 69, 72). Yet Parry is forced to acknowledge that Barbers, like Brahmans, are considered to be *purohit*s in this Kangra village and that both receive identical gifts on certain ritual occasions (ibid., 72). These facts pose a serious problem for a conceptualization of *jajmānī* relationships structured primarily in terms of hierarchy.[19]

Even those analysts who have rejected the notion that the simple opposition of the pure and the impure is the overarching conceptual framework of Hindu society have had recourse to a rank ordering that encompasses both gods and men as the cultural basis for intercaste relations in general, and *jajmānī* relations in particular. The comments of Marriott and Inden are more or less typical:

> The codes of Hindu worship require the existence of complex local communities of castes. . . . To sponsor the worship there must be a local worshipper of means, typically a ruler or man of wealth, who can by gifts entreat a priest to mediate with the god. There must be specialists of appropriate castes—e.g., temple keeper, garland maker, cook, sweet maker, singer, musician, dancer—to feed, attend, and entertain the god. Before the worshipper can approach the god, he must prepare himself and his caste to be as god-like as possible and must remove as much as possible from his person and caste any insulting, transmissible bodily substance. He does so through bathing and through engaging the services practiced by other castes, such as those who do the work of barber, washerman, midwife, funeral priest, leatherworker, scavenger or sweeper. These castes are by their intimate receivings of bodily substance rendered subordinate to the worshipper, as a child's receiving of bodily substance renders him subordinate to his parents. . . . One effect of such worship is a ranking of all participating castes by a pattern of exchanges in which natural substances and services go up and divinely transvalued substances containing divine benefits go down. Another effect is the establishment of a solidarity of substance among all castes. (Marriott and Inden 1974, 985)

Wadley's view of the relationship between Hindu ritual and the pattern of intercaste relationships is grounded in similar assumptions about the pervasiveness of cultural constructs concerned with rank. While she argues against the idea that ranked relationships are structured simply in terms of relative purity and impurity, it is nevertheless in terms of a unitary ranked order (defined by differential power or *śakti*) that she analyzes relations both between men and gods and between *jajmāns* and their clients:

> In return for physical aid and symbolic "shelter," the client provides services for his patron—the same types of services which men often provide for their deities in *pūjā,* services which are primarily concerned with the removal of the deity's polluting bodily substances. . . . From the viewpont of the *jajmān,* the *kamīn* is a lesser, inauspicious

> being (though the degrees of "lesser" and "inauspicious" vary, of course); from the *kamīn*'s viewpoint, the *jajmān* is an auspicious being who provides shelter. (1975, 182)

In other contexts, Wadley compares the "gifts" of food given by a *jajmān* to the *prasād,* the "ritual leavings" of the gods, and the attitude of devotion (*bhakti*) toward a god with the attitudes of a *kamīn* toward his *jajmān* (ibid., 169, 182).

In Pahansu, the centrality of the Gujars in the local configuration of castes, as well as their role as *jajmān*s of the village, is not simply an empirical fact of their dominance and landholding in the village and in the region, but is implicated in the ritual life of the village in ways that are only peripherally concerned with purity and impurity and a hierarchical ordering of castes. The proper presentation and acceptance of *dān,* which ensures the well-being of the entire community, is far more important than hierarchical considerations in structuring intercaste relationships in the village. Gujars give *dān* (the most important prestation in the framework of *jajmānī* relationships) to Brahmans and *kamīn*s alike, and it is this ritual centrality, as I will call it, and this similarity of function among Brahmans, Barbers, and Sweepers in particular that provides the conceptual focus of *jajmānī* relationships as they exist today in Pahansu.

This configuration, this way of construing intercaste relationships, seems to be implicit in the prestation patterns that have been reported from many villages elsewhere in the Indian subcontinent (see, e.g., Majumdar 1958 and Hiebert 1971). Yet, in Pahansu, in contrast to the villages that have provided much of the ethnographic data for the discussions of caste and *jajmānī* relationships—Wiser's and Wadley's Karimpur and Marriott's Kishan Garhi—the centrality of the dominant caste seems to be more explicit, more frequently foregrounded, and more salient, just as the prestation patterns appear to be somewhat more elaborate there. I think that the history of landholding in these other villages and their demographic structure may account for the manner in which the ritual centrality of the *jajmān* is less obvious to the ethnographer, and perhaps slightly less significant to villagers themselves, than is the case in Pahansu.

In Karimpur in 1925, when Wiser studied the village, Brahmans comprised approximately one-fourth of the total population. There were forty-one Brahman households, of which thirty-eight earned their livelihood as farmers and the principal landholders of the village (Wiser 1936, 19, 22). In 1969, when Wadley conducted fieldwork in the same village, Brahmans again comprised roughly one-fourth of the population, holding 54 percent of the land (Wadley 1975, 19–21). Brahmans, then, were the principal *jajmān*s from whose grain piles the *jajmānī* prestations were made. Statistics on landholdings of other castes are not given, though it is said that the caste of Kachi farmers had substantial holdings as well. Wadley's brief account of the history of landholding in the village, based on oral histories and the Mainpuri District Settlement Reports, indicates that Brahmans had come into control of the village lands after the defeat of Thakurs at the hands of Muslim rulers, and that revenue settlements in the nineteenth century had consistently been made with one or two *zamīndar*s rather than with the actual cultivators. This tenurial pattern facilitated just the sort of transfers of proprietary right that Stokes would have predicted, with the result that, though the Brahmans still hold slightly more than half the land, landholding does not define them as a caste opposed to others in the village in the way that landholding and *jajmānī* relations define the position of Gujars in Pahansu.

In Kishan Garhi, the village in Aligarh District studied by Marriott, the land was held largely by Brahmans as tenants of absent Jats whose ancestors had seized the village in the seventeenth century. In 1952, after the implementation of the Uttar Pradesh Zamindari Abolition and Land Reform Act, Brahmans paid slightly more than one-half of the land revenues that were due from the village (Marriott 1968, 135). Kishan Garhi was said to be a Brahman village just as Pahansu is said to be a Gujar village and is sometimes even referred to as Pahansu Gujar.

Thus in Karimpur and Kishan Garhi, Brahmans are not only the "highest" caste, but also the principal *jajmān*s and landholders. Because of this empirical coincidence of hierarchical position and position as *jajmān*s, everything may appear as if prestations to *kamīn*s flowed "down" and services were rendered to *jajmān*s in connection with their superior hierarchical status. Data from villages like Pahansu in which Brahmans depend mostly on their priestly occupations and are not landed *jajmān*s allow us to see that intercaste relationships may be ordered in terms other than rank and the opposition of purity and impurity. The order of castes grounded in rank or hierarchy and that grounded in what I have termed the centrality of the dominant caste of *jajmān*s are analytically and culturally distinguished, and they are acted upon in distinct contexts of village social life. The facts of Gujar dominance in southwestern Saharanpur District—the tenurial patterns and clan organization and the concentration of landholding in the Gujar caste—were historical preconditions for the development of Gujar centrality in the organization of the ritual life of the village and their position in the local configuration of castes, and for the degree to which they define themselves, as a caste, as givers of *dān*.

Kinship

In the attempt to uncover some aspects of a South Asian semiotic of exchange, or at least, the semiotic aspects of giving and receiving in Pahansu, attention is necessarily drawn to kinship as well as to intercaste relationships. It is of course well-established that distinct categories of prestations can be said not only to characterize particular kinship relations (Dumont 1966; Vatuk 1975) but to be constitutive of those relationships (Marriott 1976; Inden 1976; Inden and Nicholas 1977). Two sets of interrelated problems in the analysis of these prestations present themselves in the ethnographic literature.

In general, when accounts of intercaste prestations and ritual services involved in *jajmānī* relationships have been given in the literature, the system has been analyzed exclusively from the point of view of the dominant landholding caste. Insofar as such castes are deemed to be the principal *jajmāns* of the village, such emphasis is not altogether unwarranted. Yet it is the case that people of other castes, even if they are not landholders, make a number of the prestations that we have come to think of as being given by landholders to their *kamīns*, and they also require the ritual services, particularly at life-cycle rituals, that they themselves perform for the dominant caste. Virtually nothing has been reported concerning how and by whom, for example, the services performed by a Barber at weddings and funerals are carried out in Barber weddings and funerals or whether the usual prestations are made in such situations. These services and the roles of giving and receiving are, it turns out, performed in Pahansu by specified kinsmen. This in itself is hardly surprising; it has been suggested before, by Das and Uberoi (1971), that some sort of structure of kinship reciprocity might exist at this level of the system. But as the data presented in chapter 4 will indicate, the ritual services and prestations involved in such cases are ordered by principles other than hierarchy and reciprocity, much as the prestations given by Gujars to Brahmans, Barbers, and Sweepers are construed in terms of centrality rather than hierarchy. In Pahansu, the Brahman's wife-taking affines (*dhiyāne*) act as recipients to the Brahman, and the same pattern holds true for Barbers, Sweepers, and other castes who function as recipients of *dān* from Gujar *jajmāns*. Understanding the meaning of these "kinship" prestations in turn illuminates the patterns of intercaste giving and receiving.

With the exception of McKim Marriott's 1976 study, analyses of prestation patterns in North India have generally proceeded as if there were two quite separate types of giving and receiving, those having to do with caste and those having to do with kinship. Dumont and Vatuk have constructed their understandings of North Indian "kinship," for example, largely in terms of the prestations given by Brahmans (the Sarjupari Brahmans of eastern Uttar Pradesh in Dumont's case, and the Gaur Brahmans studied by Vatuk in Meerut District) to their kinsmen, particularly their affines. Yet many of the prestations that they describe, particularly the crucial ones given at the death rituals, are for all castes except

Brahmans, Sweepers, and Leatherworkers, matters of intercaste rather than kinship exchanges. What Brahmans give to their wife-taking affines, most other castes give to the Brahman *purohit* attached to them in hereditary *jajmānī* relationships.

This in itself would not be problematic for Dumont. He has argued that there is no absolute difference between the principle that governs intercaste relationships and that which governs relationships within castes, both in terms of the ranking of units within castes and in terms of affinal relationships (Dumont 1966, 1970). Most subsequent analyses of kinship in North India have followed his lead in referring terminologies, rituals, and prestations involved in affinal relationships to a principle of hierarchy (see, e.g., Vatuk and Vatuk 1976). There is, however, an implicit recourse to another principle here, one of "equality" in kinship relations, since hierarchy is said to "invade" the domain of kinship, which Dumont, based on his South Indian experience, seems to regard as characterized inherently by reciprocity. Similarly, Carter (1975), Das and Uberoi (1971), and Inden and Nicholas (1977) have maintained that principles of hierarchy and reciprocity (defined in cultural terms by Inden and Nicholas as "giving and receiving" and "sharing") can be seen to structure most aspects of kinship behavior. Following Dumont quite explicitly, both Parry (1979) and Moffatt (1979) argue that kinship relations, like intercaste relationships, are pervaded by hierarchy, and that this constitutes the continuity between intercaste and intracaste social relationships.

If, as I have already indicated, intercaste prestation patterns cannot be explicated solely in terms of a hierarchic configuration of castes, then the fact that some of these same prestations become, in certain instances, matters of intracaste giving and receiving (what I will call the permutations in gift-giving patterns) forces us to revise our notions about the extent to which these relationships, particularly affinal relationships, are structured in terms of hierarchy.

Dān *and the Transferral of Inauspiciousness*

When I left Pahansu at the end of March 1979, it was with some hesitation that I began the task of composing this monograph. I had worked out most of the analyses while I was still in the village, but it worried me that virtually all of my interpretations hinged on one crucial fact— that the significance of *dān,* and thus much of the giving and receiving that constitutes intercaste and kinship relations in Pahansu, was focused on the transfer of inauspiciousness from donor to recipient. That the dispersal of inauspiciousness structured and gave meaning to so much of Pahansu social and ritual life struck me so forcibly that it seemed inconceivable that other ethnographers had not placed it at the center of their interpretations of village life in India.

I had given much thought to this in the village too. As my Gujar friends pointed out to me that Brahmans and Barbers and Sweepers and several other castes were all alike in that they were "vessels" (*pātra*) for the removal of the inauspiciousness of the Gujar *jajmān,* as I heard my Brahman acquaintances speak of the inherent dangers of accepting *dān,* and of the *pāp* ("evil") and *viṣ* ("poison," "venom") that such prestations contained and that they daily had to accept, and as I listened to Asikaur, my Gujar "mother," admonish me, as a Gujar "daughter," never to accept food from a Brahman house because of the great difference between food obtained through work (*mehannat kī roṭī*) and food obtained as *dān* (*dān kī roṭī*), I sometimes felt as if in Pahansu the Indic world of caste and hierarchy had been turned topsy-turvy, that somehow these Gujars just weren't proper Hindus at all, and that I had stumbled into a village clearly on the fringes of Indian society.

As I began to see it wasn't the case that "centrality" had displaced hierarchy but that these were two contextually differentiated ways of construing intercaste relationships and configurations of castes in the village, I began to wonder if perhaps the ideas about the transfer of inauspiciousness in certain prestations that gave this centrality its ritual significance weren't of wider provenance in South Asia. My first thought, there in Pahansu, was that I should reread Heesterman's paper "Brahmin, Ritual, and Renouncer" (1964). A copy was sent to me from Chicago. When I read that in the *Pācavimśa Brāhmaṇa* it had been written that "he who, having accepted many gifts, feels as if he had swallowed poison" (Heesterman 1964,31), I realized Pahansu thought on the matter was not as peripheral as I had believed; many Gujars and Brahmans alike had spoken to me in precisely those terms in their descriptions of *dān* as "poison," *viṣ,* embodying the evil and sin of the donor.

In Heesterman's analysis of Vedic *śrauta* ritual, ambiguity is said to arise in the ranked relationship between Brahman and king because of the Brahman's acceptance of the king's gifts. The hierarchical relationship is temporarily reversed, according to Heesterman, because the prestations accompanying the sacrificial rituals are said to transfer "evil" (*pāp*) and impurity. Observing that in contemporary Hinduism the Brahman is conceived of as a preeminently "pure" being and not a recipient of "impurity," Heesterman has found it necessary to construct a model of historical transformation that in fact distorts the reality of social relations and the patterns of exchange in contemporary village life, or at least those that I observed in Pahansu. According to his model, in Vedic ritual, evil (which he fails to distinguish from impurity) was transferred to the Brahman with the consequence that there was a temporary reversal in the hierarchic relationship of Brahman and king. Following the "individualization" and "interiorization" of the ritual in later historical periods, when, according to Heesterman, evil and impurity were not transferred but transformed within oneself, the hierarchical order became fixed and no such reversals of rank or transferrals of evil took place. As the data on prestations in Pahansu will indicate, however, Heesterman's theory of historical transformation separates what in fact may be coexisting aspects of the relationship between Brahman and king (or Brahman and *jajmān*). These aspects are foregrounded in different contexts of social life and are not necessarily reducible to matters of "rank" on a scale of purity and impurity, precisely because, as I will argue in chapter 2, inauspiciousness (*nāśubh*) and evil (*pāp*) are quite different from "impurity." The gifts that the Brahman, the Barber, and the Sweeper accept from their Gujar *jajmāns* are imbued with inauspiciousness and evil, but impurity is not thought to be transferred in *dān*.

A few months after I formulated these ideas about the significance of what Heesterman had written of gifts given to Brahmans, I came upon a copy of the Motilal Banarsidass edition of Wendy O'Flaherty's *The Origins of Evil in Hindu Mythology* during one of my bimonthly expeditions to Delhi and the Manohar Book Service in Darya Ganj. My journal entries for the next few days are replete with quotations from that book and reflections on the relationship between O'Flaherty's descriptions of the transfers of "evil" in mythological texts, the way in which sin and evil are distributed to rivals at the end of certain rituals, to women and to affinal relatives at the *aśvamedha* sacrifice, and in later texts, to Untouchables who accept funeral offerings. Here, it seemed to me (particularly in chapter 6 of O'Flaherty's book, "The Paradox of the Evil God: The Transfer of Sin"), were some mythological paradigms that had their counterparts in the ritual and social life of Pahansu. In speaking of the transfer of evil, these texts said very little about ranked relationships between men and gods and among men, just as in Pahansu the giving of *dān* and the transferral of inauspiciousness seemed to be conceptually and contextually distinct from hierarchical orderings. Perhaps, I remember thinking, Pahansu is part of India after all.

Several months after my return from the field, I found myself reading a great many older accounts of North Indian "folklore" and "customs." In these accounts (Abbott [1932] 1974; Crooke 1896a, 1896b; Briggs 1920; and for South India, Whitehead 1921), written much before the preoccupation with "hierarchy" had established itself in Indian studies, there is evidence of a pervasive concern in ritual life for what I have called auspiciousness, as well as a concern that inauspiciousness be removed and transferred away.[20] Though the recipients of this inauspiciousness are not given with enough specificity for us to be able to establish actual prestation patterns—Briggs, for example, often says that ritual gifts are given to "relatives" or to "the menials of the family" (1920, 66)—it is clear that the removal of inauspiciousness through particular ritual actions and its subsequent transferral through gifts to kinsmen and people of other castes are indeed widespread phenomena in South Asia, despite the fact that these rituals and these prestations have been almost completely ignored in more recent ethnographic writing. Crooke, for example, gives many examples of Brahmans accepting "offerings" that are thought to remove the "sin" of the donor, with negative consequences to the recipient (Crooke 1896a, 1:171–72). The similarity of these Brahman acts of acceptance to the Barber's role in accepting prestations at the conclusion of *mūl śāntī* rituals (Crooke 1896b, 2:151–52; see below, chap. 4, for a discussion of the form of this ritual in Pahansu) and in many of the rituals of the life course is also evident in Crooke's reports.

Parry's paper "Ghosts, Greed, and Sin: The Occupational Identity of the Benares Funeral Priests" (1980) is the first extended contemporary discussion of the transmission of "sin" to Brahman recipients of *dān,* in this case, to the Mahabrahman funeral priests at the burning *ghāṭ*s of Benares. Many of the statements of Parry's informants concerning the difficulty of "digesting" (*pacnā*) the *dān* and the dire consequences of accepting it are virtually identical to the discussions I heard in Pahansu about the dangers, for any castes that might be involved, of accepting these prestations.

Pahansu Brahmans, for these reasons, are reluctant to accept *dān.* They know very well that it diminishes their *śakti* ("power") and their *tej* ("lustre"); yet within the village context it is their "appropriate obligation" (*pharmāyā*) to take *dān* from their Gujar *jajmān*s. This hesitancy, the same awareness of the dangers, also characterizes the attitudes of the Barber and the Sweeper about accepting *dān* in Pahansu.

The reluctance of the Brahman to accept *dān* has been a topic of discussion in recent Indological as well as ethnographic writing. In many cases, this reluctance has been interpreted in terms of a conflict between the ideal Brahman as an ascetic—the renouncer whose acceptance of gifts would involve him inextricably in the "hierarchical interdependence" (Heesterman 1985,189–90; 1964) of the everyday social world—and the Brahman as priest. (Fuller 1984 suggests that this idea of what Heesterman calls the "unresolved conflict" of Indian tradition, the simultaneous necessity of the Brahman's entrance into the social world to perform rituals for his *jajmān* and his renunciation of that world, is particularly appropriate for understanding the position of the Brahman in South India.) This explanation, it seems to me, accounts neither for the reluctance of non-Brahman castes to accept *dān,* nor for the nonproblematic nature, at least in Pahansu, of the Brahman's acceptance of prestations other than *dān,* some of which involve him even more in the give-and-take of social life. (Such prestations will be discussed in detail in chapter 5.)

In his 1980 paper, Parry suggested that the reluctance of the Brahman to accept *dān* should be understood in the context of what he terms the inherently hierarchic aspects of *dān*. *Dān* is given, he argues, to Brahmans as hierarchic superiors of the donor, and the "evil" that this *dān* contains can be interpreted in terms of the acceptance of the "inferior essences" of the donor. The Brahman, in this interpretation, hesitates to accept *dān* because it is given by status inferiors. The same assumption, taken almost as axiomatic, is found in the recent work of Trautmann on marriage and the Brahman theory of the gift:

> The theory of the gift participates in the theory of pollution, which has as its paradigm those biological extensions of the self, the off-scourings of the body. The theory is a relational one; the bodily extensions of inferior beings are dangerously polluting to superiors, but conversely those of superiors . . . are concrete forms of grace (*prasāda*) to inferiors. . . . The gift has become an instrument of salvation, a way of transmuting pollution, sin, and death into purity and immortality, a means, like the sacrifice, of turning *pāpman* into *śrī*. At the same time it becomes clear why the brahmin is so uneasy in his role as the conduit of purification: the gift is a danger to him, being the bodily extension of the donor, which because the donor is by definition an inferior, is defiling to him and diminishes his spiritual lustre, *tejas*, so painfully acquired and so easily drained away. (Trautmann 1981, 287)

In Pahansu, the contextual equivalence of the Brahman, the Barber, and the Sweeper as appropriate recipients of *dān*, the reluctance of all three to accept *dān*, and the fact that "sin" and "inauspiciousness" are conveyed to all three as they accept *dān* from Gujar *jajmān*s make it evident that this ambivalence about the acceptance of *dān* cannot be understood simply with reference to the supposed "inferiority" of the donor. "Religious gifts" can and indeed must be given to Sweepers and Barbers as well as to Brahmans if the well-being and auspiciousness of the donor are to be maintained. The sin and inauspiciousness of the *jajmān* are assumed by each of the recipients regardless of their hierarchical position with respect to the donor.

One final point needs to be made before we proceed with the analysis of the Pahansu data. In discussing the relationship between the position of the South Indian Brahman priest and that of his counterpart in the North, Fuller (1984, 67–71) has argued, primarily in terms of Parry's North Indian data, that the association between gifts and the transfer of sin is particularly strong in the North because in North India *dān* is said to be connected with pilgrimage places where offerings to the dead are given as *dān* (and where distinct "Brahman subcastes" such as the Mahabrahmans are specialists in the acceptance of this *dān*).[21] It is this association with death, which Fuller says is absent in the South, that he believes accounts for the highly negative aspects of *dān*.[22]

This argument is vitiated by the fact that in Pahansu inauspiciousness and *pāp*, "evil," are thought to be generated not only at death but in most life processes. Birth, marriage, death, harvests, the building of a house, and very many occasions during the calendrical cycles of the week, the lunar month, and the year are thought to generate inauspiciousness (but not necessarily "impurity") that must be removed and given away in *dān* if well-being and auspiciousness are to be achieved and maintained.

I should also like to suggest that Fuller's assertion that in the South notions about *dān* as tainted by evil and sin are absent or at least relatively unstressed may simply be an artifact of his focus on temples and temple worship. Shulman (1985) has argued quite convincingly that the very nature of the medieval South Indian polity, political dynamics, and the nature of the relationship between the king, the Brahman, and the people are grounded in this conception of the gift, *dāna*, and that many South Indian myths about kingship revolve around the necessity of removing the evil of the king and of the kingdom through prestations to Brahmans and other appropriate recipients. And there are certainly indications in the ethnographic literature that a connection between *dān* and the transferral of inauspiciousness is to be found in contemporary South Indian villages as well. (See for example Pfaffenberger 1982; Whitehead 1921; Dubois 1906; Ishwaran 1966, 58.)

Thus, while we clearly do not have an adequate ethnographic basis to enable us to make a judgment concerning the pervasiveness of these ideas concerning *dān* and the transferral of inauspiciousness, studies of Hindu textual traditions and random reports in the ethnographic literature do make it clear that the link between gift-giving and the maintenance of auspiciousness and well-being is widespread in Hindu South Asia. I have tried to suggest, in this introductory chapter, that the ideological significance of this relationship for the cultural construction of dominance is particularly evident in terms of the position of the Gujar caste in northwestern Uttar Pradesh because of a particular set of historic and demographic circumstances that have underscored the "centrality" of this caste in the local configuration of castes.

CHAPTER TWO

Auspiciousness and Inauspiciousness as Cultural Constructs

Many of the interactions among kinsmen and people of different castes in Pahansu are predicated upon cultural constructs concerned with bringing about or maintaining the well-being of persons, families, houses, and the village as a whole through the removal of inauspiciousness in the giving of *dān*. In this chapter, I will define the meaning of auspiciousness (*śubh*) and its opposite, inauspiciousness (*nāśubh* or *kuśubh*), for Hindu villagers of Pahansu through an examination of the linguistic forms, particularly verb usage, in which these constructs appear in ordinary discourse, and through a discussion of the sources of the inauspiciousness that is thought to afflict villagers at particular points in the life course, during specific astrological conjunctions, and in relation to the establishment and attenuation of connections among persons and between persons and places.

The Language of Auspiciousness and Inauspiciousness

Śubh and *nāśubh* (or *kuśubh*) are the most general terms in use in Pahansu to refer to auspiciousness and inauspiciousness; a variety of other terms, particularly for the negative qualities and substances associated with inauspiciousness, occur in everyday village talk. *Khair-khairāt*, which may be translated as "well-being achieved through gift-giving," is frequently used to characterize or elaborate upon the substantive sense of "auspiciousness," *śubh*. The term *śubh* occurs as both an adjective and a noun. Villagers perform many rituals and give *dān*, they say, "for auspiciousness" (*śubh ke māro*), and as they generally go on to say, "for one's own well-being achieved through gift-giving" (*apne khair-khairāt ke māro*); but beyond this very general usage, the occurrence of *śubh* as a noun is relatively infrequent in ordinary discourse. Much more common is the adjectival usage of the term, in which events, objects, or persons are seen as "signs" (*śakun*) of auspiciousness or "omens" (*apśakun*) of inauspiciousness; it is "auspicious," for example, to see a married woman (*suhāgan*) holding something in her lap when one is setting out on a journey; it is inauspicious (*aśubh*) to see someone sneeze or to see unrefined sugar at such a time.[1] It is, however, "auspicious" and indicative of "benefit" (*lābh*) to sneeze toward the west or to sneeze after eating.

Even these very simple and rather trivial adjectival usages of *śubh* and *aśubh* illustrate an important property of auspicious and inauspicious signs: they are contextually variable in their value. That is, what is auspicious for certain kinds of undertakings may be quite inauspicious for others.

A second adjectival usage of *śubh* and *aśubh* occurs in discourse concerning astrologically appropriate and inappropriate times for various activities. Here what is auspicious or inauspicious is not a "sign" or an "omen," but a factor that is itself either facilitating (*lābh-kārak*) and appropriate or detrimental (*hāni-kārak*) and inappropriate to the proposed activity. Pahansu villagers consult Buddhu Pandit, the most learned Brahman in the village, about the proper times (*muhūrat*) for filling their *biṭaurā*s (storage huts for cow-dung cakes), building or repairing a house, digging wells, planting their crops and plowing their fields.[2] Above all, they consult him about the *muhūrat*s or auspicious periods of time (*sāhā*) for betrothal ceremonies and marriages. All of these decisions involve complex considerations of lunar and solar days (*tithi* and *vār*), lunar months (*mahīnā*), lunar asterisms (*nakṣatra*), solar asterisms (*rāśi*), and many other astrological considerations.

The adjectives *śubh* and *aśubh* may be applied to the nine planets (*graha*) recognized in Hindu astrology, and to the seven solar days associated with them. In the abstract, that is, without regard to a specific context or activity, Candramā (the moon, associated with Monday), Budh (Mercury, associated with Wednesday), Bṛhaspati (Jupiter, associated with Thursday), and Śukra (Venus, associated with Friday) are said to be "auspicious." Sūrya (the sun, associated with Sunday), Mangal (Mars, associated with Tuesday), and Śani (Saturn, associated with Saturday) are "inauspicious." The "planets" Rāhu ("eclipse demon") and Ketu ("comet demon") are also said to be inauspicious. In these particular uses of *śubh* and *aśubh*, the terms *pāp* ("sin" or "evil") and *krūr* ("cruel") are found to occur more or less interchangeably with *aśubh*.

Despite the existence of this seemingly fixed classification of planets and days, each activity for which villagers may consider the auspiciousness or inauspiciousness of the time calls forth its own frame of reference. In other words, the "inauspicious" planets and days may in fact be "auspicious" for certain activities, and the "auspicious" ones may be "inauspicious" for some undertakings. The same is true of lunar days (*tithi*) and other units of time.

Most villagers are aware of, and constantly discuss, the solar days, lunar days, and lunar months that are auspicious or inauspicious in relation to specific activities. Nearly all villagers can list the days that are inauspicious for smearing floors with cow-dung (Tuesday, Thursday, and Saturday), auspicious for beginning the wheat harvest (Sunday or Tuesday), inauspicious for wearing new bangles (*paṛvā,* the first day of a lunar fortnight; *amāvas,* new moon day; and Wednesday), auspicious for traveling in any direction (Tuesday), inauspicious for setting out on a journey (Saturday), or inauspicious for putting on new clothes for the first time (the first or eleventh days of a lunar fortnight, a new moon day, and Tuesday). And while Saturday is commonly thought of as an inauspicious day, it is said to be a *śubh vār* (auspicious solar day) for rituals involving the laying of a foundation stone for a new house (*nīv dharnā*). Some conjunctions of activities and times are productive of inauspiciousness only for certain persons: it is inauspicious for a *suhāgan* (a married woman, literally, "one who is of good fortune") to wash her hair on Tuesday, Thursday, and Saturday, on the first and eleventh days of a lunar fortnight, and on a new moon day; if she should do this, inauspiciousness will afflict her husband. (My own disregard for this particular injunction was a source of never-ending worry to Asikaur, my Pahansu mother.) Women who have sons should not spin cotton thread on Monday or Tuesday. It is productive of inauspiciousness for a bride to be sent to her natal village on a Saturday, but a daughter may be safely sent to her conjugal village.

These considerations (*vicār*) concerning solar and lunar days are well heeded by villagers, and it is commented upon when they are not. The clothing of a young Gujar bride in Pahansu caught fire one evening as she sat before her hearth making breads, and she was severely burned. When I went to her home to apply ointment to the burns, the women of her neighborhood commented to me that this unfortunate event had probably occurred because the young woman had recently taken out a new set of clothes from her tin trunk and worn them on an *ekādsī,* the eleventh day of the lunar fortnight; the burn victim too agreed that her disregard of the dangers of *ekādsī* was probably the cause of her misfortune. One Tuesday Asikaur and Rajavati, her eldest son's wife, were spinning cotton thread in their courtyard, despite the fact that they are the mothers of sons. An older Gujar woman of their neighborhood happened to see them, and asked them, with astonishment evident in her voice, why they were spinning on such a day. They answered that they had a large quantity of cotton to spin and had decided to do the spinning in spite of the danger of *ekādsī.*

There are also sets of lunar asterisms that are particularly inauspicious for certain activities. The *pancak* ("five") asterisms—*dhaniṣṭha, śatbhiṣa, pūrva bhādrapad, uttarā bhādrapad* and *revati*—are inauspicious for journeys toward the south, for making cow-dung cakes, and for filling *biṭaurā*s with them, and they are particularly inauspicious for the performance of death rituals. The *pancak* asterisms are not inauspicious for other rituals of the life course, however. The *mūl* asterism, along with five others (*jyeṣṭha, śleṣā, māgha, revati,* and *aśvini*) associated with it, are extremely inauspicious as far as births are concerned. If a cremation must be performed at the time of a *pancak* period, or if a birth occurs during a *mūl* period, inauspiciousness (*nāśubh*) is produced and must be removed through the giving of *dān*. Most villagers are able to speak of *pancak* and *mul* and to list the activities that should not be carried out during these times, even though they would not be able to name the individual asterisms or calculate their occurrence. On a number of occasions, I was asked by women to inquire of Buddhu Pandit if a *pancak* period was in progress, particularly before the rainy season when they wanted to fill their *biṭaurā*s with cow-dung cakes.

It is perhaps in the context of marriage arrangements that villagers evince the most concern with auspicious and inauspicious solar and lunar days, lunar asterisms, and months. In every marriage negotiation that I encountered in Pahansu, Gujars consulted someone learned in astrology, usually Buddhu Pandit, to ascertain if the marriage of the couple would be auspicious, and to determine the time most "productive of benefit" (*lābh-kārak*) for the wedding. Ascertaining the appropriateness or inappropriateness of a particular marriage is accomplished through a comparison (*milānā,* lit., "mixing") of the horoscopes (*janam kuṇḍalī*) of the bride and groom. Appropriate times (*muhūrat, sāhā*) for the ceremony are determined (*śādī sujhānā,* "indicating the marriage") by eliminating the lunar months and days, lunar asterisms, and solar days that are considered inauspicious (*aśubh*) for marriages, and by eliminating various other astrologically unpropitious times, for example, when the planets Venus or Jupiter have set (*ḍūbnā,* "to be drowned") and the months, lunar days, and asterisms of the birth of the bride and groom.

The inauspicious times for marriages are listed in table 3. Most villagers are aware of and discuss the months and solar days during which marriages should not occur. Considerations concerning the lunar days, lunar asterisms, and the "ends" of certain time periods represent the more specialized knowledge of the astrologer, though I have heard Gujar men question Buddhu Pandit closely, at the time of the acceptance of a "betrothal letter" from the family of a prospective bride, as to whether these rather arcane considerations were in fact in order with reference to the day and time proposed for the marriage by the bride's family.

In these general considerations concerning the timing of a marriage ceremony, the *aśubh* times are said to be "prohibited" (*varjit*). The opposition between *śubh* and *aśubh* times is an absolute one, and dire consequences would follow, people say, if the prohibition were to be contravened. Failure to produce sons or the early death of the bride or groom

TABLE 3
INAUSPICIOUS TIMES FOR MARRIAGES

Inauspicious Months:	Sāvan, Bhādwe, Asauj, Kārttik, Pau, Cait
Inauspicious Lunar Asterisms:	*aśvini, bharaṇī, kṛttikā, ārdrā, punarvasu, puṣya, śleṣā, pūrvāphālgunī, citrā, viśākhā, jyeṣṭhā, pūrvāṣāṛha, abhijitu, śravaṇa, dhaniṣṭhā, śatbhiṣa, pūrvā bhādrapad*
Inauspicious Solar Days:	Sunday, Tuesday, Saturday
Inauspicious Lunar Days:	*amāvas* (new moon day) and the *rikta tithi* (fourth, ninth, fourteenth days of lunar fortnight)
Inauspicious "Ends":	*māsānt:* last day of any month
	tithyānt: last two *ghaṛī* of any lunar day (there are sixty *ghaṛī* in one day)
	bhānt: last three *ghaṛī* of any lunar asterism

SOURCE: Buddhu Pandit's commentary on materials found in *Jyotiṣa Sarva Sangrah,* his astrological manual. Ordinary villagers corroborated the material on months and solar days from their own experience and knowledge.

are the inauspicious results most often mentioned, while "marital good fortune" (*saubhāgya*) for the bride—having a living husband all her life—is the result of performing a marriage at an appropriate (*śubh*) time.

When horoscopes are "mixed" when a match between bride and groom is being considered, this categorization of auspicious and inauspicious is not a dichotomous or exhaustive one. Certain "mixings" are auspicious, and others inauspicious; there is also a third type of "mixing" that is said to be *pūjā kā*. Such a configuration is inauspicious, but the marriage may be performed with positive results if ritual sequences involving the giving of *dān* are carried out to remove the inauspiciousness that would otherwise afflict the bride and groom.

There is one further context for the adjectival use of *śubh* and *aśubh,* and this is in connection with *diśaśūl,* the "sharp pain, or thorn, of the directions." It is inauspicious to travel in certain directions on certain days, and although the possibility of *diśaśūl* is not generally attended to in the ordinary comings and goings to Saharanpur to sell one's sugar cane, or to the nearby town of Rampur for the Thursday market, it is almost always a factor to be carefully considered in fixing the day when a woman travels between her natal and conjugal villages, her *pīhar* and her *sasurāl.* It is probable that this concern with *diśasūl* is evidenced with respect to women's comings and goings (*ānā-jāna*) because women act as the conduits of inauspiciousness as they carry prestations from their natal villages to their conjugal villages. Most villagers could not tell me which particular directions were *aśubh* on which days; that it was a factor to be taken into account was apparent from the frequency of consultations with Buddhu Pandit about it, and the many contexts in which it became a

TABLE 4
DIŚAŚŪL

Direction:	East	West	South	North
Days:	Monday Saturday	Sunday Friday	Thursday	Wednesday Tuesday

SOURCE: Buddhu Pandit's astrological manual, *Jyotiṣa Sarva Sangrah.*

topic of conversation, particularly among women, in speculations about when a daughter would be sent back from her conjugal village for a visit with her parents, or about when female funeral guests could be expected to arrive. Villagers never seemed to bother about remembering the auspicious and inauspicious conjunctions of solar days and directions; it was easy enough to stop at Buddhu Pandit's house in the center of the village to ask him about what to do in a particular case. Table 4 outlines the diagram (*cakram,* lit., "circle" or "cycle") that Buddhu used in such consultations. The inauspicious directions are given for each solar day.

In all these examples of the use of the adjectives *śubh* and *aśubh* in connection with astrological considerations, in which what is "auspicious" is said to be *lābh-kārak,* "productive of benefit," and what is "inauspicious" is said to be *hāni-kārak,* "productive of harm," there is a contextual variability similar to that we observed in the case of "signs" and "omens": times that are auspicious for certain kinds of undertakings and events may be inauspicious for others. Yet there is a fundamental difference between these two usages. In the case of "signs" and "omens," *śakun* and *apśakun* appear as more or less arbitrary, noncausal portents (*sūcak*); in the notions of *lābh-kārak* and *hāni-kārak,* the occurrence of the terms *śubh* and *aśubh* is related, not to signs that convey information (*sūcnā denā*), but to factors (conceived in terms of substances) that are themselves facilitating or detrimental to the undertaking or the event.

How are these astrological conditions able to exert this sort of "making" or "causing" (*kārak*)? Part of the answer to this question may be found in an examination of the nouns *nāśubh* and *kuśubh,* which occur in discourse about auspicious and inauspicious causative agents, but not in discourse about *śakun* and *apśakun.*

Nāśubh and *kuśubh* appear to be used interchangeably in Pahansu; both may be translated as "inauspiciousness." These terms denote qualities and substances that themselves are the causes, or more precisely, the embodiments of ill-being. They are used in the astrological judgments of villagers concerning activities that make up the round of everyday life, in the scheduling of ritual and gift-giving, in decisions concerning the specific ameliorative techniques to be undertaken when a person, a household, or the entire village is in distress, and with regard to other events in the life course. The ways in which *nāśubh* and *kuśubh* are thought to embody, cause, and transfer ill-being are fundamental to our understanding of *dān*.

Nāśubh and *kuśubh* are the most inclusive terms in use in Pahansu to refer to a range of negative qualities and substances that may afflict persons, families, houses, and villages. A number of other terms are used to specify either the source of the inauspiciousness or the precise effects it may have on those afflicted. Below, with approximate translations, is a more or less complete listing of such terms in use in Pahansu.

kaṣṭ	distress
sankaṭ	danger
rog	disease
ḍar	terror
pāp	sin, evil
doṣ	fault
bādhā	hindrance
pret-bādhā	hindrance [caused by the presence of] ghosts
kaṛāī	difficulty

All of these terms are used for the most part interchangeably, though they may emphasize somewhat different aspects of a situation in which inauspiciousness is engendered or transferred to a particular entity. All of them are defined by villagers in ways that indicate their "otherness." These negative conditions, qualities, or substances are not produced within the boundaries (if such boundedness exists at all) of an isolated person or household or village, but arise in those situations where persons or households are separated by death or birth, joined together (as in marriage), or when other disjunctions and conjunctions are underway, as is thought to be the case during many astrological circumstances. They "come upon" and "become attached to" persons, houses, or the village as a whole at the time of such disjunctions and conjunctions, and for this reason they may all be described by villagers as *oprā*, a term that is often used to refer to "possession" by a god or ghost but has the more general meaning of "difference," "distance," or "alienation," something that is not homogeneous with oneself, that is not "one's own" (*apnā*). The verb forms used in Pahansu to describe the occurrence of inauspiciousness underscore the notion that it involves heterogeneous substances or qualities that come from outside the afflicted entity. *Nāśubh, kuśubh,* and all the nouns listed above may occur with any of the following verbs.

lagnā	to become attached
caṛhnā	to go upon

pahũcnā	to reach
uske upar ā jānā	to come upon him

These are the only verbs that are used to describe the onset of inauspiciousness in any of its forms, and they contrast, as we shall see, with verbs that are used with reference to forms of ill-being other than inauspiciousness. A clearly defined spatial imagery pervades this set of verbs and is continued in the set of verbs villagers use to talk about the ending of such conditions.

dūr ho jānā	to become far
haṭanā	to go away
utarnā	to go down off of
ṭalanā or ṭal jānā	to move away

Because, as we shall see, inauspicious qualities and substances do not "move away" without the performance of certain ritual actions, there is a corresponding set of transitive verbs that are used in referring to the actions performed in order to effect this removal.

dūr karnā	to make far
haṭānā	to cause to go away
utārnā	to take down off of
ṭālnā	to cause to move away

The verbs *denā* ("to give") and *lenā* ("to accept") may also be used in connection with the various forms of inauspiciousness. This is, as far as I am aware, a complete listing of the verb forms that occur in Pahansu talk about inauspiciousness.

Now the spatial imagery that indicates the "alien" nature of negative substances, qualities, or conditions might not be of much cultural significance were it not for two very important facts. First, the verbs I have listed here operate in marked contrast to those used with negatively valued substances, situations, or qualities other than inauspiciousness. To describe the onset of the various forms of "impurity" (*asauca, sūtak, pātak, aśuddha*), for example, the appropriate verbs are *honā* ("to be"), as in *sūtak hai* ("birth impurity is"); *mānnā* ("to observe"), as in *pātak mānte haĩ* ("they are observing death impurity"); and *phailnā* ("to spread"), which refers to the fact that *sūtak* and *pātak* may affect persons outside one's own household. For the ending of conditions of impurity, the verbs used are *khatam honā* ("to be ended") and *likaṛnā* ("to dissipate").

Illnesses caused by a disruption in the equilibrium of the three humors (the *doṣas*) within the body—*bāī,* "wind"; *pitta,* "bile"; and *kapha,* "phlegm"—or of cold and hot (*sard-garam*), seem always to involve the use of the verb *honā* ("to be"). The onset of such disorders is described in terms such as "cold-hot illness happens" (*sard-garam bimār ho jātā hai*), "because of 'wind', he becomes ill" (*bāī ke wajah se bimār ho jātā hai*), or "the body becomes dry" (*śarīr sūkhā ho jātā hai*). Descriptions that occur in ordinary discourse of the ending of illnesses caused by humoral and thermal imbalances also employ the verb *honā* with its meaning of "to happen" or "to become": "*pitta* has been stilled" (*pitta śānt ho gayā*) or "he has become alright" (*wah ṭhīk ho gayā*).

This typology of negatively valued conditions—inauspiciousness, impurity, and humoral or thermal imbalance within the body—is the major vehicle for identifying, discussing, and acting upon ill-being in Pahansu. Of these, as we have seen, only inauspiciousness is talked about in terms that represent the afflictions as originating outside of a particular person, family, house, or village, as qualities or substances that attach themselves and then must be "removed" or "made far" if well-being is to be regained.

Data concerning the ameliorative techniques employed in Pahansu in situations marked by inauspiciousness, impurity, or humoral imbalance also support the view that the use of specific verbs is significant for our understanding of auspiciousness and inauspiciousness. There are in Pahansu no life-course or calendrical rituals whose major goal is the removal of impurity or the establishment of a state of purity. Purity (*saucā, śuddha*) is, however, the goal of numerous actions that are preliminary to major ritual sequences; these actions include spreading cow-dung paste on floors and hearths, sprinkling water, and bathing. In the case of *sūtak* and *pātak* (birth and death impurity), the period of impurity must simply be waited out. It "ends" (*khatam honā*), as the appropriate verb suggests.

Bodily substances may be transmitted from one person to another; when this occurs in the context of a one-directional flow of substance, it is generally construed as a hierarchically ordered relationship, and judgments about relative "purity" and "impurity" may then be made. The well-documented ethnographic facts (Marriott 1968; Dumont 1970; Beck 1972) concerning the hierarchical implications of transactions in various media—raw foods (*sīdhā*), foods cooked in clarified butter or oil (*pakkā*), foods cooked in water or baked on a griddle without fat (*kaccā*), food leavings (*jūṭhan*), and so forth—concern the possibility of just such a transmission. What is at issue here is the linguistic and ethnographic fact that in Pahansu the transmission does not ordinarily remove a concrete "impurity" from the giver. If, for example, a Brahman were to accept *kaccā* food cooked in a Barber kitchen, or from a house in which a death had recently occurred, he would indeed incur some measure of "impurity," but the Barber or the bereaved household would not thereby lose impurity or acquire an increased measure of "purity." Such transactions of food or other items cannot, in other words, "remove" impurity; it may "spread" (*phailnā*) but it is not "moved to another place" (*ṭālnā, haṭānā*). Most significantly, there are in Pahansu no prestations that are given to remove impurity of any sort, but numerous prestations are made on a daily basis to "move inauspiciousness to another place" (*nāśubh haṭāne ke lie*).

Now the foregoing discussion is of course an insufficient account of Hindu conceptualizations of "purity" and "impurity." A full account would explore in particular the possible differences among the forms of *asaucā* (e.g., menstrual, birth, and death impurity), and the "impurity" involved in intercaste transmissions of bodily substances. While there are no doubt important differences between these impurities (see, e.g., Das 1977, 128–29; Marriott 1982), certain common characteristics are evidenced in the Pahansu data. First, impurity cannot be "removed" through any sort of transferral to a recipient, as inauspiciousness is removed through the giving of *dān*. Villagers do not speak, for example, of appropriate recipients (*pātrā*, lit., "vessel") of impurity as they do in the case of the negative qualities and substances associated with inauspiciousness. Second, forms of impurity have little if any relevance for more generalized well-being or auspiciousness. Ill-health, lack of prosperity, failure to produce sons, death, madness, family discord, poor harvests, and many of the other misfortunes about which villagers are concerned and that receive much ritual attention are never attributed to impurity or hierarchical considerations of any sort, but rather are discussed primarily in terms of the *nāśubh* that must have brought them about. Pahansu villagers also make explicit statements that auspiciousness and inauspiciousness entail a "different reckoning" (*dūsrā hissāb*) from that involved in concerns with purity and impurity, "dispositions about high and low" (*ū̃c-nīc kā bhāv*), or with health and disease as endogenous, merely "bodily" (*śarīrik*), states.

In Pahansu, techniques concerned with maintaining or restoring humoral balance in such "bodily" disorders seem to be derived primarily from the Ayurvedic system of indigenous medicine. While there are no Ayurvedic specialists in the village, these techniques are widely known, talked about, and employed, though no doubt in much simpler forms than might have been the case had there been a specialist available. There are three major types of treatment in use in the village, and these aim to increase the property of fluidity within the body, to bring about thermal or humoral balance, to "soften" (*naram kar denā*) parts of the body that have become dry and hard (*sakht*), or to open up bodily channels (*nālī*) that have become blocked. A very wide range of what we might see as either physical or psychological disorders may require such treatments.

The most common of these ameliorative techniques involves the modification of the diet to counterbalance a disequilibrium of either the three *doṣa*s or of hot and cold, or requires the ingestion of medications (*dawāī*) designed to bring about the same effect. If one is suffering, for example, from an excess of *bāī* ("wind"), one would avoid foods such as *kaṛī,* rice, and potatoes that increase *bāī;* this would be particularly advisable in the cold season (*sardī*) when levels of *bāī* in the body are likely to be high.[3] One might also eat foods that actively counteract the *bāī,* such as garlic, asafoetida, and ginger.

The second technique involves, not the ingestion of food or medicines, but the application of these to the skin. This technique is used most frequently in cases where heat (*garmī*) or an excess of *pitta* ("bile") has caused eruptions of some sort to appear on the skin. Crushed *nīm* (margosa) leaves mixed with water is one such remedy that may be applied in cases of this sort. The basis for the treatment is the notion that "cold" substances, such as the *nīm* leaves, will transmit the antidote to the build-up of the heat or the bile; they will "bring cold" (*ṭhaṇḍa pahũcānā*) to the surface of the body.

The third Ayurvedic technique in use in Pahansu is massage (*māliś* or *dabānā*). This treatment is used when a diagnosis has been made that indicates that a channel (*nālī*) that transports the humors through the body has become blocked. Massage of this type is used rather infrequently in Pahansu, but when it is deemed necessary, a Weaver woman from the neighboring village of Duharki, known to be skilled in the technique, may be called to perform the massage. The pressing and rubbing of the parts of the body in which the blocked channels are located is thought to be an effective remedy for disorders caused by such blockages.

Now the relation between the verbs used in connection with humoral imbalance and the Ayurvedic ameliorative techniques in use in the village becomes clear when we consider the etiology of such disorders in comparison with diseases and other afflictions brought about by inauspiciousness. Since humoral imbalances are often attributed to a discordance with the changes in the seasons (Zimmermann 1980), they are seen to occur partly outside and partly within the body of the patient, and they are manifested in a blockage, a drying, or an excitation of a particular humor. They do not have their origin in the mixing of negative qualities and substances with the body, and thus the appropriate remedies (and the corresponding linguistic usages) do not usually involve "removal."

"Removal" is, however, necessitated when inauspiciousness becomes attached (*lagnā*) to a person, family, house, or village. All forms of inauspiciousness are said to originate in entities and events that are "different" and "distant" from the person or other afflicted entity; they are "alien" (*oprā*), and this alien nature stands in contrast to the endogenous character of the other sorts of disorders considered here. This contrast is a pervasive one in Pahansu; nearly all illnesses, behavioral irregularities, and many kinds of misfortunes are thought to be assignable to one or the other of these categories, even though such diagnoses are seldom simply a matter of the observable symptoms in a particular case. If a diagnosis of a humoral disproportion is made, the ameliorative techniques will involve the use of medicines, diets, or massages to reinstate a proper equilibrium and flow within the body. If the etiology of a disorder or misfortune concerns inauspiciousness, however, the treatment is always the "removal" of the alien negative substances through sometimes complicated sequences of ritual acts and the giving of *dān,* which transfers the inauspiciousness to an appropriate recipient. Such attempted transferrals would never be effective in the case of a disorder caused by humoral or thermal imbalance. It is for this reason that correct diagnosis is crucial. The villager must not only determine whether the disorder in question has originated in endogenous humoral imbalances or the alien inauspiciousness; but if it is of alien origin, he must also discover the exact source of the inauspiciousness if the therapeutic action—the giving of *dān*—is to be successful, for each type of inauspiciousness requires a particular ritual, a particular type of *dān,* and a particular recipient.

The Sources of Inauspiciousness

I was able to record in Pahansu discourse eleven lexical items that functioned in very similar ways as terms for inauspiciousness: *nāśubh* (or *kuśubh*), *oprā, kaṣṭ, sankaṭ, rog, ḍar, pāp, doṣ, bādhā, pret-bādhā* and *kaṛāī.* Several important properties of these forms of inauspiciousness may be noted. First, these negative qualities and substances exhibit a principle of conservation in which the effects of *nāśubh, kaṣṭ, sankaṭ, rog,* and so on, are not susceptible to any simple diminution or palliation; the only effective ameliorative technique is to remove the inauspicious substances from the afflicted entity. Inauspiciousness must, villagers say, have its effect somewhere, and that is why it cannot simply be destroyed; it must be transferred to and assimilated by an appropriate recipient for the therapy to be successful. Second, the possible effects of inauspiciousness on persons and families are many and diverse, and the source of the inauspiciousness does not necessarily determine the precise consequences. In discussions about inauspiciousness, in speculations about the possible causes of misfortunes, in astrological consultations, and during the course of ritual preparations, villagers frequently described madness (*pāgalpan*), disease (*rog*), death, the decline of one's lineage, infertility, poor harvests, and pain (*dard*) as possible results of being afflicted by inauspiciousness or receiving it in *dān*. Symptomatically, such effects may sometimes resemble the consequences of humoral and thermal imbalance, but the etiologic differences are the decisive feature in village diagnoses. The same set of symptoms, occurring in different persons, might be attributed to humoral imbalance in one case, and exogenous inauspiciousness in another; and the services of a specialist—an astrologer perhaps—might be necessary to make such diagnoses.[4]

What, then, does it mean to say that inauspiciousness comprises specifically exogenous negative qualities and substances? What are the sources of these substances, and how precisely are they able to affect persons, families, houses, and villages? Examination of the Pahansu data indicates that there are a number of sources of inauspiciousness, the most important of which are discussed here.

General Astrological Conditions

There are certain astrological circumstances that are productive of *nāśubh* regardless of the activities in which villagers might be engaged, although the effects could indeed be exacerbated if certain actions were to be performed at those times. The most important of these times, called *parvakāl,* are the *sankrānti*s (the joining of the sun with a new *rāśi* or portion of the zodiac), new moon days (*amāvas,* literally, the "dwelling together" of the sun and moon), and eclipses (*grahaṇa*). In all *parvakāl,* there is a joining (*yog*) of heavenly bodies that results in a release of inauspiciousness. *Parvakāl* are dangerous because of this inauspiciousness, and also because, as Stanley (1977, 42) has pointed out, there is a general fluidity and potential for junctures and mixings at these times. Thus in Pahansu, *amāvas* days, *sankrānti*s (particularly *makar sankrānti*), and eclipses are appropriate days for the giving of *dān* to remove the inauspiciousness engendered by the *parvakāl* itself, and also to remove other sorts of inauspiciousness that become fluid and possess a heightened transferability at these times. Villagers say that *amāvas* and the other *parvakāl* are "dangerous" (*najuk*) days during which "bad air" is abroad in the atmosphere (*vāyumaṇḍal mẽ galat hawāe ghūmte haĩ*), bringing with it "distress" (*kaṣṭ*) and "faults" (*doṣ*) from many different sources. Because of this potential for fluidity, *parvakāl* are said to be opportune times for what is known as *ugrā kām* ("fierce work"), the transfer of inauspiciousness usually effected by "sorcerers" (*sayānā*) secretly through the use of magical devices (*ṭoṭkā*).

Conjunctions of Times and Activities

Apart from inherently "dangerous" times, there are also astrologically determined periods that may bring inauspiciousness when particular activities are undertaken. Many of these have been mentioned above in the discussion of the adjectival use of the term *aśubh*. Here, too, one finds notions of potential fluidity of inauspiciousness at certain times, and the receptivity of persons, houses, families, and villages to negative substances may be heightened by actions and events, particularly those that involve new conjunctions of persons and objects (wearing new clothes, setting out on a journey), and conjunctions and disjunctions of one person with another (in marriage, birth, and death).

Conjunctions in the Horoscope

Particular configurations of heavenly bodies in one's horoscope (*janam kuṇḍalī*) may be productive of inauspiciousness. The representation of the horoscope consists of twelve "spaces" (*sthān*), which concern salient relationships, actions, and events in one's life. The positions of the planets (*graha*) and constellations (*rāśi, nakṣatra*) at the moment of birth can be mapped on the twelve spaces of the horoscope, and the effect of the heavens on the life course can then be known (see fig. 6).

When asked to construct a horoscope, Buddhu Pandit uses two astrological manuals for ascertaining the effects of various planetary configurations.[5] Ordinary villagers discuss the inauspiciousness generated by these configurations in terms of the auspicious and inauspicious planets. This classification in fact has a great deal of relevance in this context. The astrological manuals frequently make the distinction; if, for example, an "evil" planet (Sūrya, Mangal, Śani, Rāhu, or Ketu) falls in the seventh space of a girl's horoscope, it is said she will become a widow. If one of these planets falls, at the time of birth, in the tenth or fifth spaces, inauspiciousness in the form of "distress" (*kaṣṭ*) results; the presence of Śani and Sūrya in these spaces gives *kaṣṭ* to the father, Rāhu gives *kaṣṭ* to the mother, Mangal gives *kaṣṭ* to the brother, and Śani gives *kaṣṭ* to the child.

However, the astrologer is concerned with more than the simple presence or absence of inauspicious planets. Particular configurations of heavenly bodies are at issue. If, for example, a "cruel," inauspicious planet coincides with the *lagan* (the "space" of the *rāśi* at one's birth), and another falls in the fourth space, the inauspiciousness is somewhat mitigated and the child will survive it. The mere presence of one inauspicious planet in a particular space may not produce inauspiciousness unless a particular auspicious planet falls in another space. If the inauspicious *graha* Rāhu occupies the eighth place, for example, and the moon occupies the first, inauspiciousness is produced that will result in the child's death at the age of twelve.

Ordinary villagers do not possess this detailed knowledge of planetary configurations in the *janam kuṇḍalī*. Buddhu Pandit's astrological manual contains this information in the form of Sanskrit verses with Hindi

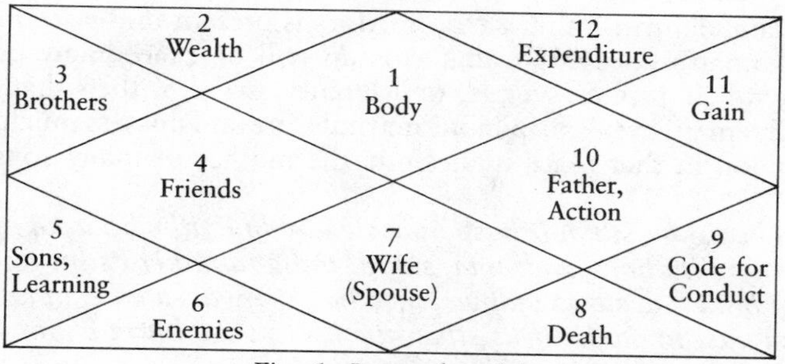

Fig. 6. *Janam kuṇḍalī*

translations. Each verse and its prose rendering considers a specific, partial, horoscopic configuration. A typical Hindi rendering is as follows:

> *lagan mẽ śani, 6 candramā, 10 mangal mẽ ho to uske pitā kī mṛityu ho yā kaṣṭ ho.*
>
> If Saturn is in the *lagan*, the moon in the sixth space, and Mars in the tenth, death or distress will afflict the father.

These verses are arranged in two sections in the manuals, paralleling the actual uses, in Pahansu, to which knowledge of the *janam kuṇḍalī* is put. The first section deals with the auspiciousness and inauspiciousness that may affect the child, the parents and brothers, and occasionally, the mother's brother. The example given above is found in this first section. The second section, labeled *strī kuṇḍalī phalam* ("fruit of the wife's horoscope"), contains verses that follow the same form as those in the first section but deal with the inauspiciousness that affects a woman's marital life. Three examples follow.

1. *jis strī ke sūrya saptam ho to wah pati ko tyāg de, candramā ho to sundar ho, budh ho to saubhāgyavatī, bṛhaspati ho to sarva sukh vālī, śukra ho to bhog bhogne vālī bhāgyavatī ho.*

   That woman in whose seventh place the sun falls will leave her husband; if the moon is in that place, she will be beautiful; if Mercury is in that place, she will remain in the auspicious marital state; if Jupiter is there, she will possess all happiness; and if Venus is there, she will enjoy good fortune.

2. *sūrya, śaniścar, rāhu, ketu aur mangal ye graha dūsre sthān mẽ sthit hõ to yah strī atyāt daridra aur dukhītā hotī hai. bṛhaspati, śukra, yā budh ho to wah strī saubhāgyavatī aur adhik dhanvatī honī cahiye aur candramā bahut putravatī kartā hai.*

If the sun, Saturn, Rāhu, Ketu, or Mars is present in the second space of a woman's horoscope, that woman will be exceedingly poor and sorrowful. If Jupiter, Venus, or Mercury is there, then that woman should remain in the auspicious marital state and possess much wealth. The moon in that place makes one the mother of many sons.

3. *jis strī ke aṣṭam sthān bṛhaspati athwā budh baiṭhe hõ uskā apne pati se viyog rahtā hai; candramā, śukra, tathā rāhu-ketu sthit hõ to uskā maraṇ hotā hai. sūrya vidhvā kartā hai, mangal sadacaraṇ karne vālā banātā hai aur śaniścar us sthān mẽ hõ to uske putra bahut hõ tathā wah strī apne pati kī pyārī hotī hai.*

That woman in whose eighth place Jupiter or Mercury falls will live apart from her husband; if the moon, Venus, Rāhu, or Ketu is present there, she will die. The sun in that space makes one a widow, Mars makes one act virtuously, and if Saturn is in that space, she will have many sons and be beloved of her husband.

Two important characteristics of inauspiciousness are evidenced in these examples. First, the usage patterns of the adjectives *śubh* and *aśubh* do not always tell us of the sources of inauspiciousness; in these examples, auspicious as well as inauspicious *graha* may be the sources of negative qualities and substances by virtue of their positions in the *janam kuṇḍalī*. Otherwise, as Buddhu Pandit pointed out to me, the necessity for giving the *dān* of the auspicious planets would never arise. Second, the inauspiciousness generated by the heavenly bodies may afflict, not only the person whose horoscope has been cast, but the spouse, the parents, the siblings, and the mother's brother as well.

Inappropriate Matchings of Persons and Places

Settling in a new village or town involves, in the indigenous conceptualization, a matching of the person with these places, and inappropriate matchings may result in inauspiciousness.[6] Ordinary villagers do not have a comprehension of the techniques used by the astrologer to determine whether the match will be auspicious or inauspicious, but they are aware of the sort of mapping of village to person that is involved. The mapping is carried out in the following manner.

Beginning with the lunar asterism (*nakṣatra*) that corresponds with the first letter of the name of the village, the twenty-eight *nakṣatra*s are mapped onto the "body" in the order in which the asterisms appear in the heavens.[7] Thus, taking Pahansu as an example, Buddhu Pandit would start with *uttarā phālgunī,* the asterism that is associated with the Hindi syllable *pa,* and map the *nakṣatra*s as has been done in table 5.

Having constructed the *nakṣatra* "body" in this way, the astrologer

TABLE 5

Settling in a Village: Matchings of Asterisms and the Body for Pahansu

Part	*Nakṣatra*s
māthā (forehead)	*uttarā phālgunī, hasta, citrā, svāti, viśākhā, anurādhā, jyeṣṭha*
pīṭh (back)	*mūl, pūrvāṣāṛhā, uttarāṣāṛhā, abhijitu, śravaṇa, dhaniṣṭhā, śatbhiṣā*
hṛday (heart)	*pūrvā bhādrapad, uttarā bhādrapad, revatī, aśvini, bharaṇī, kṛttikā, rohiṇī*
pāv (feet)	*mṛgaśirā, ārdrā, punarvasu, puṣya, śleṣā, maghā, purvā phālgunī*

then notes the *nakṣatra* that corresponds to the first syllable of the name of the man who wishes to settle in the village. If that *nakṣatra* has "fallen" (*paṛnā*) on the forehead or heart, then the match between village and person is propitious, and the man's family will prosper there; if it falls on the back or the feet, inauspiciousness will afflict him if he settles in that village. In this procedure, the lunar asterisms are arrayed in an order specified by the particular village, and this ordering determines where the person's own name-asterism will fall. It is in this particular matching of the person with the village that the potential for auspiciousness or inauspiciousness lies.

Inappropriate Conjunctions of Spaces and Times

Astrological considerations that precede house-building and well-digging are examples of a concern with inauspiciousness that may be produced if inappropriate matchings of spaces and times are made.

Deciding on a propitious time and place to dig a well in one's fields involves a mapping of times (the *nakṣatra* days) onto the space of the fields, similar to the way in which asterisms are mapped onto a "body" before one decides to move to a new village.[8] If a Pahansu farmer wants to dig a well on his land, he is likely first to consult Buddhu Pandit about a good time and place for the well-digging. Buddhu Pandit first looks for an auspicious time (*muhūrat*) at which the *nakṣatra, tithi* (lunar day), and *vār* (solar day) are all auspicious for this activity. The auspicious asterisms, according to Buddhu Pandit, are *hasta, citrā, svāti, dhaniṣṭhā, śatbhiṣā, śleṣa, maghā, uttarā phālgunī, uttarāṣāṛhā*, and *uttarā bhādrapad.* Auspicious lunar days are the second, third, fifth, seventh, tenth, thirteenth, and fifteenth days of the lunar fortnight. Auspicious solar days are Monday, Wednesday, Thursday, and Friday. After selecting a day based on these criteria, Buddhu Pandit carries out the second step, which involves a mapping of the day's *nakṣatra* (the *din nakṣatra*) onto the space

aśvini, bharaṇī, kṛttikā NORTHEAST **Auspiciousness**	*mṛgaśīra, ārdrā* EAST **Inauspiciousness**	*punarvasu, puṣya, śleṣā* SOUTHEAST **Auspiciousness**
pūrvā bhādrapad, uttarā bhādrapad, revatī NORTH **Auspiciousness**	*rohiṇī* CENTER **Auspiciousness**	*maghā, pūrvā phālgunī, uttarā phālgunī, hasta, citrā* SOUTH **Inauspiciousness**
dhaniṣṭhā, śatbhiṣā NORTHWEST **Inauspiciousness**	*uttarāṣāṛhā, śrāvaṇa* WEST **Inauspiciousness**	*svāti, viśākhā, anurādhā, jyeṣṭha, mūl, pūrvāṣāṛhā* SOUTHWEST **Auspiciousness**

Fig. 7. Auspicious and inauspicious conjunctions of times and spaces with reference to well-digging

defined by the boundaries of the fields in which the farmer wishes to dig a well. The farmer gives a rough map (*nakṣā*) of his fields to Buddhu Pandit, and Buddhu superimposes a diagram (*cakra*) of the directions over this. The squares of the diagram are propitious or not propitious for the digging because of their conjunction with the various asterisms. If the day's *nakṣatra* falls on a square that is unfavorable, then another day is chosen. Inauspiciousness (*kuśubh*) is produced if one acts in the context of an unfavorable conjunction of times and spaces. These auspicious and inauspicious conjunctions are shown in figure 7.

Here again we find that, out of context, the simple description of a lunar asterism or direction as being "auspicious" or "inauspicious" does not correspond to its actual effect. When conjoined with certain asterisms, for example, the easterly direction, generally said to be "auspicious," produces inauspiciousness; generally inauspicious asterisms, such as *mūl*, produce auspiciousness when conjoined with the inauspicious southwest direction. It is the specific relation of the times and spaces here that may produce inauspiciousness for the farmer, his fields, and the quality of the well water.

Propitious or unpropitious alignments of times and spaces may also occur when a foundation is laid for a new house. As in the foregoing case, it is not simply certain directions or spaces, or certain times, that generate inauspiciousness; rather, it is their conjunction that must be attended to.

In Pahansu, the digging of the foundation and the laying of the foundation stone (*nīv dharnā*) are accorded the most attention when a house is to be built or repairs are to be made to an old one. Certain times are said to be auspicious for this regardless of the spatial orientation of the house. The lunar asterisms *pūrvāṣāṛhā, punarvasu, puṣya, mṛgaśīra, śravaṇa, dhaniṣṭhā, śatbhiṣā, uttarā phālgunī, hasta, citrā, svāti, mūl, revatī, anu-*

rādhā, and *aśvini,* the months of Sāvan, Baisākh, Kārttik, Phālgun, and Mangsar, and the solar days Monday, Wednesday, Thursday, Friday, and Saturday are all auspicious for the digging and the laying of the foundation stone, according to Buddhu Pandit. When, for example, a Brahman man of Pahansu wanted to rebuild a section of his house after it had been destroyed by heavy monsoon rains, he consulted Buddhu about the best time to lay the new foundation stone. Buddhu first noted the foregoing fixed considerations, and eliminated some of these because of other considerations that involve a mapping together of spaces and times similar to those that are involved in well-digging and settling in a new village. He then consulted his astrological manual and told the Brahman about Śeṣnāg *vicār,* the "considerations about Śeṣnāg," and the manner in which inauspiciousness would afflict the house and its occupants if the digging were to be carried out improperly. Śeṣnāg, the "remainder snake," on whose body the earth is said to rest, shifts his position from time to time, and this movement must be taken into account. During the months of Bhādwe, Asauj, and Kārttik, the head lies in the east; in Mangsar, Pau, and Māgh, it is in the south; in Phālgun, Cait, and Baisākh, it is in the west, and in Jeṭh, Aṣāṛh, and Sāvan, the head of the snake lies in the north. Accordingly, the back (*pīṭh*) and tail (*pū̃ch*) of Śeṣnāg also lie in particular directions. Reading from his astrological manual, Buddhu Pandit told us of the results (*phal*) that one could expect if the digging and the placing of the foundation stone were to be done in these directions at these times:

> *yadi śeṣnāg ke sir par khudvāve, to mātā-pitā ki hāni hoy aur pīṭh par khudvāve, to bhay rog pīṛā ho, pū̃ch par khudvāve, to tīn gotra kī hāni hove aur jo khālī jagah par khudvāve, to strī, putra, dhan ityādi kā lābh ho.*
>
> If one digs over Śeṣnāg's head, there will be harm to one's parents; and if one digs over the back there will be fear, disease, and pain; and if one digs over the tail there will be harm to the three *gotra*s. But whoever digs over an empty space will obtain the benefits of wife, sons, and wealth.

In order to determine exactly where the digging and the placing of the foundation stone should be done, the position of Śeṣnāg beneath the earth, as illustrated in figure 8, is mapped onto the plot of land on which the house is to be built. During each three-month period, Śeṣnāg moves ninety degrees clockwise, and the "empty space," where the digging should always be done, changes accordingly.

The consequences of not taking the movements of Śeṣnāg into account are generally thought of, by ordinary villagers, in terms of failure to pro-

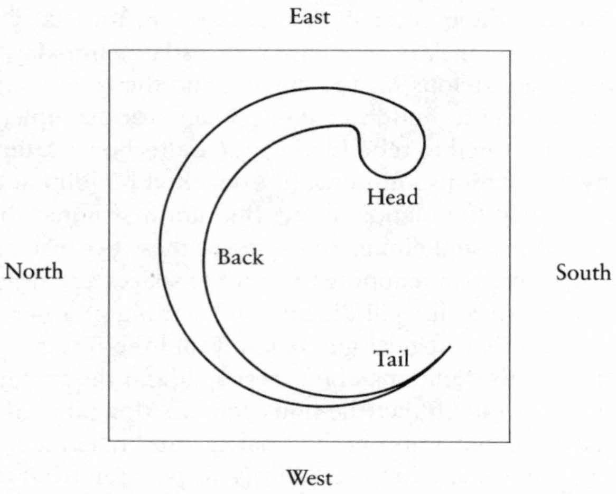

Fig. 8. Śeṣnāg's position in the months of Bhādwe, Asauj, and Kārttik

duce offspring, particularly sons. Many years before my arrival in Pahansu, Pitambar, a Gujar landholder, built a fine new house for his family just behind the house of Telu Ram and Jabar Singh in which I lived. He failed, however, to consult an astrologer about these matters, nor did he give the *dān* that is necessary at the time of building a house. The many misfortunes that his family has suffered since are still attributed by many people of the village to Pitambar's disregard of Śeṣnāg *vicār*. Narendar, Pitambar's father's brother's son's son, had lived in this house for some time, but about ten years before my arrival in Pahansu he had built a new house for himself far from the other houses of his *kunbedār*s, near the Camar (Leatherworker) neighborhood at the northeastern end of the village. Once when I was attending the rituals that are performed at the completion of a new house (at the home of another Gujar landholder), several people began to speak of the house that Narendar had built ten years before, and the fact that he, like Pitambar, "didn't do anything" to ensure the auspiciousness of the house. He had failed to take care that his house was oriented properly with respect to Śeṣnāg, and he had failed to give *dān*, and this was the reason that his wife Kaushal had not been able to conceive and bear children.

Inauspiciousness and the Night of the Gods in Pahansu

That the gods are the source of many of the sufferings of men is a commonplace theme in Hindu mythology. While sometimes in village myths and in other textual traditions evil and suffering are sent by the gods as a sort of punishment for the sins of men against gods, it is often the case that evil and inauspiciousness are given to men by the gods simply to rid themselves of these noxious qualities and substances. The well-known myth of the distribution of Indra's sin of brahmanicide (a version of which is translated in chapter 3) is perhaps the paradigmatic version of this theme, as O'Flaherty (1976, 146–60) has pointed out.

Many of the rituals oriented toward deities are, in Pahansu, concerned with "removing" and making far" the evil and inauspiciousness sent from the gods at various points in the yearly calendrical cycle. The distribution of these various rituals at different times of the year may tell us something of their meaning insofar as the sources of inauspiciousness are concerned. Figure 9 illustrates the yearly cycle of seasons, lunar months, and the *āyaṇa*s, the periods of time between the summer and winter solstices. The *uttarāyaṇa* is the time of the sun's northward movement, and the *dakṣiṇāyana* is the time in which the sun moves in a southward course (see Pugh 1983 for further details).

Uttarāyaṇa is sometimes said to be a "day of the gods" (*devatāõ kā din*) and *dakṣiṇāyaṇa* a "night of the gods" (*devatāõ kā rāt*); for this reason one should do "auspicious work" (*śubh kām*) in the *uttarāyaṇa* half of the year. The middle four months of the *dakṣiṇāyaṇa*—Sāvan, Bhādwe, Asauj, and Kārttik—represent the time in which the gods are said to sleep, and they are inauspicious for many activities, particularly for betrothals and weddings. Indeed, in these months, no weddings occur in the village. Yet this four-month period is filled with ritual activity, and most of the rituals of the yearly cycle occur during this period.

Many of these rituals are oriented toward the gods and involve the giving of *dān* to remove the inauspiciousness that has been transferred to human beings when the gods are asleep. Only one ritual of the yearly cycle that involves a god as well as the giving of *dān* occurs outside these four months (the ritual of Holi in the month of Phālgun). There are several other rituals of the yearly cycle that are addressed to deities, but they do not occur during this time, and they do not involve the giving of *dān* to remove inauspiciousness. They are relatively unimportant in Pahansu, though in other regions of northern India they seem to assume greater prominence. These include the "nine nights" (*naurātrī*) of the goddess in the month of Cait, and the "night of Śiva" (*śivrātrī*) in the month of Phālgun.

karśā (hot season)				*camāsā* (rainy season)				*jaḍa* (cold season)			
uttarāyaṇa (cont.)				*dakṣiṇāyaṇa*						*uttarāyaṇa*	
Phālgun	*Cait*	*Baisākh*	*Jeṭh*	*Asāṛh*	*Sāvan**	*Bhādwe**	*Asauj**	*Kārttik**	*Mangsar*	*Pau*	*Māgh*

**Inauspicious lunar months in which the gods "sleep" and no weddings are held*

Fig. 9. Aspects of the yearly cycle in Pahansu

At the time of weddings, then, when the presence of the gods is desired for the well-being of the bride and groom, the gods must be "awake." Thus betrothals and marriage rituals are not performed in the four months of their sleep. But the rituals that through the giving of *dān* remove the inauspiciousness of the gods from human beings are celebrated in this four-month period, because it is at this time that the inauspiciousness and evil of the gods is transferred to men. (These rituals of the calendrical cycle will be discussed in detail in chapter 4.)

Birth, Marriage, and Death and the "Connections of the Body"

Inauspiciousness circulates spontaneously among related persons, villagers say, by means of the "bodily connection" (*śarīr kā sambandh*) that, quite literally, "binds" them together. This connection is, of course, an indigenously defined relationship; one shares such a connection with many persons, including the people of one's own *kunbā,* one's spouse, one's mother's brother, and so forth. But there is no *śarīr kā sambandh,* according to my informants, with one's married sisters, daughters, and father's sisters, or with their offspring; with these persons there is only a "relationship" (*riśtā*).[9] The apparent paradox of this statement will immediately be noted: a man is said to have a "bodily connection" with his mother's brother, but a mother's brother is said specifically *not* to have such a connection with his sister's son. Thus, in the villagers' view, *śarīr kā sambandh* is not necessarily a reciprocal form of relatedness. Now villagers mentioned this idea of a "bodily connection" with one's mother's brother primarily in the context of discussions concerning the spontaneous flow of inauspiciousness from sister's son to mother's brother. If, for example, a person has become afflicted by inauspiciousness because of an unpropitious birth at the time of a *mūl* asterism or because of the death of his mother or father, it will affect people of his own *kunbā,* and his mother's brother as well. Inauspicious substances spontaneously move in the direction of one's mother's brother, informants say, but not in the direction of one's sister's son, or of married sisters, daughters, or father's sisters, precisely because with those people there is no *śarīr kā sambandh.* We can see clearly, in this example, how "bodily connection" is related to inauspiciousness: the connection functions as a channel, as it were, for the movement, but not for the "removal," of the negative substances and qualities from one person to another.

Because these "bodily connections" serve as channels for the spontaneous flow of inauspiciousness, the points at which such connections are created (marriage), attenuated (death), or transformed (birth) are the points in the life course at which inauspiciousness is thought to circulate among persons. A small detail of the marriage ritual illustrates this point. Just before the *pherā,* the "circling" of the fire that indissolubly unites a bride and a groom, ends of the clothing of the two are tied together with a strip of white cloth, one and one-quarter *gaj* (about a yard) in length, called the *kānjol*. A Sanskrit *mantra* recited at the time the *kānjol* is tied describes the function of this "tying" or "connecting" (*bāndhnā*): the cloth is tied "to protect the two masters" (i.e., the bride and the groom), *dampatyoh rakṣaṇārthaya,* from the inauspiciousness that is put into circulation as a result of their joining together. The tying of the *kānjol* both unites them and contains the negative qualities and substances set in motion by their union. This cloth is then given as *dān* to the Brahman priest (*purohit*) of the groom's family, who thereby takes away the inauspiciousness it contains. The way in which the *kānjol* is made to absorb the inauspiciousness will be discussed in greater detail in chapter 4. The point to be noted here is simply that the very act of creating a new connection (and the marriage ritual is indeed thought to create a "bodily connection" between bride and groom) is fraught with the possibility of inauspiciousness.

Connections of the body also serve as conduits for the spontaneous flow of inauspiciousness from a recently deceased person to those with whom he shared a *śarīr kā sambandh,* and several ritual actions are performed after a death to terminate the connection so that the flow of inauspiciousness may be stopped. Immediately after the cremation, the men of the deceased's *kunbā* pick up a pebble and stand with their backs to the smoldering funeral pyre. They throw the pebble over their right shoulders, in order that, as villagers say, "connection won't remain" (*sambandh na rahe*) with the dead man. This act is called "dropping the pebble" (*kãkrī ḍalnā*) and is seen as being so potent that it is used as a metaphor for breaking "connections" in other ways as well. Thus, in the midst of a quarrel with his kinsmen, a villager may shout, "We have thrown down a pebble" (*hamne kãkrī ḍāl dī*). This "saying" (*kahāvat*) signifies that for them, at least at the time of their anger, the "connection" has been severed. In the context of the cremation, though, the breaking of the connection is done explicitly so that the inauspiciousness of the dead man, the *pret-bādhā* ("ghost hindrances"), will not flow back to the living through the channel of the bodily connection. But of course these connections are not usually broken so easily and so definitively. In Pahansu, the many rituals connected with death, and the many *dān* prestations that are made immediately after death and in the following year, have as their primary purpose the removal of the inauspiciousness of the *pret* from his living kinsmen and the gradual termination of the *śarīr kā sambandh* that unites them. The termination of the connection is most difficult when a death occurs "out of time" (*akāl mṛityu*), that is, when a person dies at a young age without having produced a son. In such cases, extraordinary measures must be taken to remove the *pret* from the household of his kin, and to sever the connection by establishing the *pret* in a shrine in the fields. (For further discussion of the problem of the lingering ghost, see Gold 1984, 86–108.)

Hamāre Ghar Mẽ Kleś Rahe: Afflictions in the House and the Problem of Diagnosis

Dān is most frequently given to remove the inauspiciousness that regularly afflicts one at specific times in the life course and in the calendrical cycle, even when the symptoms of this inauspiciousness have not yet presented themselves. However, *dān* of many sorts is also given when a specific set of symptoms has been diagnosed as originating because inauspiciousness has become "attached" (*lagnā*) to a person, a household, or a village. Because each type of inauspiciousness, that is, inauspiciousness from specific sources, must be removed with a specific kind of *dān*, and because illness resulting from humoral imbalance will not be cured through the giving of *dān*, diagnosis is a crucial part of any ameliorative action. In this section, I will discuss a number of incidents in which Pahansu people suffered illness, infertility, familial discord, and unforeseen death, and the manner in which they set about discovering the causes of their misfortunes, so that appropriate action, often involving the giving of *dān*, could be taken.

Amar Singh and the Pater Khurd Paṇḍit

Amar Singh Pradhan, an important Gujar landholder in Pahansu, had been ill for some time, with what appeared to be tuberculosis. Convinced that his sickness had been brought about by the presence of ghosts (*bhūt-pret*) and their inauspiciousness, Amar Singh summoned Agyaram Shastri, a Brahman from the village of Pater Khurd, who is renowned in the villages around Pahansu for his *jyotiṣī kā kām*, "astrology work." The *paṇḍit*, as he is called, took two *pīpal* leaves, placed some turmeric between them, and placed them in Amar Singh's hands. When the *paṇḍit* opened the leaves, he divined that Amar Singh's problem had not arisen from the presence of *bhūt-pret*s or the "fury of the gods" (*devī-devatā kā prakop*) and therefore that the giving of *dān* was not an appropriate treatment in this case. Rather, he said, Amar Singh's illness was a "bodily illness" (*śarīrik bimārī*) and should therefore be treated with medicines (*dawāī*).

Sudesh and the Sasurāl Devatā

Sudesh, the only child of Omkar, a Gujar man of Pahansu, returned from her husband's village just a few weeks after her *cālā* (the return to the husband's village a while after the wedding, at which time sets of cloth and other items are given to the groom and his family as a second "dowry," *dān-dahej*). When I went to Omkar's house to see her, she was suffering from a fever and complained that her legs were in pain; she kept clutching her abdomen and moaning, and her right hand and leg trembled and shook almost constantly. Many women of her neighborhood came to see her, and they discussed the nature of Sudesh's affliction. A few, clearly in the minority, were calling it a "matter of *karma*" (*karma kī bāt*), that is, a matter of the actions that Sudesh must have performed in her previous births. Interpreting difficulties and afflictions in this way generally has, in Pahansu, the pragmatic implication that ameliorative measures are few and difficult. Other women waited to judge what the source of Sudesh's affliction might be, though none of them seemed to feel that her illness was of purely "bodily" origin. Later that day, Sudesh began to speak incoherently, but in her near delirium the women heard her say, "I am B.A. pass." At that point, nearly all the women with whom I spoke were convinced that Sudesh was suffering from the inauspiciousness of a *bhūt,* specifically the *bhūt* of Mangi, the son of a Gujar woman who had been living in Pahansu with his mother's brother and had been found dead, hanging from a mango tree, several years before. (Mangi had in fact passed his B.A. exams before he died.)

Mela, mother's brother of Mangi, had consulted a *sayānā,* a man adept in dealing with *bhūt-pret*s, at the time of Mangi's untimely death. The *sayānā* had driven iron stakes into the ground at the four corners of Mela's house, to prevent the ghost from taking up residence in the house in which he previously lived. He had also done a *kārnī karwānā* to ensure that the wandering ghost should be removed from the house and be reborn in another womb, and that the inauspiciousness occasioned by his ghostly form should be transferred to a Brahman through the giving of *dān*. But it was possible, in the estimation of many people in Pahansu, that these procedures had not been successful and that Mangi had returned to trouble Sudesh. For several days there was much talk in the village of the powers of *sayānā*s, the way in which, perhaps, this *bhūt* might be trapped in a clay pot by a *sayānā,* "bound" (*bāndhnā*) by the power of *mantra*s, and then buried in an uninhabited place outside the village. Or perhaps the *sayānā* might, they thought, actually struggle with the *bhūt,* attempting through his acquired power (*siddhi*) to bring it under his influence, to force the *bhūt* to become his "client" (*mauvakīl*).

Because the *bhūt* that they thought was bringing the difficulties to Sudesh was not of her own or her husband's *kunbā,* it would not be possible to remove the inauspiciousness simply through the giving of *dān*. The *bhūt* himself had to be conquered by the *sayānā,* who is knowledgeable, not in the giving of *dān* to remove the inauspiciousness of one's own *devatās*, the ghosts of one's own house, but in the control of unknown or alien ghosts. The day after Sudesh returned to her father's house, he indeed took her to a *sayānā* in another village. I was not present at that consultation, and I do not know what method of diagnosis the *sayānā* used. But he did pronounce that Sudesh's illness and delirium were not caused by the ghost of Mangi. He apparently questioned Sudesh and her father and discovered that Sudesh had failed to make an offering at the shrine of a *pitri devatā* of her husband's family, a properly enshrined former *bhūt*, when she went there at the time of her *cālā*. A set of cloth from the *dān-dahej* is normally offered at such a shrine by the new bride, and then it is given as *dān* to the Brahman priest of the groom's household. Sudesh's difficulties were due, he said, to her failure to give this *dān*. And so the very next day, Omkar took Sudesh back to her *sasurāl* to make these offerings to the *pitri-devatā* and to give the *dān* to her husband's Brahman.

"I Don't Know Where He's Wandering": The Death of a Son and the Sorrows of a House

The joint family of Illam, Hukma, and Kanta, Pahansu Barbers, had, in the early months of my fieldwork and in the previous year or so, suffered many sorrows. Two years before I arrived in the village, Illam's elder son, Sirpal, had died at about twelve years of age. Shortly thereafter, as Illam's wife told me, two of her own sisters, a sister's son, her mother, and an infant child of Hukma had died. And then, around the time I arrived in the village, she lost another son at birth. Their fortune, she sometimes said, had indeed been spoiled (*kismat bigaṛ gayā*).

One afternoon I went to their house to pay a visit and found that the wives of Illam and Kanta had been crying. Hukma's wife had been taken violently ill, so much so that Illam had arranged for a taxi to take her to a hospital in Saharanpur. Her hands and feet had become cold, they said, and her stomach had swollen. As soon as she had given me this news, Illam's wife, again in tears, told me that she had had a dream the night before about Sirpal, her son who had died two years before.

In her dream, Illam's wife had gone to the *jangal*, an uninhabited area beyond the village, with some fruit tied in the end of her shawl (her *pallā*). Two other women were with her. She saw her son there in the *jangal*, and she told him: "Go home now. Your father will be angry if you don't go home." So she sent the boy home. But then she realized that she herself did not know the road back to the village, so she asked the two women to tell her the way. But the women said that it was getting dark, and that if she tried to walk home, some thief might come and snatch away her fruit; so, they said, she should lie down on a cot that was there in the *jangal* and spend the night there. But Illam's wife told the women in her dream that she had already sent her son on his way home, and so she too had to go. Just at that point, she woke up and she thought for a moment that she saw Sirpal behind the door of the inner room of their house. She cried out, "Where is Sirpal?" and woke Illam from his sleep.

Illam's wife cried as she told me this dream and, as she finished the narration, sobbed, "I don't know where he's wandering, or what house he has taken birth in" (*patā nahī̃ kahā̃ phirtā, kis ghar mẽ janam liyā*). She spoke of the boy's past actions (*bacce kā karma*) that perhaps had caused his early death.

She seemed to make a connection between her dream, the death and the probable "wandering" of Sirpal, and the sorrows that had beset their family; before I could say anything to her as she finished recounting the dream and its aftermath, she told me again that within two years after Sirpal's death, her sister, her mother, her sister's son, and the two infants born in their household (her own son, and Hukma's child) had also died.

I know that it was very difficult for Illam and his family to think of the son they loved as a *pret*, a wandering ghost who was now, perhaps, the source of the inauspiciousness that was afflicting their own house as well as Sirpal's maternal kin. About four months after the dream, Illam's daughter Kaushal was married. During the *bān* ritual, preliminary to the giving of the daughter in marriage to the groom, songs about the brothers of the bride are sung by the assembled women. At this point in Kaushal's *bān*, she burst into tears and could not be comforted. A week later, as Kaushal prepared to depart for her *sasurāl*, her mother embraced her and began to wail, calling out Sirpal's name. Illam's mother and Hukma's wife also embraced and wept. Finally Illam came to tell his wife to stop crying, but he too burst into tears. The brother of Hukma's wife finally came forward and tried to stop all of this, saying that Illam's other son, his mother, and his father were all alive, and that everything else was now well in the house. Then one of Kaushal's mother's brothers came to lift her into the waiting car for the farewell.

About the time of his wife's dream, Illam consulted with Buddhu Pandit and his father, Raghu, to arrange for the performance of a *pāṭh*, which would be done, Illam said, to "obtain happiness, to make far suffering" (*sukh prāpt karne ke lie, dukh dūr karne ke lie*). My ethnographic objectivity failing me at that moment, I could not bring myself to ask him if the *pāṭh* was intended to rid the house of the inauspiciousness of the *pret*, but that this was indeed its purpose became clear when the *pāṭh* was performed in Illam's courtyard.

For nine days, Buddhu Pandit recited *mantras* in an inner room of Illam's house, where sets of cloth that would later be given as *dān* were kept, as well as a small pile of sand in which some barley seeds had been planted at the beginning of the nine-day *mantra* recitation. (The seeds were expected to sprout and take root by the time the recitation was completed.) On the ninth day, a *havan* (fire sacrifice) was performed, with Illam and his brothers acting as the patrons, the *jajmāns* who would give the *dān* at the conclusion of the ritual. Illam gave Raghu fifty-one rupees as a *dakṣiṇā* payment, and as he accepted this money, Raghu led Illam in the recitation of a Sanskrit *sankalp* ("resolution") in which he referred to the astrological coordinates of the ritual (the *rāśi,* the *tithi,* and the year of this acceptance) and announced that the *dān* and *dakṣiṇā* were being given in order to rid Illam's house of the inauspiciousness of the *pret.* In the concluding act of the *pāṭh,* then, Illam gave Raghu one and one-quarter rupees and a set of cloth (a *joṛā*) as *dān,* placing the latter on Raghu's head. This *dān,* they hoped, would rid their house of the inauspiciousness and bring about the "auspiciousness of the whole family" (*sārā parivār kā kalyāṇ*).

Mamchand's Son and the Caudasvālā

The son of Mamchand, a Gujar landholder in Pahansu, had not been eating and had lost consciousness several times. The people of his neighborhood were convinced that a *dev-pitar,* a brother of Mamchand's father who had died without offspring and who had been enshrined at a "place" (*thān*) in the fields, had brought this about. This diagnosis—that "otherness had happened" (*oprā ho gayā*)—was confirmed when Mamchand took his son to a wandering "*paṇḍit* from the hills" (*pahāṛī paṇḍit*) who told him that his son should offer a set of cloth at the place of the *caudasvālā,* "the one of the fourteenth" (the phrase used to describe the *dev-pitar* in question, who had died on the fourteenth day of a lunar month). The son should then give that cloth as *dān* to the family Brahman on the new moon day of the month of Kārttik.

Trouble in the Head, Anger in the House: The Sorrows of the Washermen

There are two Washermen houses in Pahansu, built close together in a lane on the east side of the village. In one, Kamala, a "daughter" in Pahansu, lives with her husband, her son, and his wife; in the other house, another "daughter" of the village lives with her husband and son. After their marriages both women had come again to live in Pahansu, their natal village, because there had been no male heirs to take up the work of serving the Gujar *jajmāns* of the village. Both women complained of the "affliction" (*kleś*) that had been besetting their households: "Afflictions remain in our house" (*kleś rahe hamāre ghar mẽ*), as Kamala would often say. The two women seemed to feel that there might be some connection between the sorrows of their two households.

In Kamala's house, she said, there was much "anger" (*gussā*); her son showed anger and did not heed his mother's words, and he had insisted on becoming "separate" (*nyārā*) from his parents in matters of cooking and household expenditures. In the other house, the son of the woman of Kamala's natal *kunbā* had "trouble in the head" (*sir mẽ taklīf*) and had been tearing his clothes and behaving as if he were "mad" (*pāgal*). His mother had taken him to the small government clinic in Pahansu, where the doctor had told her that her son's troubles were caused by "heat" (*garmī*) in his head. But the women did not accept this endogenous diagnosis. When they discussed their troubles, it was always in terms of the possible sources of inauspiciousness that may have afflicted them. Perhaps, Kamala would speculate, an "evil planet" (*burā graha*) was exerting its influence on them; perhaps some *dev-pitar* or other, one who had had no offspring, had brought about the "anger" in her house. Because Kamala did not know which planet it might be, or which *dev-pitar* might be causing the discord in her house, she could take no action. *Dān* could not be given until the exact source of the inauspiciousness was determined.

Punno's Cattle and the Rajput's Wife: Motions of the Planets and Trouble in the House

There had been, Punno's wife told me, some "trouble" (*kaṛāi*) in their house. Punno is a Gujar man in Pahansu, one of the *barsohevāle* (see chap. 1). Two of their water buffaloes had died in rapid succession, and this loss (*hāni*) presented great difficulties for them. Suspecting that the "motions of the planets" (*grahacāl*) had brought this about, they consulted Raghu Pandit and asked him to "look in the almanac" to find out the cause of their misfortune. Raghu did so, and he found that the planet Saturn (Śani) was the source of the inauspiciousness that had afflicted them, causing their cattle to die. As the women of Punno's house told me, the "motions of the planets" can affect many aspects of one's life: "The motions of the planets may come upon one's body, one's cattle, one's fields, or one's children" (*grahacāl apne śarīr pe ho jā, ḍangarõ pe, apnī khetī pe ho jā, yā apne baccõ pe ho jā*). Raghu told Punno's family that a Śani *pāṭh* had to be performed: *mantra*s would be recited by Raghu each morning for nine days in an inner room of their house, and then *dān* would be given to remove Saturn's inauspiciousness. (The *pāṭh* and the *dān* that was given are described in chapter 4.)

One day as I sat in Buddhu Pandit's courtyard, three Rajput men from across the Yamuna River in Haryana came to see him, to have some "astrological work" (*jyotiṣī kā kām*) carried out. There was, they said, *āpatti* (distress, a predicament) in their house. The wife of one of the men had an illness (*rog*) and they wanted to know what the treatment should be, and what the "facilitating" (*lābh-kārak*) and "detrimental" (*hāni-kārak*) days for it might be. Buddhu looked into his almanac and found that *bṛhaspativār* (Thursday), the day of the planet Bṛhaspati, would be an appropriate day to make a small offering of yellow rice to the planet Jupiter, an offering that would then be given to their own Brahman *purohit* as *dān*. More serious, however, was the fact that Buddhu determined that Śani was also implicated in the woman's illness. Buddhu said that *dān* would have to be given to a man of the Dakaut caste to rid the woman of the inauspiciousness of Saturn.

The diagnostic procedure that Raghu and Buddhu used in these cases involved the "name constellation" (*nām rāśi*) of the afflicted person. Determinations (*sujhānā*) based on the name of a person rather than on the time of birth appear to be common in North Indian astrological practice. I heard many people mention this method when they spoke of consulting an astrologer, and Buddhu Pandit and Raghu used it frequently, particularly in cases of illness. The astrological manual that they used (*Jyotiṣa Sarva Sangrah*) says that for the purpose of marriage and other "auspicious work" (*śubh kām*), including setting out on a journey, calculations based on the birth *rāśi* should be used; for subjects concerning "country, village and house, employment and business," one should consider the name and not the time of birth.

If someone comes to him, Buddhu says, and asks, "What is my fortune?" (*merī kismat kaise hai*), with respect to some sorrow (*dukhī*) or illness (*rog*) that is afflicting him, Buddhu will "take out the *lagan*" (*lagan nikālnā*) and in that way construct a *kuṇḍali;* the *lagan* will not be the *rāśi* (solar asterism) of one's birth, but the solar asterism that corresponds with the first sound of one's name. That asterism is then placed in the first "space" (*sthān*) of the *kuṇḍali,* and the other asterisms take up their places in sequential fashion, just as would be the case if the birth *lagan* were being used. Planetary positions and their influence can also be determined in terms of the positions of the solar asterisms in the specific configurations in the *kuṇḍali*. (The correspondences between sound and asterism that provide the starting point for these calculations are listed in the almanacs and astrological manuals that Buddhu Pandit uses.)

Another diagnostic method that Buddhu and Raghu use less frequently involves the time that the question about the illness or sorrow or distress was originally asked. In this procedure, the lunar day, the solar day, the lunar asterism, and the exact time that a question is asked indicates the source of the inauspiciousness that has afflicted a person or a household. The ordinal number of each of these—the lunar day, solar day, lunar asterism, *pahar* (there are eight *pahar*s in a twenty-four hour period), and *lagan*—are added together and then divided by eight. If there is a remainder (*bacnā*, "to be unused or unspent") of zero or two, this indicates that an ancestor god (*pitri-devatā*) is the source of the inauspiciousness, the "hindrances" (*bādhā*) that have caused the difficulties. If the remainder is seven or three, this indicates that a deity (*devatā*) is the source; if four or six, the source is a "ghost" (*bhūt*); and if the remainder is one or five, this outcome indicates that the "motions of the planets" (*grahacāl*) are the source of the inauspiciousness.

The point, then, is that by whatever means—dreams of dead sons, divination with turmeric and *pīpal* leaves, consultations with *sayānā*s, astrological determinations based on time of birth, one's name, or the astrological coordinates of the time a consultation is held—the source of the inauspiciousness that has afflicted a person, a family, or a house must be determined before any ameliorative procedures can be carried out. Each inauspicious substance or quality must be removed through a particular ritual procedure, and through a particular set of *dān* prestations. The structure of the ritual action that is thought to "move away inauspiciousness" (*nāśubh haṭānā*) is the subject of the following chapter.

CHAPTER THREE

The Structure of Ritual Action

The removal of negative qualities and substances—inauspiciousness—from a person, family, house, or village necessitates a complex sequence of ritual actions and prestations that derive their meaning partly from more general Hindu cultural principles concerning givings and receivings of many kinds, in many different contexts. A number of recent analyses of ritual exchanges in South Asian social life have made it clear that in indigenous thought about many transactions, they are not simply matters of abstract relations between actors as givers and receivers, but also effect a transformation of the natures of both actors, or sets of actors, involved (see particularly Marriott 1976, 111–12).

Numerous studies of ritual in both domestic and temple contexts (e.g., Appadurai and Breckenridge 1976; Wadley 1975; Babb 1975; Inden 1976) have established that givings and receivings are fundamental components of almost all Hindu ritual. The most common kinds of exchanges examined in these studies consist of offerings made to deities in the context of *pūjā* worship, which are then transvalued and returned to the worshiper, and others, in the form of *prasād,* the leftover food of the deity that becomes imbued with powerful substances of the deity. *Prasād* is sometimes understood as an "honor" (Appadurai and Breckenridge 1976), but it is more generally an exchange between men and gods that is understood in terms of a difference in rank, power, and quality of coded substance between the donor (the deity) and the recipient (the worshiper) (Marriott 1976, 112). Gods receive offerings from men, but return them, imbued with their own substance and powers, and the transaction is thus unequal, with the deity reciprocating in a higher medium. Babb (1975) focuses on the functions of ritual distributions in establishing ranked relationships between men and gods on the one hand, and on the neutralization of rank distinctions among the worshipers on the other, as they together partake of the *prasād* of the deity. Thus *prasād,* like most transactions in the South Asian social world, has been understood in terms of a ranked relationship between the parties involved in the exchange; and further, all prestations made in the context of worship or ritual activity, or other ritualized modes of bestowal and acceptance, have been interpreted according to this idiom. Thus the basic structure of ritual action, in this model, is a reciprocal relation between two parties: the worshiper makes offerings of cloth, food, incense, and so forth, and receives the more valuable *prasād* or boons (see Wadley 1975) from the deity, resulting in or establishing a hierarchical relation between the two.

Östör (1980) has postulated a more complex set of relations as the fundamental structure of ritual action. He proposes a tripartite structure of *pūjā* in which the basic relations are between the deity (*devata*), the worshiper (*jajmān*), and the priest (*purohit*) who officiates at the *pūjā* on behalf of the *jajmān*. In the Bengali rituals he analyzed, the category of *jajmān* may be an individual, or a household, line, caste, neighborhood, or community; but in each case the relations to the deity and to the priest remain the same and have the same transactional implications. The priest offers food, service, respect, and honor to the *devata* on behalf of the *jajmān*, and is thereby simply an intermediary between them. The threefold structure is ultimately, for Östör, dominated by relations of hierarchy, in terms of both the worshiper-deity relation, and the worshiper-priest relation. Only the "purity" and hierarchical position of the Brahman *purohit* allow him to approach the deity, and this is apparently, in Östör's analysis, the sole reason for his participation in the ritual actions. In this model, as in the previous ones alluded to above, the transactional structure is completed when the worshiper receives the transvalued offerings back from the deity. The homology of this last exchange with relations between men is explicit:

> *Prasād* (leavings of the goddess) are sacred (*pabittra*) because they were touched by the goddess. *Prasād* is the *ēto* (polluted food) of the goddess, but for men it is the most sacred food. In the same way, at home a wife may eat the *ēto* of her husband, and children that of their elders. Sometimes the lowest castes take the *ēto* of the Brahmans. (Östör 1980, 86)

In all of these interpretations of Hindu ritual activity, a ranked relationship between worshiper and deity, enacted transactionally, is seen to account in full for the structure of the ritual.

However, in Pahansu, ritual prestations and the structure of ritual action in general are founded upon a more complex set of cultural constructs. Most important, aside from *prasād*, there is another type of ritual prestation, a kind of *dān* that is called *caṛhāpā* or *pujāpā*.[1] While *prasād* may, in Pahansu, be distributed to the worshiper or to anyone else regardless of caste or kinship relation, *caṛhāpā* must be given to a designated recipient, either to a particular kinsman of the *jajmān* or to a person of a particular caste. More rarely, it can be deposited in certain geographical locations. The efficacy of the whole set of ritual actions depends upon the proper disposition of this prestation. In rituals involving a deity, food items or sets of cloth are offered directly to the image of the deity before being given to the designated recipient, and in rituals in which deities do not figure, various manipulations of the items are performed before they are given. But in both cases, rituals involving the giving of *caṛhāpā* exhibit a common structure.

The purpose of this chapter is to isolate and describe this structure shared by ritual sequences that are performed in a wide range of contexts and that have seemingly diverse aims and functions. It should be noted that nearly all of the life-cycle and calendrical ritual sequences I observed in Pahansu involved the giving of *caṛhāpā*.

Caṛhāpā as a category of prestation has been virtually ignored in the ethnography of Hindu caste, kinship, and ritual, despite the fact that such prestations constitute an almost daily and very substantial redistribution of grain, cooked and raw food, cloth, cash, and other items along the lines of both kinship and intercaste relationships, and despite the fact that the giving of the *caṛhāpā* is the crucial and culminating point of nearly all ritual sequences.

The giving of *caṛhāpā* has two culturally postulated functions. First, in any ritual for a deity, the giving of the *caṛhāpā* to the appropriate recipient (conceived of in this context as a vessel or receptacle, *pātra*) enables the god to appropriate the offering. Second, whenever *caṛhāpā* is given to the appropriate *pātra* (whether or not deities are involved) after the prescribed ritual manipulations, the negative qualities and substances characterized as "inauspiciousness" in the previous chapter—"afflictions" (*kaṣṭ*), "danger" (*sankaṭ*), "disease" (*rog*), "inauspiciousness" (*nāśubh*), "demerits" (*pāp*), and "faults" (*doṣ*)—are transferred from the donor (i.e., the *jajmān*, the person who performs the ritual or has it performed) to the recipient. If not given to the appropriate recipient at the appropriate time and place, the negative qualities will even more virulently beset either the giver or the receiver or both.[2]

What is given as *caṛhāpā* is also called *dān*, and *dān*, villagers say, is always given to remove some form of inauspiciousness (*nāśubh haṭāne ke lie*) and transfer it to the recipient.[3] Through the giving of the *dān*, the negative qualities "come out" (*utarnā*) of the donor, and then have their effect on the recipient in the form of illness, death, or other misfortune, or in the form of a diminishing of one's internal "power" (*śakti*).

It should be emphasized that the contrast of *caṛhāpā* and *prasād* is an absolute one. *Prasād* is never thought of as a vehicle for the transferral of inauspiciousness, nor is it ever referred to as *dān*. Linguistic usages, particularly in the matter of verb correspondence, emphasize this contrast. *Prasād* is always "distributed" (*bāṇṭnā*), while *caṛhāpā* or *dān* is always "given" (*denā*).[4]

Let us examine the process of transferral, the giving of *caṛhāpā*, in more detail. First, the provenance of this transferral should be noted. While there have been numerous attempts to delineate "levels" (Mandelbaum 1966; Babb 1975; Wadley 1975) of Hindu ritual in terms of purpose or domains of ritual associated with life and auspiciousness on the one hand, and death and inauspiciousness on the other (Das 1977), the transferral of inauspiciousness appears to be the basic structuring feature in all of the many rituals that have so often been seen as belonging to opposed types. A structure of transferral—the basic sequence of actions and prestations—is found not only in rituals oriented toward deities, but also in the contexts of astrological practices (*jyotiṣ*); birth, marriage, and death rituals; "sorcery" (*ṭonā*); agricultural rituals; house-building ceremonies; and in practices concerned with the removal of specific diseases caused by inauspiciousness.

In all of these various transferral sequences, the performer of the ritual, who makes the prestations and from whom the inauspiciousness is removed is, in Pahansu, termed the "sacrificer" (*jajmān*). Depending on the type and source of the inauspiciousness involved, the recipient of the prestations, the *pātrā*, may be a Brahman *purohit*, a Barber, a Bhangi Sweeper, a wife-taking affine, a man of the Dakaut *jāti*, or a particular spatial configuration or location. There is, however, nearly always an intermediate transfer: the prestation is first made to the source of the inauspiciousness—usually a deity or a particular kinsman—before being "given onward" (*āge denā*) to the final recipient, the *pātrā*. This pattern, and the specific ritual sequences in which such transferrals are accomplished, will be examined more closely in chapter 4. The present discussion will focus on the basic forms, the component actions as it were, through which the transferrals are effected.

Vrat and Udāpan

Vrat is a complex ritual form, found as a component in many ritual sequences, involving a number of elements: fasting, the reading or telling of a story (*kathā*) about the efficacy of the particular *vrat*, and the giving of gifts (*dān*) at the conclusion of the ritual. The making of this final prestation, and the accompanying ritual manipulations of the items given, is termed the *udāpan*. In previous analyses of *vrat*, the most important element, the *udāpan*, has been ignored, and thus a transaction between men and gods sometimes described in the *kathā*s, an exchange of service and devotion for mercy and boons, has been taken as the fundamental feature of this ritual action (Wadley 1975). I have, however, shown elsewhere (Raheja 1976) that what is at issue in *vrat* performances is primarily a transformation of the person, effected through a variety of ritual actions, of which worship of or exchanges with a deity is only one. This exchange relationship is complementary to a general transformation of the person effected in the *vrat* as a whole. In the present context, I am concerned to show that the structure of this ritual component—*vrat* and its accompanying *udāpan*—is an instantiation of the general paradigm of the disarticulation and transferral of inauspicious qualities and substances, whether or not a deity is involved in a particular *vrat*.

The paradigm of transferral in *vrat* is clearly articulated in the ritual sequence and the story (*kathā*) of the *vrat* of Bṛhaspati (the planet Jupiter), which women may perform on Thursdays for the well-being of their husbands. Women in Pahansu keep this *vrat* either for an entire year, or during the months of Kārttik, Sāvan, or Cait, whenever afflictions or illnesses of their husbands are diagnosed (by themselves or by an astrologer) as having been caused by the inauspicious influence of Jupiter.

Women performing this *vrat* fast during the entire day, and they refer to this practice as the *tap* (heat generated by austerities) necessary for the success of the disarticulative phase of the *vrat*. Sometime during the course of the morning, each woman listens to or reads a *kathā* detailing the efficacy of the *vrat*, while holding grains of *chanā* (chick peas) in her hand. At the conclusion of the story, these grains are given as a first *caṛhāpā* to the Brahman *purohit* of the woman's conjugal family. At the conclusion of the *vrat*—after one year or one month has elapsed, during which time the fast would have been kept each Thursday—the *udāpan* is performed in the following manner.

The following items are placed over an image of Bṛhaspati drawn on the ground with turmeric, circled counterclockwise with water (this action is called *mīnasnā*), and then given as *caṛhāpā*, once again to the Brahman *purohit* of the woman's conjugal village:

1 1/4 *ser* (a unit of measurement) of chick peas
1 1/4 *ser* of wheat flour
1 1/4 *gaj* (a *gaj* measures about one yard) of yellow cloth
1 set of men's clothing (a *joṛā*)

By making these prestations in one and one-quarter measures, the woman effects a transferral of the inauspicious qualities or substances that have attached themselves to her husband.[5] A precise mythological parallel to this transferral, and to those that occur with the performance of any *udāpan*, is found in the *kathā* for the *vrat* of Bṛhaspati.[6]

> One day Indra was sitting very proudly on his throne, and many gods, sages, celestial musicians, and others were present there in his court. Bṛhaspati entered the court at that time, and everyone stood to show respect to him. But because of his own pride, Indra did not stand, although he always used to show respect to Bṛhaspati. Bṛhaspati under-

stood Indra's action to be disrespectful to him, and so he got up and went away. Indra was very sorrowful at this and said: "Look, I have been very disrespectful to the *guru* [Bṛhaspati is said to be the *guru* of the gods], and a great fault has beset me. It was only because of the blessings of the *guru* that I first obtained my glory, and now because of his anger all of this will be destroyed. I should therefore go to him and beg for his forgiveness, from which his anger will be stilled and my auspiciousness (*kalyāṇ*) will be assured."

Thinking in this way, Indra went to that place. Because of his yogic power (*yogbal*), Bṛhaspati knew that Indra was coming to seek forgiveness, but because of his anger he did not think it appropriate to give him a boon, and so he disappeared. When Indra didn't see Bṛhaspati at his house, he lost hope and returned.

When this news became known to Vṛṣvarṣa, the king of the demons, he took permission from his own *guru* Śukrācarya and surrounded the city of Indra. And, because of the absence of their own *guru*'s mercy, the gods of the city began to be killed and defeated. They went then to Brahma and with humility told him the whole story and asked him to save them from the king of the demons.

Brahma said: "You have committed a great offense and angered the *guru* of the gods. There is one way to assure your well-being in this. Viśvarupa, the son of the Brahman Tvaṣṭha, is very wise and possesses the heat of great austerities. Your auspiciousness can be assured if you make him your *purohit*."

Hearing this, Indra went to Tvaṣṭha and with great humility said: "Become our *purohit,* and our auspiciousness will be assured."

Tvaṣṭha gave his answer: "The power of the heat of one's austerities (*tapobal*) is diminished from becoming a *purohit*. But you have acted with great humility, and so my son Viśvarūpa will become your *purohit* and protect you."

Acting then on the order of his father, Viśvarūpa became the *purohit* and tried to assure Indra that he would be victorious and remain on his throne. Viśvarūpa had three mouths. He extracted juice from the soma plant and drank it with the first mouth. With the second mouth he drank intoxicating liquors, and with the third mouth he consumed grain and other things.

After a few days, Indra said: "By your mercy I would like to do a sacrifice (*yajña*)." Then, according to the order of Viśvarūpa the sacrifice began. One day a demon said to Viśvarūpa: "Your mother is the daughter of a demon; therefore for our auspiciousness you should be making offerings in the name of demons. This is the proper thing for you to do."

Viśvarūpa accepted the words of the demon, and at the time of making offerings at the sacrifice he slowly pronounced the name of the demons as well. Because of this, the fiery energy (*tej*) of the gods did not increase.

Indra learned of this, and became very angry, and cut off the three heads of Viśvarūpa. The liquor-drinking head became a black bee, the soma-drinking head became a pigeon, and the grain-eating head became a partridge. Just when he killed Viśvarūpa, Indra's form changed, from the effect of murdering a Brahman. But the evil (*pāp*) of murdering a Brahman was not removed even when the gods accumulated one year of expiation.

At the gods' entreaty then, Brahma, together with Bṛhaspati, divided that Brahman-murder into four parts. The first part was given to the earth, and for this reason, the earth is uneven and in many places seeds cannot be sown. But with that, Brahma gave the boon that wherever holes should appear on the earth, they would on their own become filled after some time. The second part of the Brahman-murder was given to treeṣ, and as a result gum and sap flow from trees. For this reason, all sap and gum except fragrant resins are considered to be impure (*aśuddha*). But the trees were given the boon that even if the tops become dry and withered, the roots sprout again. The third part of the Brahman-murder was given to women, and for this reason women become menstruous (*rajasvalā*) each month, and on the first day are equal to Cāṇḍālas, on the second they are equal to Brahman-killers, on the third day they are like Washerwomen, and on the fourth day they become pure (*śuddha*). They were given the boon that they may obtain offspring. The fourth part of the Brahman-murder was given to water, because of which scum and algae come to the top of water. The boon was given to water that whatever thing it might be placed in, the weight of that thing would increase.

Indra thus became free of the evil (*pāp*) of Brahman-killing. In this way, whatever human being reads or listens to this *kathā*, all of his evil (*pāp*) will be destroyed by the mercy of Bṛhaspati.

In this *kathā*, the inauspiciousness—the *pāp* afflicting Indra because of his actions—cannot simply be forgiven, destroyed, or wiped away. It must be transferred away and have its effect on the recipient. The effect is hinted at in the early episode, when Tvaṣṭha refuses to become the *purohit* of the gods, which would entail receiving gifts from them, to remove Indra's *pāp*, because the power of the heat produced by his austerities would be diminished by this acceptance.[7] The consequences of receiving the *pāp* from the gods are delineated further in the final episode of the story, as the effects on the earth, trees, women, and water are described. Indra becomes free of the inauspiciousness, but in this closed universe in which no human or divine powers or sins are ever destroyed, the *pāp* is recycled and exhibits its consequences elsewhere.

At the end of the *kathā*, the transferral of Indra's *pāp* is explicitly compared to the transferral of the inauspiciousness from the performer of the *vrat*, which is said by the women of Pahansu to be accomplished by the giving of the *udāpan* prestations to the Brahman *purohit* of the conjugal family.

A second type of *vrat* illustrates other aspects of the performance of this ritual. In order to remove sin and evil (*pāp*) from their parents and to assure their own future marital auspiciousness (*suhāg*),[8] unmarried girls in Pahansu observe a *vrat* called *candan chaṭh* ("moon sixth") on the sixth day of the dark half of the month of Bhādwe. On this day, they fast throughout the day, and in the morning they take six grains of wheat in their left hands and listen to the story of the efficacy of the *vrat*. Following the *kathā,* the six grains of wheat are given as *caṛhāpā* to the Brahman *purohit* of the family, along with a payment (*dakṣiṇā*). Following the girl's marriage, the *udāpan* is performed by the family of the bride, who send the following items as the final *caṛhāpā* to the conjugal village (*sasurāl*) of their daughter:

six *ser* of fried breads (*pūrī*)
six *ser* of sweetmeats (*halvā*)
six *ser* of cooked pumpkin
six *ser* of cooked potatoes
ornaments: nose-ring and toe-rings, six glass bangles
padõ kā dān: one pair of shoes; two full sets of cloth, one for a man and one for a woman; brass pots

The fact that inauspiciousness is being removed from the parents of the bride through this prestation is indicated not only by villagers' statements but also by the items given in the *udāpan*. In a great many such ritual sequences, sets of clothing corresponding to the gender of the person from whom the negative qualities and substances are to be removed are given as the *caṛhāpā*. Thus in the Bṛhaspati *vrat* that a woman performs for the well-being of her husband, a set of men's clothing is given in the *udāpan,* while in the *candan chaṭh vrat* both men's and women's clothing is given. Here we should note that although it is the daughter of the house who performs the initial actions of the *vrat,* her parents make the prestations after she has been married. In the *bṛhaspati vrat,* however, a wife both performs the initial actions and also makes the prestations for the benefit of her husband. This pattern will emerge again and again in the ritual sequences to be discussed in chapter 4. Wives may make prestations to remove inauspiciousness from themselves, their husbands, and other conjugal kin, and from their sons. As daughters, women may initiate the *vrat,* but they must make themselves available as recipients rather than acting as donors when the *udāpan* is to be given.

Below I translate, first, the story for the *candan chaṭh* (or the more Sanskritic *candan ṣaṣṭhī,* as the printed text reads) from a popular pamphlet (published in Meerut District and purchased in a bazaar near Pahansu) that explains the performance of this ritual, and second, the very similar *sūrya ṣaṣṭhī vrat* that is performed on the sixth day of the bright half of the month of Bhādwe.

The Story of *Candan Chaṭh*

The Bard spoke: At the conclusion of the Mahabharata war, Yudhiṣṭhara the son of Dharma asked a question of his elder kinsman Bhīṣma. The king Yudhiṣṭhara said: "Kindly tell about the greatness of the sixth-day *vrat* that produces merit (*puṇya*) and saves unfortunate women from hell." Then Bhīṣma said: "Nāradajī, the beloved of Viṣṇu, was wandering through the worlds (*lok*) and one time arrived in the world of Brahmā, and began asking Brahmā questions. Nārada said: 'O Brahmā, tell from what actions (*dharma*) birth in good lineages (*śreṣṭha kul*) results, and about a *vrat* that produces fruit. O Lord! Tell about a *vrat* that produces merit, saves women from hell, gives happiness (*sukh*) and good fortune (*saubhāgya*), and gives devotion (*bhakti*) and release (*mukti*).'

"Brahmājī spoke: 'O son Nārada. Men and women who do the twelfth-day [of the lunar cycle] and sixth-day *vrat* do not take birth in hell or in lowly wombs.'

"Then Nārada said: 'O Master! Tell about the method of performing this most excellent merit-granting *vrat;* it is my greatest wish to hear it.'

"Hearing Nārada's reverent speech, Brahmā said: 'I will give the account of the greatness of this most excellent *vrat* that should be performed by women. Gangā, Sarasvatī, Revā, Parvatī, Devkanyā, Urvaśī, Indrānī, Ahilyā, Gauri, Śāṇḍalī, Rohinī, Lakṣmī, Tārā, Rambhā, Tilottama, and many other women devoted to their husbands (*pativrata*) are present in the world of Viṣṇu. Whose story (*kathā*) should I tell? Listen, O best of ascetics.

" 'One time on Mount Kailāśa Śankarjī [Śiva] was sitting telling such stories to all the women, when, from among them, Pārvatī began to respectfully ask Śankarjī to tell them about a *vrat* from which they could receive good fortune (*saubhāgya*), all good qualities (*sarva guṇa*) and all the mind's desires. Then the great god said: "I will tell you the method of performing the greatest *vrat* on the sixth day of the dark half of the month of Bhādwe. O beloved! It is proper for women to remove all other matters from their minds. O fulfiller of wishes! Listen to the story of the greatness of that *vrat*. O one of great fortune!

" ' "On the Citrakūt mountain in the Mālva territory there lived a Brahman learned in the Veda, in teaching, in medicine, in grammar, and in all the six parts of the Veda. On that day of the lunar cycle, a Brahman named Śrīdhar stopped in the garden, O beautiful one! It was the time of the rites for ancestors (*śrāddha*). The Brahman named Śrīdhar invited many Brahmans and began himself to prepare the food.

His invited guests, the great sages Vyāsa, Bālmīki, Garga, Gautama, Pārāśara, and many great ascetics came. The Brahman's wife was very beautiful, youthful, devoted to her husband, and filled with modesty. The Brahman said to her: 'O beloved, listen! O beautiful one! On the lunar day of the ancestral rites for one's mother and father, the act of feeding Brahmans gives one the fruit of a *rājasūya* and an *aśvamedha* sacrifice.' This woman of *dharma* devoted to her husband began carefully to prepare several varieties of fried breads, spinach, mango powder, pickles, many kinds of flavorful fruits, yogurt, milk, ghee, and many other types of food. When the food was ready, the invited Brahmans arrived, and having bathed and washed their feet, began to perform the ancestral rites. Just when the food was ready and the rites had begun, the Brahman's wife by chance began to menstruate (*rajasualā ho gaī*) and out of shame concealed the fact of her menstruation (*rajodharma*). Having eaten the food she had touched, the Brahman guests were satisfied and pleased. The Brahman saluted them and gave them payment (*dakṣiṇā*) according to his ability. Then he circumambulated them and had them depart. In the course of time the wife died. But despite being a *sati* [woman who dies on the funeral pyre of her husband], because she had fed impure (*aśuddha*) food to Brahmans, she suffered in hell from the punishment of Yama and was reborn in the family of a Cāṇḍāla, but she remembered her previous birth. This woman who concealed her menstruous faults (*rajodoṣa*) had been born as a dog and as a pig that had offspring; and finally in her seventh birth, she was reborn in a human womb and became a Cāṇḍāla woman of evil actions.

"'"In the city of this Cāṇḍāla, the son from her former birth [as the Brahman woman] also lived; he knew the Vedic texts, he was humble, and he was a Brahman who studied and taught, gave gifts (*dān*) and received gifts, did sacrifices for himself and for others, and thus was devoted to the six actions of a Brahman. At the end of a sacrifice for all the gods (*vaiśvadeva yajña*), the Cāṇḍāla woman came to his house to eat the rice of the *bali* offerings. Then the Brahman became angry and reprimanded her, saying 'O Cāṇḍāla woman! Go away from my house, because simply from seeing you I become impure. After seeing a Cāṇḍāla one doesn't become pure until one sees the sun again. After being touched by a Cāṇḍāla one is purified only by bathing in the Ganga.' Hearing his words, the woman went away crying from his house.

"'"That night the Cāṇḍāla woman to whom he had spoken, his mother who had taken birth as that Cāṇḍāla, appeared to that Brahman in a dream. She said: 'O son! Are you awake or asleep? I am tormented by the fearful pain of hell.' Hearing this, the son from the previous birth said: 'O mother! Because of what evil (*pāp*) have you taken birth in the womb of a Cāṇḍāla? I am very surprised. Tell me, what is the meaning of this?' The mother said: 'Your father respectfully did the ancestral rites. A hindrance came into it because at the time of preparing the food I became menstruous and I kept the great evil (*mahāpāp*) secret. O son, because of that I have had to become a Cāṇḍāla, and I had to suffer the unbearable torments of Yama, the king of *dharma*.'

"'"Hearing these words of his mother, the son said: 'O mother! If you know a way to bring about your release (*mokṣa*), tell me and I will try to do it.' His mother said: 'O son! the sixth day of the dark half of the month of *bhādrapad* is the most pure (*pavitra*) of all lunar days (*tithi*) and of all the junctures (*tīrtha*). O son! I can be freed from this Cāṇḍāla birth from the effect of a Brahman's performance of the *vrat* of this sixth-day, and his giving of its merit (*puṇya*) to me.' Seeing the suffering of his mother in this dream, the son got up from his sleep, and remembering his mother's words, he began to think that the sixth-day *vrat* is better than other austerities (*tap*) and fasting (*upvās*). Thinking this, the Brahman took permission from the ascetics and after bathing and making the resolution with speech, mind, and action, began to give the fruit of the greatness of this *vrat* to his mother. From the effect of that merit, his mother, who had been born in that Cāṇḍāla womb, attained heaven. Whatever woman performs this *vrat* will likewise not be born in a low family (*nīc kul*)."'

"Nāradajī spoke: 'O Brahmā! Now tell the manner in which this *vrat* is to be performed. I am asking you what the *mantra*s are for this sixth-day *vrat*, and which deity should be worshiped.'

"Then Brahmā said: 'Taking saffron-colored sandalwood paste, flowers of one's native land, fruit, red sandalwood paste, incense, lamps, and nourishing food offerings (*puṣṭikārak naivedya*), worship (*pūjā*) should be done. At dawn libation offerings should be given with pomegranates, coconut, and other fruits. And then, maintaining good conduct, in the eighth part of the day before sunset, one should bathe and keep the senses in control. One should go to a river, a tank, or a deep well and bathe, or bathe in the house. One should go to the house of one's *guru* and should not go among women. Then, making an image of copper or an eight-petaled lotus on a red plank, Varuṇa and the other deities should be worshiped. Varuṇa, Sūrya, Vedānga, Dhāta, Indra, Ravi, Garbhasti, Aryamā, Skanda, Savitā, Divākar, Aditya: these twelve were produced from the ascetic Kaśyapa. Saffron, lotus flowers, red sandalwood paste, *kuśa* grass, perfumed water, sesame, and rice should be mixed and kept in a copper vessel. Then the sun, master of the senses, should be worshiped, and water offerings with red sandalwood paste should be made twelve times for the twelve names of the sun (*sūrya*). Foodstuffs, potables, things to be licked and things to be sucked, payment (*dakṣiṇā*), and raw foodstuffs should be given to Brahmans, and they should be worshiped. After this, one should dismiss Sūrya Narāyāṇa. At the time the moon rises, one should mix white sandalwood paste and milk in a libation vessel covered with cloth and offer these to the moon. Then one should eat a meal of wheat-flour fried breads, other breads, cow's milk, curds, ghee, and sweetmeats, but salt should not be eaten. Then on the twelfth day of the lunar cycle the *udāpan* should be done: one should give gifts (*dān*) of shoes and cloth, and a *dakṣiṇā,* to Brahmans, and have them eat a meal. Raw foodstuffs should also be given to those Brahmans to whom it is appropriate to give raw foodstuffs, and then, for the success of the worship of the moon, have a Brahman pronounce that the *pūjā* has been successfully completed.'

"Whatever human being reads this story (*kathā*) or hears it receives the fruit of one hundred gifts of a cow (*gaudān*); from the effect of the greatness of this *vrat,* one receives happiness in this world and an auspicious state in the next world."

Sūrya Ṣaṣṭhī Vrat Kathā

Nāradajī spoke: "O Lord God Sūrya! Tell the method of performing *sūrya ṣaṣṭhī*. Tell which *mantra*s are used for the worship." Then the lord Sūrya said: "O great sage! Listen to that which, upon hearing, all desired fruits are obtained. The sixth day of the bright half of the month of *bhādrapad* is the giver of *dharma, artha,* and *kāma;* therefore the *vrat* of that day should be performed. It is appropriate that all men and women do this highest *vrat*. The eyes, ears, mind, and other senses should be kept in control, and one should bathe in the afternoon. One should bathe as convenient, in a river, tank, or at one's house, and then a saffron and red sandalwood paste image of Sūrya Nārāyaṇa should be made. If there is a lack of red sandalwood paste and saffron, the image may be made from white sandalwood paste. Beautiful Vedic and Puranic *mantra*s should be read, and the Light-Giving Lord (*bhagvān bhaskar*) should be invoked into the image with incense, flowers, and unbroken rice. Sūrya should then be worshiped with devotion and a resolute mind. Greeting Sūrya, water offerings should be made at noon and in the afternoon. A meal (*naivedya*), with ghee and four kinds of foodstuffs should be given and in the morning Sūrya should be worshiped with an attentive mind. Payments (*dakṣiṇā*) of gold should be given to a learned Brahman, and with a concentrated mind one should listen to this lovely story from the mouth of that Brahman. While listening to the story, the hands should be joined in respect and devotion. The meritorious effect of this best of *vrat*s is the increase of sons and grandsons. Whatever stupid or unlearned person abandons this *vrat* without doing the *udāpan,* in that person's house misery will remain for one hundred thousand years, that is, misery will always remain in his house. Wise human beings should do the *udāpan* according to their capacities. The *udāpan* should be done when six years have passed."

The sage then said: "O god Sūrya! Now tell about the method of performing the *udāpan* of this *ṣaṣṭhī vrat,* because you are the remover of all of my ignorance." Then the lord Sūrya said: "O Nārada! Listen to the method of performing the *udāpan*. Cover seven water pots and seven sacred threads, and seven sweetmeats made from ghee and sugar with silken cloth, and place these with a payment (*dakṣiṇā*). According to one's capacity, a golden image should be made of this increaser of good fortune (*saubhāgya vardhak*), Lord Sūrya, giver of light. According to one's wealth, cloth, ornaments, pots, and so forth, should be given to Brahmans, and Sūrya should be worshiped with many kinds of edible substances."

Nāradajī then asked: "Who on this earth has performed this worship of Sūrya?" Sūrya said: "The worship was done by the proper method first by Anasūyā, and from its effects she received her desired good fortune (*saubhāgya*). The leprosy and other diseases caused by evil (*pāp rog*) of whatever person performs this *ṣaṣṭhī vrat* are destroyed. One should bathe, give gifts (*dān*), perform austerities (*tapasya*), meditate, do sacrifices (*homa*), feed Brahmans, and give gifts of buffaloes and horses according to one's capacity in order to please Sūrya. The sons and wealth of whatever person performs this sixth-day *vrat* of the month of *bhādwe* will increase; whatever things are desired will be obtained, enemies will be destroyed, and many kinds of diseases (*rog*) such as smallpox, boils, pimples, and fever are destroyed. Rising at dawn, one should meditate on Sūrya and give gifts (*dān*) of grain according to one's capacity. Whatever person does this *sūrya ṣaṣṭhī vrat* for five years, his fiery energy (*tejas*) will become like that of Sūrya, and after leaving his body will obtain the world of Sūrya (*sūrya lok*) for sixty-thousand years."

In the texts for these two *vrat*s, the sequence of actions in the ritual is clearly elucidated. Because of sin or evil (*pāp*), a person suffers either ill-birth or disease, and the *vrat* is described as the appropriate way of removing these afflictions and assuring one's happiness and well-being. The primary elements of the ritual as it is performed in Pahansu and described in these texts are the performance of austerities (*tap*)—the fasting—from which "heat" is produced and the giving of *dān* at the *udāpan,* the concluding actions of the ritual in which the inauspiciousness is transferred to the recipient. In the case of this *candan chaṭh vrat,* a deity is only very peripherally involved, and the *caṛhāpā* items given in the *udāpan* are given directly to the appropriate *pātra*. The structure of the ritual and prestation sequence, however, remains the same as when a deity is invoked as a conduit for the *dān* prestation.

In other *vrat* rituals, deities may be more directly involved in the transferral sequence. The *vrat* of Saturday (*śanivār*), performed in order to remove the inauspiciousness generated by the planets Śani (Saturn), Rāhu ("eclipse demon"), or Ketu ("comet demon"), is one such ritual. The following is a partial translation of a Hindi manual for the performance of this *vrat*.

The Story of the *Vrat* of Saturday

The *vrat* of Saturday is performed for the pacification (*śānti*) not only of the cruel planet Śani, but also for that of Rāhu and Ketu, whose actions are like those of Śani. Many people also do this pacification *vrat* in order to please the Lord Śiva. This *vrat* is begun in the bright [waxing] fortnight of the month of Śrāvana.

The Procedure (*vidhi*):

After rising on a Saturday morning and finishing the daily actions of bathing and teeth cleaning, the performer of the *vrat* should make the resolution (*sankalp*). Then iron or glass images of Śani, Rahu, and Ketu should be made and a worship ceremony (*pūjā*) should be conducted in the proper manner. Blackened unbroken rice, black cloth, black flowers, and black sandalwood paste should be used. It is best if the *pūjā* is done beneath a *pīpal* tree. After the *pūjā*, the image should be circumambulated to the right (*pradakṣiṇā*) seven times. After the circumambulation, the tree should be bound with thread, and the god Śani should be petitioned. A small bowl filled with mustard oil, black sesame seeds, and black cloth should be given in *dān*. Black barley, black gram, and black sesame should be used. If possible, a black cow with a black calf should be given in *dān* to a Brahman who is an appropriate receptacle for this *dān*. If possible seven such cows should be given.

The Story (*kathā*):

One day the great king Daśarath was told by the royal astrologer that when the planet Saturn would leave the *kṛttika* lunar asterism (*nakṣatra*) and move into the *rohini* lunar asterism, ten years of fearful famine would fall upon the earth, during which time people would die from the scarcity of food and water, and lamentation and tumult would result. Hearing this from the astrologer, the great king Daśarath was filled with anxiety and so asked his teacher, the sage Vaśiṣṭha, for a way to prevent this calamity. But even Vaśiṣṭha did not know of a way to remove the influence of Śani. Dasárath, however, knew nothing of despair, and so he donned his weapons and ascended to the world of the lunar asterisms (*nakṣatra lok*).

When Śani was preparing to move from *kṛittika* to *rohini,* Daśarath blocked his way. The god Śani had never before seen a king as brave as Daśarath. He said to the great king: "O lord of kings! I am very pleased at the sight of your unearthly heroism. Until today, all the gods, demons, and human beings who have confronted me have been burned up, but because of your irrepressible fiery energy (*tej*) and fierce austerities (*ugra tap*), you have been spared. Now I will grant you whatever boon you ask."

The great king Daśarath said: "O great king, I entreat you not to enter the *rohini* asterism."

The god Śani accepted King Daśarath's entreaty, and told him about the proper manner (*vidhi*) of performing the *vrat* of Saturday, which removes the suffering and misery of the world. Then Śani said: "This *vrat* will protect whoever is enduring suffering caused by me or my friends Rāhu or Ketu. All of their afflictions will be removed by this *vrat*."

The king Daśarath then left the world of the lunar asterisms and returned to his own capital, Ayodhya. There in his kingdom he promulgated this *vrat* of Saturday, and ever since then this *vrat* has been in use.

In this text, the *udāpan* is not mentioned in the story, but it is prescribed in the *vidhi,* the section in which the proper manner of performing the ritual is set forth. According to the text, it should consist of a *dān* of various items that have first been brought into contact with the body of the person afflicted by the planetary configuration (for details of this process in rituals performed in Pahansu, see chapter 4) and then offered to the deity Śani. In the *udāpan* these items are given as *dān* to the appropriate *pātra*. In cases such as these, as in the Bṛhaspati *vrat,* the inauspicious qualities and substances are first returned to their source and then given on to an appropriate final recipient; the deity himself does not assimilate the inauspiciousness but acts only as an intermediary between the *jajmān* and the *pātra,* the recipient of the *dān*.

In certain other *vrat*s, there is no giving of *dān* as *caṛhāpā* at the conclusion of the ritual, despite the fact that both informants' statements and the ritual texts indicate that the *udāpan* prestations are absolutely crucial to the success of most rituals and the well-being of the performer of *vrat*s. The *vrat* of Satyanārāyaṇa is typical of this very small subset of *vrat*s. Unlike most other *vrat*s, that of the god Satyanārāyaṇa is not prescribed by almanacs (*pancāng*) for any particular time of the year. The stories that are read by the Brahman officiant exemplify its performance at points either of special difficulty or of special prosperity in the life of the *jajmān*. In Pahansu, one might typically decide to perform the *vrat* upon the completion of the construction of a house, upon the acquisition of wealth or other property, or following a marriage or childbirth; some relatively wealthy Gujars in the village arrange for the worship to be done annually, to ensure the continual well-being of their households.

As in the rituals involving the giving of *caṛhāpā* to an appropriate recipient, here, too, auspiciousness is ensured through the transferral of inauspiciousness. The performer of the Satyanārāyaṇa *vrat* fasts during the day (the fasting is again referred to as *tap*), and in the afternoon a worship (*pūjā*) of the deity is carried out under the direction of the Brahman officiant. Offerings of water, food, cloth, and other items are made to an image of the deity, and each item is offered in one and one-quarter measures called *sawāī*—one and one-quarter *ser*, for example. The *kathā* is then read by the priest, and finally *āratī* is performed. For this part of the ritual, a small clay lamp is placed on a brass tray, and this is passed around to everyone present as *ārati* songs are sung. In these songs, the performer of the ritual is said to be afflicted by negative qualities and substances that must be "removed": "sin" or "evil" (*pāp*), "disease" (*rog*), "distress" (*kaṣṭ*), and "faults" (*doṣ*). In the case of the *vrat* of Satyanārāyaṇa, the transferral is not made through the giving of *dān* to a human recipient, but through a transferral to the deity himself. Satyanārāyaṇa is referred to in the songs as *haraṇā* or *hartā*, "the one who seizes," or as *dhāraṇa* "the one who takes upon himself" the evil of the *jajmān*. The deity himself "makes far" (*dūr karnā*) the inauspiciousness and takes it upon himself as he receives the *sawāī* offerings.

The words of these songs, then, make it clear why *dān* or *caṛhāpā* is not given at the conclusion of this *vrat:* it is the deity who takes upon himself and assimilates the negative qualities and substances and so a further transferral or "giving onward" is unnecessary for the efficacy of the ritual.

In Pahansu domestic and calendrical ritual, it is quite rare for the deity himself to assimilate the negative substances rather than passing them on to a human *pātra*. Indeed, there is only one other example. In a case of "hindrances" (*bādha*) and inauspiciousness caused by the planet Śani, an alternative to the Śani *vrat* and the giving of Śani *kā dān* is for the afflicted person to go to a temple in which an image of the god Hanuman has been installed facing toward the south (*dakṣiṇā mukh*). (Such an image is found in the little-used Pahansu Śiva temple, and in the temple of Śakumbhari Devi in the Siwalik Hills, to which many people in Pahansu travel on pilgrimage.) The afflicted person circles the image forty times in a clockwise direction, and in this way "the hindrances are removed" (*bādhā dūr ho jā*) and absorbed by the image, and thus no *caṛhāpā* is generated.[9] However, this method of removing the inauspiciousness of Śani is not often employed in Pahansu; most people, especially Gujars, prefer to give the *dān* of Śani when they are so afflicted.

The giving of one's sins and afflictions to a deity who "seizes" them and removes them from the worshiper seems to be characteristic of *bhakti* ritual; this is particularly apparent in the case of the Satyanārāyaṇa *vrat*. Gujars in Saharanpur District are relatively isolated from *bhakti* influence, and this may account for the fact that transferrals of inauspiciousness to a deity are so uncommon in village ritual, and it may also account in part for the pervasiveness of transferrals to human recipients in Pahansu. *Caṛhāpā* is not generated in *bhakti* ritual forms, and this seems to be the major point of difference between domestic and calendrical ritual in Pahansu on the one hand and *bhakti* worship on the other.

In the latter, *prasād* is distributed, but the ritual centrality of a *jajmān* who disposes of his inauspiciousness through the donative act is completely absent.[10]

We have thus isolated three variations in the structure of transferral in *vrats*. In the first, in which a deity is involved as both the source of the inauspiciousness and the intermediary through which it is removed, the sequence of the transferral that removes inauspiciousness is as follows:

jajmān → deity → { Brahman *purohit*
(donor) wife-receivers
(or other appropriate recipient)

In the second, which involves no deity, the prestation sequence is a simple one:

jajmān → { Brahman *purohit*
(donor) wife-receivers
(or other appropriate recipient)

The third and much less common type consists in a direct transferral to the deity himself, who "takes upon himself" and assimilates the negative qualities and substances:

jajmān → deity

In the performance of the first two types of *vrat,* there are two distinct sets of actions. The first is the keeping of the *vrat* itself, which involves primarily the inner "heating of the body" (*śarīr ko tapānā*) of the performer through various ascetic practices. During this time, the acceptance of any *dān* would dissipate this heat; thus one should not accept any *pujāpā* during *śarīr ko tapānā*. The "heating" predisposes the body to both disarticulation and mixtures (Marriott 1976), and therefore the acceptance and assimilation of *dān* during such a time would be easily accomplished but would reduce this "heat," just as a Brahman's "fiery energy" (*tej*) is diminished by the acceptance of *dān* prestations at any time. The actions that bring about the *tapānā,* the "heating," in this first phase of the *vrat* are disarticulative: they separate the negative substances from the person. People in Pahansu say that from fasting and performing the *vrat* itself "afflictions come out" (*kaṣṭ utar jā*). Then, from giving the *udāpan,* "the afflictions are removed" (*udāpan karne se kaṣṭ dūr ho jā*). It is for this reason that the performance of the *udāpan,* the making of the *caṛhāpā* prestations, is so crucial; the negative qualities that are separated from the person are extremely dangerous until they have been "moved away" (*dūr karnā, haṭānā*) and assimilated by the appropriate receptacle.

The two-phase process of disarticulation and removal is a feature not only of *vrat,* but of most other Pahansu ritual as well. The *vrat-udāpan* may stand alone as a mode of transferral of inauspiciousness, or it may be found as a component of more complex sequences, which will be examined in detail in chapter 4, as they occur in life-cycle, calendrical, and harvest rituals. In the remainder of this chapter, we will briefly survey other components and modes of transferral.

Ṭakkarpūrat, Pūrat Pūrnā

Spatial configurations may be implemented in the transferral of inauspiciousness, and this emerges most clearly in the case of *ṭakkarpūrat* prestations. Designs called *ṭakkarpūrat* ("protection from harm") are drawn with flour on an area of the ground that has first been smeared with cow-dung paste. The act of drawing itself is called *pūrat pūrnā,* "drawing protection." The design takes the form of a square oriented toward the cardinal directions, with two transverse lines crossing in the middle (see fig. 10).

The intersection of the two transverse lines is generally positioned over the household *okhlī,* a small plastered depression in the earthen floor of the house that is used as a mortar for husking and grinding operations. The *okhlī* is nearly always found in an inner room of a house or near the threshold (see fig. 11). The square itself is sometimes interpreted as a "protection from harm man" (*ṭakkarpūrat ādmī*), in which case a few additional lines will be added to represent the head and the limbs, as in figure 10, part B.

The disarticulation of inauspiciousness involved in the use of these *ṭakkarpūrat* designs is accomplished through the catalytic agency of "heat," just as in the *vrat* ritual sequences. This heat is engendered in several ways. The actions of husking and grinding are said to produce heat, which is then partially contained in the *okhlī.* In fact, the possible locations of the *okhlī* are themselves the "hottest" parts of the house; it is in the inner rooms of a house that the heat-releasing actions of sexual intercourse and childbirth occur, and the threshold, because of the comings and goings through it, is also "hot," just as a crossroads (*caurāī,* a place where four roads meet) is hot. The design of the *ṭakkarpūrat* itself is ho-

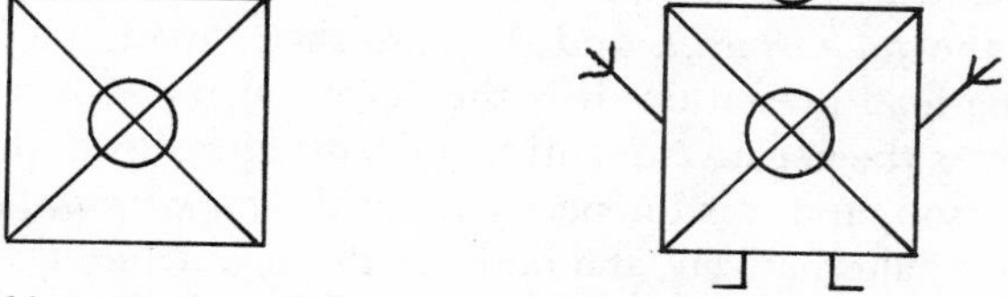

A. *Ṭakkarpūrat* over *okhlī* B. *Ṭakkarpūrat ādmī* over *okhlī*

Fig. 10. Pahansu *ṭakkarpūrats*

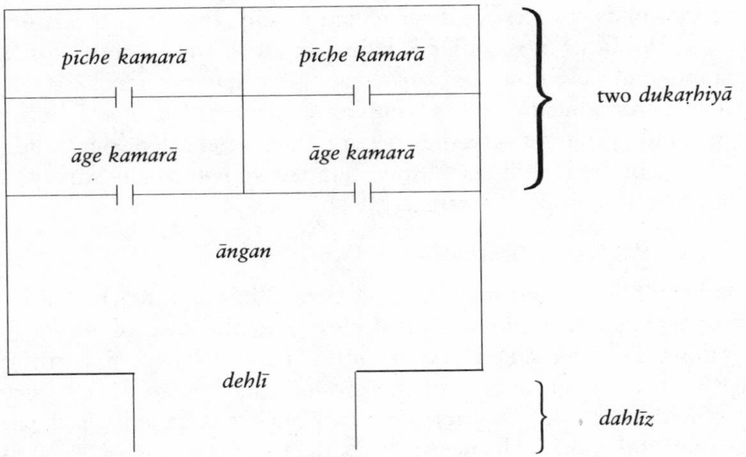

Fig. 11. A typical Gujar house in Pahansu consists of a *dahlīz,* a small enclosed area at the threshold (*dehlī*) of the house; just beyond the *dahlīz* is the *āngan,* the courtyard in which the cooking, bathing, and most other household activities are carried out; off the courtyard are pairs of rooms, from one to four, called *dukaṛhiyā.* There is only one doorway leading to the courtyard for each *dukaṛhiyā.* The room nearest the courtyard is the "front room" (*āge kamarā*) and the inner room is the "back room" (*pīche kamarā*).

mologous to a *caurāī* as well. The crossroads is thought of as going out to the four directions, just as do the transverse lines of the directionally oriented *ṭakkarpūrat,* which meet and form a "crossroads" over the *okhlī.* Finally, we should note, a crossroads is thought of as an appropriate dumping place for some specific types of *dān.*

After this design has been drawn with flour over the *okhlī* (by the Barber's wife, or by the wife of the family's Brahman priest), the brass tray containing the leftover flour and some unrefined sugar is placed just outside the square, and the subject of the ritual (from whom inauspiciousness is to be removed) is seated over the center of the *ṭakkarpūrat.* Various other ritual actions may be performed then; and at the end, the tray of leftover flour and sugar is given as *caṛhāpā* to an appropriate recipient.

Inauspiciousness and "hindrances" are here disarticulated by the "heat" of the *ṭakkarpūrat,* and they are then "made far" (*dūr karnā*) through the final prestation. It is the "heat" at the center of the design that separates the negative qualities and substances from the body of the afflicted person, and it is the perimeter of the *ṭakkarpūrat*—the four directions—or, alternatively, the body of the *ṭakkarpūrat ādmi,* that absorbs this inauspiciousness, which is transferred through the flour that is given as *caṛhāpā.*

Husking (koṭnā), Winnowing (pachornā), and Churning (bilonā)

The analogies between the agricultural and domestic activities of husking, winnowing, and churning on the one hand, and on the other, the disarticulation of negative qualities and substances—the removal of the chaff from the wheat as it were—are obvious. Their iconicity is relevant in their interpretation in the ritual context, but it is not only because of this obvious resemblance that the actions of husking, winnowing, and churning are so often found in transferral sequences. All three of these actions are thought to produce "heat" as they accomplish various kinds of separations in domestic operations; hence they are used in ritual sequences as well to effect separations of inauspiciousness from the subject of the ritual. On a number of occasions, the items to be given as *caṛhāpā*, into which the negative qualities are to be transferred, are actually placed in a winnowing basket (*chāj*) and "winnowed," and *wārpher* (which is discussed below) is also sometimes performed with items placed in a winnowing basket. Rice to be given as *caṛhāpā* is frequently placed in a vessel over the household *okhlī* and ritually husked with a pestle (*mūsal*). Finally, the churning rope and staff (*netī* and *raī*) appear in a number of ritual sequences performed for the separation and removal of inauspiciousness.

Dhok mārnā

Perhaps the simplest disarticulative ritual action is *dhok mārnā*, which is found as a part of longer ritual sequences in many contexts. It consists of dropping grains of wheat or rice, or unrefined sugar or flour, from one's hand before an image or onto items that are to be given in *dān*. The grain, flour, or sugar is then given as *caṛhāpā* to an appropriate recipient, thus removing inauspiciousness from the performer of the ritual.

Wārpher and Chuwānā

In both *wārpher* and *chuwānā*, the disarticulation of inauspiciousness is accomplished by bringing objects into contact with, or into a particular spatial relationship with, the body of the afflicted person. The word *wārpher* is derived from two verbs: *wārnā*, "to make an offering to ward off inauspiciousness," and *phernā*, "to circle."[11] *Wārpher* occurs most frequently during the course of wedding rites, but also in connection with rituals of childhood, and it consists in the circling of small dishes of grain or other items over the head of the subject of the ritual, from whom the inauspiciousness is to be removed. Through this action, "hindrances" are said to be removed from the body; the grain or other item is then given to the appropriate recipient as *caṛhāpā*. It is thus referred to as a "*dān* of the body" (*śarīr kā dān*) or "*dān* that has been touched [to the body]" (*chuā huā dān*).

Chuwānā may be translated as "the touching" (a causative form of the verb), and like *wārpher* it is a disarticulative action performed for a person afflicted with some form of inauspiciousness, usually, in this case, disease (*rog*) or pain (*dard*). To perform *chuwānā,* a dish of grain or *sawā rupiāh* (one and one-quarter rupees) is waved over the body of the afflicted person; the articles are touched first to the feet, then moved upward to the head, and finally brought downward again toward the feet. (The first upward movement is referred to as *lagānā,* "the applying," and the downward movement is called *utārnā,* "the taking off.") Alternatively, these items may be circled seven times, in a counterclockwise movement, before the afflicted person. These movements separate the inauspiciousness from the body and cause it to be absorbed (*sokhnā*) by the coins or the grain. These things must then be kept out of the reach of children, to whom the negative qualities might be inadvertantly transferred, until they are given to the appropriate recipient, who thereby assimilates the danger they contain and moves it away (*haṭānā*) from the afflicted person. The significance of the two movements of *lagānā* and *utārnā* will be more fully explicated in chapter 4, but below I describe several other directionally oriented disarticulative actions that occur as part of longer transferral sequences in Pahansu.

Mīnasnā

Mīnasnā is the sprinkling of water, in a counterclockwise direction, around items that are to be given as *dān* or *caṛhāpā*. This circling with water is part of a number of ritual sequences performed for the removal of inauspiciousness. The direction here is of primary importance. A clockwise movement, the "straight" or "direct" (*sulṭā*) movement, is inappropriate; the sprinkling must always be done *ulṭā,* in the "reverse" direction, if the transfer of negative qualities and substances into the *caṛhāpā* items is to be successful. When instructing villagers as to the proper performance of rituals that include *mīnasnā,* priests and astrologers in Pahansu frequently stress that after a *mīnasnā* has been performed, no one should touch these articles before they are given to the appropriate recipient; inauspiciousness will be transferred to the first person who comes into contact with the *caṛhāpā* items. When the *dān* is given to the designated recipient, water is poured out from the same vessel used in the *mīnasnā.*[12]

Nackār and sevel

Villagers say that *nackār* and *sevel,* which differ only in the direction of the transfer of inauspiciousness, are like *wārpher* in that they bring about the removal of inauspiciousness and "hindrances," which then must be transferred through the making of prestations. The person who is to perform a *nackār* (always a woman) touches the end of her shawl (the *pallā*), first to her own head and then to the items into which the inauspicious qualities are to be transferred. Through the performance of *nackār,* the woman removes inauspiciousness both from herself and from her husband or sons. *Nackār* is almost always preceded by a heating and thereby disarticulative fast, a *vrat.*

The way in which *nackār* transfers inauspiciousness to the items to be given in *dān* is graphically depicted in the *kathā* of the festival of *karvā cauth* that is told in Pahansu. In this story, a woman restores her husband to life when she touches the end of her *pallā* to plants and trees along the road she travels. The vegetation, she discovers, dries up and withers, but her husband returns to her. (The text of this story is translated in chapter 4.)

Sevel may be performed either by a woman or, in some rituals, by a Brahman priest. Like *nackār,* it is performed using the *pallā,* but in this case it is touched first to the head of another person, then to a tray containing various articles to be appropriated or eaten by the person who performs the *sevel,* or by a third person designated as the appropriate recipient of the prestation. *Sevel* is performed, it is said, for the auspiciousness (*śubh*) of the person whose head is first touched, from whom inauspiciousness is to be removed. The inauspiciousness is transferred to the items in the tray, and then these things are received as *dān* by the Brahman, the woman who may have performed the *sevel,* or in the case of a Brahman ritual, by certain kinsmen.

The woman who performs *nackār* first touches her *pallā* to her own head and then to the items to be given in *dān,* and she thereby removes negative qualities and substances from herself or from those with whom she shares bodily substance, most particularly her husband and sons. In the case of *sevel,* this action is performed for another person, for the auspiciousness of the person whose head is first touched by the *pallā.*

The *pallā* is seen in very many instances as the appropriate place to receive items that are given in *dān,* and also as the place where inauspiciousness is likely to collect. Once when I visited a Bhangi house for a *chaṭṭhī* ritual (performed on the sixth day after a birth) I was asked, before I entered the confinement room, to wave my own *pallā* over the smoldering embers of the hearth. I had "wandered in the village," the women said, and I should wave my *pallā* in that way to discharge whatever loose inauspiciousness might have collected there in my wanderings, so that it would not afflict the mother and the child.

Wārpher and *chuwānā, nackār* and *sevel* are performed, people say, "for protection, and for well-being achieved through gift-giving" (*rakṣā aur khair-khairāt ke māro*). When the *dān* is given, "hindrances are made far" (*bādhā dūr ho jā*).

The Use of Disarticulative Substances

Like actions, certain substances may also act as disarticulative agents. In such cases, certain food items, water and earth from various locations, roots and herbs, cloth of particular colors, and so forth, are brought into contact with the body of the afflicted person—but never consumed by that person—in order to effect a separation of the inauspiciousness.[13] These substances may be used in conjunction with one of the ritual actions described above.

In the use of these substances, one of two basic principles may be involved. First, it is thought that in many cases the "heat" produced by certain ritual actions may be replaced by the inherent heat of certain substances (one never finds foods described as cooling used in this way). Mustard seed and mustard oil, a combination of "seven grains" (*satanajā*)—mixtures of grains always being more heating than any grain alone—and unrefined sugar are examples of heating substances that may effect the desired disarticulation.

Second, substances corresponding in some way to the nature of the negative qualities and substances themselves may attract inauspiciousness and thus draw it away from the body of the afflicted person. This is most obvious in the case of inauspiciousness and "faults" (*doṣ*) engendered by planetary configurations. Each planet has its own nature, and the inauspiciousness engendered by it partakes of this nature. Certain foodstuffs, metals, flowers, and colors share a similar nature, and they therefore are capable of drawing out the inauspiciousness in a particularly efficacious fashion.

Bathing with water mixed with such substances is sometimes part of the disarticulative phase of ritual sequences. The baths always begin at the head and proceed downward over the body—the *utārnā* "removing" or "taking down" direction—and are followed by *caṛhāpā* prestations for the removal of the negative qualities just separated from the body. Each type of affliction requires its own set of substances to draw out the negative qualities through the bathing.

If the disarticulative actions of a particular ritual sequence do not involve a touching of the *caṛhāpā* items to the body of the afflicted person—as in the case of these directionally oriented baths—this contact will take place following the disarticulation of inauspiciousness: cloth may be placed on the head or a pair of shoes may be worn, for example, and then given as *caṛhāpā*. Among the most potent of these transferral-effecting actions is the casting of one's reflection into a vessel of mustard oil. The contact with the item to be given as *dān,* the oil, removes the inauspiciousness that has been made to "come out" (*utarnā*) through various disarticulative actions. When the negative qualities have been transferred to the oil, it is given to the appropriate recipient as *chāyā kā dān,* the "*dān* of the reflection."

So far we have traced inauspicious qualities and substances through the disarticulative and removal phases of ritual sequences. We shall now examine the final phase of the transferral process in which these qualities and substances are assimilated by the recipient of the *caṛhāpā.*

The recipient of the *dān* or *caṛhāpā,* the *pātra* ("vessel"), is said to "take the afflictions" (*kaṣṭ lenā*) of the donor or *jajmān* upon himself. Villagers explained that such prestations are made whenever "suffering" (*dukh*), "anguish" (*kleś*), or "afflictions" (*kaṣṭ*) beset one, and through this action the negative qualities will come upon the recipient (*us ke ūpar ā jātā hai*) and may bring harm to him (*nuksān pahũcānā*): "The faults of another come upon him" (*dūsre ke doṣ uske ūpar ā jātā hai*). These negative qualities and substances must be assimilated by the recipient, rearticulated as it were, following the disarticulation accomplished through the actions that precede the giving of the *caṛhāpā.* This rearticulation on the part of the recipient is said to be a "digestion" (*pacnā*) of the *dān* and the inauspiciousness.[14]

If the *caṛhāpā* is not properly "digested" by the recipient, the inauspicious qualities contained within it begin immediately to exhibit their negative consequences in him and in his family: disease will afflict them, they may become mad (*pāgal*), their "lineage" will gradually fall (*vaṃś din par din girtā rahegā*), the intellect will be ruined (*buddhi bhraṣṭ ho jayegī*), sin and evil will come upon them (*pāp caṛhnā*), and their "fiery energy" (*tej*) will be decreased.[15] Ordinary digestion of food is said to occur by the action of "heat" in the stomach (*peṭ kī garmī*), and the "digestion" of *caṛhāpā* is accomplished in much the same fashion. Heat produced by austerities (*tap, tapasya*) is a prerequisite for the successful assimilation of the inauspiciousness of the *caṛhāpā* prestations, and if this heat is present the negative qualities will be rearticulated without disastrous consequences to the recipient.[16] Nevertheless, each acceptance of *caṛhāpā* has its destructive effects, because the "digestion" of the *pāp, doṣ,* and *kaṣṭ* dissipates the internal power (*śakti*), *tej,* and "heat" (*tap*) of the recipient. Brahman recipients must then replenish their power by daily austerities, the recitation of *mantra*s, and so forth,[17] and other categories of recipient do so through other means.

Among the most important of these alternative modes of heat production on the part of the recipient are the simple activities of householdership (*grihasthī*): grinding, husking, churning, and sexual intercourse, and so forth. It is frequently stipulated—by informants and in popular ritual texts—that *dān* and *caṛhāpā* are to be given to a married person: to a Brahman householder who has a wife (one who is *sapatnī*), to the wife of one's family Barber, or to one's married daughters and their husbands, for example. In contrast, widows are not generally considered to be appropriate recipients of such prestations.

In all of the ritual actions that are said to "remove inauspiciousness," the "coming out" (*utarnā*) of the negative qualities and substances from the *jajmān* is accomplished through disarticulative procedures that often involve the generation or application of inner "heat," and this is followed by the "removal" (*haṭānā, dūr karnā, ṭālnā*) of the inauspiciousness in the *caṛhāpā* items. The prestation is made then to an appropriate recipient, the "vessel" who takes the *caṛhāpā* and its load of inauspiciousness upon himself in a very literal way, by placing cloth on his head, by consuming foodstuffs, or by wearing clothes or shoes. This process is effected in all of the ritual procedures discussed in this chapter. These procedures are components of larger ritual sequences enacted in life-cycle, calendrical, and harvest rites and when ill-being has been diagnosed as being brought about by the negative substances characterized here as inauspiciousness. In each such ritual, there is a specified *pātra,* and these various recipients are almost always involved in either kinship or intercaste relationships with the *jajmān* donor. Chapter 4 will examine these ritual contexts and the nature of the social relationships that are implicated in the ties between donors and recipients in Pahansu.

CHAPTER FOUR

The Ritual Contexts of *Dān* and the Ritual Construction of Gujar Centrality

In chapter 3, we examined a number of isolated ritual actions through which inauspiciousness is said to be "taken out" (*utārnā*) before being "made far" (*dūr karnā*) or "removed" (*haṭānā, ṭālnā*) through the giving of *dān*. In this chapter, we will focus on the larger ritual sequences of which these procedures are a part: rituals of the life course, rituals of the harvests, calendrical rituals, and the ameliorative rituals that are performed when inauspiciousness has been identified as the cause of specific afflictions in the village. We shall consider especially the manner in which particular kinsmen and persons of particular castes are related, in Pahansu, as donor and recipient of *dān* and *caṛhāpā*, and the implications of this for the anthropological understanding of kinship, caste, and dominance in more general terms.

The Rituals of Pregnancy, Birth, and Childhood

Even before the birth of a child, there is a great deal of concern for safeguarding the mother and the child from the dangers of inauspiciousness. Among the precautions that are taken in this respect is the avoidance of *dān* or *caṛhāpā* in any form during one's pregnancy. Gujar women in Saharanpur District generally remain in their conjugal villages for the delivery, where their husbands' mothers counsel them not to eat any of the sweets or other foods that may be sent as *dān* from their natal villages at that time. The pregnant woman should not partake of these foodstuffs because in her "weak" (*kamjor*) condition she may not be able to withstand the dangers that accompany such prestations. Should she visit her *pīhar*, her natal village, during her pregnancy, she must also avoid the *caṛhāpā* generated at any ritual occasion there, which as *dhiyānī* (married "daughter" or "sister," specifically in her capacity as recipient of *dān*) she would ordinarily be obligated to accept.

During the pregnancy, illnesses and discomforts not diagnosed as caused by disproportions in the consumption of "hot" and "cold" foods or by imbalances in the three humors (*doṣ*) are generally assumed to be caused by the inauspiciousness of the *dev-pitar* ("ancestor gods") of the conjugal family, particularly those that died without producing offspring of their own. I was told that when Simla, a wife in the Gujar house in which I lived, was pregnant with her first child, she suffered from pain in her teeth and gums. Convinced that this condition had been brought about by the actions of her own husband's first wife's son, who had died childless many years before, Asikaur, Simla's husband's mother, advised Simla that the only way to rid herself of the pain would be to remove it through the giving of *dān*. Asikaur performed a *chuwānā* ("causing to touch") for Simla by taking a handful of wheat, waving it over Simla from feet to head, and then in the reverse direction from head to feet. (Asikaur and Simla demonstrated this for me.) The grains of wheat were then tied in a knot in the end of Simla's shawl (her *pallā*) until the fifth day of that lunar month (the afflicting *dev-pitar* had died on the fifth day in the lunar cycle). On that day, grains of wheat were taken to the shrine in the fields that had been established for the *dev-pitar,* and *dhok mārnā* was performed with them. These grains from the *chuwānā* were then given as *dān* to the wife of the family Brahman *purohit,* to effect the final transfer of the pain that had been afflicting Simla. The women of the household explained to me that it is the *pharmāyā* ("obligation") of the Brahman woman to accept the grains of the *chuwānā,* and when such a prestation is necessary in a Brahman household, the grain would be given to a *dhiyānī* of the Brahman family.

The first occasion at which prestations are made to ensure the well-being of both mother and child is during labor. Women in the household of the *jaccā,* the woman who is about to give birth (this term is used to refer to the woman for forty days after the birth as well) circle *sawā rupiāh* (one and one-quarter rupees) over her body in order to remove the pain, to remove the hindrances to a speedy delivery, and to avert again the danger occasioned by the presence of the *dev-pitar. Chuwānā* is performed the same way it was for Simla (or, alternatively, the coins are circled seven times counterclockwise over the woman), and the coins are given to the wife of the family's Brahman *purohit.* In this case, as in the case of the *chuwānā* that Asikaur performed for Simla, the inauspiciousness that caused the pain will be transferred to the recipient. However, at the time of birth, the *jaccā* is in a condition of birth impurity (*sūtak*), and during this period Brahmans will not accept any prestations from the households of their *jajmān*s. The coins are therefore kept out of the reach of children in a niche in the wall, and they are given to the Brahman's wife after the *sūtak* has ended. Only the inauspiciousness is transferred then and not the *sūtak*. As in the case of the *chuwānā* prestations that may be made earlier in the pregnancy, the *dhiyānī* of the family are the appropriate recipients in the case of a Brahman birth.[1]

In cases where the delivery of the child seems to be particularly slow in coming, one further prestation may be made, as I myself witnessed. When Santroj, another of the wives in the household in which I lived, was about to give birth for the first time, it seemed to Asikaur that the labor had been going on too long, so she brought a small container of grain and a set of clothes that Santroj had previously worn, and performed a *chuwānā* with them. The grain and the clothes were then placed underneath the cot on which Santroj was lying, to be given later to the Sweeper midwife.

At the time of a birth, it is essential for all castes that a *dhiyānī*, usually the *jaccā*'s *nanad* (husband's sister), be present in the house. She must generally return from her conjugal village (her *sasurāl*) for this event. The first ritual role performed by the *dhiyānī* is *cūcī dhulāī*, the washing of the breasts of the *jaccā*. On the day after the birth (preferably forty hours after the birth has occurred) the *dhiyānī*, in order to "purify" (*sūci karnā*) the breasts before the child is nursed, brings a small earthen saucer of cow's milk and stalks of grass to the confinement room. With the stalks of grass she sprinkles cow's milk on the breasts of the new mother, first the right and then the left. This simple act of "washing" is indeed thought of as making the breasts *sūci*, "pure." But it accomplishes more than this. A ten-*paisā* coin is placed in the earthen saucer before the washing, and this is taken by the *dhiyānī* woman to remove the "dangers" (*sankaṭ*) occasioned by the presence of the ancestor deities. It is only because she removes this "danger" by receiving the coin that a *dhiyānī* must perform the *cūcī dhulāī*, for as we shall see in chapter 5, it is not specifically "the work of *dhiyānī*" (*dhiyānī kā kām*) to perform purificatory functions.

Indeed, the two separate ritual functions that are involved in the *cūcī dhulāī* are marked by two separate prestations. At the time of the washing, the *nanad* receives the coin (or occasionally a piece of silver jewelry) that has been placed in the milk. It is said to be the *pharmāyā* ("obligation") of the *dhiyānī* to accept this as *dān*. On the day she returns to her *sasurāl*, however, she receives five, seven, or nine sets of cloth (*joṛās*), a sum of money (generally from five to fifty rupees), and perhaps an additional piece of jewelry (*ṭūm*). These gifts, in contrast to the previous *dān* prestation, are called *lāg* or *neg*, words used to refer to prestations made in payment for the performance of ritual and other services. They are most definitely not *dān*, and the *nanad* may quite properly ask for a certain amount of money, or a certain ornament from the *jaccā*, because in this case it is the "right" (*hak*) of the *nanad* to receive these things as *neg*, rather than her "obligation" to accept them, as it is in the case of the *dān* that she receives. The existence of these two separate prestations, and the attendant linguistic distinctions, permit us to separate two culturally postulated functions of the *cūcī dhulāī:* the purification of the breasts, a service for which the *nanad* is compensated by the *neg*, and the removal of danger from the mother's milk, effected through the acceptance of the coin from the earthen saucer.[2]

It is the *pharmāyā* of the *dhiyānī* to accept another prestation on the day after the birth. On this day, the *jaccā* receives her first food following the birth, a liquid mixture of warm clarified butter, sugar, and ground *ajwāyan* (anise-like) seeds called *cuwānī*. (This is said to be a "hot" mixture, and it therefore gives strength to the *jaccā*.) It is usually the husband's mother who prepares the *cuwānī*. When it is ready, she divides it into two portions, takes an ember from the hearth, and sprinkles a bit of the *cuwānī* from the first portion onto the ember, as a *dhok mārnā* to Bhūmiyā, the god of the village site, to the goddess Kālī, and to the ancestor deities. The first portion is then *pujāpā* and is given to the *dhiyānī*, who must drink it before the remaining portion is given to the *jaccā*. This is done so that the dangers that are brought on by these deities will not affect the new mother and the child, but will instead be transferred to the *dhiyānī*, whose obligation it is to accept these dangers for the well-being of her brother's wife. The same procedure is followed a few days later, when a preparation of browned wheat flour, clarified butter, coconut, almonds, and sugar called *sāndhā* is made for the *jaccā*. Like the *cuwānī*, the *sāndhā* is a "hot" (*garam*) food that restores the "strength" (*tākt*) of the *jaccā*.

The well-being and auspiciousness of the mother and child are further secured on the sixth day after birth at the ritual called simply *chaṭṭhī* ("the sixth").[3] A number of different prestations are made on this day so that "distress" will not afflict the child and the family as a whole (*kaṣṭ na pahũcnā*). These prestations are accompanied by separate ritual sequences that should be performed before the father sees his child, lest he be afflicted by this *kaṣṭ*, the inauspiciousness of birth, before it is removed.

The first sequence of ritual actions and prestations is concerned with the goddess Bemātā, who is said to place the body of the child into the mother's womb. On the sixth day after birth, she comes to write the "fate" (*takdīr*) of the child on its forehead. Her *lekh* ("writing") indicates what "sequence of actions" (*karyākram*) the child will perform in his life, and what "merits and transferrals of evil" (*pun-dān*) will be produced through those actions.

As the following story that is told about Bemātā in Pahansu indicates, and as the ritual actions concerned with the goddess imply, *lekh* is not simply a reflection of a previously determined fate; Bemātā herself may influence the well-being of the child:

> Seven girls were spinning thread in a house. At that time someone died in the village, and one of these Brahman girls began to say: "What kind of a woman is this who let her husband die?" A Brahman was

standing in the lane and heard this. This Brahman had a son, and a *paṇḍit* had told him that this son would die when his twelfth year was completed. So that Brahman did the boy's marriage with that girl [who had spoken of a woman's ability to maintain her husband's life].

So when that boy's twelfth year was completed, he was lying on a cot. That girl [his wife] lit a clay lamp and put it at one of the feet of the cot. She put some grain at another, and a vessel of water at the third. And she herself sat at a foot of the cot.

When Yamrāj [the god of death] sent his emissary (*dūt*), that clay lamp said: "This is my three-hour watch (*pahar*) and for one and one-quarter *pahar*s I won't let the boy go." And the grain too spoke in this way, when the one and one-quarter *pahar*s (*sawā pahar*) was finished. And the emissary returned, and again had to go away. Then the *pahar* of the water came, and the emissary returned, but the water too spoke in this way.

Then Yamrāj Bhagvān called Bemātā and asked: "What kind of a *lekh* have you written? I sent an emissary and he hasn't returned with the boy." Then Bemātā went to the house of that boy, and his wife began to massage the legs (*ṭāng bhīcānā*) of Bemātā, and so that old woman said: "May your husband live, may your brothers live, may you have sons, and may you be a *suhāgan* [auspiciously married woman] in your old age."[4] Then Bemātā said [to the Brahman boy]: "Let's go. I have come to take you. Bhagvān is calling you." But the boy's wife began to say: "You said 'may your husband live' and 'may you have sons' but now you are taking him away. So how will he live, and where will the sons come from?"

So Bemātā went to Yamrāj Bhagvān [without the Brahman boy] and said: "Because of my words [the words of the blessing] I will be made a liar if I bring the boy. So take my own son in place of that boy." So Bemātā's own son died, and she made her own son's wife a widow (*rāṇḍ*). And the Brahman boy lived.

Bemātā's son's wife was very angry at this. And so now the old husband's mother (*būṛhiyā sasū*) gives sons to people, and her son's wife gives daughters. [Both the mother and the son's wife are Bemātā, villagers say.]

In this story, Bemātā is forced to act as the intermediary in the transferral of death from the Brahman boy to Bemātā's own son, after death is rebuffed by the lamp, the grain, the water, and the wife at the feet of the boy's cot. The sixth-day rituals concerned with Bemātā that are performed in Pahansu effect the same sort of transferral, although to a different recipient, and in a somewhat different manner than that depicted in the story.

In the afternoon of the sixth day after a birth, the midwife (*dāī*) returns to the house in which the birth had taken place. The women of the house assist the mother, the *jaccā*, in preparing the items necessary for the *chaṭṭhī* ritual. *Sawā pā̃c ser* (five and one-quarter *ser*, about eleven pounds) of grain is placed in a large brass tray, and a set of cloth (a *joṛā*) is placed over the grain. A tray with some sugar and flour is also prepared. An earthen lamp filled with mustard oil is placed, along with some other items, at a leg at the "head" (*sirānā*) of the cot in the confinement room on which the birth took place, and on which the mother has been lying with her child. Five piles of fried breads are also prepared, one for Bemātā and one for each leg of the cot. The midwife meanwhile fashions a small, rough cow-dung image of Bemātā and wraps it in a cloth. The mother takes the child in her arms and squats down at the head of the cot. The midwife puts a bit of the sugar and flour before the earthen lamp; she then puts some of the grain in the mother's hands, and directs her in performing *dhok mārnā* to Bemātā seven times. All of the items used in this *dhok mārnā* are left in the confinement room overnight; the legs of the cot, it is said, should not be unguarded during the sixth night. These items are given, as the *pujāpā* of Bemātā, to the midwife on the following day, when it is said that the *bidā* ("departure") occurs. The midwife thus becomes the *pātra,* the receptacle for the *kaṣṭ* that would otherwise afflict the child and its family. In the story, Bemātā is the intermediary who transfers death from the Brahman's son to her own; in the ritual sequence she is again the intermediary. The offerings that are made to Bemātā contain the inauspiciousness, which is ultimately received by the midwife in the *pujāpā.*

Both the *kathā* and the ritual actions of *chaṭṭhī* represent the *lekh* as something that cannot simply be wiped away or retracted by Bemātā or by Yamrāj. Once it has come into being, it must have its effect somewhere; and so, in the story, when she is tricked by the wife, in order to prove her blessing true, Bemātā must provide a substitute to fulfill the *lekh* and accept the consequent death. The actual process of transferral is left unstated in the story, as it is in many of the North Indian myths connected with such ritual practices; Bemātā simply tells Yamrāj to take her own son instead of the Brahman boy. The objects guarding the bed in the story—the lamp, the vessel of water, the grain, as well as the wife—convey similar messages to Yamrāj that the boy should not be taken away.

In the ritual sequences, on the other hand, the transferral is a substantial one: the five and one-quarter *ser* of grain, the earthen lamp, and the cow-dung image of Bemātā themselves absorb the inauspiciousness of the *lekh.* As in the story, Bemātā herself is an intermediary in the transferral process. Her image receives the *kaṣṭ* through the *dhok mārnā,* but when the midwife accepts the grain and the other items of the *pujāpā,* the inauspiciousness is "given onward" to her.

Immediately following the *dhok mārnā* to Bemātā on the sixth day, the *jaccā* is led to the threshold of the confinement room to perform a second ritual and prestation sequence. *Sawā pā̃c ser* of husked rice, *sawā pā̃c ser* of unrefined sugar, and a complete set of cloth (a *teḷn*), including a *tukrī* (a long skirt worn by women when they visit other houses in their conjugal villages) are placed in a large brass tray.[5] The *jaccā,* again with the child in her arms, takes a handful of the rice, and an older woman of the house, usually her husband's mother, directs her in the performance of a *dhok mārnā* to the ancestor gods of the house, exactly over the threshold. The mother and child then return to the cot in the confinement room. The rice, the sugar, and the *teḷn* from the *dhok mārnā* are given as *pujāpā* to the sister of the *jaccā*'s husband, her *dhiyānī,* so that *kaṣṭ* from the ancestral deities will not afflict her, her child, or the other people of the house. The cloth, the rice, and the sugar are spoken of as "the *pujāpā* of the threshold" (*dehlī kā pujāpā*). It is important, people say, that all of these items be taken to the conjugal village of the recipient; by removing them across the threshold, and on to another village, inauspiciousness is transferred away from the house.

At the time of these sixth-day rituals, women of the *kunbā* in which the birth has occurred bring small dishes of unhusked grain to the house and do *wārpher* with them over the head of the child. This action is said to remove *pāp* ("evil," inauspicious results of actions) and *bādhā* ("hindrances") from the child that may be present as a result of past actions (*karma*). The grain is then given as *caṛhāpā* to all of the *kamīn*s of the household.

On the same day, a set of prestations called *kevkā* is sent from the mother's *pīhar,* her natal village. (*Kevkā* is always sent for the birth of the first child and the first son, and it may be sent for other births as well.) One of the most important items in the *kevkā* is *sawā pā̃c ser* of *sāndhā.* Other items are also sent. A typical Gujar *kevkā,* sent for the wife of Mange, the son of Hirdha, included the following items:

Five and one-quarter *ser* of *sāndhā*
Two *joṛa*s for the mother
Nine *joṛa*s for the newborn son
One for the child's father's brother
One for the child's father's father
One for the child's father's mother
One for the child's sister
One for the child's father
One for each of the child's father's two sisters
One set of bedding

A similar set of prestations, called *cūcak* (from *cūcī,* "nipple") is given to the mother as she returns to her *sasurāl* after her first visit to her *pīhar* after the birth. Usually this first visit occurs about three months after the birth. Villagers, when they speak of this visit, say that she goes to her natal village "to accept the *cūcak*" (*cūcak len jā*). When Kamlesh, the daughter of Pahel Singh, left Pahansu to return to her conjugal village after her visit, she took the following items with her as her *cūcak:*

Fifteen *joṛa*s for the newborn son
Nineteen for herself
Fifteen for the men of her *sasurāl*
Eleven for the women of her *sasurāl*
Three ornaments (*ṭūm*) for herself (a gold necklace, a gold nose stud, and silver toe rings)
Eleven brass vessels

All of these prestations may be termed *dahej,* as are wedding prestations. But within both the *kevkā* and *cūcak,* discriminations are made. The sets of cloth for the newborn child and for the mother are given separately (*nyāre-nyāre*), women always insisted, from those for the *aglī,* "the next ones," the people of the daughter's *sasurāl.* This is so because, in these contexts, one does not give *waise hī joṛe* ("sets of cloth 'like that'"), that is, sets of cloth that are *dān,* to one's daughter and her child, but only to the *aglī.* The term *aglī* is used, as we shall see, only in relation to the *bhāt* prestation given by the mother's brother at the time of a wedding, the wedding *dahej* prestations, the *cālā* (return of the bride to her *sasurāl* for the second time), the *cūcak,* and the *kevkā.* The term itself foregrounds the notion of "giving onward," *āge denā,* an idea that appears again and again in the context of prestations that transfer inauspiciousness from donor to recipient. The inherent dangers of accepting the *kevkā* and the *cūcak* are indicated by the fact that sets of cloth and *sāndhā* from them must always be "given onward" in two ways. First, before the *sāndhā* is given to the *jaccā* in her *sasurāl,* a portion of it is taken out and given to her husband's sister (*nanad*), as her *dhiyānī;* only then is it safe for the *jaccā* to consume it. Furthermore, when the *nanad* returns to her own conjugal village, she takes sets of cloth from the *kevkā* and *cūcak* with her as *dān,* for herself and for her husband. Second, a *joṛā* from both sets of prestations is taken to the shrine of the ancestor deity of the *jaccā*'s *sasurāl,* to be offered there and given as *pujāpā* to the Brahman *purohit* of the family. In these, as in so many other similar prestations, the sequence of giving, then, is from "wife-givers" to their *dhiyānī,* who then "give onward" to their own *dhiyānī* or to another appropriate recipient, here the Brahman *purohit.* In each case, the "giving onward" is done for one's own well-being, auspiciousness, and protection.

There is one other postpartum ritual that is performed by Gujars in many villages in Saharanpur District, and by several castes in Pahansu (though not by Gujars), to ensure the well-being and auspiciousness of the mother. A small cow-dung square is plastered over the threshold of the house, and the *jaccā* places a few grains of rice and some turmeric on it. This is done ten more times in the lanes of the village, as the *jaccā* makes her way to a village well. Another cow-dung square is made there, and a *dhok mārnā* is performed for Khwājā, a vaguely characterized deity associated with wells. Then a Water-carrier woman brings two small pots of water, and the *jaccā* places some coins in each of them. The two pots are placed on the mother's head and circled, as a *chuwānā*. The water is then poured out and the coins are given as *caṛhāpā* to the Water-carrier. This is done, villagers say, to remove the *kaṣṭ* of the mother that may be caused by Khwājā. It should be noted here that the *pātra* for this *dān,* the Water-carrier woman, corresponds to, or has some affinity with, the source of the *kaṣṭ,* the deity associated with wells and water. Such correspondence of the *pātra* and the source of inauspiciousness is typical of the rituals and prestations analyzed here and will be discussed in more detail in the concluding section of this chapter.

The transferrals of inauspiciousness from the child, his own *kunbā,* and the *kunbā* of his mother to *ḍhiyānī,* to the midwife, to *kamīn* castes, and to Brahmans are procedures that occur at all births. There are also a number of possible circumstances at birth that may necessitate extraordinary ritual actions and prestations to remove afflictions and inauspiciousness from various sources from the child, the mother and the father, the house, the *kunbā,* and occasionally from the child's *nānā* (mother's father), *nānī* (mother's mother), and *māmā* (mother's brother).

The birth of a first son following the birth of three daughters is said to cause *kaṣṭ* to the child and to the parents. Indeed, it may cause the death of the child. Telu Ram, my "brother" and patron, had been born after three daughters, and he was therefore called a *tīkun* (from the word "three"). This was a long-awaited son for Nyadar and Asikaur, his parents. Nyadar had been married previously and had had one son. His wife died, and shortly thereafter his son drowned in the village pond. (This son is now enshrined as the *pācimvālā,* "the one of the fifth lunar day," in Telu Ram's fields.) Nyadar was already of quite an advanced age, probably around fifty years old, at the time his son drowned, and he went to great lengths to secure another bride so that a son and heir could be provided. He was married to Asikaur, a young girl at the time, and she gave birth to three daughters in rapid succession. Nyadar was one of the leading men of the village and had one of the largest landholdings in Pahansu. He, as well as the other men of his *kunbā,* were anxious that a son should survive to inherit the land when Nyadar died. They did not want the land to pass out of the *kunbā,* as it might if a future husband of one of the three daughters were to inherit the land as a *ghar jamāī* ("daughter's husband of the house"). And so, when Telu Ram was born in inauspicious circumstances as a *tīkun*, a number of measures were taken to ensure his well-being. (These were described to me by Asikaur and Telu Ram himself, who had heard the story many times from his father. Nyadar died just two years before my arrival in the village, at an age estimated to be ninety-two.)

Telu Ram had been placed in a winnowing basket (*chāj*) on *sawā ser* (one and one-quarter *ser*) of grain, and the winnowing basket and its contents, including the child, had been dragged across the courtyard of the house and then given as *dān* to the family's Sweeper. This Sweeper woman kept the basket and the *sawā ser* of grain (about two pounds), and the *kaṣṭ* besetting the child was transferred to her. She then returned the child to Asikaur and Nyadar, and they and the child were thus freed of the inauspiciousness generated in the circumstances of the birth. But she could not simply "give" the child back to his parents, as this would return the *kaṣṭ* to them. The baby had to be "bought" (*mol lānā,* lit., "taken for a price"). Asikaur and Nyadar gave money and grain to the Sweeper woman as "payment" for the child, and Telu Ram says that one of his names is in consequence Molhar, "one who has been bought." Such a child is also called *chāj ghasīṭū*, "dragged in the winnowing basket."

But Asi and Nyadar didn't stop there. Asi says that she put *sawā ser* of mustard oil (*kaṛvā tel,* "bitter oil") and *sawā ser* of unbroken black gram (*uṛad dāl*) in the drain of the house. And this is the origin of the name Telu, "of the oil." (These quantities of oil and black gram are frequently used to remove inauspiciousness.) The iconicity of the drain, leading out of the house, is obvious. Finally, to remove the last trace of inauspiciousness, Nyadar gave a small parcel of land as *dān* (a *dān* of land is called *dohlī* and is only given by Gujars in extraordinary circumstances) to a Pahansu Brahman. The parcel of land was *sawā bīghā* and was given, according to Asi, *khair-khairāt ke nām,* "for well-being achieved through gift-giving."

There are a number of astrological circumstances of birth that may necessitate the transfer of inauspiciousness in *dān*. If a child is born under the *mūl* lunar asterism, afflictions and faults will come upon the child itself, as well as upon the father, the mother, mother's brother, mother's father, mother's mother, or the entire family, should they ever see the child.[6] Depending upon the precise time of birth within the time of the *mūl nakṣatra,* the *kaṣṭ* could beset (*pahũcnā*) any of these persons.[7] It is said that the child shares the qualities (*guṇ*) of these persons and has a "bodily connection" (*śarīr kā sambandh*) with them, and it is for this reason that they may be afflicted by the *mūl doṣ* ("faults" engendered by *mūl*).[8]

In order to "make far" these faults, a series of ritual actions and prestations called *mūl śānti* should be performed in the month following the child's birth, on the day that the same *nakṣatra* again occurs.[9] In fact, the ritual is rarely performed in this way. More typically, if illness or some other adversity strikes someone in a family and a Brahman or an astrologer is consulted to ascertain the source of the misfortune, the horoscope of the child may be found to indicate that the *mūl nakṣatra* is the source of the difficulties. The *mūl śānti* might then be performed in order to remove the *doṣ*. But even if the full *mūl śānti* ritual is not deemed necessary at the time of birth, villagers say that the inauspiciousness of a *mūl* birth is so great that the men of the house may not enter the confinement room or see the child for *sawā mahīne,* one and one-quarter months, nor may the mother and child leave the room before that time. (This contrasts with the six days of such precautions in the case of an ordinary birth.)

I never witnessed a *mūl śānti,* but Buddhu Pandit described it in detail to me. The first step is the recitation of the *mantra* appropriate to the *mūl* asterism. The *mantra* is said to be recited by the Brahman *purohit* twenty-eight thousand times over a period of several days. The Brahman comes to the house of the *jajmān* and recites these *mantra*s as he sits alone in the confinement room.

On the day of the main ritual events, the Brahman again comes to the house of the *jajmān* before dawn to prepare the *vedi* (spatial configurations drawn on the ground with flour, turmeric, and other colored powders) for the ritual.[10] Designs drawn with flour, limed turmeric, black sesame seeds, and powdered myrtle leaves are always made whenever a fire sacrifice is to be performed. To the north of this ordinary *vedi,* five additional ones are made: cow-dung is smeared over five squares laid out in the cardinal directions, with one in the center, and over these squares an eight-cornered form (*āṭh koṇ kā ākār*) is drawn with rice flour or barley flour. Over these, a small amount of "seven grains" (*satanajā*) is placed. Four pots are placed over the outer *vedis,* and over the fifth one, the center one, a basket containing another pot with holes in the bottom is placed.

The ritual begins as the *jajmān* is seated facing east, and the Brahman facing west. The *jajmān* holds some rice and a little water in his right hand as he makes the resolution (*sankalp*) to perform the ritual. All the deities depicted in the *vedi* are then invoked and worshiped.

Following these preliminary actions, the Brahman officiant asks the *jajmān* to touch each of the pots that have been placed in the four cardinal directions. Then, in the eastern pot, the Brahman places the following items:

white sandalwood paste (*safed candan*)
red sandalwood paste (*lal candan*)
various herbs and roots

mustard seeds
a protective wrist thread

In the second, the southern pot, the priest places

"five nectars" (*pācāmṛit*): clarified butter, yogurt, milk, water from the Ganges river, honey
"seven grains" (*satanajā*)
fluid from the head of a male elephant (*hāthī kā mad*)
water from "junctures" (*tīrth jal*): from the Ganges, from the Yamuna, from the ocean

In the third, the western pot, the priest would place "the seven earths":

earth from the path of an elephant
earth from the place where a pig has trampled
earth from the doorway of a "king" (*rajdwār*)
earth from a place where a cart has stood
earth from a cow pen
earth from a crossroads
earth from a river bank

The fourth, the northern pot, should contain the following:

the "five jewels": a pearl, diamond, coral, blue sapphire, and ruby
five kinds of leaves
water from twenty-seven wells
pebbles from twenty-seven villages (*kheṛe kī kākar*)

Finally, in the central pot, in the bottom of which twenty-seven holes have been bored, the Brahman places

ek sau auṣadhi (one hundred herbs and roots that are said to "remove disease")

Most of the items to be placed in the pots are easily available in the village; I neglected to ask Buddhu Pandit how he goes about obtaining the more exotic ones. Substitutions for prescribed ritual paraphernalia and substances are made in many rituals and would probably be made in this case.

A small silver image in the shape of a man, which represents the *mūl* asterism, should be placed on the top of the last pot. The image is worshiped, and offerings of cloth, red sandalwood paste, black flowers, and cooked rice with sugar should be made to it. The offerings and the image itself are given as *caṛhāpā* to a Brahman, usually the family *purohit*. The *purohit* of the family may sometimes refuse this *dān* because of the extreme inauspiciousness that is involved, in which case another Brahman willing to act as the *pātra* would have to be found. If the *purohit* does consent to accept it, he may do so because the *dān* given at the beginning of the ritual is not as *krūr* ("fierce," "destructive") as the *dān* to be given later in the same ritual.

The giving of this first *caṛhāpā* is followed by a fire sacrifice (*havan*), which is performed in the usual manner. Following the *havan*, a small lamp made from dough (a *langārī*) with four wicks ("four-mouthed," *caumukhā*) is filled with mustard oil and lit. This lamp is said to "protect all directions" (*diśā rakṣā karnā*) when offerings of yogurt, black lentils, and black soot are placed upon it. In the Sanskrit *mantra* recited by the priest, the lamp is addressed as the "guardian of the space" (*kṣetrapāl*) that, by "consuming the offerings" (*balīn bhakṣat*), "separates and removes the causes of hindrances" (*vighnavicchedahetur jayati*) to the success of the *mūl śānti* as a whole. After the offerings are made at this point in the ritual, the lamp is taken away and disposed of in the village pond. (The same sort of dough lamp with four wicks is used in a very similar fashion by women in Pahansu on the night of Kārttik *amāvas*, the new moon day of the month of Kārttik.)

As soon as this preliminary transferral of obstacles is completed, the third and most crucial transferral sequence of the *mūl śānti* is begun. The Brahman officiant pours water through the holes in the center pot over the *jajmān*, his wife, and the child who was born under the *mūl nakṣatra*, moving upward over their bodies from their feet to their heads. In the accompanying Sanskrit *mantra*, this is called the "anointing" (*anulepana*). The three are then seated on the beam of a plow that has been placed over a *ṭakkarpūrat* made with flour by the Barber's wife, and they are covered with a blanket. The Brahman ties the pot with the holes in it to three large pestles (*mūsal*) so that the latter will support the pot as it is held above the *jajmān*. The four directionally oriented pots with their various contents are filled with water, and by turns the water and other substances from each of these is poured through the sieve-like pot over the heads of the three seated on the plow. This bathing is, in the long accompanying *mantra*, called *abhiṣek viniyog*, "the bath of disjoining." The plow and the pestle used here iconically represent the effects of this bathing: the separation out of the body of the faults engendered by the *mūl* birth.[11] In the *mantra*, the negative qualities to be removed are referred to as *doṣ* (faults) and as *yakṣma* (disease, affliction). The Brahman, reciting the words of the *mantra* as he performs the bathing, says that these faults and afflictions are being manifested, uncovered, brought to the surface (*vivṛhāmi*) as he pours the contents of the pots over the *jaj-*

mān. The bath removes the *doṣ* and the *yakṣma* first from the head and then from the arms, the internal organs, the genitals, the legs, and finally the feet. As in the *chuwānā* performed over the body of a woman in labor, the afflictions are here separated from the body through procedures involving a reversal of directionality; the *anulepana* moves up the body, while the bathing from the four pots moves in the opposite direction from the head to the feet.

The text of this *mantra*, which I have translated from the Sanskrit, is as follows:

> Aum. I bring afflictions to the surface from the eyes, from the nostrils, from the ears, from the chin, from the top of the head, from the forehead, and from the tongue. From the neck, from the breastbone, from the spine, from the organs of perception and cognition, and from the arms, I bring afflictions and faults to the surface. From the bowels, from the anus, from the rectum, from the heart, from the internal organs, from the liver, and from the intestines, I bring afflictions to the surface. From the thighs, from the knees, from the heels, from the toes, and from the buttocks, I make the dormant afflictions appear and bring them to the surface. From the penis, from the body hair, from the nails, from the whole self, I bring the afflictions to the surface. From all the sections of the body, and all the body hair, I bring afflictions engendered in all parts of the body to the surface.

At the conclusion of the "bath of disjoining,"[12] the *ṭakkarpūrat* flour and the blanket that covered the parents and the child are given to the wife of the family Barber, for they too contain some of the inauspiciousness of the *mūl* birth.

Then the *jajmān* and his wife and the child bathe with clear water and, still wearing their wet clothes, they perform the final actions of the *mūl śānti*. A small brass dish filled with clarified butter and containing a ten-*paisā* coin is brought and the three cast their reflections into the dish. The faults and afflictions "brought to the surface" of the body during the "bath of disjoining" are in this way transferred to the dish, which is then given as "the *dān* of the reflection" (*chāyā kā dān*), along with several rupees as "payment" (*dakṣiṇā*), to a man of the Dakaut *jāti*, a caste of very low "Brahmans" resident in a village near Pahansu. This caste is termed Brahman simply because of their function as recipients for a number of similar prestations (e.g., the *dān* of the planets Śani, Rāhu, and Ketu, and certain *dān* given at particular points in the lifecourse) that also transfer negative qualities from donor to recipient.

It is said that if Gaur Brahmans (the Brahman *jāti* resident in Pahansu) were to accept the kinds of *dān* given to Dakauts, disastrous consequences would follow, in the form of "sickness" (*rog*), loss of quality of one's family and lineage (*bekhāndānī*), inauspiciousness (*nāśubh*); and the "faults" would attach themselves to that Brahman (*doṣ lagegā*). The permutational possibilities of the acceptance of these gifts are illustrated by the fact that when the celestial dispositions are such that a Dakaut himself must give this *dān,* he gives it to his *dhiyāne,* the husbands of his married daughters, sisters, and father's sisters.

While I did not observe a performance of the *mūl śānti* ritual in Pahansu, I have included a rather lengthy description of it here for several reasons. First, although it is only occasionally performed, when the inauspiciousness of the *nakṣatra*s is deemed to be extreme, the villagers are well aware of its importance as an ameliorative technique. One day Asikaur and I were speculating as to whether a *pancak* period of *nakṣatra* inauspiciousness might be in progress. Asi wanted to fill up her *biṭaurā*s (storage places for cow-dung cakes) before the rainy season set in, and it is productive of great inauspiciousness to do this in a *pancak* period. She was telling me of the possible inauspicious consequences of filling the *biṭaurā* at such a time, and she spoke of both the *mūl* and the *pancak nakṣatra* days as "not good days, very bad days" (*acche din nahī̃ haĩ kharāb din haĩ*); and then she spoke of the "great faults" (*baṛā doṣ*) that will come if a child is born during a *mūl* period, and the actions that must be taken if such a birth occurs:

> *pun-dān kare. admī ā nahī̃ sakte bagaṛ mẽ bahū bāhar nahī̃ jā saktī sawā mahīne mẽ. baṛā doṣ hogā. baṛā pun-dān kare aur baṛā havan kare.*
>
> One should give *dān*. Men may not come into the courtyard for one and one-quarter months, and the son's wife [i.e., the *jaccā*] cannot go outside. There will be faults. One should give a very big *dān* and do a big fire sacrifice.

My second reason for giving so much of the detail of the *mūl śānti* ritual lies in the fact that its very elaborateness (in contrast with some of the simpler disarticulative rituals and prestations) makes it possible for us to discern some of the culturally defined mechanisms through which inauspiciousness is always removed. The elaboration of these techniques in the *mūl śānti* exists no doubt because of the extreme inauspiciousness involved, and the care that must be taken to ensure its complete removal; one must give a "big *dān*" and do a "big *havan,*" as Asi pointed out. We have in the *mantra*s for the *mūl śānti* a particularly explicit formulation of the disarticulative processes that occur in the simpler rituals as well, even in the quickest performance of a *chuwānā* or a *wārpher*.

Although I did not see a *mūl śānti* in Pahansu, I was able to observe the performance of a "big *dān*" and a "big *havan*" similar to the ritual that was described to me. This was in connection with the planetary configurations in place at the time of the birth of Asikaur's son's son, Arvind.

As we have seen, the positions of the planets (*graha*) in the various spaces (*sthān*) of the horoscope (*janam kuṇḍalī*) at birth affect specific aspects of the child's well-being, as well as that of his parents and siblings. To "move away" (*ṭālnā*) the faults and the afflictions that may be engendered by the presence of the nine planets in the spaces of the horoscope, elaborate ritual sequences, culminating in the giving of gifts to particular recipients, are necessary. The inauspiciousness of each planet must be removed with a specific kind of *dān*. Buddhu Pandit provided me with a detailed list, but most villagers know about the differences at least in a general way. According to Buddhu Pandit, the following items should be given in *dān* to remove planetary "faults":

Sūryā (sun): unrefined sugar, red cloth, gold, copper, red sandalwood paste, red flowers, clarified butter, a reddish cow, rubies, red coral

Candramā (moon): white rice, camphor, silver, clarified butter, white sandalwood paste, white cloth, yogurt, white flowers, refined sugar, pearls, a white bullock

Mangal (Mars): coral, copper, unrefined sugar, red flowers, clarified butter, red cloth, red sandalwood paste, a reddish bullock, gold, saffron, red lentils (*masūr dāl*)

Budh (Mercury): green lentils (*mūng dāl*), brass pots, gold, clarified butter, green flowers, green cloth, ivory, emeralds, unrefined sugar, camphor

Bṛhaspati (Jupiter): turmeric, yellow cloth, clarified butter, yellow flowers, yellow lentils (*cannā dāl*), gold, unrefined sugar, yellow fruits, saffron

Śukra (Venus): white cloth, rice, cows, gold, silver, white sandalwood paste, clarified butter, refined sugar, diamonds, yogurt, white flowers

Śani (Saturn): black lentils (*uṛad dāl*), sesame, mustard oil, black cloth, iron, black shoes, black cows, black blankets, black flowers, gold, blue sapphires

Rāhu ("eclipse demon"): gold, black cows, sesame, mustard oil, black cloth, iron, black mustard seeds, goats, "seven grains" (*satanajā*), black blankets, blue sapphires, black flowers, glass

Ketu ("comet demon"): sesame, mustard oil, gold, knives, "seven grains," black blankets, iron, black flowers

The characteristics of these *dān* items are said to correspond to the nature (*svabhāv*) and "habits" (*ādat*) of the various planets. The planets are thought of as being of a particular *varṇa* and are classified in the following way:

Bṛhaspati, Śukra	Brahman
Mangal, Sūryā	Ksatriya
Budh, Candramā	Vaisya
Śani, Rāhu, Ketu	Sudra

The categorization of the kinds of things to be given as *dān* is congruent with this *varṇa* classification: black objects for the Sudra planets, green or white for the Vaisya, red for the Ksatriya, and white or yellow for the Brahman. Now, as we shall see, the *dān* items for the various planets must, before they are given, be brought into contact with the body of the person afflicted with the planetary inauspiciousness, and then, having taken into themselves the *doṣ* and *kaṣṭ* engendered by the planet, they are given as *dān* to the appropriate recipient. We might therefore infer—correctly—that negative qualities and substances can only be transferred into objects that are partly of the same nature as the source of those qualities and substances; indeed, the colors that are involved are always, in Indic discourse, thought of as partaking of the natures of the four *varṇas*.

If the planetary configurations that are mapped on a child's *janam kuṇḍalī* indicate an early death or that afflictions will beset the child or his parents, the necessary sets of prestations are made in the appropriate ritual contexts. Or, as is often the case, planetary inauspiciousness may be found to be the cause of current illness or misfortune, and the prestations then would be given to remove that specific complaint.

When a *janam kuṇḍalī* was cast for Arvind (the eldest son of Telu Ram) at his birth, it was found that Rāhu occupied the eighth place ("death") and Candramā the first ("body"). This configuration portended death for the child in his twelfth year, unless the proper prestations were made. Telu Ram did not hesitate to arrange for a consultation with an astrologer from a nearby village to discuss the performance of the required ritual, but he did remark to me that perhaps what was in one's "fortune" (*bhāgya*) and "actions" (*karma*) would take place regardless of the planetary *dān* that might be given. But Telu Ram's wife, Rajavati, would have none of this interpretation. There *is* "benefit" (*phāyadā*), she insisted, and of course the *dān* was given.

When the astrologer-*paṇḍit* arrived from the village of Pater Khurd, I was permitted to sit in on the consultation. The *paṇḍit* first told us why very particular items had to be given to remove the inauspiciousness of Rāhu and Candramā:

> If afflictions and danger are over someone, particular *dān* must be given. Just as for different illnesses there are different medicines, in this way, for different afflictions there is different *dān*. For different planets there is different *dān*.

He then told us of the items to be given in Arvind's *dān*. Since two planets had engendered the inauspiciousness besetting Arvind, two sets of *dān* prestations had to be made. To remove the inauspiciousness of Rāhu, the following items had to be given to a man of the Dakaut *jāti:*

a small blue sapphire (*nīlam*)
a small amount of gold
sawā pā̃c ser of black lentils (*uṛad dāl*)
sawā ser of *kulthī*, a kind of gram
a black water buffalo (a soot-blackened dough image of a water buffalo, fashioned by Asikaur, Arvind's father's mother, was actually given)
black shoes
sawā ser of mustard oil
sawā gaj (about one yard) of black cloth

The *dān* that would remove the inauspiciousness of Candramā was to be given to a Brahman:

a set of clothing that had been worn by Arvind (five items, yellow or white in color)
seven and one-quarter *ser* of flour
two and one-quarter *ser* of refined sugar
sawā pā̃c ser (five and one-quarter *ser*) of rice
sawā pā̃c ser of clarified butter, into which a small amount of salt was to be placed

The *paṇḍit* explained that the salt had to be placed "quietly, secretly" (*cūp-cāp se*) in the butter, because if the Brahman recipient knew about it, he would not accept the *dān*. Salt, he said, is a substance that induces afflictions (*kaṣṭ-kārak*) in the recipient when it is given in *dān;* benefits (*lābh*) accrue to the donor, while faults and "fear" (*ḍar*) attach themselves to the person who accepts salt in *dān*. The "coming distress" (*ānevālī āpatti*) of Arvind would be removed by this prestation. Both sets of prestations, the *dān* of Rāhu and the *dān* of Candramā, were referred to by the *paṇḍit* as *sankaṭ-kaṛāī kā dān* (*dān* of dangers and difficulties), and through the giving of these items to the Dakaut and the Brahman, the negative qualities and substances would be "removed" and "made far" from Arvind and transferred to the recipients: "the difficulties of Rāhu will come upon them" (*rāhu kā kaṛā caṛh jā*).

Arvind's *cācā*, his father's younger brother, wrote on a slip of paper all of the items that were to be given in *dān*, and during the following weeks several trips to Saharanpur were made in order to obtain the right sort of black shoes, the black iron container (a *tassalā*), an inexpensive sapphire, and so forth.

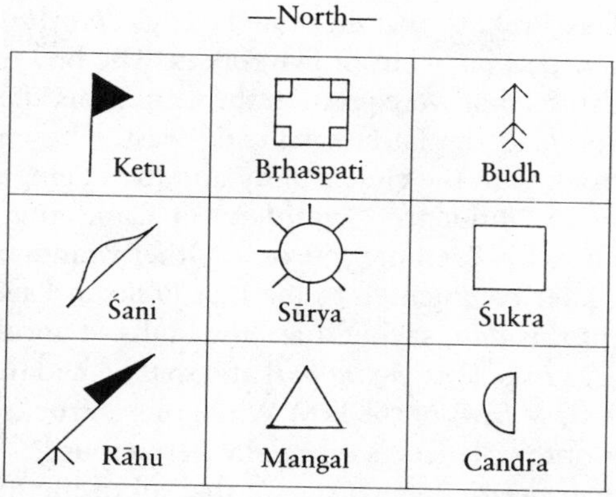

Fig. 12. Buddhu Pandit's representation of the nine planets

Two days before the Saturday on which the Rāhu *dān* was to be given, the *paṇḍit* returned to Pahansu to begin the recitation of "the great death *mantra*" (*mahā mṛityu mantra*), eleven and one-quarter thousand times, as he put it. This is, he said, a "death-removing" (*maut haṭānā*) *mantra.* After a preliminary worship of all of the planetary deities, the *paṇḍit* indicated that Buddhu Pandit, who was assisting in the performance of the ritual, should begin the recitation of the *mantra.* The astrologer-*paṇḍit* from Pater Khurd then asked that the items for the Candramā *dān* be brought into the inner room of the house where the recitation was being done.

While Buddhu Pandit continued to recite the *mantra,* Arvind was brought into the room. The *paṇḍit* from Pater Khurd gave Arvind some water to sip; touched water to his cheeks, nose, eyes, ears, shoulders, and knees; and then sprinkled the remaining water in the small vessel over the boy's head. Water was also sprinkled over a diagram on the floor representing the nine planets (see fig. 12).[13]

The *paṇḍit* next placed water and some stalks of grass in Arvind's right hand, with the left hand touching the right. Then the boy followed the priest in the recitation of the *sankalp,* the resolution to perform the ritual and give the *dān.*The words of the *sankalp* describe the purpose of the ritual and locate the boy in terms of the astrological coordinates at the time of the ritual (the lunar day, solar day, year, and so forth) and also in terms of "genealogical" space as the *got* of the donor—Khūbaṛ—is recited.

Meanwhile, a layout (*vedi*) had been prepared on the ground for a *havan.* The offerings were made for this fire sacrifice, and upon its completion, the items for the Candramā *dān* were placed before Arvind as he sat facing east. The set of cloth (the five yellow items) was placed on his head as he was made to recite a second *sankalp* for the giving of this particular *dān*. Then Prakash Pandit, the family's *purohit,* received the clothing and a *dakṣiṇā* payment of five rupees. The boy then circumambulated the foodstuffs that were given in the Candramā *dān,* and gave the food to the *purohit,* as the latter sat facing west. These prestations, by coming into contact with the child's body and then being given away, removed the negative "influence" (*prabhāv*) of Candramā from the boy and transferred it to his Brahman *purohit*. Other Brahmans, particularly Buddhu Pandit, later commented to me that Prakash Pandit was foolish to agree to accept this *dān,* saying that "the faults of another come upon him" (*dūsre ke doṣ uske ūpar ā jātā haĩ*) and that he had thereby accepted the afflictions (*kaṣṭ le liyā*) of the boy. While this is true, they agreed, for all *dān,* the *dān* of the planets is especially pernicious.[14]

Precautions had been taken to ensure that all of the inauspiciousness would indeed be transferred into the items to be given in *dān*. While these things were being brought into contact with Arvind's body, his right foot rested on a stone, so that the negative substances being removed would not flow into the earth.

The recitation of the *mahā mṛityu mantra* continued for two more days. On the third day of the recitation, Saturday, preparations for the giving of the Rāhu *dān* began at about ten in the morning. Asikaur, Arvind's *dādī* (father's mother), made a small dough lamp (*cūn kā dīyā*) with four wicks and filled it with mustard oil, the "bitter oil." Asi then made a small image of a water buffalo from dough and rubbed it with soot.

The *cūn kā dīyā* was lit, and all of the items to be given in the Rāhu *dān* were placed before it. The same preliminary procedures as for the Candramā *dān* were performed by the boy, including the recitation of a *sankalp*. Then, as Arvind held the sapphire in his hand, the black cloth for the *dān* was placed on his head, he put on the black shoes, and he was made to cast his reflection into the iron vessel filled with the *sawā pā̃c ser* of mustard oil. While he did this, his right foot again rested on a stone. As soon as he had cast his reflection into the oil, he removed the cloth and the shoes and placed them on the ground. He sprinkled water around them in a counterclockwise (*ulṭā,* "reverse") direction. This circling further separates the *kaṣṭ* from the child. During the initial consultation, the *paṇḍit* had been very specific and emphatic that the circling was to be done in the "reverse" direction, not in the "straight" (*sulṭā*) or clockwise direction. After the circling, no one else should come into contact with the *dān* articles; the Dakaut recipient, who had arrived in Pahansu just as the ritual began, came forward to collect them himself as soon as the circling had been done. (As he came forward to take the articles, the Dakaut asked Telu Ram to help him carry them away. Telu Ram, aghast at the request, told him that no one in the house would touch the *dān* articles after the circling.) The Dakaut's acceptance of this *chāyā kā dān* ("the *dān* of the reflection") facilitated the final removal of the planet's inauspiciousness from the child. The other items necessary for the Rāhu *dān* were also given, along with a *dakṣiṇā* payment of one rupee. The *dān* items were given to the Dakaut precisely at ten-thirty in the morning, at the time when, according to Buddhu Pandit, the maximum transferral of *kaṣṭ* to the recipient could take place.

A *havan* was then performed in the courtyard of the house, at the conclusion of which, Buddhu Pandit gave Rajavati a coconut and a one-rupee note that had been placed near "Varuṇa," established in a pot of water near the *vedi*. He placed this in her *pallā* and told her to keep it because it was "good fortune"; Rajavati locked it in her tin trunk. The inauspiciousness had been given away, but the auspicious residue was to be kept in the house.

At the conclusion of the *havan,* the *paṇḍit* from Pater Khurd received Rs. 101 as *dakṣiṇā,* and Buddhu Pandit received Rs. 51.

The rituals concerned with the removal of the *mūl doṣ* that were described to me by Buddhu Pandit and those concerned with the removal of planetary inauspiciousness exhibit very similar characteristics.

In both, the separation of the *doṣ* and the *kaṣṭ* from the locality (*kṣetra*) proceed in very similar ways. In both cases, a dough lamp with four wicks corresponding to the four directions is fashioned to absorb any of the inauspiciousness that may have been transmitted to the locale of the house in which the afflicted person lives. The four directions beyond the house are in this case embodied in the *pātra,* the receptable for this particular inauspiciousness. The "directions" are not only contained in the lamp, but the lamp is also to be disposed of "outside" (*bāhar*), beyond the house, according to the advice given to Asikaur by Buddhu Pandit.

The same congruity or similarity is evident in the removal of *kaṣṭ* and *doṣ* from the body of the afflicted person. In both the *mūl śānti* and the planetary ritual, the substances that are brought into contact with the body for the "disjoining" resemble in some way the source of the affliction. This is particularly clear in the case of the Rāhu and Candramā *dān* items, since the *dān* items of each planet are explicitly said to correspond to the nature of the planetary deity itself. This also seems to be the case in the *mūl śānti* ritual; the number twenty-seven recurs in the enumeration of the substances used in the "bath of disjoining," indicating, perhaps, that there is a homology between the twenty-seven lunar asterisms as the source of the *doṣ* and the earth from twenty-seven villages and water from twenty-seven wells.

The directional orientation of the "disjoining" is also identical in the two rituals: in the *mūl śānti mantra* that I have translated, the "bringing to the surface" is described as proceeding from the head to the lower portion of the body, and in the Rāhu *dān* sequence the cloth must first be placed on the head before the shoes are worn. Wearing these articles and removing them in the specified sequence removed the *kaṣṭ* from the boy before the items were given as *dān* to the Dakaut. This movement from top to bottom, whenever it occurs (in the *chuwānā,* in the *mūl śānti* and planetary rituals, or in wedding and harvest rituals) is called *utārnā* ("to bring down off of"), and it effects the removal of the inauspicious substances from the afflicted person, the bride or groom, or from the grain heap. In the case of both of the astrological rituals, the final transfer is effected through the *chāyā kā dān* prestations (also referred to as *śarīr kā dān,* the "bodily *dān*") that are given to the Dakaut.

The planets influence the well-being of persons, not only by their positions at the time of birth, but also by their continually changing positions through time. Whenever during the course of one's life, one is faced with what is diagnosed as an astrologically engendered "distress" (*āpatti*), *dān* must be given, although it is not always given at the conclusion of such elaborate ritual procedures as those just described. Somewhat simplified versions of the Rāhu *dān* ritual are frequently performed in Pahansu in connection with the inauspiciousness of the planet Śani. In other circumstances, particularly in the case of the non-Gujar castes, an astrologer may advise a course of action that involves a different sort of *dān.* If, for example, Śani, Rāhu, or Ketu is found by a *paṇḍit* versed in astrology to be the source of someone's misfortunes, the victim may be advised to place oil in an iron vessel, to place something made of copper into it, and to take it with him to a crossroads. There, on a Saturday, he should stand facing south, cast his reflection into the oil, and then secretly place the vessel and its contents at the crossing of the roads. This too is termed *dān* because, villagers say, although the afflictions are not transferred to a *khās pātra* (a "special recipient"), they are nevertheless transferred to whomever stops at the crossroads. As in the case of the *ṭakkarpūrat* and the lamp with four wicks, the four roads of a crossroads provide a spatial configuration capable of absorbing and then transferring inauspiciousness.

These properties of crossroads are very often utilized in cases of diseases that afflict young children, especially when the appropriate procedure is the making of a *ṭoṭkā.* A *ṭoṭkā,* as villagers put it, is any object that transfers afflictions from one person to another; it is used "if there is some affliction over one, in order to transfer that affliction to another" (*agar kisī bhī ādmī ke ūpar kaṣṭ hai, kisī dūsre ādmī ko kaṣṭ pahũcāne ke lie*). This device is used when the intended recipient is unaware that the transfer is being made and thus may be unprepared to accept it. The *kaṣṭ* is "moved away" (*kaṣṭ haṭānā*) and transferred (*pahũcānā*) to the first person who comes upon the objects at the crossroads. There is a "saying" (*kahāvat*) that I heard several times in the context of discussions about the *dān* of the crossroads, where unwholesome things are often found: *koṛhī caurāī mẽ mute kare,* "Lepers piss at the crossroads."

If a small child is suffering from vomiting or diarrhea, threads are tied to a cow-dung cake and it is circled several times over the child's head. This is called a *chuwānā.* To move away the illness of the child, the cow-dung cake is placed in a crossroads, and the *kaṣṭ* will then afflict the next child who passes by. Another method of accomplishing this transfer is to place an earthen lamp filled with oil, some rice, and some sugar wafers (*batāssā*), along with some of the child's used clothing, in a winnowing basket; to perform the *chuwānā* over his head with these things; and then to place the basket with its contents at a crossroads.

Dakauts are the recipients of one other type of prestation pertaining to the development of a child. If a child's first tooth appears in his upper jaw, faults, afflictions, and "difficulties" (*kaṛāī*) will come upon (*caṛhnā*) his mother's brother, because of the "connection of birth" (*janam kā sambandh*) he and the child share. To move away the inauspiciousness and "to cause the faults to come down" (*doṣ utārne ke lie*), the mother's brother prepares a mixture of wheat flour and unrefined sugar (this is called *kasār* and is very often used in *caṛhāpā*), places it in a small brass bowl, and ties it up in a red cloth. He then goes secretly to the conjugal village of the sister whose child has been the source of the inauspiciousness besetting him and throws the package of *kasār* over the wall of her house. (He will later make the same gesture—with a set of cloth—at the weddings of this sister's children.) He does not enter the house, however; if he did, people say, the inauspiciousness would remain with him (*nāśubh lagnā*). Instead, the negative qualities and substances are removed with the *kasār,* which must not remain in the sister's house any longer than necessary. The *kasār* is then given onward, explicitly as *dān,* to a Dakaut as soon as possible. The mother's brother does not give the packet directly to the Dakaut himself; if he did so, people said when I asked, the "difficulties would not come out" (*kaṛāī nahī̃ utar jā*). They are only transferred if they are given first to the sister's son, that is, returned to their source. If this prestation in the form of the *kasār* is made in the proper manner, "the difficulties come down" from the mother's brother (*kasār dene se kaṛāī utar jā*).[15] We will observe this pattern of giving to one's *dhiyānī* and then having that prestation "given onward" to another recipient in a great many other contexts.

If a child has difficulty in learning to walk, ritual prestations are made in order to remove the "hindrances" that are preventing him from doing so. Small fried cakes (*pūṛā*) are prepared and placed at the feet of the child. An earthen lamp is lit, *dhok mārnā* is performed, and the cakes are sent, along with a few sets of cloth, as *caṛhāpā* to the child's maternal grandparents. Although they otherwise would never accept cloth or food items from the house of a married daughter, it is their "appropriate obligation" (*pharmāyā*) to accept these "cakes of the feet" (*pāõ pūṛe*) as *dān* so that their daughter's child will be able to walk. This is the only instance I ever recorded in which *dān* was given to one's "wife-giving" people; it is clearly an anomaly. I was able to elicit no explicit reason for this reversal of the usual directionality in the giving of *dān*.

Early childhood health problems are often attributed to the negative influence of two goddesses, both called "mother" (*mātā*), who have shrines on the periphery of the habitation site of the village. (See chap. 1, fig. 5.) The first, referred to as the "village-site mother" (*gām-kheṛī mātā*) or the "smaller mother" (*choṭī mātā*) has a shrine on the northeast outskirts of Pahansu's habitation site, in what is now the Leatherworker neighborhood. (Before the expansion of the habitation site, the shrine was in the fields.) The shrine itself actually consists of seven small connected shrines, for *gām-kheṛī mātā* is said to be a composite of seven sisters. The second goddess, the "big mother" (*baṛī mātā*), is the goddess of smallpox and is referred to in this way, villagers say, because she gives more "difficulties" to children than does *gām-kheṛī mātā*. The shrine of this second goddess is located within the confines of a Gujar cattle pen and men's sitting place (*gher*), but when the shrine was originally built, the land there was *goyrā*, agricultural land immediately outside the boundaries of the habitation site. The shrine is located at the southeastern edge of the *abādī*, the present habitation site.

When *baṛī mātā* inflicts sorrows (*dukh denā*) on children, this is called *karaunī*. There are a number of ways that the afflictions caused by the *karaunī* can be removed from the child. For instance, if a child is suffering from *murāre* (a skin infection thought to be caused by this goddess), *chuwānā* is done with seven balls of dough, and then these are offered to the goddess and given as *pujāpā* or *dān* to a Sweeper woman. Or *sawā ser* of rice may be used for the *chuwānā*, then kept in the house until the illness has been transferred to the rice and the child is well. This rice is also given as *pujāpā* either to a Sweeper woman or to a Brahman woman. If a child has eye problems, sweet fried cakes called *chilṛā* are prepared and *chuwānā* is done by waving the cakes over the eyes seven times. To remove the *kaṣṭ*, the cakes are given to a Brahman as the *pujāpā* of the "big mother."

It is the *pharmāyā* of Sweepers to accept flour and salt from their *jajmāns* each Monday, the day on which the *gām-kheṛī mātā* may be approached. The Sweeper woman simply comes to the house of the *jajmān* sometime in the afternoon, and the flour and salt are put into her outstretched *pallā* without any particular ritual actions. But if a child in the household is ill, the flour and salt may be given to the Sweeper after having been circled, in a *chuwānā*, over the head of the child to remove the "affliction" of the village-site mother. In either case, the flour and salt that are given are called *caṛhāpā*.

To remove the *kaṣṭ* with which the *gām-kheṛī mātā* afflicts sons, particularly one's eldest son (*jeṭhā jākaṭ*), women who have given birth to a male child in the past year offer a full set of cloth (a *teln*) to the goddess in the course of a ritual called *badhāvā,* which is performed in the month of Bhādwe. This is then given as *caṛhāpā* to a Sweeper woman. (*Badhāvā* may also be performed for the ancestor deities and for Bhūmiyā, "the one of the land," who is the "protector of the site," the *khetrapāl.* The shrines of these deities are all located outside of the Pahansu habitation site.)

A *badhāvā* (the term is defined in the *Bṛhat Hindī Koṣ* dictionary as *mangalācār,* "actions for auspiciousness"), unlike most other rituals, involves two separate trips to the shrine of the deity. In the morning, wives of the village go to the shrine to perform *dhok mārnā* and to give the *pujāpā* prestations. In addition to receiving the *teln* as *dān,* the Sweeper woman sometimes brings one of her own live chickens and does a *wārpher* with it over the heads of the children of the women performing the *badhāvā.* The Sweeper woman also receives *pujāpā* from all the women who have sons, regardless of their age, in the form of packets called *kandhelī.* For each son, a mother prepares a packet of fried *pūṛā* cakes, and another packet containing uncooked cotton seeds (*binauliyā*) and *satanajā,* the "seven grains" often used in the removal of inauspiciousness. These items are made into packets by wrapping them in banyan tree leaves. When all of the *dān* items have been offered to the goddess and given to the Sweeper woman, the women who have performed the *badhāvā* return home in small neighborhood groups, singing the songs of the ritual (*badhāve gīt*), which describe its performance. They sing of each woman in their party, and the sons who have come from her womb.

Āsī kī kokh
badhāve mẽ bali gayī.
Jisne jāyā
Telu pūt
Jabara pūt
Rajendar pūt
Ashok pūt
badhāve mẽ bali gayī.

The womb of Asi
has made an offering in the *badhāvā.*
That which gave birth to
the son Telu
the son Jabara
the son Rajendar

the son Ashok
has made an offering in the *badhāvā.*

In the late afternoon, a second trip is made to the "mother's place," the *mātā kā thān.* This time, it is a more casual party, consisting mainly of young daughters of the village. They sing no songs, but go simply to distribute the *prasād* of the goddess in the form of *baklī* (soaked chick-pea gram) and to give a dish of grain as payment to the Sweeper who has played the drum for the day's ritual events.

The Sweeper women themselves perform this *badhāvā* very early in the morning before any of the other women, and they give the *badhāvā pujāpā* to their *dhiyānī.* Aside from *dhiyānī,* there are in general three possible "receptacles" for diseases and afflictions of childhood: Brahmans, Sweepers, and Dakauts, who are, in this context, seen by Gujars as equivalent *pātra,* recipients of *dān.* These four, along with the family Barber, are also the appropriate receptacles for inauspiciousness on the occasion of marriage.

Marriage and the Giving of *Dān*

An almost universal assumption in the study of marriage and affinal prestations in North India has been that hierarchy is the dominant ideological feature structuring all aspects of the relationship between "wife-givers" and "wife-receivers." While there has been some debate over the question of whether the ranking precedes the marriage or is a consequence of it, the pervasiveness of this ideological construct has not been questioned (see Vatuk 1975, 159).

Through their analyses of marriage prestations, both Vatuk (1975) and Dumont (1966) have demonstrated that important aspects of North Indian kinship relations are articulated through various kinds of prestations. They have also demonstrated the salience of the "alliance" aspects of affinal relationships, that is, the particular valuation and elaboration of the enduring relationship between wife-givers and wife-receivers. It was Dumont who in 1966 first detailed the way in which relatives of at least two successive generations are identified by virtue of their roles as wife-givers and wife-receivers. While the inaccuracy of his formulation of the relationship in terms of concrete "groups" (the *khāndān,* or local descent group) has been demonstrated (Vatuk 1975; Inden and Nicholas 1977), the significance of the relationship itself and the importance of the gift-giving it entails are not in doubt.

Difficulties emerge when Dumont begins to discuss the content of this relationship in North Indian society. Both he and Vatuk have detected certain hierarchical elements in the affinal relationship among the Uttar Pradesh Brahman castes that they studied, and they have interpreted marriage, postmarriage, and funeral prestations in terms of hierarchy: the gifts are given, they assume, precisely because of the "superiority" of wife-receivers over wife-givers.

The data that Vatuk and Dumont adduce in this connection are limited in two ways. First, as I pointed out in chapter 1, they have limited themselves to an analysis of prestations within an arbitrarily drawn domain of "kinship," and consequently they have been unable to perceive the wider cultural meaning of many of these prestations. Second, there has not been an adequate specification of the ritual contexts of the prestations, or of the linguistic aspects of the gift-giving situations. Most important, it has not been taken into account that many of these prestations are *dān,* and that as such they involve transfers of inauspiciousness in which it is the obligation of wife-receiving people to act as recipients for the well-being of those who are related to them as wife-givers.

Tambiah's analysis (1973) of marriage prestations in South Asia also assumes, following Blunt (1931, 70), that hypergamy, a ranked relationship between wife-givers and wife-receivers, is ideologically central in the conception of marriage as *kanyā dān,* the "gift of a virgin," and in the "dowry" that accompanies the *kanyā dān*. Tambiah sees this status superiority of wife-receivers over wife-givers as being related also to his central argument that dowry in India and Ceylon "connotes female property or female right to property which is transferred at a woman's marriage as a sort of pre-mortem inheritance" (Tambiah 1973, 64). The following analyses of marriage prestations in Pahansu demonstrate not only that the hypergamous ethos may be contextually distinct from *kanyā dān* and the "dowry" (*dāt, dahej*), but also that Tambiah's conceptualization of the dowry as a "pre-mortem inheritance" for the daughter does not accord with linguistic and ritual data concerning these prestations.

For many castes in northern India, a ranked relationship between lower wife-givers and higher wife-receivers is a marked feature of intracaste social organization. This relationship may sometimes appear as a formalized ranking of clan groupings, and differences in status are created or expressed in explicit and pronounced tendencies toward clan hypergamy. Clan rankings appear in such castes as the Kangra Rajputs studied by Parry (1979, 200–205), and once existed among Marwari Rajputs as well (Stern 1977, 71–76). In other castes, such as the Kanya-Kubja Brahmans of central Uttar Pradesh, there is elaborate intracaste social differentiation and hierarchization comprising such formal elements as "clans" or Brahmanic *gotra*s, place of origin, ritual titles, wealth, and so forth (Khare 1960, 1972).

In some areas of North India, hypergamous directionality in marriage is manifested in an explicit formulation that brides should be given in a north or west direction: "the girl from the east, the boy from the west" (Karve 1968, 125; Marriott 1955, 180). Marriott has also found in Kishan Garhi, a village dominated by Sanadhya Brahmans and Jats, that there is an assumption of and an actual tendency toward villagewide consistency in the categorization of affinal villages as wife-receivers or wife-givers, as "higher" or "lower" (ibid., 178).

For other castes, such as the Gaur Brahmans of western Uttar Pradesh, and the Pahansu Gujars, there is no formalized system of rank within the caste, and it is only the marriage itself that establishes the hierarchic superiority of wife-receivers over wife-givers (Vatuk 1975, 159), a superiority defined, not in terms of bounded patrilineal descent groups (such as "clans" or "lineages"), but in terms of a shifting perspective that unites past givers and receivers as givers in relation to the wife-receivers at a new marriage (ibid., 194). Thus givers and receivers are ranked only with respect to each other and only with regard to a specific marriage.

Among the Gujars of western Uttar Pradesh, formalized designation of hypergamous entities within the caste is minimal. While certain clans are often thought of as having more prestige (*izzat*) than others—the Khūbaṛ *got,* for example, is said to be much respected because of the Landhaura Khūbaṛ "kings" of southeastern Saharanpur District—and while such considerations are certainly relevant in marriage negotiations, all clans intermarry in all directions and there is no explicit or implicit formulation that they should not.[16]

While there is, within the Gujar community of Saharanpur and Muzaffarnagar districts, some hesitancy in giving daughters to villages to the south, to Meerut and Bulandshahar districts in particular, villages as a whole are never classified as wife-givers or wife-receivers to one another, and daughters are sent and wives received between two villages as a matter of course. Immediate reversals of directionality among families are avoided, but such avoidances are phrased as applying not to *got*s or villages, but to relatively small segments of *kunbā*s. Reversals of direction, if they do occur, are termed *āṭā-sāṭā* or *adlā-badlā.* (The second word in each of these phrases means "exchange," and this notion is pragmatically and pointedly emphasized by the phonetic reduplication in each phrase.) Gujars do not discuss their aversion to *āṭā-sāṭā* as an undesirable reversal or neutralization of a ranked relationship that might have previously existed between wife-givers and wife-receivers. They say they avoid exchange because such marriages suggest the "taking for a price" (*mol lānā*) of a bride, a transaction that contravenes the fundamental purposes of *dān,* inasmuch as inauspiciousness can never be transferred in a reciprocated exchange. The well-being and auspiciousness of the givers of a bride are only assured when the marriage is a *kanyā dān,* an unreciprocated gifting away of a daughter.

While Gujars do conceptualize the affinal relationship between segments of two *kunbās* as asymmetrical, with the groom being an honored guest, they are markedly disinclined to think of the *dān-dahej* and other subsequent prestations to *dhiyānī* and *dhiyānā* in terms of hierarchical considerations. When I asked Gujars about a relationship between rank and affinal prestations, they always pointed out that the groom, like Brahmans, Barbers, and Sweepers, must "spread out the begging bag" (*jholī pasārnā*) to accept *dān* and that it is his obligation to do so. In affinal as in intercaste prestations, Gujars thus stress the ritual centrality of the giver of *dān* rather than his hierarchical position vis-à-vis the recipient.

Below I will examine the Pahansu data on the prestations that are given at the time of a marriage, both to the family of the groom and to the Brahman and *kamīns* of the families of the bride and groom, and discuss the way in which auspiciousness is procured and inauspiciousness removed through the giving of these prestations. I will suggest in this section, as well as in the concluding section of this chapter, that hierarchy must be understood as a cultural construct that may be implemented and foregrounded only in some contexts of social life; it is not necessarily the foregrounded aspect of relationships when the giving of *dān* is at issue. With respect to Pahansu Gujars, we find that the giving of *dān* at a marriage is crucially important and ritually elaborate, despite its dissociation from the hypergamous ethos. Thus, while *kanyā dān* may for some castes have an ideological connection with status differences between wife-givers and wife-receivers, this connection is not universal in North India, and it is not the central issue in the cultural definition of *kanyā dān* and other affinal prestations in Pahansu.

In Pahansu as elsewhere in northern India, marriage is conceived of explicitly as a *dān, kanyā dān,* "the gift of a virgin." This *dān* is given in the context of the central rite of marriage, the *pherā,* the circling of a fire. But there are many other subsidiary prestations that are made in the drawn-out course of the marriage rituals. We will examine all of these prestations in the order in which they occur in Gujar weddings in Pahansu, noting where these differ from the rites of marriage in other castes, particularly the Brahman.

When the negotiations for the marriage have been completed, after the initial approach has been made by the family of the bride or by a go-between (*bicauliyā*) acting on their behalf, the first prestations from the bride's "side" (*pakṣ*) to the groom's side are sent on the occasion of *sagāī,* a betrothal ceremony at which the "letter" (*ciṭṭhī*) that formally opens the sequence of *dān* prestations is sent. The *ciṭṭhī* also announces the lunar day and precise time that have been determined as the auspicious astrological coordinates for the wedding rituals.

Several weeks before the date fixed for a Gujar wedding, the Brahman and the Barber of the girl's family are sent to the village of the groom. (In the case of Brahman and Barber weddings, *dhiyāne* of the family are generally sent.) The bride's Brahman and Barber take with them another *ciṭṭhī*, a large sheet of paper on which is written the formal marriage proposal and the astrological information. *Sawā rupiāh* (one and one-quarter rupees) are placed in the letter, along with some turmeric and some rice, and it is rolled up and tied with red and yellow protective threads (*ḍorī*). The Barber and the Brahman also take the first gifts that are to be given: a few sets of cloth for the groom and the women of the house, and a sum of money that ranges from Rs. 101 to Rs. 1001. At the groom's village, then, men of the *kunbā* and the neighborhood gather in the *baiṭhak* (men's sitting place) of the groom's family. The groom's Barber makes a *ṭakkarpūrat* design on the ground there, and a wooden stool is placed over it. The groom, wearing a shawl, is seated on the stool while his family Brahman conducts the worship of the nine planets and several other deities. Then the groom holds out the end of his shawl, in a gesture called *jholī pasārnā* ("spreading out the begging bag," a phrase used idiomatically in other contexts to mean simply to beg or to accept *dān*, a fact stressed especially by Gujar informants when they discuss the betrothal ceremony). The Brahman priest of the bride's family puts the *ciṭṭhī* and the sets of cloth in the end of the groom's shawl. (We have already noted that *dān* is very frequently received in the *pallā*.) As the groom sits holding the cloth and the *ciṭṭhī*, men of the *kunbā* perform *wārpher* by circling coins over his head, and these coins are given to the groom's Barber. The Barber also receives the leftover flour from the *ṭakkarpūrat*. Both of these prestations remove and give onward some of the *kaṣṭ* that may afflict the groom as a result of his acceptance of the *dān* from the bride's family.

Meanwhile, the women of the *kunbā* have gathered in the courtyard of the groom's house, where a second *ṭakkarpūrat* has been constructed at the threshold by the Barber's wife. Before the *ciṭṭhī* may be opened, the groom carries it, still in his *pallā*, into the house. He stands on a wooden stool over the *ṭakkarpūrat*, and the women perform another *wārpher*, this time with dishes of grain they have brought from their own houses. This grain and the *ṭakkarpūrat* are given to the Barber's wife. (In Barber weddings, all of these *wārpher* articles and the flour are given to the *dhiyāne* and *dhiyānī* of the groom's family.) It is only after these protective actions have been performed that the *ciṭṭhī* may be opened and read; the groom returns to the *baiṭhak*, and his Brahman reads the letter aloud. Much concern is often evinced at this time by the men of the groom's family about the astrological coordinates of the time that has been proposed by the bride's family for the giving of the *kanyā dān*. When they have satisfied themselves that the time is not an inauspicious one, the one and one-quarter rupees in the *ciṭṭhī* are taken out of the letter and kept in the groom's house. Because of the inauspiciousness that it may contain, it may not be spent or otherwise used by the family; it is kept in a large clay pot called a *maṭ* for four or five years, after which it is usually given in the *ciṭṭhī* of a sister of the groom, or melted down to provide silver for ornaments to be given to the *dhiyānī* of the groom's family. (Old silver rupees are often sent in the *ciṭṭhī*.) Inauspiciousness is thus transferred from wife-givers to wife-receivers, later to be "given onward" (*āge denā*) to their own wife-receivers.

Five, seven, or nine days before the wedding ceremony, the second set of ritual actions and prestations begins at the homes of both the bride and the groom.[17] In the morning or early afternoon, the women of the *kunbā* gather in the courtyard for the *halad* ("turmeric") rituals. The wife of the Barber ties red protective threads on two winnowing baskets, two large earthen pots, and two long pestles. She also ties protective threads on the right wrists of the seven married women who will perform the actions of the *halad*. Then the Barber woman prepares a *ṭakkarpūrat* over the household *okhlī,* the small plastered hole in the earthen floor of the house that is used as a mortar in husking and grinding operations. *Sawā daīs ser* (ten and one-quarter *ser*) of rice (the quantity may be reduced to five and one-quarter *ser* for all but the oldest child in the family) is then put in a pile over the *ṭakkarpūrat* and the *okhlī*. A large brass tray containing a five-*paisā* coin, a few pieces of turmeric, and salt is placed near the rice. As Brahman women sing appropriate songs *(halad ke gīt)*, the seven women approach the pile of rice in pairs and pound (*masalnā*) it with the pestles, as if to husk it. (The rice that is used is in fact husked rice.) When all seven women have done this (the last woman alone) the same women, again in pairs, each place seven handfuls of the rice into the winnowing baskets and "winnow" (*pachornā*) it, shaking the baskets seven times. When all seven have done the winnowing, they join hands, two by two, and transfer the rice with their interlocked fingers into the larger of the two earthen pots. The salt from the brass tray is also placed in this pot. The rest of the articles from the tray are placed in the smaller pot. These pots, and the winnowing baskets and pestles, are taken to the threshold of an inner room of the house, and the flour from the *ṭakkarpūrat*) is given to the Barber woman. The seventh woman (who performs all of the actions alone) touches the ends of the two shawls she must wear for this ritual to all of the items seven times, in the action called *sevel*. Everything is then taken to a corner of the inner room, where the small pot is placed over the larger one on top of a pile of grain. The pots remain there until after the wedding, when the rice and the grain is given as *caṛhāpā* to the family Brahman *purohit*. (Brahmans give these things to their *dhiyānī* and *dhiyāne*.)

It is said that the disjoining acts of the *halad*—the "husking" and the "winnowing"—preliminary to the giving of the rice are performed in order to separate and remove any *kaṣṭ* that may be engendered by the presence of the ancestor deities, the *dev-pitar,* in the house at the time of a wedding. The winnowing basket in particular is frequently used in such ritual operations, and it is of great importance in the *halad* as the means by which the negative qualities and substances—the "chaff" as it were—are separated from that which is auspicious. Since such transferrals are made at the time of a wedding to one's *dhiyānī* and *dhiyāne,* it is not surprising to find Khare commenting that "the winnowing pan [in eastern Uttar Pradesh] is strongly associated with the idea of affinity, in that it accompanies a newly-wed woman and reappears whenever she formally moves between her father's and husband's homes, or whenever she gives birth to a child" (1976, 212).

At the time of the *halad,* the women of the *kunbā* also bring dishes of black lentils (*uṛad dāl*), which are emptied out over a *ṭakkarpūrat* made by the wife of the family Brahman *purohit,* who afterwards takes away the *ṭakkarpūrat* flour. The black lentils will be used later in the course of the wedding rituals, in connection with the ancestor deities.

The pots of the "winnowed" rice are kept in the inner room of the house until all of the wedding ceremonies have been completed; a number of *dhok mārnā* and other ritual actions performed in this room during this time remove inauspiciousness from the bride or groom and transfer it into those pots. Of particular importance to their well-being are the rites of the *bān,* which culminate in such a transfer to the pots of rice.

The term *bān* refers specifically to the application of oil and milk, and then a mixture of oil, turmeric, and barley flour, to the bodies of the bride and the groom, in their respective courtyards. In the afternoon, on the day of the *halad,* women again gather in the house of the bride or the groom, bringing small dishes of unhusked grain with them. The Barber woman prepares all of the items necessary for the *bān;* she brings two small earthen dishes, puts a few stalks of grass and a five-*paisā* coin in both of them, and then puts mustard oil in one and milk in the other. She also grinds *sawā ser* of barley flour and makes a paste of it with additional quantities of mustard oil and turmeric powder. Then a brass tray with flour and unrefined sugar is brought, and the Barber woman makes a *ṭakkarpūrat* on the ground in the courtyard of the house. A wooden stool is put over it, and the bride or groom is seated on it. The same seven women who performed the *halad* acts of disjoining come forward, and in pairs they touch the body of the bride or groom with the stalks of grass dipped in the oil and in the milk. The two women sit close together in front of the bride or groom, and they join hands left to left and right to right. They pick up stalks of grass from the earthen dish and dip their right hands into the oil and the left into the milk. They anoint first the feet, then the knees, then the shoulders, and finally the forehead, in such a way that the left side of the body is anointed with the oil, and the right side with the milk. (The laterality involved here may indicate that it is the left side of the body that contains the greatest inauspiciousness, since oil is used generally to remove and contain the most pernicious forms of inauspiciousness; I cannot say this with any great certainty, however, as I have no Pahansu exegesis on this point.) The anointing is called *bān lagānā* ("applying the *bān*") or *bān caṛhānā* ("making the *bān* go up"), and the directionality of this ritual may be compared to the *anulepana* of the *mūl śānti* ritual and the sequentiality of the prestations in the ritual of the Rāhu *dān* described earlier in this chapter. Here, the reversal of directionality, the "taking down off of" movement, is found to occur later in the course of the wedding rites, as we shall see. At the conclusion of the first *bān,* the Barber's wife rubs the mixture of barley flour, oil, and turmeric on the body of the bride or groom. When this is finished, she rinses the paste off and washes the hair with yogurt and water.

The bride or the groom then stands on the wooden stool over the *ṭakkarpūrat* and is given a brass plate containing a four-wicked dough lamp filled with mustard oil, a few grains of uncooked rice, some turmeric, and a ten-*paisā* coin. As the bride or groom holds this brass plate, the seventh woman performs a *sevel:* she touches the end of her shawl first to the head of the bride or groom and then to the plate that holds the burning oil lamp. All of the assembled women do *wārpher* with the dishes of grain they have brought. The grain and the flour and sugar from the *ṭakkarpūrat* are given to the Barber's wife, or to *dhiyānī* in the case of a Barber wedding. When the *wārpher* has been completed, the bride or groom carries the brass plate to the inner room where the two earthen pots containing the rice and other *halad* items have been kept. The tray with the lamp is put on the floor before these pots. *Dhok mārnā* is then done by the bride or groom, and the tray is placed over the pots. The coins from the lamp are given to the Barber woman, or to *dhiyānī* in a Barber wedding.

The *bān* rituals continue for five, seven, or nine days, until the day of the wedding—the *bān* of the bride should be for two days less than that of the groom, and the number of each is determined by the *rāśi,* the solar asterism of the bride (see table 6).[18] On the day of the wedding, the last *bān* (*ākhrī bān*), the "removing" or "taking down" of the *bān* (*bān utārnā* is performed. For the groom, the last *bān* is done the day before the wedding, just before the groom's party, the *barāt,* sets out for the bride's village.

On the day before this last *bān* is to be done, women gather in the courtyard of both the bride and the groom for a *dhok mārnā* to the ancestral deities. This day is called *bhalwāī kā din,* the day on which *bhalle* are prepared. *Bhalle* are small fried cakes made from the black lentils that

TABLE 6
Rāśi and Bān

Rāśi	Number of *Bāns* for the Bride
dhan *sinha* *vriṣa* *kumbh*	5
kanyā *tulā* *mīn* *meṣ*	7
makar *vriścak* *mithun* *kark*	9

were brought to the house by the women of the *kunbā* at the time of the *halad*. After frying, the *bhalle* are soaked in water in an earthen pot, covered, and placed in the inner room of the house where the *halad* items have been kept. They will be used later in the course of the wedding rites. These cakes are prepared by the wife of the family Brahman, and for the *dhok mārnā* itself, she makes fried breads (*pūṛī*) from *sawā ser* of wheat flour. Then she takes two small flat earthen dishes and places a bit of the flour previously set aside and a five-*paisā* coin in each dish. The two ends of a thick, many-stranded protective thread (*doṛī*) are placed in the dishes. The Brahman woman takes these things into the inner room and attaches them to the wall with some cow-dung paste. On the wall, these are the "forms" (*ākār*) of the ancestral deities, and the place where they are established (*thāppā*) for the duration of the wedding rites, and where their inauspiciousness is contained.

As Brahman women sing songs (*git*) of the *bhalwāī* day, a small dish of grain containing an earthen lamp filled with clarified butter is set on the floor before the *thāppā*. The women of the house and of the *kunbā* come before the *thāppā,* the lamp is lit, and a brass plate filled with the fried breads made from the *sawā ser* of flour is brought into the room. The women then do *dhok mārnā* with some grain, and a small piece of one of the breads is dropped on a burning ember. The grain and the breads become the *pujāpā* of the ancestral deities and are given by Gujars to their Brahman *purohit,* and by all other castes to their *dhiyānī*. At the conclusion of all of the wedding rites, the *thāppā* is removed from the wall, and the coins in the earthen saucers are given to the same recipients.

The purpose of this long sequence of actions and prestations is the removal of the inauspiciousness of the ancestral deities, the *dev-pitar,* from the bride and groom at the time of the wedding, and the transferral of it to the *purohit* through the intermediacy of the *thāppā* on the wall. A similar ritual, called *manḍhā,* is carried out by the men of the *kunbā* on the following day.

For this ritual, the men assemble in the courtyard of the house or in the men's sitting place. The Barber of the family prepares a cow-dung paste square on the ground, and the Brahman *purohit* draws a *vedi* over this. Using flour and variously colored powders, he makes figures representing the nine planetary deities, Śeṣnāg ("remainder snake"), the "seven sages," and Ganeṣa, the god of auspicious beginnings. (The flour for the *vedi* and some unrefined sugar are kept on a brass plate near the *vedi,* and these will be taken by the *purohit* at the conclusion of the *manḍhā.*) Several of the *bhalle* prepared on the previous day are enclosed in two small earthen saucers. The two saucers are tied together with a thick *ḍorī* to enclose the *bhalle,* and the package that is formed is also called the *manḍhā.* This is placed on the ground near the *vedi,* and the men sit around it. Following the directions of the Brahman *purohit,* they sprinkle rice and turmeric over the deities represented on the ground. The *manḍhā* is then put on the *vedi* itself, and more rice and turmeric are sprinkled. Then very long plant stalks are brought to the courtyard, and five of the men tie the stalks together and fasten the *manḍhā* to them. This is affixed to the lintel of the main door of the house, over the threshold, where it remains until the day after the wedding. During the course of the wedding, the *mandhā* is said to contain any *bhūt-pret*s (wandering ghosts) and their inauspiciousness that may bring harm to the bride or groom. The *manḍhā* in a Gujar wedding is taken down and disposed of by the Brahman *purohit,* while in a Brahman wedding, this task must be done by a *dhiyānā.*

As soon as the *manḍhā* is tied over the door, the final *bān* is performed. On each of the days preceding the central wedding rites, *bān lagānā* had been done as on the first day of the *bān.* But for the *bān utārnā,* "the taking off of the *bān,*" the ritual actions are not carried out in the courtyard, but in the darkness of the inner room where the pots of the *halad* rice have been kept. The same preparations are made and the same actions performed, but for the "taking off" and "removing" of the last *bān,* the directionality of the anointing with the oil and the milk is reversed. The seven women start at the forehead; then the shoulders, knees, and feet are touched with the milk and the oil in the same manner as in the *bān lagānā,* and the stalks of grass are put back in the earthen dishes. The rubbing with the mixture of barley flour, oil, and turmeric is performed as in the *bān lagānā.* The brass tray, still containing the dough lamp with four wicks, rice, turmeric, and a ten-*paisā* coin (a few sweet fried breads have also been added) is put in the hands of the bride or groom, and a piece of red cloth measuring *sawā gaj,* called the *candoyā,* is put on the head. The seventh woman then does *sevel* as in the previous *bān,* and all of the assembled women again do *wārpher* with dishes of grain. The grain from this *wārpher* is given to the Barber's wife as before. The *dhok mārnā* before the *halad* pots is again done in the same way, except that before the *dhok* is done, the red cloth, the *candoyā,* is taken from the head of the bride or groom and placed over the pots, and the *bān* tray is set down on top of this. On the day after the central rite of the *kanyā-dān,* the *pherā,* the *candoyā* is given as *dān* to the Barber's wife (to a *dhiyānī* in a Barber wedding); the coins from the lamp and the sweet cakes from the tray are given as *dān* to the family Brahman (to a *dhiyānī* in a Brahman wedding); and the oil lamp with four wicks, which may not be kept in the house because of its accumulated inauspiciousness, is disposed of in the village pond.

Immediately following the *bān utārnā,* the bride's or the groom's mother's brother breaks the small earthen dishes that contained the milk and oil and gives the five-*paisā* coin he had earlier placed in these to the Barber's wife. Here, as in so many other rituals, the breaking of the container in which items for *dān* and *caṛhāpā* have been kept signifies their transferral to the recipient. Finally, the Barber is given the clothes that the bride or groom had worn throughout the *bān* sequence, clothes that now contain some of the inauspiciousness loosened in the *bān utārnā.*

The overall sequence of these *bān* rituals effects a series of transfers of inauspiciousness to the Barber and the Brahman of the household in which the ritual is performed. There are a number of smaller and subsidiary transfers (e.g., the *ṭakkarpūrat dān* and the various *wārphers*) that occur within the context of the most crucial one, the removal of inauspiciousness that occurs with the *bān utārnā.* At the first *bān,* the direction of the anointing with milk and oil was from feet to head, and in the final *bān,* the "taking off," the direction is from head to feet. This is precisely the same pattern that we observed in the *mūl śānti* baths and the various *chuwānā*s. This reversal in the *bān,* as well as the replacing of the grass stalks in the earthen dishes containing the coins to be given as *caṛhāpā,* transfers negative substances from the body to the coins, which are then given to the Barber's wife. The "husking" and the "winnowing" of the *halad* rice and its subsequent bestowal, as *dān,* upon one's Brahman or *dhiyānī* effect the crucial transferral of inauspiciousness created by the presence of the ancestral deities at the time of the wedding.

When the *bān utārnā* has been completed, the family's Brahman *purohit* ties a *kangan* on the right wrist of the bride or groom. The *kangan* is a protective bracelet in which are tied five items that are said to attract and absorb inauspiciousness: areca nut (*supārī*), an iron ring, a shell (*kauṛī*), a small splinter of wood from a *nīm* tree, and a variety of small mustard seed called *raī*. All of these items are tied in red cloth.[19] For a bride's *kangan,* the small red pouch is tied with seven knots to a red and yellow thread, and for a groom's it is attached to a silver bracelet given by the groom's sister. (The sister gives this bracelet, villagers say, simply because "one asks one's *dhiyānī* for a protective bracelet" [*dhiyānī par te kangan māngte*].) When the *kangan* has been tied on the wrist, the women who are present do *wārpher* with dishes of grain, which are then given to the Barber's wife. (The disposal of the inauspiciousness that collects in the items tied in the *kangan* will be discussed below.)

Immediately following the tying of the *kangan,* preparations are begun for receiving the *bhāt*. The prestations made by the mother's brothers of both the bride and the groom are called *bhāt,* and the mother's brothers make this prestation, it is said, for their own auspiciousness (*apne śubh ke māro*); the *bhāt* is in fact *dān*. Soon after the betrothal ceremony, the mother of the bride or groom goes to her brother's house to give the "invitation" for the *bhāt;* this is called *bhāt nyautnā*. Until the *bhāt* is actually given, the mother's brother may not enter the conjugal house of his sister, for if he did, inauspiciousness would afflict him there *(nāśubh lagnā*), just as it would if he were to enter his sister's house before giving the *kasār* as *dān* when a child's upper tooth is the first to appear. In any event, a wedding, like the appearance of an upper tooth, is a time when, to maintain his own well-being, the mother's brother goes to the village in which his sister has been married and gives ritual gifts.

The mother's brother arrives at his sister's village on the day of her daughter's wedding, or in the case of a son's wedding, on the day the marriage party sets out for the bride's village. He may not enter the house immediately, but must wait until the *bān utārnā* has been completed. The Barber's wife prepares a *ṭakkarpūrat* over the threshold of the entrance to the house, and a wooden stool is placed over it. The mother of the bride or groom, wearing her *tukrī* (a long skirt that may be worn only by a married woman in her conjugal village—a woman would normally never wear such a skirt within the confines of her husband's house, however) and two shawls, waits just inside the door. Because she waits for her brother in the *tukrī,* it is evident that she is to receive the prestations as "other" (*dūsrī*) to him, a woman who has by virtue of her marriage become of another house and *kunbā*. In other circumstances, much shame would be felt by a woman in appearing before her brother in this skirt. (The significance of this contextually stressed "otherness" of the sister will be discussed in detail in chapter 5.)

The mother of the bride or groom, as she stands at the door, holds a large brass tray containing some husked rice mixed with turmeric, a five-*paisā* coin, and the dough lamp with four wicks made for the *bān*. The wife of the family Barber stands at her side holding a basket of *laḍ-*

*ḍū*s, ball-shaped confections made from sugar and chick-pea flour. The mother's "brothers" (including a number of men from her natal *kunbā,* sons of her brothers, and perhaps her own mother's brother as well) approach the threshold of the house with the gifts to be given in the *bhāt,* and one by one they stand over the *ṭakkarpūrat.* A number of preliminary prestations are made as they stand there. The first is a *joṛā* for the wife of the Sweeper attached as *kamīn* to the house of the sister's husband. This set of cloth is thrown over the wall of the house, and the Sweeper woman picks it up herself. This *joṛā* is called the *phalsā* ("doorway," "boundary"), and the action of throwing it into the sister's house is termed *phalsā caṛhānā,* "causing the *phalsā* to go up" or "offering the *phalsā.*" This prestation is referred to as *dān,* and it is given by the mother's brother "on his own behalf" (*apnī taraf se*), "for his own well-being achieved through gift-giving (*apne khair-khairāt ke māro*). No matter what else is given in the *bhāt,* the first prestation is always the set of cloth given to the Sweeper.

The mother of the bride or groom then puts a *tilak,* a mark of rice and turmeric, on the forehead of her "brother," and he in turn puts a full set of cloth, a *teḷ* that includes a *tukrī* and two shawls, on his sister's head.[20] Other items in the *bhāt*—sets of cloth, and money and jewelry if a daughter is to be married—are placed in the brass tray containing the dough lamp. The brother himself holds the tray while his sister performs a *sevel* with the ends of the two shawls that she wears: she touches first the brother's forehead, then the *bhāt* items in the tray, and finally her own forehead. This sequence of touching iconically implements the transferral of inauspiciousness from the brother himself, to the items of the *bhāt* in the tray, and finally to the recipient, the sister as she receives the prestations. Then the sister does a *wārpher* over his head with the *laḍḍū*s, which are given as *caṛhāpā* to the Barber woman. In a Barber wedding, they are given to *dhiyānī.* (In a Sweeper wedding, these sweets of the *wārpher,* laden with inauspiciousness, are given to *dhiyāne,* and they say that "whoever is the *pūj* eats the *laḍḍū*s" [*jo pūj haĩ ve khāve*]. For a discussion of the meaning and contextual implementation of the word *pūj,* see below, 152–53).

Each brother or brother's son steps forward in this way to give the *bhāt* and to have the protective ritual actions performed, and then all of the *bhāt* gifts are taken over the threshold into the house. As the last *bhāti* (giver of the *bhāt)* steps off the *ṭakkarpūrat,* the Barber woman receives the leftover flour and unrefined sugar as *dān.*

In this set of *bhāt* prestations, the mother's brothers of the bride or groom ensure their own auspiciousness by giving gifts at the threshold of their sister's house. The removal of inauspicious substances is effected by the manner in which the *bhāt* is received by the sister, and by the protective actions and processes (the *ṭakkarpūrat*, the *wārpher*) at the door. The *bhāt* rituals also make it clear that a man's "well-being achieved through gift-giving" is ensured, not simply through his relationship with his own sister, but also through the relationship he maintains with the *kamīns* of her conjugal household, insofar as they are the recipients of the *phalsā* cloth and the *laḍḍūs* and the *ṭakkarpūrat* flour.

The *bhāt* prestations received in Pahansu at the wedding of the daughter of Sevaram, a fairly prosperous Gujar landholder, included the following items:

the *phalsā*, a set of cloth for the Sweeper
one *telṇ* for the bride's mother (placed on her head)
one *telṇ* for the bride's father's mother
three pieces of jewelry (*ṭūm*) for the bride: silver toe rings, silver ankle bracelets, and a gold necklace
Rs. 505
twenty-one *dhotī* (inexpensive *sārīs*) to be given onward in the "dowry" (*dāt*)
fifteen brass vessels
one set of cloth for the bride, to be worn at the *pherā*
one set of cloth for the bride to be worn at the *cālā*, her second return to her conjugal village
one set of cloth for Sevaram, the bride's father
four sets of cloth, one for each of the bride's brothers
three sets of cloth, one for each of the bride's brothers' wives
one set of cloth for the daughter of the bride's brother
one set of cloth for the groom

These gifts are of the same nature as those given both at the *cālā* and in *cūcak* and *kevkā*, the prestations that these men have already sent to the *sasurāl* of their sister upon the birth of her children. In these contexts, and only in these contexts, particular sets of cloth are sent for specific persons (other than the sister, her husband, and her children) in the sister's *sasurāl*. The recipients are called the "next ones" (*aglī*). On other gift-giving occasions, such as the wedding *dāt*, sets of cloth are simply "counted out and given" (*ginke dete haĩ*), and the word *aglī* is not used. (For further discussion of this point, see pp. 141–42.) In all of the instances where the term *aglī* occurs, it functions as an index of that aspect of the relationship concerned with the acceptance of inauspiciousness, just as the term *dhiyānī* does.

The *bhāt* prestations are given in other castes in much the same fashion. Brahman *bhāts* must always include a bed, however, a point whose significance I will discuss below in relation to gifts given by Brahmans at the time of a death.

Immediately following the giving of the *bhāt,* the bride's family *purohit* and the men of her *kunbā* go to the place in the village where the members of the groom's party have been lodged, usually in one of the Gujar *caupāls* ("meeting places"). The Brahman *purohit* carries a large brass tray containing five sweets, some rice, turmeric, stalks of grass, a *caddar* (a man's large shawl), and a one-rupee note. The groom is seated on the ground in front of the *purohit,* who prepares a *vedi* with representations of Ganeṣa, the planets, and several other deities. The priest puts some rice in the hands of the groom and the men of his *kunbā,* and they throw it over the representations of the deities. Then the priest places a mark of rice and turmeric on the foreheads of these men. The shawl is placed over the groom's shoulder and down his lap, to form a *jholī,* a "begging bag." The one-rupee note is placed in it, and a further prestation, usually of Rs. 101, the first of the *dahej* prestations, is also put in the end of the shawl. The groom is then given a piece of one of the sweets in the tray, and the Brahman priest of the groom receives the remaining ones. The one-rupee note is wrapped in the shawl from the brass tray, and this is given as *dān* to the *purohit* of the groom's family.

This brief ritual is called *barāt lenā* ("receiving the groom's party"), and it represents the reopening of the gift-giving to the groom's side (*var pakṣ*), the first of a number of prestations to be made during the course of the wedding. As in the betrothal ceremony, the items to be given are placed in the groom's shawl, emphasizing the nonhierarchic aspects of the relationship between the side of the bride and the side of the groom. The fact that the shawl from the tray and the one-rupee note are given to the groom's *purohit,* through the intermediacy of the groom, is another indication that the affinal relationship entails a unidirectional transferral of inauspiciousness from the bride's family and village to those of the groom, since this type of mediated transfer is so common in the giving of *dān*. As in the giving of the *bhāt,* where the bride's mother's brother gives a set of cloth to the sister's Sweeper, here too the relationship is not simply between the families of the bride and the groom, but between the bride-givers and the *kamīns* and *purohit* of the bride-takers as well.

In the next sequence of prestations in the wedding, at the *bār dwārī* ("entering the door"), there is an apparent reversal of the transfer of inauspiciousness. As the groom prepares to enter the bride's house for the first time, inauspiciousness is removed from him and given to the *kamīns* of the bride's family. Before the groom approaches the door, another *ṭakkarpūrat* is drawn over the threshold of the house and a wooden stool is placed over it. The bride's Brahman *purohit* stands at the door to await his arrival, holding the brass tray with the dough lamp used at the time of the *bhāt*. On the tray, in addition to the lamp, is some turmeric and rice, a ten-*paisā* coin, one rupee, and five *laḍḍūs*. As the groom steps up on the wooden stool, the *purohit* does a *wārpher* with the rupee note and gives it to the bride's family Barber. Then the priest performs a *sevel* just as the mother of the bride has done for her brother: he touches the end of his shawl first to the groom's forehead, then to the brass tray, and then to his own forehead. Then he takes the ten-*paisā* coin from the tray and keeps it. The sequence involved in the *sevel,* and the Brahman's removal of the coin from the tray, effect the transfer of *bādhā* ("hindrances") from the groom to the *purohit* himself. In a Brahman wedding, a *dhiyānā* of the family (usually the bride's *bahenoi,* her elder sister's husband) performs the *sevel* and receives the coin. A *dhiyānā,* it is said, must do this simply because he is *pūj,* the appropriate recipient of *pujāpā.*

The *purohit* breaks a small morsel from one of the *laḍḍūs* and puts it into the groom's mouth so that, people say, he will not step down from the stool with an empty mouth (*khālī mū̃h nahī̃ utarte conkī par te*). The Brahman then receives the rest of these sweets. Finally, as the groom steps off the stool, the stool itself is given, in all castes except Gujar, to a *dhiyānā* of the bride's family, for the well-being and auspiciousness of the groom.

All of the *bār dwārī* prestations are accompanied by ritual actions that transfer inauspiciousness from the groom to the *kamīns*, *purohit,* or the *dhiyāne* of the bride's family. This is one of only two times that a transfer of negative qualities occurs in this fashion, and one of two times in the life of a groom that a *wārpher* or *sevel* or other protective actions will be done on his behalf in the village of his wife. This apparent anomaly may be resolved if we keep in mind the fact that the term *dhiyānā* (and the "otherness" it implies) is not constituted solely in terms of its referential applicability regardless of the context of its use. The meaning of the term is in large part contextually ordered, indexing as it does particular aspects of the affinal relationship, that of the "appropriate obligation" of the husbands of one's *dhiyānī* to accept *dān* and *caṛhāpā* for the well-being and auspiciousness of the donor. Only in quite specific instances, then, is this term found to occur. At the *bār dwārī,* the groom would never be referred to as *dhiyānā,* even though his appropriateness in other situations as a recipient of *dān* has already been established in the ritual of the betrothal and in the *barāt lenā.* At the *bār dwārī* it is, rather, the *bahenoi* (sister's husband) and *phūphā* (father's sister's husband) who, in the case of Brahman and Barber weddings, are called *dhiyānā;* and this is so precisely because of their acceptance of the *wārpher* money and sweets, and the wooden stool.

Why, then, should the negative substances adhering to the groom be transferred to the *kamīns* and *purohit* or *dhiyāne* at the *bār dwārī*? In effect, this appears to classify the groom with the people of the bride's house (and perhaps also with the bride's mother's brother), in opposition to the *kamīns* and the *dhiyāne* of the house, even though he is becoming a *dhiyānā* himself. At one level, the spatial aspects of the ritual may provide an explanation. Thresholds and village boundaries are very often the points at which negative substances and qualities enter or are transferred from the house or village, and there are many actions and prestations that restrict the entrance and facilitate the exit of inauspiciousness at these places. The *bār dwārī* is such a ritual; it takes place over the threshold of the bride's house, as the groom enters it for the first time. Rather than receiving prestations as he leaves the house, as he later will do, prestations are made on his behalf in order to ensure that inauspiciousness not come into the house. *Dhiyāne* (for Barbers, Brahmans, and Sweepers) and the Barber and the Brahman (for Gujars) are the appropriate recipients of this inauspiciousness. The bride's house does not function as the recipient, or even as an intermediary, in this transferral because in fact the ritual is done for the auspiciousness of its inhabitants.

All *dān,* villagers say, is given to remove *sankaṭ* ("danger"), *kaṣṭ* ("afflictions") and *pāp* ("sin," "evil") from the donor. The central rite of the wedding ceremony is itself referred to as *kanyā dān,* the *dān* of a virgin daughter. Like other *dān, kanyā dān* removes *pāp* and *sankaṭ* from the family of the donor. It brings the greatest *sankaṭ,* villagers say, for a daughter to remain in her father's house after she has begun to menstruate. She must be given as *dān* (*uskā dān kar denā cahiye*) because to allow her to remain in her father's house would be productive of inauspiciousness and misfortune. It is also the case that inauspiciousness is transferred to the groom and his family through their acceptance of the *kanyā dān* and the prestations that accompany and follow the gift of the virgin. This idea appears to have a very long history in Indic texts. In a Ṛg Vedic hymn describing the marriage of Sūryā (daughter of the sun) and Soma (verses of which are used in marriage rituals even today) there is a similar inauspiciousness attached to the blood—here the blood of defloration—of the bride. The marriage gown on which the stain of blood appears causes her own family to prosper, but her husband's family is "bound in the bonds," and her husband himself may become "ugly and sinisterly pale" if he comes into contact with it. Diseases also result from the transferral of blood from the bride's own people to the groom's family. "It [the blood] burns, it bites, it has claws, as dangerous as poison is to eat." As we shall see, some of the inauspiciousness of the acceptance of the *kanyā dān* is, in Pahansu, passed on to the groom's *purohit,* and this is the case in the Vedic hymn as well: "Throw away the gown, and distribute wealth to the priests. It becomes a magic spirit walking on feet, and like the wife it draws near the husband. . . . Only the priest who knows the Sūryā hymn is able to receive the bridal gown."[21] I want to suggest in this discussion of the *kanyā dān* rite that similar ideas structure the *pherā* as it is performed in Pahansu, as well as the manner in which the prestations that accompany the *kanyā dān* are handled by the groom's family.

One thing should be made clear before we proceed. The meaning of marriage is not, of course, exhausted by the paradigm of the transferral of inauspiciousness in the *dān;* wife-takers are not in all contexts referred to as *dhiyānā* and the bride is not looked upon merely as a conveyor of sin and evil. The reciprocal aspects of the relationship between the family of the bride and the family of the groom are indexed by the use of the term *riśtā* ("relationship") and the reciprocal term for kin related through marriage, *riśtedār* ("holder of a relationship"); indeed there are many prestations that are referable to this aspect of the relationship. (These will be discussed in detail in chapter 5.) Similarly, for many castes, there is an important hierarchic aspect to the relationship between the family of the bride and the family of the groom. Yet it is the case, as I will suggest, that in the ritual actions so far discussed, and in those that comprise the *kanyā dān,* neither of these aspects of the affinal relationship come to the fore. Rather, it is the oriented transfer of inauspiciousness that is most clearly enacted and expressed in these rituals and the accompanying prestations, and this transferral is not comprehensible in terms of the possible hierarchic aspects of the relationship.

In the ritual core of the wedding, the *pherā* ("circling") or the *kanyā dān,* the transferral of inauspiciousness structures the actions at two levels; these levels will be intertwined in the description of the *pherā,* but two points should be kept in mind. First, the overall structure of the *pherā* is an instantiation of the basic paradigm of transferral outlined in chapter 3, and second, within this overall sequence of ritual actions and prestations, there are other specific prestations that transfer inauspiciousness to recipients other than the groom and his *kunbā.*

Like the *dān* that follows *vrat*s and other ritual actions, the *pherā* and *kanyā dān* are preceded by fasting on the part of certain persons in the close family (*nijī parivār*) of the bride: her mother, father, older sisters, brothers, father's mother, father's father, brothers' wives, father's brothers, and father's brothers' wives. On the day the groom's party arrives in their village, these persons (or at least one of them, embodying their unity) do not eat foods made from grain. Fasting is here, as usual, an act of disjunction analogous to the *mūl śānti* baths or the winnowing in the *halad.* It should be noted that the persons who fast before the *kanyā dān* include only those to whom the bride will be *dhiyānī* after the marriage; this is highlighted by the fact that older, but not younger, sisters may undertake the fast; a younger sister, after her own marriage, is *dhiyānī* to an older one, but the reverse is not true.

After the *bār dwārī,* then, at the time the Brahman of the bride's family has determined to be appropriate for the *kanyā dān,* he prepares the *vedi* for the *pherā* in the courtyard of the girl's house.

The priests of the bride's family and of the groom's, men from both "sides" (*pakṣ*), and the groom himself are seated around this *vedi.* Preliminary worship of all the represented deities is performed, and the groom is ceremonially welcomed by the bride's father. The first *dān* is then given: after the appropriate *sankalp* (resolution), *gau dān,* "the *dān* of a cow," is given in the form of a sum of money to the groom. A small sum of money for *dakṣiṇā* ("payment") is presented with the *dān.* Immediately following the *dān,* the groom may make a prestation from this money received in *dān* to his own *purohit;* the Sanskrit *sankalp* that is recited for the *dān* to the *purohit* says that it is given "to remove the faults caused by the acceptance of a cow" (*gau pratigraha doṣa nivāraṇārtham*). This instantiation of the very general structure of transferral from wife-givers to wife-receivers (as *dhiyānā*) to Brahman (or Dakaut) as *purohit* makes very explicit, through the words of the *sankalp,* the precise meaning of the "giving onward" (*āge denā*) of the *dān* that one receives: to remove the "faults" engendered by the act of receiving that prestation.

Embers for the sacrificial fire are brought (in a new brass vessel) and the fire is lit. The bride's mother's brother then leads the bride herself, heavily veiled, into the courtyard, and seats her at the side of the groom. The father of the bride (or perhaps the oldest man in the *kunbā*) is directed by the *purohit* in the recitation of the *sankalp* for the *kanyā dān.* A resolution is also necessary for the giving of the *dakṣiṇā* that accompanies the gift of the virgin, the "payment" for the groom's acceptance of the *dān.* While the first *sankalp* that is recited at this time facilitates the giving on the part of the donor, the second *sankalp,* the "installing of the *dān*" (*dān pratiṣṭhā*), effects the actual transfer to the groom. In both of these resolutions, the groom is referred to as the "protecting groom" (*śarmanne var*) because of his role as recipient of the *dān.* The groom pronounces, in a *mantra,* that the *dān* has been received and assimilated and says to the bride's father, in Hindi, "May auspiciousness be yours" (*tumhārā kalyāṇ ho*). He thus indicates that it is the auspiciousness of the bride's family that is being assured through the acceptance of the *kanyā dān.*

Immediately following his acceptance of the *kanyā dān,* the groom makes a *sankalp* for a *gau dān* to his own *purohit.* The resolution again refers to the purpose of this *dān:* "to remove the faults caused by the acceptance of a wife" (*bhāryyā pratigraha doṣa nivāraṇārtham*). A sum of money is given to the *purohit* of the groom's side as *gau dān.* The *purohit* is also referred to in the *sankalp* as one who protects (*śarmanne*) through his acceptance, in the same way that the priest of the Ṛg Vedic hymn receives the blood-stained bridal gown in order to protect the husband from its evil. A *dān pratiṣṭhā dakṣiṇā* accompanies this *dān* to the groom's *purohit*.

Then the bride's mother's brother again steps forward and provides *sawā gaj* (one and one-quarter measures) of white cloth called a *kānjol*. The end of the bride's shawl is tied to the clothes of the groom with this piece of cloth. When the cloth is tied, small stalks of grass, a few grains of rice, and a ten-*paisā* coin are placed in the knot. This cloth remains tied to the bride's clothing until the *maṇḍhā* at the groom's house is taken down several days after the *pherā*. It may not be kept in the house after that, because of the inauspiciousness that it contains; it is given to the *purohit* of the groom's family, and Brahmans give it to a *dhiyānā*. (This too seems to be a striking parallel to the role of the priest in the Ṛg Veda who accepts the bridal gown.) The Sanskrit *mantra* recited by the bride's *purohit* as the *kānjol* is tied states that this action is *dampatyoh rakṣaṇārthaya*, to "protect the two masters" (i.e., the bride and the groom) from any inauspiciousness that would affect their future offspring (*santān*), their wealth (*dhan*), and longevity (*āyu*), inauspiciousness that arises precisely because of the joining together of the bride and the groom: the tying of the *kānjol* both unites them and contains the negative qualities thereby set loose.[22]

After the cloth has been tied, a fire sacrifice is performed in the usual way, with men from the bride's side and the groom's participating. When the last offerings (*āhuti*) have been made into the fire, the bride and the groom rise and stand facing east, the bride in front of the groom. The bride's brother stands to the northeast of the fire with a winnowing basket (*chāj*) filled with parched rice (*khīl*). He divides the rice into four portions and puts one of these into his sister's hand. She in turn gives it to the groom, who then drops it into the fire. This is done three times in all, and Sanskrit *mantra*s accompany each sequence.

Then, with the bride still in front of the groom, the couple circles the fire in a clockwise direction (*parikrama* or *pherā*) three times. The brother of the bride takes the one remaining portion of the parched rice from the winnowing basket, gives it to his sister, and she herself makes the offering into the fire. (In all four of the circumambulations, brothers of the bride, including many men of her *kunbā*, by turns lead her around the fire.) In light of the sequentiality of prestations to *dhiyānī* and *dhiyāne*, and the meaning of gifts to them, the iconicity of the winnowing basket should by now be obvious. Its conjunction with the *pherā*, in the course of which the bride is said to become *parāyī*, "other" to her natal kin, is particularly interesting. After the third *pherā*, transfer of the parched rice is made from the brother's winnowing basket to the sister and then to the groom, who offers it into the fire. The bride does not offer it herself; she is an intermediary, as it were, between her brother and the man who is just then becoming her husband. At the fourth *pherā,* however, she offers the parched rice into the fire herself. No longer a half-transformed intermediary, she is now "of another house" (*begāne ghar kī*), and thus when she receives a prestation from her brother, she receives it as a person of her husband's family, as a *dhiyānī* to her brother, and offers the *khīl* into the fire on her own and her husband's behalf. As we will see, this pattern is replicated in the "giving onward" of certain marriage and postmarriage prestations.

At the conclusion of the *pherā,* an additional prestation is sometimes made. A dish filled with clarified butter is brought and a ten-*paisā* coin is placed in it. Both the bride and groom are made to cast their reflections into it. This *chāyā pātra* ("reflection vessel") is then given to a Dakaut, with an appropriate *sankalp*. Whenever a *chāyā dān* is given, the purpose, as we have seen, is to remove from the donor negative substances engendered by particular circumstances. The words of the *sankalp* once again describe the purpose of the *chāyā dān:* "to remove the various afflictions" (*nānākaṣṭ nivāraṇārtham*) caused by the marriage (*vivāh karmaṇah*), this *chāyā dān* is given to the Dakaut. The recipient is again referred to as a *śarmanne,* "protecting," Brahman, which sets up a specific contextual equivalence between the Dakaut, the groom, and the family Brahman *purohit* (and for Brahmans, the *dhiyāne*): all "protect" insofar as they receive prestations that remove inauspiciousness from the donor. In the context of these prestations in the course of the wedding ritual, all recipients are referred to as *śarmanne* in the Sanskrit resolutions.

When the *pherā* sequence has been completed, the bride and groom are led into the inner room of the bride's house where the *thāppā* for the ancestral deities has been made and the pots from the *halad* kept. Before the *thāppā,* the *kangans* of both the bride and groom are removed from their wrists. The tying of the white cloth and its contents (*kānjol bāndhnā*) and the tying of these bracelets (*kangan bāndhnā*) share the same function: to contain the inauspiciousness (*nāśubh*) generated in the course of the *pherā*. And just as the contents of the *kānjol* are disposed of later by being given to a Brahman or *dhiyānā,* so too are the negative qualities of the *kangan* transferred through a sequence of actions and prestations. When the *kangans* have been taken off the wrists, they are placed in the bride's hands with several of the *bhalle* (black-lentil cakes) prepared earlier; she drops these things into the groom's hands, and he lets them fall into the water into which the *bhalle* have been soaking. This is done seven times for the well-being, it is said, of the bride and groom (*śubh ke māro*); the negative qualities are thereby transferred into the water, and thus into the *bhalle* themselves. The *bhalle* that have been put into their hands are given as *dān* to the Barber's wife, and those remaining in the pot are later given to the family's Brahman or, in the case of Brahman weddings, to *dhiyāne*.[23]

After the inauspiciousness of the *kangans* has been removed in this way, the bride and the groom exchange bracelets; the silver one is put on the bride's wrist, and her string *kangan* is tied on his. A brass tray containing some uncooked rice, turmeric, three *bhalle*, and a ten-*paisā* coin is then brought into the room. An older woman married into the bride's family (a *baṛī bīr*) does *dhok mārnā* into this tray, and the contents are given by Gujars to their Brahman *purohit*. (The expression that I heard in this connection was that these articles "go upon the Brahmans," *brahmanõ pe jā*.) Finally, the women of the house do *wārpher* over the heads of the bride and groom with dishes of grain they have brought, and this grain is given to the family Barber.

During the *pherā*, the groom is the recipient of several prestations from the bride's father: the *gau dān*, the bride herself, and a sum of money also called *kanyā dān*. In Gujar weddings in Pahansu in 1977–79, the *kanyā dān* prestation was typically Rs. 1,100. On the morning following the *pherā*, at a ceremony called *paṭṭā* the groom receives further gifts that are also referred to as *dān*.[24]

There are in fact two *paṭṭā*s, and in each of them there are different accountings of the prestations that are made. After the marriage (*śādī*), a bride generally visits her conjugal village for a brief period of several days, during which time the marriage is not consummated. She returns to her natal village, and then goes back to her husband's house in the first, third, or fifth year after the wedding, but never in an even year, as this would engender inauspiciousness for her natal family. The return to the *sasurāl* is called *cālā* ("the going") or *gaunā*. At the astrologically appropriate time, the groom's party again goes to the bride's village for the *cālā*, and a second *paṭṭā* is held. After this *paṭṭā*, the bride returns to her husband's house, this time to consummate the marriage. Occasionally the *śādī* and *cālā* are performed at the same time, in which case there will be only one *paṭṭā*. But if this is the case, there will still be two sets of prestations made, one set for the *śādī* and one for the *cālā*.

The prestations made at a fairly representative Gujar *paṭṭā* at the wedding of Mukhiya's daughter in Pahansu included the following items:

twenty-five brass vessels
five sets of cloth for the bride
one set of bedding
thirty-one sets of cloth "for the *sās*" (husband's mother), including five *teḷ*, (such *joṛā*s are in fact distributed within the groom's family)
one set of clothing for the groom
a bicycle
gold rings for both the bride and groom

gold rings for the groom's parents
gold earrings for the bride
silver ankle bracelets and toe rings for the groom's mother
a watch for the groom
Rs. 1,001

At the combined wedding and *cālā* of Sevaram's daughter the following items were given at the *paṭṭā:*

fifty-one brass vessels for the wedding
twenty-one brass vessels for the *cālā*
fifty-one sets of cloth for the wedding *dāt* ("for the *sās*")
thirty sets of cloth "for the next ones" (*agliõ ke*), for specific recipients in the girl's *sasurāl,* for the *cālā*
twenty-five sets of cloth for the bride
seven sets of bedding
a bed
a "dining set"
a "sofa set"
a steel wardrobe
a steel trunk
a suitcase
assorted fans, baskets, stools, etc.
a motorcycle
seven silver ornaments for the bride
five gold ornaments for the bride
five silver ornaments for the groom's parents
two silver ornaments for the groom's father's mother
gold rings for the bride and groom
Rs. 3,001

All of these items may collectively be called *dahej,* and this term is also used for the *cālā* prestations as a whole, and for the *cūcak* and *kevkā* gifts given after a birth. For several days prior to the wedding, all of these things are spread out in cots in the courtyard of the bride's house, and the Barber's wife announces to all of the neighbors and women of the *kunbā* that they should "go to see the *dahej*" (*dahej dekhan jā*). The term *dahej* is also used in the context of discussions about the negative aspects of receiving; Gujars say that "*dān* should go from the house" (*ghar se dān jānā cahiye*), and that they want to give *dahej,* but that they do not like to receive it.

Within the set of *dahej* prestations, however, distinctions are made. The sets of cloth (excluding those given for one's own daughter) and brass vessels that are given at a wedding *paṭṭā* are termed *dāt*. Although the sets of cloth are distributed within the groom's family, they are not earmarked by the bride's family as being for specific recipients; thus they may easily be, and indeed are, "given further" by the groom's mother. They are simply "counted out and given" (*ginke dete haĩ*), and the *dāt* is thus referred to as thirty-one *kī,* forty-one *kī* or fifty-one *kī dāt.*

It is important for the well-being of the bride and her husband's family that some of these items in the *dāt* be "given onward" in various ways. It is particularly necessary for the women there to take one of the sets of cloth from the *dāt* to the place in the fields where the ancestral shrines are located. The set of cloth is first placed on the top of the small shrine, then taken off and given as *pujāpā, pūj ke,* to the groom's family *purohit.* Sets of cloth from the *dāt* are also given to *kamīn*s and to *dhiyānī,* who return to their *pīhar*s for the weddings of their brothers and brothers' sons, when *dān* comes into the house. *Dhiyānī* always receive brass vessels from the *dāt* as well.

At the *cālā paṭṭā* of his only daughter, Sansar, Sukhbir and his wife gave the following items to the groom's family:

eight *ṭūm* (pieces of jewelry) for Sansar, including ankle bracelets, a ring, a necklace, toe-rings, and a nose ornament
Rs. 2,000 for additional ornaments
eleven brass vessels
thirty-one sets of cloth for Sansar (including one *teḷ*)
fifteen sets of cloth for the "next ones" (*aglī*), including a *teḷ* for the *sās*
one full set of clothing for the groom
five sets of bedding
one set of cloth for the groom's elder brother's son
one set of cloth for the groom's elder brother's daughter
miscellaneous household goods, including a steel trunk, a sewing machine, and steel eating utensils

Here again, the sets of cloth that are given to one's daughter are kept separate from those that are given for the groom's family; they are even carefully laid out on separate cots in the bride's courtyard as the women of the *kunbā* come to view them. At the *cālā* of Sansar, her *dādī* (father's mother) said to me over and over as I stood in their courtyard writing down each item that was laid out on the cots that the sets of cloth given to one's daughter were "separate" (*alag-alag*) from those given to the *aglī*: "We give separately to our girls" (*ham apnī laṛkī ko nyāre-nyāre de*). (It should be noted that the daughter is not called *dhiyānī* in this context.) Each of the sets of cloth for the "next ones" is in fact earmarked for a specific recipient in the family of the groom or their *dhiyānī*.

When the bride goes to her *sasurāl* after the *cālā,* a set of cloth must again be offered at the shrine of the *dev-pitar*s. This would have been done after the *śādī,* but at that time it would not have been the bride who offered them, but the older wives of the groom's *kunbā*. But after the *cālā,* the bride herself offers this set of cloth (earmarked by the bride's family as being for the particular *dev-pitar* as one of the "next ones"), and she gives it herself to the Brahman *purohit* of the groom's family. She is now completely "of another house" (*begāne ghar kī*) to her natal kin, and not simply an intermediary, and so she may make these offerings on behalf of her husband and the people of her *sasurāl*.[25] This difference between the offerings to the *dev-pitar* from the marriage *dāt* and from the sets of cloth for the "next ones" from the *cālā* replicates exactly the distinction we have noted in the *pherā* offerings: only after the final circumambulation of the fire does the bride offer the parched rice directly into the fire on behalf of her husband.

The overall sequentiality in the gift-giving may also be related to the gradual transformation of the daughter from "one's own girl" (*apnī laṛkī*) to intermediary to *dhiyānī*. In the first set of wedding prestations of cloth, the daughter receives cloth that is altogether separate (*nyāre-nyāre,* as the women insisted that I record in my notebook), and the *joṛā*s for the groom's family, the *dāt,* are simply "counted out and given." The latter are *dān,* while *joṛā*s given to the daughter are not. In the *cālā* prestations, the sets of cloth for the daughter are again separate from the others, but this time sets of cloth are sent for specific relatives of the groom as "the next ones" (*aglī*), and not simply "counted out." Again, only the gifts to the groom's family are *dān,* but the daughter, the bride, moves closer to the people of her *sasurāl* as she takes the set of cloth for the *dev-pitar* and offers it herself. At the *kevkā* and *cūcak* prestations that are sent at the birth of the daughter's first child, the daughter receives proportionately fewer sets of cloth, while the *aglī* again receive specific *joṛā*s as *dān*. After the birth of the first child, however, the daughter and her husband receive the *dān* prestations from her natal kin. She herself is completely "other," and there is no need for her natal kin to send *dān* to the *aglī* after that. They send *dān* to their daughter who is now their *dhiyānī,* and she may "give onward" cloth from such *dān* for her own auspiciousness and that of her husband.

It may also be the case that the prestations of the *cāle ke dūsre* ("*cālā*'s second," the return to the conjugal village after the *cālā*) mark another point in the on-going transformation of the daughter to *dhiyānī*. At the *cāle ke dūsre* of the daughter of Hirdha, a Gujar landholder, the following prestations were sent from Pahansu:

twenty-one sets of cloth for the daughter
two sets of bedding
six sets of cloth for the husband's mother

one for the husband's father's mother
one for the husband's father's sister
one for the husband's sister
one for the husband's father's younger brother's wife
one for the husband's father
one for the husband's father's younger brother
one for the husband's father's sister's husband
one for the husband's sister's husband
one for the husband's younger brother
one for the husband

All of the sets of cloth except those for the daughter and her husband are said to be "for the next ones," just as in the *cālā*. In all of the wedding prestations that are made prior to the *cāle ke dūsre,* the giving of brass vessels is essential. The fact that they are never given in the *cāle ke dūsre* may indicate that the wedding prestations have come to a close.

We return, then, to our description of the ritual events immediately following the *pherā*. The *paṭṭā* prestations are made early in the morning of the day following the *pherā*. The men of the groom's party and of the bride's *kunbā* assemble in the *gher* (men's sitting place and cattle pen) of the bride's father. All of the *dahej* items are displayed on cots there, and a senior man of the bride's *kunbā* holds a tray with the jewelry and cash that are to be given. The groom sits on the ground facing north (the position a Brahman always assumes as he accepts *dān*), wearing a shawl with the end coming down over his right shoulder to form a *jholī,* a "begging bag." As in the betrothal ceremony, this posture is called *jholī pasārnā,* "to spread out the begging bag." The bride's family *purohit* places a spot of turmeric powder on his forehead, and the men of the bride's *kunbā* throw rice into the *jholī*. Then the cash and the jewelry are placed into the *jholī,* and this concludes the *paṭṭā*.

In Brahman weddings, the *dahej* is given in a different manner, and the variation here is indicative of the different constructions placed upon the affinal relationship. We have noted that the terms *dhiyānī* and *dhiyānā* occur in contexts in which the acceptance of *dān* is foregrounded in the relationship between wife-givers and wife-receivers. While there are a number of occasions on which Gujars give *dān, pujāpā,* and *caṛhāpā* to their *dhiyānī,* they do not give *dān* to the husbands of these women (their *dhiyāne*) except at the wedding, *cālā, kevkā,* and *cūcak*.[26] Correspondingly, it is only in these contexts that the term *dhiyānā* is used by Gujars; in other contexts other terms are used to refer to these men. Thus, for Gujars, the *paṭṭā* does not set a precedent for the continued giving of *dān* to the groom. The Brahman ritual in which *dahej* is given, however, directly prefigures many future prestations of this sort.

The Brahman act of bestowal is called the *śayyā dān,* the *dān* of a bed, and it takes place in the courtyard of the bride's house. A Brahman *bhāt,* unlike that for a Gujar wedding, must always contain a bed, and at the *śayyā dān* this bed is placed in such a way that the head (*sirānā*) points toward the south and the foot toward the north. All of the *dahej* items are placed on or near the cot, and the bride and groom are seated on it, facing north, the direction for the receiving of *dān*. The father and the mother of the bride are tied together with a piece of cloth, and this tying is called *ganṭhjoṛā bāndhnā,* "tying the pair in a knot." Facing east, the father ties a protective thread on the eastern leg of the cot. He takes water, a few grains of rice, and a ten-*paisā* coin, and touching this to the leg of the cot he recites the *śayyā dān sankalp* and then gives the thread and the coin to the groom, thus transferring the bed and the *dahej* items to him.

Now a bed is an essential item in a number of *dān* prestations, including the very inauspicious *dān* that is given after a death has occurred.[27] Gujars, as well as all other castes except Brahman, Leatherworker, and Sweeper, give this *dān* to their Brahman *purohit;* these other castes give it to men related as *dhiyānā*. Thus, in the Brahman wedding prestations, the ritual elaboration of the giving of the bed seems to prefigure the *dān* that will follow. Similarly, a Sweeper *dahej* must always include a bed as well.

The *paṭṭā* (or *śayyā dān*) is followed by a ritual sequence called *dhān boāī,* "the sowing of the rice." A wooden stool is placed over the remains of the *vedi* made for the *pherā,* and it is covered with a thick white sheet. The groom stands on this stool, and the bride, again heavily veiled in two shawls, is carried into the courtyard by her mother's brother and seated at the groom's feet. The bride's brother and his wife enter the courtyard, and the ends of their clothing are tied together with a white cloth. The wife of the bride's family Barber is also present, holding a winnowing basket into which the bride's brother has placed *sawā rupīāh* (one and one-quarter rupees) and *sawā ser* of rice. (The one and one-quarter rupees are placed in the winnowing basket, it is said, so that it will not be empty at any time: *chāj khālī na rah jā*. Inauspiciousness, *nāśubh,* would remain with the brother and his wife if this were to happen.) As the brother and his wife circle the bride and groom in a counterclockwise direction, the Barber woman gives a handful of the rice from the *chāj* to the groom, who throws it over his right shoulder in such a way that it falls into the white cloth tied between the brother and his wife. This circling, and the dropping of the rice, is repeated seven times. Then the grain and the *sawā rupīāh* are given by the brother to the Barber's wife. She keeps them, except for a handful (*muṭṭhī*) of rice that she gives back to the groom. (In a Barber wedding, a *dhiyānī* holds the *chāj* and receives the prestations.) The groom throws half of this handful of rice back over his head,[28] and this is said to affect his own fields (*khet*); he accepts the handful and receives the inauspiciousness of his wife's father's fields. He has become a *dhiyānā* (*dhiyānā ban gayā*) in the course of the *pherā,* people say, and therefore the proper "recipient' of this handful of rice. (This is one of the very rare contexts in which Gujars refer to their daughter's or sister's husband as *dhiyānā.*) By his action, "hindrances" are removed from the fields of the wife's father, whose rice harvest will increase (*dhān baṛh jāyegā*). Then the groom throws the rest of the rice in his hand forward, and this is said to be for the positive increase of grain in the fields of the wife's father. As he throws the rice forward, the groom should say, "May my wife's father's rice become established in all the directions" (*mere sūsar kā dhān jame cārõ khūnṭ mẽ*). Villagers say afterwards that "the boy has sown our rice and gone away" (*laṛkā hamārā dhān bokar gayā*).[29]

The role of the groom as recipient, as *dhiyānā,* is foregrounded even more clearly in the *dhān boāī* of Brahman weddings. In Gujar weddings, one man and his wife circle the bride and groom, usually her brother and his wife or perhaps her father's younger brother and his wife. In the Brahman ritual, this is done by a number of people: father's brothers, father's father, and other men of the *kunbā,* and also by the bride's mother's brother. The circling may not, however, be performed by a *dhiyānī* or *dhiyānā.* This dichotomization of kinsmen, corresponding as it does to the categorization found in so many other prestation contexts, indicates very clearly the directionality of the transfer of inauspiciousness; a *dhiyānā* may never act as the donor of such prestations in relation to his own wife-givers, nor to their *dhiyāne.*

After the *dhān boāī,* the groom remains standing on the wooden stool as the bride's sisters' husbands (her *bahenoi*s) and father's sisters' husbands (her *phūphā*s) by turns stand next to him. The *bahenoi* and the *phūphā* are the "previous grooms" (*pahale damād*), and it is as such, according to villagers, that they join the groom on the wooden stool. The women of the bride's house (her mother, father's brothers' wives, brothers' wives) come by turns and, holding the brass tray from the *bān* (now containing the dough lamp with four wicks, some of the *bhalle,* one and one-quarter rupees, and some rice and turmeric), apply a *tilak* spot on the foreheads of all the "grooms" and place a rupee on the tray. Then the brother who performed the *dhān boāī* steps forward, again applies *tilak* to the men, and touches two five-*paisā* coins to the forehead of the groom. Other men of the bride's *kunbā* also do this and place the coins on the tray. The groom receives this money himself, for the auspiciousness of the donors. When he steps down from the wooden stool, he unties one of the strings with which the *manḍhā* had been tied.

The groom leaves the house then, and he goes with the men from his own village to the boundary (*sīmā*) of the bride's village for the departure ceremony (*bidā*). The bride's mother's brother meanwhile carries her into a water-buffalo cart (or in some cases, a car rented for the occasion) waiting just outside the door of her house and seats her there. All of the men of her *kunbā* escort her to the village boundary, and each gives her a rupee. She then joins the groom's party. As they are about to leave, the groom's father throws some coins over their heads, "for his own well-being" (*apne khair-khairāt ke māro*) as they begin the journey home. This is called *mūṭh mārnā* ("to cast a spell"), and it is referred to as *dān*. From throwing these coins "difficulties come out" (*kaṛāī utar jā*) from the groom's party. The coins may be picked up by *kamīns*. This *mūṭh mārnā* is done in all weddings except those of the Gujar caste. Gujars say that they do not do this because there is no special recipient (*khās pātra*) for this *dān,* and therefore the *kaṛāī* may not be appropriately transferred. The same reason is also given for the fact that Gujars are less likely to place *dān* items at a crossroads, for instance, than to give them to a Brahman, *kamīn,* or Dakaut. These alternate ways of giving *dān,* without a "special recipient," do not emphasize the ritual centrality of the donor, and this also may be a factor in Gujar reluctance to make such incomplete prestations.

When the bride arrives at her conjugal village after the journey, she is taken to the threshold of the groom's house, where she and the groom are met by the women of the household. The groom's mother, wearing two shawls over her head, holds the brass tray from the groom's *bān;* the dough lamp with four wicks is lit using mustard oil, and one and one-quarter rupees are placed on the tray. The rope from the household churn and two small pots, one containing mango leaves and the other water, are kept nearby. The bride and the groom are once again tied together with the *kānjol* cloth, and they stand together over the threshold. The churning rope (*netī*) and the two pots are held over the bride's head, and the groom's mother puts a *tilak* spot (from the *bān* tray) on the two pots, and on the groom's forehead. Then she waves the two pots over their heads seven times. This is said to be a *wārpher* or *chuwānā*. She does this, villagers say, so that any *kaṣṭ* or inauspiciousness from *bhūt-prets* that the new bride brings with her shall be removed from the pair and transferred into the water. Then, despite the assembled women's ritual protests to the groom that he should not allow his mother to drink this water (*apnī mā̃ ko yah pānī na pine de*), she drinks it and thus takes upon herself the *kaṣṭ,* for the well-being of her son and of the household. Then, all of the women present do *wārpher* with dishes of grain, and this grain is given to the Barber's wife. Finally, the groom's sister blocks the entrance of the bride into the house, and the groom pays her a small sum of money (called *neg*) so that she will allow them to cross the threshold.

This discussion of the marriage rituals and the prestations that are made in the course of them has focused on those aspects of the rites that involve the maintenance of well-being and auspiciousness through the giving of *dān*. I have tried to show that nearly all of the ritual actions of wedding rituals in Pahansu are indeed performed in order to remove inauspiciousness and transfer it to a recipient. The central transfer is the *kanyā dān* itself, through which the groom takes upon himself "faults" in order to promote the auspiciousness (*kalyāṇ*) of the bride's natal kin. Surrounding this central act, there are numerous other prestations that serve to pass on some of this inauspiciousness, to remove inauspiciousness from others who may share in the negative substances that may be loosened at this time (e.g., the mother's brother), or to move away the inauspiciousness that may hinder the *kanyā dān* itself, particularly the inauspiciousness of the ancestor deities and wandering ghosts.

Gujars certainly do not see the giving of these prestations as a matter of hierarchical status; they give such prestations, in the course of a wedding, to the groom, to the Barber, to the Sweeper, and to the Brahman, and they do not interpret the gifts in terms of the relative superiority or inferiority of these recipients. It is, rather, the obligation of the recipients, as *pātra,* to accept these prestations for the well-being and auspiciousness of the *jajmān,* the family of the bride. Hierarchical status is not the foregrounded aspect of the relationship here. We will return to this issue in the concluding sections of chapter 5, as well as in the final section of this chapter.

Death: Breaking "Connections" and the Giving of Gifts

Inauspiciousness flows, as we have seen, through the "connections of the body" (*śarīr kā sambandh*) between persons, and when these connections are transformed (at birth) or attenuated and created anew (at marriage), inauspiciousness flows over, as it were, and must be channeled and removed. Death, the time when "bodily connections" begin a process of gradual termination, is also a time of great inauspiciousness for the *kunbā,* and particularly the household, of the dead person. The rituals of death, and the subsequent rituals concerned with the existence of the deceased as a "ghost" (*bhūt*) or as an ancestral deity (*dev-pitar*) are, in Pahansu, concerned largely with removing and transferring this inauspiciousness.

Every death produces inauspiciousness in the form of *bādhā* ("hindrance") and *ḍar* ("fear"). The inauspiciousness of death is largely a result of the dead person's continued existence as a disembodied *pret,* and it is therefore often referred to as *pret-bādhā*. A number of prestations are made in the days following a death to remove *pret-bādhā*. "In living, in dying" (*jīne mẽ, marne mẽ*), villagers say, gifts must be given to Brahmans, to *kamīn*s, and to *dhiyānī* to accomplish this removal.

On the day of a death, after the body has been prepared for cremation, it is placed on a stretcher (*arthī*) made from the branches of a *nīm* tree and then taken to the threshold of the house. The women of the *kunbā* stand at the feet of the corpse and do *pair pūjā* (*pūjā* of the feet): they place some coins or a dish of grain at the threshold (*anāj caṛhānā*), and this is given as *pujāpā* to the family Barber to begin the process of removing inauspiciousness from the house itself. (In the Barber and Sweeper *jāti*s, this *pujāpā* prestation is given to a *dhiyānā* of the house.) Occasionally the women will also place a set of cloth over the body, and then this is given to the Barber as well. But nowadays, according to villagers, the Barber is often reluctant to accept the *joṛā* because of its extreme inauspiciousness; in the past, he would simply have been ordered to take it by his *jajmān*. But "the times have changed" (*zamānā badal gayā*), Gujars say, and now the *joṛā* is usually burnt with the body.

The *pair pūjā* is done, villagers say, "according to relationship" (*riśte ke anusār*): it is done only by women to whom the deceased is an older relative (*apne se baṛā nātā ho*), because certain kinds of inauspiciousness generally tend to flow "downward" to one's juniors. At the death of a younger person, there would not be as great a danger of inauspiciousness to the older person, and so the prestation is not made.

After the *pair pūjā,* the body on the stretcher is carried out of the house on the shoulders of four men and taken to another "threshold," the boundary (*sīmā*) of the village. The family Barber brings a broken earthen vessel in which he has prepared four balls of dough (*cūn kā piṇḍ*). Just outside the boundary of the village habitation site, the stretcher is placed on the ground. (Inside the house or the village, the stretcher must never rest directly on the ground. Sheaves of wheat, *gehū kī pūlī*, are placed under it so that the *nāśubh* of the body will not be transferred to the ground on which it rests; these stalks are afterwards given to the Barber of the dead man's family, as are his clothes.) The Barber places the balls of dough at the four corners of the stretcher, and the four men put their feet on the earthen vessel and break it. The four balls of dough are simply left outside the boundary of the village, where, villagers say, animals will find them and eat them. The breaking of the earthen vessel in which the *piṇḍ* has been prepared has precisely the same significance as the breaking of the *bān* dishes by the mother's brother in the course of the wedding rites: it effects the transferral of inauspiciousness to the proper recipient, here simply the space outside the village and the animals who may eat the *piṇḍ*. (The same procedure is repeated on the tenth day after death, though of course in the absence of the corpse.)

In death, as in birth, particular astrological circumstances may exacerbate the inauspiciousness that afflicts certain kinsmen. It is productive of extreme inauspiciousness for the family of the dead man if the cremation (*phūknā* or *dāh karnā*) is performed during a *pancak* period, the five solar days (*vār*) during which the moon is seen to pass through five particular asterisms.

In a *pancak* period, then, five small figures in the shape of men are fashioned from stalks of grass. These are positioned on the corpse: one on the head, one at each of the hips, one at the genitals, and one at the feet. These figures, called *putlā* ("body"), represent the five asterisms, and by placing them in contact with the corpse, the faults engendered by the *nakṣatra*s are turned back upon them from the dead man. When the cremation fire is lit, offerings (*āhuti*) of clarified butter are put in the fire for each of the five *nakṣatra*s. Though it would normally be avoided, if a cremation must be performed in such a period, Buddhu Pandit told me, a complex ritual sequence similar to the *mūl śānti* ritual may be performed on the thirteenth day after the death. After a *havan,* the men of the *kunbā,* as *jajmān*s, are sprinkled with water from five pots containing substances similar to those used in the *mūl śānti* "bath of disjoining." In order to also rid the house and the village space of *pancak doṣ,* ten earthen lamps are filled with mustard oil and lit. A few black lentils are placed in the lamps through the performance of *dhok mārnā,* and in this way the lamps absorb the *doṣ* from the "ten directions." Then a dough lamp with four wicks is also filled with mustard oil and lit, and a few more black lentils are dropped in it as *kṣetrapāl dān* ("*dān* to protect the site"). A Sanskrit *mantra* will be recited at this point by the Brahman priest, a *mantra* in which the lamp is entreated to "eat the offering for the protection of the directions" (*diśo rakṣat bali bhakṣat*) in order that the family of the dead man may enjoy long life. The dough lamp, having absorbed the *pancak doṣ* that has afflicted the house and village, is then taken out of the house and submerged in the village pond. Finally *gau dān,* "the gift of a cow," usually in the form of a sum of money, is given to a Dakaut, who is referred to in the *mantra*s as a "protecting Brahman" (*śarmanne brahman*).

We now return to the ritual sequences performed at any death, regardless of astrological circumstances. On the third day after the burning of the body (the day is called *tījā,* "the third"), the four men who carried the body out of the village (the *kāndhīyā,* from the word for shoulder) and the man who set the fire to the cremation pyre (usually the eldest son of the dead man) go again to the cremation ground, accompanied by the family Barber. They take with them four small earthen saucers, an earthen lamp filled with mustard oil, milk, honey, some flour, white cotton string, and four small pieces of wood. The Barber first puts the pieces of wood in the four corners of the space where the body was burnt, and the string is wound around this rectangle. Milk and honey are placed in the saucers and these are positioned inside the square at the four cardinal directions. The oil lamp is also put inside the space, at the southern side, and the flour is sprinkled inside the space. The tying of the thread around this space represents a tying down or "binding" (*bandhan*) of the wandering *pret*s of the locality, so that they will accept the things that have been offered (*caṛhānā*) there. These things, the milk, the honey, and the flour, are simply left in the cremation ground as the *caṛhāpā* of the *pret*s. The bounded space itself becomes the *pātra* for the inauspiciousness.

The bones of the corpse are then collected (*phūl cūgnā,* "gathering flowers") and wrapped in a red cloth. People of Pahansu often make a trip to Haridwar to place these "flowers" in the Ganges River. The ashes are also gathered up and deposited in a river or some other flowing water.

After the *phūl cūgnā,* the Barber and the five men return to the house of the dead man. The Barber spreads cow-dung paste in a square over the spot where the body had lain while it was still in the house. It is around this space that women gather for thirteen days for the ritualized wailing with covered heads that is called *pallā lenā*. The Barber gives each of the *kāndhīyā* men an iron nail, and as they hold these, he puts some yogurt and unrefined sugar in each corner of the square. Then the *kāndhīyā* men each pound a nail into the floor through the piles of yogurt and sugar. The yogurt and the sugar are in this way offered to the disembodied *pret* who may still be lingering in the house despite the "dropping of the pebble" (*kākarī ḍālnā*) by the men of the *kunbā* at the cremation, an action that is performed so that "connection won't remain" (*sambandh na rahe*) with the dead man. The offerings are made to remove the inauspiciousness of the *pret,* so that "there won't be any bad effects of the *pret*" (*pret kā burā asar nahī̃ hogā*) on the living or in the house. The iron nails driven into the offerings absorb the *pret-bādhā*, in the same way, villagers say, that the iron rings that mothers sometimes place in their children's pockets or around their necks absorb *nazar* ("evil gaze") and other inauspiciousness that might afflict the child.

These *tījā* actions are called *kārnī karwānā,* and they may be much more elaborate in the case of the death of a young person who has no offspring (*aulād*), one who has many more lingering attachments and unfulfilled desires and with whom it is more difficult to break the "connection." In these *tījā* "prestations," there is no human *pātra;* the spaces themselves, or the iron nails, replace a human relationship as the appropriate channel or recipient.

On the thirteenth day after the death (the *terāhmī*), however, further prestations are made to remove the inauspiciousness of death and these are given to particular human recipients. After the twelfth day, the deceased no longer exists as a *pret,* but has at least begun the transformation into an ancestral deity, and it is perhaps this fact that accounts for the difference: he is no longer "disembodied," and so it is necessary that a "body" assimilate the inauspiciousness.

Early in the morning of the thirteenth day, the Brahman *purohit* of the dead man's family arrives at the house and prepares a *vedi* for a fire sacrifice. Wife-givers to the dead man's family—men of his wife's natal *kunbā* as well as the dead man's mother's brother—bring a full set of cloth, a staff, five brass pots, and a pair of shoes, and place these on a basket of grain.[30] A brass tray of uncooked food (*sīdhā khānā*), including rice, flour, lentils, sugar, salt, and chili is also brought by the men. The food on the tray is actually only a very small part of the total quantity of these foods that is given. There should be, in total, thirteen measures (e.g., thirteen *ser*) of each food, one for each of the days that the dead man has existed as a *pret*. That this is not given simply to sustain the *pret* and nourish him (as has sometimes been suggested) is evidenced by the fact that it is given after the thirteen-day period has come to an end. The connection lies elsewhere: the gifts of food are not given to sustain and nourish the *pret* body, but to remove the inauspiciousness generated by the *pret* during those thirteen days.

These food prestations are called *kaṛvā cūn,* "the bitter flour." The same set of items, except for the *kaṛvā cūn,* is also collected by the dead man's own *kunbā,* and these are also placed near the *vedi*. The man from the dead man's *kunbā* who lit the funeral pyre, and a man from his wife's natal village, sit at the *vedi* facing east, and the *purohit* of the dead man's family sits facing north. The *purohit* then conducts a preliminary worship of the deities represented in the *vedi.*

The foodstuffs and other articles that have been brought to the *vedi* are then given as *dān*. The *purohit* ties a protective thread on the wrists of the donors, gives them rice, turmeric, water, and a twenty-five *paisā* coin to hold in their right hands, and he then leads them in the recitation of the *dān sankalp* as they touch the items that are to be given. The men take a bit of the *sīdhā khānā* from the brass tray and place it in a pile of smoldering embers (*angārī*) that has been brought to the room for this purpose. This action offers the food to the dead man. Again they take some rice and water in their hands and sprinkle it around the *dān* items. This circling of the water is called *mīnasnā,* and the *dān* items may then be referred to as *mīnsāī* or *pujāpā*. (Alternatively, the men may take rice, water, and *sawā rūpiāh* in their hands, bring these into contact with the *dān* items, and then put the rice and the money near the *angārī*.)

All of the *dān* items, and the coins used in the *sankalp* and the *mīnasnā,* are then given to the family Brahman *purohit* of the dead man, who may sometimes indicate that he accepts them with great reluctance.[31]

In the case of Brahman and Sweeper deaths, the same prestations, also referred to as *martak* (from the Hindi word for death)—cloth, brass vessels, the *karvā cūn*—are given to the *dhiyāne* of the dead man. In the case of a married woman, the donors are her own brothers and the men of her husband's house, and the recipients are her husband's sister's husband and father's sister's husband, their *dhiyāne*. This is the same pattern described by Vatuk (1975) for the Gaur Brahmans of Meerut District and by Dumont (1966) for the Sarjupari Brahmans of eastern Uttar Pradesh. Both Dumont and Vatuk analyze these prestations as "kinship" gifts and fail to see, perhaps because they worked primarily among Brahmans, that the gifts are part of a much wider universe of action and meaning. Further, both Vatuk and Dumont (more particularly the latter) argue that the gifts are given to wife-taking affines because of their higher status, and because they are "fit to be worshipped" (Dumont 1966, 94). In support of this argument, Dumont cites the usage of the term *pūj,* which he translates as "worshipful."

Now we have already noted several instances of the occurrence of this term in Pahansu discourse. At the *bār dwārī* when the groom enters the house of the bride for the first time, the Brahman or *dhiyānā* who performs the *sevel* and thus takes upon himself the inauspiciousness that the groom may bring with him is referred to as *pūj;* he does it, people say, because he is "our *pūj*" (*hamārā pūj*). And in a Sweeper wedding, the *dhiyānī* who receives the *phalsā* from the *bhāt* (given "downward" in other castes to a Sweeper) does so precisely because, Pahansu Sweepers told me, she is the *pūj* of the family. The other contexts in which the term appears in ordinary talk in the village also seem to indicate that the primary implication of the term is that the person who is *pūj* has an obligation to accept *pujāpā*. I heard the term *pūj* most frequently in Pahansu in discussions of the acceptance of these very inauspicious death prestations. When, for instance, I asked Gujar villagers why they give the *martak pujāpā* to their Brahman *purohit,* while Brahmans give it to *dhiyāne,* they generally replied in much the same way as Bugli, an old Gujar woman: "There is terror (*ḍar*) in *martak;* why should we give it to our *bahenoi* or *phūphā* when we can give it to our Brahman? Our *dhiyāne* are not our *pūj*, Brahmans are our *pūj*." And so I asked Brahmans why they give *martak* to their *dhiyāne,* and they answered: "Who else would take it? That is why they are our *pūj*." Indeed, no one else may be willing to accept such prestations, but the Brahman *purohit* and the Brahman's *dhiyāne* are obligated to take them. In all cases, then, the usage of this term in Pahansu indexes and foregrounds that aspect of the affinal or intercaste relationship concerned with this obligation. Hierarchy is simply not the salient issue when we find Sweepers and Brahmans using the term in reference to death prestations, and when Gujars say emphatically that the husbands of their *dhiyānī* are not their *pūj* because they do not give inauspicious gifts to them (though a Gujar's *dhiyānī* may in some contexts be called *pūj* as she receives *dān*). The use of the term *pūj* is a function of the configurations of kinsmen and castes involved in the giving and receiving of *dān* and *caṛhāpā*, not of the hierarchical relation of one caste to another.

Sweeper informants were perhaps the most explicit as to the meaning of the *martak* prestations that they give to their *dhiyāne*. They often commented to me that while Gujars give *pāp* to Brahmans, they themselves, through *pun-dān*—*dān* given to establish "merit" (*pun*) through the removal of *pāp*—give the *pāp* engendered by death to their *dhiyāne:* "Giving *dān* we take 'evil' from ourselves and give it to *dhiyāne*" (*dān karke apnī taraf se dhiyāne ko pāp dete haĩ*).

Particularly important for my argument concerning the usage of the term *pūj* and the contextual separability of the hierarchic paradigm and the paradigm of the transferral of inauspiciousness through gifts to wife-taking affines is evidence that the terminology and gift-giving patterns described above appear even when the "hypergamous ethos" is inverted. Dumont (1964) discusses this question when he reviews Fürer-Haimendorf's data (1959) on Hindu Chetri marriages in Nepal, in which girls of higher status (*jharrā*) may marry men of lower (non-*jharrā*) status. "Even after the wedding," writes Fürer-Haimendorf, "they give ritual gifts (*dakṣiṇā*) of the type given to Brahmans for the sake of acquiring merit." Similarly, the *jharrā* bride is still *pūj* to her natal family even though, according to Fürer-Haimendorf, "she experiences a drop in status in terms of the purity-pollution scale which affects commensality." Dumont, presumably in order to preserve his view of the pervasiveness of the ideology of hierarchy in all contexts of the social life of Hindu South Asia, tries to minimize the importance of the husband of lower status, arguing that the marriage should not in fact be seen as "hypogamous" since the non-*jharrā* men are sometimes regarded as being formerly *jharrā*. He finds it necessary to argue in this way because, according to him, "it clearly does not make sense to make gifts to inferior people . . . as one does to Brahmans."

Dumont's observation is clearly problematic for Pahansu in light of the data on the permutations in the prestation patterns, where Brahmans, Sweepers, and Barbers alike receive such prestations, and where there are such clearly delineated contextual equivalences drawn between wife-takers as *dhiyāne* and Brahmans, including the very low-ranking Dakauts. My suggestion here is that an understanding of the manner in which the various aspects of relationships—exemplified in gift-giving and terminological patterns—are intertwined in various historical and geographical circumstances, within particular castes and in specific contexts of social action, may help us to explicate local systems of kinship and marriage, as well as the overarching meanings in terms of which variations are ordered and assume significance.

By the analysis I am proposing, then, the death prestations are an instance of the same sequential structure we have observed in so many other contexts: wife-givers make prestations to wife-receivers, as *dhiyānī* and *dhiyānā,* who in turn give them on to their Brahman *purohit,* to a Dakaut, to certain *kamīn*s, or to their own *dhiyānī* or *dhiyāne.* Indeed, informants themselves often observe the similarities among these types of gifts. They comment, for instance, that *bhāt* comes from a woman's *pīhar,* her natal village, at the marriage of her children, and at death the *kaṛvā cūn* is sent from the same place, for the same reasons.

As I pointed out in the discussion of the Brahman *paṭṭā,* there are even more pointed correspondences between the gifts given by the mother's brother at marriage and those that are given after a death. For Brahmans, first of all, both the *bhāt* and the *terāhmī* prestations include a bed. At the *paṭṭā,* it will be remembered, the mother and the father of the bride circle the bed (given by the mother's brother in the *bhāt*) on which the bride and groom are seated. In some villages in Uttar Pradesh, though not in Pahansu, a separate prestation called *śayyā dān,* the *dān* of a bed, is made after a Brahman death, just as in the concluding actions of the wedding rituals. For the death *śayyā dān,* a Mahabrahman, Dakaut, or other low-ranking "Brahman" caste that specializes in the acceptance of *dān* is seated on the bed and the *jajmān* (the son of the dead man) walks around the bed seven times.[32] As he does so, he recites a *mantra* pronouncing:

> *yāni kāni ca pāpāni janamāntarkṛtāni ca*
> *tāni tāni praṇaśyati pradakṣiṇā pade pade*
>
> Any evils that are produced between births,
> those and only those are removed at every step of the circumambulation.

After this circumambulation, the bed is given as *dān* to the Mahabrahman or to the Dakaut, transferring the *pāp* described in the *mantra* to him. The major difference between this ritual circling of the bed after death and that performed at a Brahman *paṭṭā,* aside from the fact that the recipients are different, is that in the latter case the foot of the bed points toward the north, while in the death ritual it points toward the south, the direction associated with death and the *pret*s.

The *śayyā dān* is a very explicit transferral of inauspiciousness, and it is similar to the *martak* given in Pahansu at the thirteenth-day rituals to the *purohit* or, in the case of a Brahman death to *dhiyāne. Padõ kā dān,* (lit., "*dān* of the feet"), as this *martak* is sometimes called, should also include a bed. *Padõ kā dān* is a phrase sometimes used to refer to any *dān* consisting of brass pots, sets of cloth, a bed, shoes, and foodstuffs. As we shall see, it is also given to one's Brahman *purohit* (or *dhiyānā*) at the establishment (*sthāpanā*) of a shrine in the fields for an "ancestor" who, because he died without offspring, is causing difficulties for a family. The *dān* is given to remove this "distress" (*sankaṭ*) from the family. *Padõ kā dān* is also the prescribed prestation for the *udāpan* (the concluding *dān*) of certain *vrat*s.

In all of these cases of the giving of the *padõ kā dān,* it is not the hierarchical position of the recipient vis-à-vis the donor that is the foregrounded aspect of the relationship; nor are the gifts seen as "honoring" the recipient in any way. Rather, the primary concern is that the prestations be given to an appropriate *pātra,* and these *pātra* for very similar prestations are hierarchically extremely heterogeneous.

In Pahansu, on the afternoon of the thirteenth day, after the *martak* prestations have been made, the men of the *kunbā* of the dead man and the other "relatives" (*riśtedār,* both wife-givers and wife-receivers) assemble in the men's sitting place for the turban-tying (*pagṛī bāndhnā*) ceremony for the eldest son of the dead man. The *purohit* of the family brings a brass tray containing rice, turmeric, a red protective thread, and a small stone representing the god Ganeṣa. A portion of the rice is set aside for a *tilak,* and the rest of it is separated into nine piles in the tray to represent the nine planets. The *purohit* first conducts a brief worship of these deities and then places a *tilak* on the son's forehead and the thread on his wrist "for protection" (*rakṣā ke lie*). The son's mother's brother then steps forward with a turban and a sum of money, usually eleven rupees, and places them on the tray. The son then puts on the turban and takes the money from the tray. The mother's brother then goes immediately to the house where his sister, the widow, waits for him at the threshold, just as she had earlier waited for him at the marriages of her children. He takes with him several sets of cloth that he has brought from his own village (the woman's *pīhar*) and he places them on her head, again, just as he had done at the *bhāt*. These sets of cloth are called *raṇḍāpe ke kapṛe* ("the cloth of widowhood"). *Raṇḍāpe ke kapṛe* may also be sent from the natal villages of her son's wives (such villages are referred to as the widow's *samdhānā*s), but never from the conjugal villages of her daughters. That is, *raṇḍāpe ke kapṛe* may only be sent to the houses of one's *dhiyānī.* This cloth must be worn by the widow; its *nāśubh* is so great that no one else may wear it. And the widow herself may not simply put the cloth away or dispose of it; she must wear it so that inauspiciousness will not attach itself (*nāśubh na lag jā*) to her brother.

Several months after the *terāhmī* the widow may stop wearing the clothes. Their inauspicious qualities prevent their being kept in the house, however, and so they must be given onward. "Taking off the clothes of widowhood" (*raṇḍāpe ke kapṛe utārnā*) may be done in one of two ways. If a woman's family can afford it, they may send her to Haridwār, where she will tie a ten-*paisā* coin in the *pallā* of the *oṛhnā* (the shawl) that came with the "cloth of widowhood" and give the coin and the cloth as *dān* to a Sweeper of that place. Or the cloth may simply be taken to a river bank (usually the Yamuna) and disposed of there. The similarities between the giving of the *raṇḍāpe ke kapṛe* and the *bhāt,* and the way in which both of these must be "given onward," are obvious. Each of these prestations is, as we have seen, given by the mother's brother for his own "well-being achieved through gift-giving," so that "inauspiciousness will not be attached" to him at the marriages of a sister's children or at the death of her husband.

While the widow is receiving this cloth on the thirteenth day after the death of her husband, women of the *kunbā* and women who as *riśtedār* have come from other villages for the *terāhmī* assemble in the courtyard of the house. The family Barber's wife brings a brass vessel filled with water and places it in the middle of the courtyard. One by one the women wash their hands in this water and place a five-*paisā* coin in the vessel. When all of the women have finished, the Barber's wife takes all of this money, which is called "the coins of the hand-washing" (*hāth dhone ke paise*). Villagers were quite explicit about the significance of the hand-washing and the giving of the coins. They said that this is not done to remove death impurity (*pātak*); the coins that are given are like the "grain of the *wārpher*" (*wārpher kā anāj*) given to the Barber at the wedding, in that the prestation removes inauspicious hindrances from the donor and transfers them to the recipient.

In the month following the death, on the lunar day (*tithi*) on which the death occurred, *karvā cūn* (this time the "bitter flour" is in the form of wheat flour mixed with unrefined sugar) is again sent to the house of the dead man by his mother's brother or wife's brother. The Barber then distributes this "bitter flour" to all of the houses of the dead man's *kunbā,* but they do not consume it because of its great inauspiciousness; instead, they give it to their own Barber, who may in turn, instead of eating it himself, feed it to a cow. This may be repeated on the lunar day of death for twelve months.

One year after the death, according to lunar calculations, *dān* is once again given to the family Brahman *purohit*. The ritual sequence in which this is done is called *barsī* or *barsoḍhī* (from the word for "year") or *joṛ* ("the joining"). The latter term indicates that it is at this time that the dead man is said to join the company of the *dev-pitar*, and it is only after this that the ancestor rites of *kanāgat* may be performed for him. The *barsī* ritual is essentially the same as the morning rites of the *terāhmī* day, and *padõ kā dān* consisting of a bed, five brass pots, a pair of shoes and *sīdhā khānā* (raw foodstuffs) is again given to the family Brahman (or to a *dhiyānā* in the Brahman and Sweeper castes), for the well-being of the mother's brother and the wife's brother, and for that of the *kunbā* of the dead man.

After the dead man has become a *dev-pitar,* the ritual actions of *kanāgat* may be directed to him. During the dark half of the month of Asauj, offerings are made to the *dev-pitar*s up to the third generation, on the lunar day on which the death of the particular ancestor occurred. The fortnight is a time of extreme fluidity of inauspiciousness and danger. It is also characteristic of this time that transferrals of many kinds occur willy-nilly, and a number of precautions are taken to ensure that bodily substances and inauspiciousness are transferred only in appropriate ways. For example, there is a strictly adhered to prohibition against women coming and going between their *pīhar*s and their *sasurāl*s. "Coming and going is stopped," women say, *ānā-jānā bandh hai,* lest inauspiciousness be transferred to the ancestors or others. Wives of a house also should not wash their hair during the fortnight of *kanāgat* because "sin" and "evil" might in that way be transferred to the *dev-pitar*s and remain with them, instead of being given on as *pujāpā.*

During *kanāgat,* on the night before the lunar day of death of a particular *dev-pitar,* a wife of the house (never a daughter) spreads a square of thin white mud just outside the threshold of the house. Three small piles of rice are placed inside the square, and the wife does a *dhok mārnā* with these grains. The grains of rice are simply left outside the door, beyond the threshold. The next morning, several food items are prepared: rice, lentils, breads, and a rice pudding (*khīr*). Portions of these foods and one and one-quarter rupees are placed on a brass tray, and some burning embers and a pot of water are placed in the courtyard. After keeping a fast, a male descendant of the dead man or woman (a woman's *kanāgat* is done only at her conjugal village) takes a handful of the water and sprinkles it in a counterclockwise movement around the tray of food. This circling is called *mīnasnā.* As he does this, he says a Hindi *mantra* of the following sort:

aum pācim vālā parbābā
jis lok mẽ ho
yah ann padārth prāpt ho.

Aum. Great-grandfather of the fifth lunar day,
whatever world you are in,
may you receive these food substances.

Then he holds a few grains of uncooked rice in his right hand and with the left pours out the rest of the water in the pot over the right. The coins and the food from this tray are then given as *pujāpā* (or *mīnsāī*) to the Brahman *purohit* or to one's *dhiyānī*. Bugli, an old Gujar woman, the mother of Mangal Singh and Sukhbir, said this of the *mīnsāī:*

> *mīnsāī laṛkõ ko na de, na bahū. unkā pharmāyā nahī̃ hai. laṛkā apne ghar kā hai, laṛkī dūsre ghar jayegī, begānī ho jayegī. Laṛkī apnī pūj māne. Laṛkā kāṛh de phīr laṛkī ko denī cahiye. jo dhiyānī hai wah khā sake. laṛkõ ka pharmāyā nahī̃ hai.*
>
> *Mīnsāī* is not given to one's son, nor to the *bahū*. It is not their obligation to take it. The son is of one's own house, and the daughter goes to another house and becomes "other." Daughters are accepted as one's *pūj*. The son "takes out" [the *mīnsāī*] and should then give it to the daughter. Whoever is *dhiyānī* can eat it. It is not the obligation of sons.

The structure of Bugli's statement is, I think, very important for understanding the meaning of the term *pūj* and its relation to the *kanāgat* prestations. The giving of the *pujāpā*, the *mīnsāī*, is here very explicitly predicated on the fact that the daughters, one's married *dhiyānī*, are "other." Once more, what is at issue here as a condition of their appropriateness as *pātra* and for the usage of the term *pūj* is not the possible hierarchical aspect of the relationship, but the "otherness" of the married daughter. *Dān*, like the *kaṣṭ* and inauspiciousness that it transfers, must be "moved away" if the rituals and prestations are to be efficacious. A Brahman woman in Pahansu put this another way:

> *byāhī huī ko pūj ke de sakte haĩ ve dhiyānī haĩ. Apnī laṛkī ko nahī̃ dete. acche nahī̃ mānte. agar pujāpā apne ghar mẽ dete haĩ to kyā phāyadā hai?*
>
> We can give *pūj ke* [i.e., *pujāpā* prestations] to the married ones [the daughters] but not to our own [unmarried] girls. That wouldn't be good. If we give *pujāpā* in our own house, then what is the benefit?

The distinction between "the other" as daughter and "one's own" as son in Bugli's statement above is replicated here, at another level, in the definition of one's married daughters as "other" and one's unmarried daughters as "one's own girls." The emphasis in such contexts upon the "otherness" and the "going away" of the married daughter corresponds, it would seem, to the common instruction in Hindi ritual manuals to "give the *dān* [to a Brahman or other recipient] and have him depart" (*dān dekar bidā kare*). Indeed the same word, *bidā*, is used for the bride's departure from her *pīhar* the day after her wedding. The very structure of the rituals involving *dān* and *pujāpā* and their efficaciousness depends upon the transferral of inauspiciousness in this way, beyond one's house and *kunbā* and village. This structure is exhibited in the remarks that Bugli and the Brahman woman made about the *kanāgat mīnsāī.*

On *amāvas,* then, the new-moon day and the last day of *kanāgat,* the same food items are prepared and laid out on sixteen leaf plates. *Mīnasnā* is performed and a bit of the food from each plate is put on some embers, and the remainder is put on the roof of the house for crows. The food is given as the *pujāpā* of the "forgotten scattered ancestors" (*bhūle bisare pitri*) for whom an individual *kanāgat* is no longer performed. Those ancestors who have been "scattered" and with whom the household has only a tenuous "connection" (*sambandh*) require only a very "scattered" and unconnected *pātra.*

There is one further type of prestation that may be made to remove the inauspiciousness of a *bhūt* or a *dev-pitar.* It concerns those whose deaths have occurred "out of time" (*akāl mṛityu*), those who, because they were not "satisfied" (*santuṣṭi*) and had no offspring, are unable to "take another birth" (*dūsrī janam nahī̃ le sakte*). Their continued presence in the house may be a source of "afflictions" (*kaṣṭ*) and "trouble" (*pareśānī*) to those living there; they "wander and turn" (*ghūmnā-phīrnā*) and bring inauspiciousness with them.

In Sikandarpur, a neighboring village (*guwāṇḍ*) of Pahansu, such a death had occurred, and some time later the family began to suffer from various "troubles." At first they did not know the source of their difficulties, but then, they said, the "one who had died" began to speak from the mouth of a daughter, and they realized that a *sthān* ("place") had to be constructed for him in the fields outside the village.

The shrine was constructed for "the one whose age was not complete" (*jiskī āyu pūrī nahī̃ huī*), but the wandering, turning ghost still had to be established in it. The Sikandarpur family asked Buddhu Pandit and Raghu to perform the necessary ritual, and it was at this point that I came to know of the situation. Buddhu and Raghu went to Sikandarpur for eleven days to do the *gayatri jap,* the recitation of the *gayatri mantra* that is preliminary to establishing the ghost in his "place." On the final day, I went to Sikandarpur with Buddhu and Raghu to observe the "establishing."

The shrine, a simple white domed structure a few feet in height, had been built next to another such shrine, not far from the Sikandarpur Bhūmiyā shrine. Beneath this "place" a snake made from silver had been buried because, I was told, the *ātma* ("soul," "spirit") of one who suffers a death "out of time" often "assumes the form of a snake" (*sāmp kā rūp dhāraṇ karnā*).

Before this shrine, Raghu began to cook the lentil soup, rice, and rice pudding that would be offered there, while Buddhu continued the recitation of the *mantra.* Buddhu then made the preparations for a fire sacrifice. Meanwhile the women of the house arrived, bringing with them the sets of cloth, shoes, walking stick, brass vessels, and other items that were to be offered. They did the "bathing" (*nahānā*) of the shrine with milk and water, applied a *tilak* of rice and turmeric, and then did *nackār* to the side of the shrine, touching their *pallā*s to it. They put the sets of cloth and the brass vessels on top of the shrine, and the shoes and walking stick in back of it. All the while, they entreated the ghost in this way: "Ancestor god, accept your place" (*pitri devata apnā sthān grahaṇ karo*). The women of the house then retreated to the shade of the nine-foot sugarcane growing nearby, while the men of the family, led by Buddhu Pandit, performed a *havan* in front of the shrine. At the conclusion of the *havan,* Buddhu Pandit received *sawā sau rūpiāh* (Rs. 125) as the *dakṣiṇā* payment for the *mantra* recitation, and the *pujāpā*—the items that were offered at the shrine—were given as *dān* to the Brahman *purohit* of the family. It was pointed out to me that these items were the same as those given in the *martak* prestation. They were given at the shrine to remove the *kaṣṭ* that had been engendered by the presence of the wandering ghost.

There are very many such shrines in the fields around Pahansu, and the *dev-pitar*s that are enshrined there receive offerings whenever they have afflicted someone of their own *kunbā,* and during *kanāgat.*

Death rituals, like those of marriage, may have a number of culturally postulated meanings and functions. The foregoing discussion focuses on one of the most important aspects of the death rituals: the transfer of inauspiciousness from the wife-givers and the *kunbā* of the deceased to a Barber, a Brahman *purohit,* or the *dhiyānī* and *dhiyāne* of the deceased, or, in the early stages of the rituals, to a particular space. It is clear, for example, that the numerous prestations are not given to remove the "impurity" of death (*pātak*). *Pātak,* as we noted in chapter 2, is not "transferred" or "removed". It simply "ends" (*khatam honā*) or "dissipates" (*likaṛnā*) after a certain period of time or after bathing; prestations are not required in this process. Second, as we have noted here, many of the death prestations have their exact counterparts in the rituals of marriage, which do not involve any sort of "impurity." And finally, the "terror" of accepting *martak* is unconnected with *pātak* since the period of death impurity ends before the giving of *martak,* the subsequent monthly *kaṛvā cūn* prestations, and the *dān* at *barsī.* For these reasons, the Brahman's reluctance to accept these prestations, and the statements of Gujars that they would not want to give such things to their sisters' husbands and fathers' sisters' husbands cannot be explained by an association with death impurity. Nor would such an explanation account for the same hesitation about accepting other kinds of *dān* and *caṛhāpā.*

The distinction between the two functions of *caṛhāpā* discussed in chapter 3—the transfer of inauspiciousness back to its source and then onward to a *pātra,* and the appropriation by the deity or other being of the offerings—is also pertinent to our understanding of the death rituals. The giving of *dān* to the appropriate *pātra* transfers the inauspiciousness of death and it also ensures that the *pret* or the *dev-pitar* accepts the items and foodstuffs that are given (*usko prāpt ho jā*). The first function of the giving has hitherto been overlooked in the analysis of Hindu death rituals, and the second has been seen as providing the only underlying logic of the gift-giving. Thus, for example, Dumont (1966) writes that the wife-takers simply "impersonate" the dead man and thus facilitate his appropriation of the offerings. In that analysis, there is not a three-term structure of the type outlined in chapter 3 and illustrated again in figure 13, but simply a single transfer from donor to dead man (that is, to wife-takers). Dumont nowhere explains why it should be that a man of a wife-taking category is called upon to impersonate a man of his wife's natal village. It is precisely because the *dān* must be "given onward" (*āge denā*), that is, outside of one's own *kunbā* and village, that a *dhiyānā* is obligated to accept these prestations, just as he accepts inauspiciousness when he receives the gift of a virgin. In my analysis, the first function of *caṛhāpā* is simply not reducible to the second.

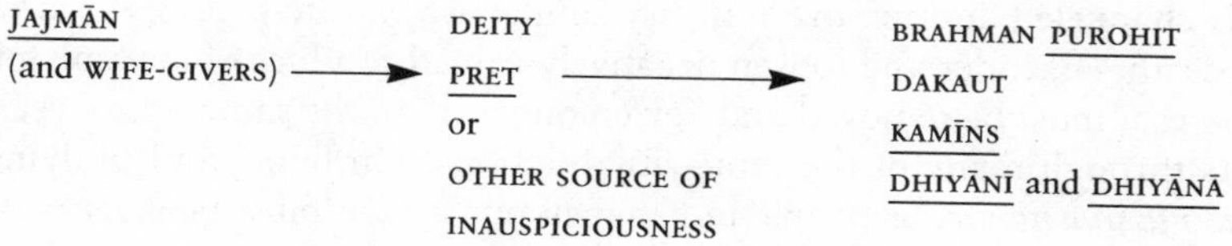

Fig. 13. The transferral of inauspiciousness

Similar problems are also encountered in discussions of death rituals in classical Hindu texts. In Knipe's account (1977), the pots, the bed, the clothes, and so forth, are given to a Mahāpātra ("great receptacle") Brahman, a very low-ranking Brahman caste similar to the Dakauts who live in the villages around Pahansu. Knipe characterizes the Brahman's role simply as a "silent watchful stand-in for the *preta*" and interprets his low status in light of his association with the impurity of death, even though, by Knipe's own account, the Brahman receives the gifts after the period of death defilement has come to an end. Knipe sees the gifts themselves simply as a way of maintaining the deceased in his afterlife and of satisfying his every need: the second function of *caṛhāpā* as it is given in Pahansu. In Knipe's account, as in that of Inden and Nicholas (1977), the death rituals merely provide for the creation and sustenance of the body of the *pret*. While this is no doubt an important aspect of some death rituals, in Pahansu this theme is remarkably inconspicuous, particularly because the rituals of the *piṇḍa dān* are not performed there, at least not by Gujars. In Pahansu, the most significant aspect of the death rituals and the prestations is the transferral of the inauspiciousness engendered and made to flow by the "breaking of the connection," through the "giving onward" of the offerings to the appropriate *pātra*. Rather than being simply identified with the *pret,* this *pātra,* the recipient, is a distinct entity in the structure of the ritual action.

This analysis of death rituals in Pahansu bears on another recent attempt to understand the conceptual structures that underlie Hindu ritual action. Das (1977) also argues that the opposition of the pure and the impure is not an encompassing dichotomy in Hinduism. Through an examination of death rituals as they are described in the Sanskrit *gṛihya sūtrā*s (compendia of household rituals), she maintains that an equally important and fundamental opposition is that between life and death. In her analysis, rituals concerned with the passage of time, rites of initiation, rites of pregnancy, and rites of marriage are opposed to death rituals, rites to ghosts and ancestors, and rites to serpents. The former, according to Das, are rituals concerned with life and auspiciousness, and the latter are rites associated with death and inauspiciousness.[33] Yet as I have attempted to demonstrate, inauspiciousness is generated in all of these contexts, and it is channeled and removed in very similar ways. Life processes, as well as death, engender and loosen negatively valued residues of inauspiciousness that must be removed and "given onward" to the same sets of recipients through many of the same ritual actions. "In living and in dying," *jīne mẽ marne mẽ,* as people in Pahansu put it, *dān* must be given.

Prestations at the Harvests and the *Barkat* of the Grain

The agricultural year is divided into two six-month periods (*chamāī*), roughly the time between the two major harvests. The most important agricultural rituals occur at the harvests: *sāvanī* is the rice harvest that generally occurs in the month of Kārttik, and *sāṛhī* is the wheat harvest in the month of Baisākh. From each of these harvests, the cultivator, as *jajmān,* makes a number of prestations to ensure the increase and auspiciousness of the grain.

The Brahman's portion of the harvest in what has been considered as the *jajmānī* "system" of distributions is distinguished from that of other castes by being called *sāvṛī* ("of the pile"). The shares of the harvest received by other castes are called *phaslānā* (from *phasal,* "harvest") and are given for quite a different set of reasons (these *phaslānā* prestations will be discussed in chapter 5). The *sāvṛī* is given to the cultivator's Brahman *purohit,* not as payment for services rendered during the course of the year, nor as a token of his material dependence on the *jajmān,* as Pocock (1962) has suggested. Instead, the Brahman's portion of the grain is given to him, as *dān* or *caṛhāpā,* in the course of a sequence of ritual actions performed at the threshing place for the "increase" (*barkat*) and auspiciousness of the harvests.

After being threshed and winnowed, the harvested grain (both rice and wheat) is gathered into piles (*rās* or *sāvaṛ*). The winnowing basket is first placed at the south end of the pile of grain. Facing north, the *jajmān* cultivator picks up the *chāj* with his right hand (with the left hand touching the right wrist), turns it on its side, and takes it around the circular pile in a clockwise direction, marking the pile with small indentations with the basket as he goes. This is repeated in a counterclockwise direction, and finally clockwise once again. The marks of the first circling are made at the bottom of the pile, the second midway up, and the last around the top of the pile. This procedure is called *cāng lagānā,* "applying the *cāng*". (The *Bṛhat Hindī Koṣ* dictionary defines *cāng* as "a wooden mallet with which lines are drawn on a pile of grain at the threshing place; an implement for marking lines on a pile of grain; a line drawn all around an afflicted [*pīṛit*] place of the body".) The *chāj* is once again placed to the south of the pile, and the *jajmān,* facing north, performs a *dhok mārnā* with a handful of grain from the pile. Then the *cāng utārnā* ("taking down the *cāng*") is performed: the grain pile is circled as in the *cāng lagānā,* but the directional sequence is reversed; the first circling is done at the top, the second around the middle, and the last around the bottom of the pile. Both the *cāng lagānā* and the *cāng utārnā* encompass alternations of clockwise and counterclockwise movements, but the most salient reversal is that between the *lagānā* movement upward and the *utārnā* movement down the pile.

After the *cāng utārnā,* the *jajmān* returns to the south of the pile and again does *dhok mārnā.* He then fills the winnowing basket with grain and goes around to the north of the pile, where he places the *chāj,* taking care that the mouth of the basket faces toward the east. The basket, filled with grain, remains in that position until the weighing of the grain in the pile is completed, sometimes with the help of the family's Brahman. The basket of grain is then given to the *purohit* as his *sāvṛī,* as the *caṛhāpā* of the grain pile. Such prestations are, in total, a substantial amount of grain, and these winnowing baskets of rice or wheat from each pile at the threshing place are the only portions of the harvest that the Brahman receives. But it is of the essence of this prestation that the quantity of grain that is given not be weighed, calculated, or haggled over. I estimated, however, at the wheat harvest, that each winnowing basket contained about five kilograms of grain. All of the Pahansu Gujar cultivators, as far as I could determine, gave *sāvṛī* in just this way (I witnessed many such rituals in the Pahansu fields), but the amounts of grain that were given varied, both because of differences in the harvests and in the amount of land each Gujar cultivated, and also because the *jajmān* could gather his grain into any number of piles and give one winnowing basket of grain from each.

The Brahman receives his portion of the harvest, the *sāvṛī* or *caṛhāpā*, in this way in order to ensure, it is said, that the harvest will be auspicious and bountiful (*anāj kā barkat ho jā*) and that any inauspicious "hindrances" in the grain will be transferred to him through the grain in the winnowing basket. The winnowing basket not only separates the grain from the chaff (an operation performed just before the *cāng lagānā*); it is also the instrument through which the auspiciousness of the harvest (its *barkat*) is ensured through the removal of the inauspiciousness (the *bādhā*). The verb forms used to describe this ritual—*lagānā* ("applying") and *utārnā* ("taking down off of")—parallel the verb forms used in the characterization of the *bān* ritual, in which inauspiciousness is removed from the bride and from the groom. The pile of grain is ritually constructed here in the same way that the body is constructed in the *bān* and in other ritual procedures, for example, the *chuwānā:* through a movement from bottom to top and then, in a reversal of directionality, from top to bottom. In all of these cases, the ritual actions precede the making of a prestation and remove ("take out," "bring to the surface") certain negative substances from the object undergoing the ritual, whether it is a human body or a pile of grain. The ritual congruence of the two reminds us of the nature of the gift. In the *sāvṛī,* it is a portion of the grain itself that is given, just as in many other prestations it is part of oneself (the inauspicious part) that is given, through the cloth that has been worn or the items that have touched the body before being given to the proper recipient.

A few Brahmans have small parcels of land in Pahansu, but none of them cultivate on a scale that enables them to make distributions from the harvests. I did ask Brahmans if they would themselves give *sāvṛī* if they were the cultivators of the soil. Their reply was that of course they would, for the *barkat* of their harvests, and they would give it to their *dhiyānī.* This answer belies Pocock's assumption that the shares of the harvest given by landholders to village Brahmans are simply "payments" for their priestly services or tokens of their temporal dependence on the *jajmān.*

The Brahman is not the only recipient in Pahansu of prestations that ensure the *barkat* of the harvests. On each day of both the wheat and the rice harvests, the family Barber goes to the fields of his *jajmān* to receive *muṭṭhī*, a "handful" of the rice or wheat still on the stalks. He takes them to his house, threshes them by beating them on the ground (*anāj cetnā*), and then uses the grain in his own household. This prestation, like the *sāvṛī*, is never weighed; nor is it ever referred to as *phaslānā*, the shares of the harvest that are given in exchange for the work that the Barber and other *kamīn*s perform for the cultivator during a *chamāī*. The similarity of *muṭṭhī* and the *sāvṛī* is explicit. Illam Nai, a Pahansu Barber, and I were talking about the *muṭṭhī* one day as his wife did the *anāj cetnā* in their courtyard. He remarked that "Brahmans receive *sāvṛī* and we receive *muṭṭhī*," and that both are given for the same reason, for the auspiciousness and *barkat* of the grain: "from giving to *kamīn*s the grain increases" (*kamīnõ ko dene se anāj baṛhegā*).

Some Pahansu wives reported to me that in their natal villages, *muṭṭhī* is also given to one's Sweeper, and a few older informants recalled that this was once the custom in Pahansu as well. Today members of the Dom *jāti*, another of the castes like the Dakaut that specialize in the acceptance of *dān*, sometimes come to Pahansu from the nearby village of Nawada to receive *muṭṭhī* from Gujar fields. In this context they refer to the cultivator as their *jajmān*.

The distinction between the grain received by the Barber and that received by the Brahman *purohit* for the *barkat* of the harvest resembles a distinction we have already observed in the death rituals: the Barber receives the prestations to remove inauspiciousness from the thing that is in process or transition or that is being separated (the dead man as *pret*, the grain as it is cut and harvested) and the Brahman receives a similar prestation, but in both cases after the separation has been completed. A similar distinction has been noted in regard to the roles of the Barber and the Brahman in death rituals in the city of Banaras, though not with respect to prestations (Kaushik 1976).

Further prestations are also made to ensure the auspiciousness of the harvested grain after it has been weighed and brought into the storage rooms of the house. During each harvest, the *sāṛhī* and the *sāvanī*, the wife of the Gujar cultivator goes to the field shrine of the family's *dev-pitar*s, and together with the wife of the family's Brahman *purohit* she cooks some of the new rice or makes breads (*roṭī*) from the new wheat. Portions of this food are placed on a brass tray and put before the *dev-pitar*, at the "mouth" of the shrine. The shrine itself is "bathed" (*nahānā*) with milk, turmeric marks are put all around the door or "mouth," and an earthen lamp is lit. *Dhok mārnā* is done with some of the grain, and then a bit of the cooked food is put onto some burning embers. The wife of the cultivator performs these actions, and she may often be joined by her children and by her husband, who may come to the shrine from the nearby fields. The food from the tray is then given as *pujāpā* to the family

Brahman or his wife. (This ritual in the fields is generally done on the lunar day on which the *dev-pitar* in question died.)

A similar ritual is performed by the wives of Gujar cultivators at the shrine of the village god Bhūmiyā, the "protector of the site" (*khetrapāl*). This shrine is located to the north of the Pahansu habitation site. At the *sāvanī* harvest, a sweet rice preparation is made, and at the *sāṛhī* wheat harvest a sweet pancake preparation called *chilṛa* is made from the newly harvested grain. These things are offered at the Bhūmiyā shrine and given as *pujāpā* to the family Brahman *purohit* in order to remove inauspiciousness from the grain, inauspiciousness that may cause the grain to be depleted even after it has been stored in the house.

We have so far seen two types of evidence that *dhiyānī* and *dhiyāne* are, like Brahmans, Barbers, and Doms, involved in the protection of the harvests and the auspiciousness of the grain: (1) the *dhān boāī* ritual during the course of the wedding rites and (2) statements by Brahmans that if they were the cultivators of the soil they would give the *sāvṛī* prestation to their *dhiyānī*. A comparison of two yearly rituals, both concerned with the auspiciousness of one's work—whether of agriculture, barbering, or priesthood—reveals further correspondences.

People in Pahansu repeatedly drew parallels between two yearly rituals, *pāyatā* ("direction of the feet") and *godhan* ("cow wealth"). The former occurs on the tenth day of the bright half of the month of Asauj, and the latter about three weeks later on the first day of the bright half of the month of Kārttik.

On "direction of the feet" day, *pāyatā,* women of the Barber and Brahman castes in Pahansu spread cow-dung paste in a large square in the courtyard of their houses and prepare ten fresh cow-dung cakes (*gosā*). The *gosā* are placed over the prepared square in a curved arch pattern. Then the women make *ṭakkarpūrat* designs with flour inside the arch, and finally they attach legs, head, and arms to the *ṭakkarpūrat* figures, again using flour. It is important that the feet of this figure should point toward the south. Burning embers and an earthen lamp filled with mustard oil are placed inside the *ṭakkarpūrat* figure, and the brass tray with the *ṭakkarpūrat* flour, some unrefined sugar, and one and one-quarter rupees is kept on the ground just outside the figure. Occupational implements—the razor of the barber and the Brahman's priestly paraphernalia—are placed inside the designs. Household implements such as the churning staff and pestle may also be included. Then the lamp is lit, and a daughter or a sister of the family ties protective threads on the wrists of the men of the household. The men do *dhok mārnā* with unhusked rice at the *ṭakkarpūrat*. The rice from this *dhok mārnā,* and the tray of flour, sugar, and one and one-quarter rupees are then given to the Brahman *purohit* by the Barbers, and to *dhiyānī* by Brahmans.

Villagers often comment that while Brahmans and Barbers protect their occupational implements on *pāyatā*, Gujars do so on *godhan*. Two days before *godhan*, on the thirteenth day of the dark half of Kārttik, Gujar women take two mustard oil lamps to the place where the "feet" of a *ṭakkarpūrat* man will be drawn on *godhan*. The next evening, in the midst of the other activities of Kārttik *amāvas* (see below, 173–75), Sweeper men and boys go from house to house in the village, beating on their drums "to awaken *godhan*" (*godhan jagāne ke lie*); the Sweepers receive two breads from each of their *jajmāns* for performing this service.

The next afternoon, the wife or sister of the family's Leatherworker cowherd, or another Camar woman with whom there has been in the past a hereditary *jajmānī* relationship, comes to the cattle pen (*gher*) of the Gujar cultivator where the two lamps had been lit the night before. She goes there to make fresh cow-dung cakes and to prepare the *godhan ṭakkarpūrat*. She makes thirty *gosā* and arranges them, in piles of three each, in the same manner as the *pāyatā* design. A *ṭakkarpūrat* with head, feet, and arms is also drawn with flour and turmeric, within the *gosā* arch, again with the feet toward the south. Small cow-dung figures of cows and water buffaloes are fashioned, and these are placed within the *ṭakkarpūrat*. Finally, she makes small cow-dung representations of the household vessel used for boiling milk and of the churning pot, and these too are placed within the *ṭakkarpūrat* outline, along with a cow-dung representation of the family's *bālḍī* (cowherd).

In the evening, when all of the men of the family have returned from the fields, two new lamps are placed at the feet of the *godhan ṭakkarpūrat*, and some coals are placed beneath them. Finally, a big armload of the newly harvested sugarcane crop, the household churning staff (*raī*), the household pestle (*mūsal*), the plow, a digging implement (*phāvaḍā*), and the silver ornaments of the women of the house are placed inside the design. Protective threads are tied on the wrists of the men of the house, and a brass tray of foods—breads, rice pudding, and unrefined sugar—is brought from the house. The men perform a *dhok mārnā*, and the grain from this is given to the Camar, in the *pallā* of the shawl. The Camar also receives the tray of food and a stalk of the sugarcane as *dān*, as the *godhan pujāpā*. This prestation not only protects the household and agricultural implements, but also removes inauspiciousness from the sugarcane harvest. The harvest should never begin more than a few days before *godhan*, villagers say, and no one should chew the raw cane—a favorite village treat—or process the cane in any way until after the giving of the *pujāpā*. As soon as this had been done in the household in which I witnessed the *godhan*, stalks of sugarcane were taken into the house for the first time, and the children who had been eagerly anticipating the conclusion of the ritual were finally permitted to chew the cane.

There is no story (*kathā*) recited during the performance of this ritual, as there is for some of the rituals of the calendrical cycle, but there is an associated story (*kahānī*) in which the mountain Gobardhan that protected the inhabitants of the Braj district from the wrath of Indra plays a central role.

> One day the lord Kṛṣṇa saw that throughout Braj many kinds of sweets and special foods were being prepared. When he asked about the reason for this, he was told that preparations were underway for the *pūjā* of the god Indra, so that being pleased he might let the rains come at the appropriate times. Hearing this the lord Kṛṣṇa began to speak ill of Indra, saying that the *pūjā* should be performed only for those deities who were present to receive the offerings. Hearing this, the cowherds of Braj replied that Kṛṣṇa should not speak ill of the god Indra, because it is only because of Indra that the rains come. Kṛṣṇa answered by asking what power (*śakti*) Indra had to make it rain, and saying that it is the mountain Gobardhan that makes the rains come and therefore *pūjā* offerings should be made to the mountain instead of to Indra.
>
> Hearing the words of Kṛṣṇa, the residents of Braj stopped worshiping Indra, and began to do the *pūjā* of Gobardhan mountain. But when Indra saw that his own *pūjā* had come to an end, he ordered that heavy rains should fall and destroy the whole village. Seeing these terrifying rains, the inhabitants of the village became frightened and worried, and said to Kṛṣṇa: "Now Indra wants to destroy the whole village. What should we do?" Hearing this, Kṛṣṇa said to the people: "All of you go with your cattle to the shelter of Gobardhan and there you will be protected." All of the cowherds went to the foot of the mountain. There Kṛṣṇa lifted up Gobardhan on the tip of his finger and held it in that way for seven days while the cowherds and the cattle sat beneath the mountain. Indra's fearful rain fell on Gobardhan, but not a single drop fell on the cowherds who sat beneath it.

In this story, Gobardhan absorbs, as it were, the destructive rains,[34] thus diverting them from the cowherds and the cattle. The mountain is also, as Kṛṣṇa points out, present to receive the offerings. In the Pahansu *godhan* ritual, the *ṭakkarpūrat*, explicitly identified with Gobardhan, absorbs the inauspiciousness of the cattle and the family cowherd (as well as of the sugarcane and the household and agricultural implements) that are placed within it. A particular space is implicated in both the myth and the ritual: a concrete geographical configuration in the story, and a square figure oriented to the directions in the ritual.

Just as the auspiciousness of the sugarcane crop is ensured at *godhan*, and the *barkat* of the grain ensured by the giving of *muṭṭhī* and *sāvṛī*, so too is the productivity of small plots of cotton enhanced through a specific *caṛhāpā* prestation. A number of Gujar women in Pahansu set aside small plots of land for the growing of cotton, and it is their responsibility to look after the entire productive process, from planting to the spinning of thread. It is also their responsibility to ensure the auspiciousness and the "increase" (*barkat*) of the cotton. When a woman goes to her plot of land (*bāṛī*) to pick the cotton for the first time in the season (*bāṛī phuraknā* or *bāṛī cugnā*), she takes with her four handfuls of a mixture of unrefined sugar and uncooked husked rice, or some puffed rice (*khīl*). Standing in the center of the field, she first does a *dhok mārnā* with a bit of the rice and sugar, and then throws a handful of the mixture toward each of the four directions, saying:

dūsre gām kī bāṛī cakanācūr
hamārī bāṛī khile bambūl.

Let the cotton fields of other villages be destroyed,
let our own cotton fields blossom like the acacia tree.

This "prestation" to another village is made, as Asikaur put it, "to protect one's own thing" (*apnī cīz bacāne ke lie*) and to guard the auspiciousness of the cotton as it is picked. One cannot ensure the productivity of one's own field unless this *caṛhāpā*—the rice and the sugar—is transferred out of the field and on to another village, just as it is transferred to human recipients in the case of the other harvests.

Protecting the House and the Village: Placing the *Nī̃v* and Kālī *Kā Bhẽṭ*

A house in its physical aspects is not separate from those who live in it; the inauspiciousness of persons may affect the house, and the inauspiciousness of the house, resulting from the time and space of its construction, may also affect the well-being of its inhabitants.

There are certain times and astrological circumstances (the five *pancak* lunar asterisms, particular days of the week, certain lunar days, and so forth) that are inappropriate for a house-building. Inauspiciousness will be engendered if building commences at those times. Avoidance of these periods is always the first consideration when a man in Pahansu consults Buddhu Pandit about the appropriate time for laying the foundation for a new house or for beginning repairs to an old one. "The placing of the foundation" (*nī̃v dharnā*) refers not simply to the bricks that support the walls of the house, but to certain items that are placed in that foundation to remove the inauspiciousness and "sorrows" (*dukh*) that afflict both the house and the occupants as the dwelling is constructed. Aside from the general astrological considerations, there are two other factors that must be taken into account before the *nīv* may be placed. The earth (*prithvi*) is said to "sleep" (*sotī hai*) during certain *nakṣatra* periods and to be awake (*jāgnā*) during others. A well or a house foundation should never be dug when the earth is sleeping, as this is the time when the inauspiciousness that the earth has absorbed is most likely to seep into the house that is being built, just as the inauspiciousness of the gods is most easily transferred to men during the "night of the gods," when the gods are asleep in the months of Sāvan, Bhādwe, Asauj, and Kārttik. The second consideration involved in the placement of the *nīv* is the position of Śeṣnāg under the earth, already described in chapter 2.

The *nīv* itself consists of five bricks on which are placed a small bit of silver, some unrefined sugar, and mustard oil. The oldest person of the household should position these things beneath the foundation of the house because, as people in Pahansu said, a great deal of inauspiciousness attends this process and it is likely to shorten one's life (*umar gaṭh jayegī*). The *nīv* must always be placed over an "empty space" (*khālī jagah*), the one cardinal direction in which Śeṣnāg's head, back, or tail is not at that time situated; otherwise disease, terror, and afflictions will beset the occupants of the house just as they will if *dān* is given to an inappropriate *pātra*. In fact the appropriate direction for the *nīv* becomes the *pātra* for the silver, the sugar, and the "bitter oil" that absorbs the inauspiciousness of the house site and transfers it to that directionally specified space. There are actually two nested representations of directionality involved here. The *nīv* is placed in a particular direction, a particular quadrant of the house site, but in itself also represents the four directions around a center (see fig. 14). The spatial configuration of the bricks acts as a *pātra* in precisely the way that a *ṭakkarpūrat* (also a representation of the directions) takes into itself the inauspiciousness of the space in which a ritual is to be performed or prestations made. The house rests on a *nīv* just as a person sits on a *ṭakkarpūrat*.

Before it is occupied, the house is protected from inauspiciousness in one other way. For the "well-being achieved through gift-giving" (*khair-khairāt*) and the auspiciousness (*śubh*) of the occupants, a *dhiyānī* of the household ties a *kangan* over the threshold of the house. This *kangan*, like the one used in weddings, is a small parcel of red cloth tied with a red thread that contains an iron ring, mustard seed, a small piece of wood from *nīm* tree, betel nut, and a *kauṛī* shell. Just as in the wedding ritual, the *kangan* absorbs the inauspiciousness that may pass over the threshold into the house. At the time she ties the *kangan*, the *dhiyānī* is given a *dakṣiṇā* payment of one and one-quarter rupees.

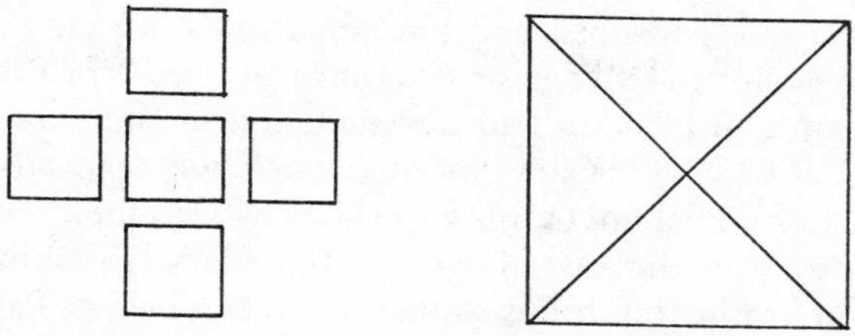

Fig. 14. Bricks of the *nīv* and the *ṭakkarpūrat*

Kālī is a dangerous goddess, a "goddess of blood" (*rakta kī devī*) through whose anger men and cattle suffer afflictions, disease, and danger, especially as a result of the spread of her inauspiciousness to particular places. There are a number of ways to avert or remove her afflictions. The simplest is to place a handful of the "seven grains" (*satanajā*) in a piece of red cloth, and to tie this packet above the entrance to the cattle-pen, the *gher*. As in other rituals in which it is used, the *satanajā* absorbs inauspiciousness, in this case, that of the goddess Kālī, thereby "protecting" (*rakṣa karnā*) the cattle within the enclosure. The importance of the site, the place that has been afflicted, is shown in the fact that the red packet is placed at the entranceway to the *gher* rather than being brought into contact with the animals themselves.

A second and more efficacious way of removing the *rog* and *kaṣṭ* involves making offerings at the village shrine of the goddess. Near the village Śiva temple there is a small shrine containing a rough stone image of Kālī. On any Tuesday (Kālī's day), but particularly in the month of Cait, women may prepare fried breads (*pūṛī*) and a sweet porridge (*lapsī*) made from browned flour, clarified butter, and unrefined sugar and take these to the shrine. They first bathe the image with milk and then light an earthen lamp filled with clarified butter. The image is then anointed with daubs of turmeric on the feet, hips, hands, breast, and forehead, in that order.[35] Here negative qualities afflicting the family and the village are being transferred to the goddess, and so the sequence of the anointing includes only the "application" (*lagānā*) direction—from bottom to top—and not the "taking down" (*utārnā*) direction. *Dhok mārnā* is performed, and a bit of the *pūṛī* and *lapsī* is placed on a smoldering ember; the remainder of the food is then given to the family Sweeper as the *pujāpā* of Kālī.

Late one evening in Pahansu when I thought that nearly everyone in the village had gone to sleep, I witnessed what was certainly the most dramatic method of removing the afflictions caused by Kālī. At about 10:30 on that Tuesday, I heard the sound of conch shells being blown, bells, drums, and a few gunshots, and loud angry voices near the boundary where the fields of the village of Pilakhni meet those of Pahansu. As it happened, cattle in Pilakhni had sickened, and the men there were performing a Kālī *kā bhẽṭ*, "Kālī's gift" (the word *bhẽṭ* seems to be a euphemism here), to rid Pilakhni of this *kaṣṭ*. They had slit the ear of a goat and were trying to drive the animal over the boundary (*sīmā*) into Pahansu, shouting and beating on drums as they went. But men of Pahansu, hearing the noise, surmised what was happening (it being the time of year when such things often happened) and a large, very angry crowd had assembled in the fields to try to turn the goat back or to send it on to yet another village. The mere presence of the goat on Pahansu soil would be sufficient to transfer the *kaṣṭ* to them, the men explained to me, and still more harm (*nuksān*) and sickness would afflict anyone who might catch the animal and consume the meat. The goat itself is the *pujāpā* of Kālī, and the men of Pahansu were not willing to permit the village to become the *pātra* for this inauspicious and dangerous *dān*. They said that the giving of Kālī *kā bhẽṭ* had been the cause of fighting among villages in the past, and would continue to be so. Often when a village does become the recipient of such a *bhẽṭ*, the inhabitants later do a Kālī *kā bhẽṭ* themselves, in order to "give onward" the *kaṣṭ* that has been received.

This scene was repeated just a week later, when the people of Madanuki village attempted to drive a *bhẽṭ* goat onto Pahansu lands. And a week after that, Pahansu Camars performed a Kālī *kā bhẽṭ*. Two young Camar girls had recently died, and the death had been attributed to the inauspiciousness of Kālī. In this instance, a young goat was taken to the village boundary, a spot of vermilion was placed on the animal, *dhok mārnā* was done (Kālī *pe dhok mār jā*, as villagers said), and the throat of the goat was slit. The carcass, the *pujāpā* of Kālī, was then placed over the boundary on the land of a neighboring village, which thus became the unwitting recipient of the *kaṣṭ* that had been afflicting the Camar community.

Pujāpā, *Sandhārā*, and *Bayanā*: The Transferral of Inauspiciousness in the Yearly Festival Cycle

The calendrical rituals in which *pujāpā*, *sandhārā*, and *bayanā*—prestations that transfer inauspiciousness—are given almost without exception occur in the months of Sāvan, Bhādwe, Asauj, and Kārttik, the inauspicious months in which weddings do not occur and when the gods are said to be asleep. This is a dangerous time for human beings, the time at which the inauspiciousness of the gods is very likely to come upon them, partly because of astrological circumstances that facilitate its flow. In all of these calendrical rites, a fairly uniform sequence of ritual acts precedes the giving of prestations that remove the inauspiciousness of the gods. (Though it is the case that a number of these rituals do not in fact involve gods at all, but are performed to remove inauspiciousness of other kinds.)

In the rites oriented toward deities (the prestation is in such cases generally called *pujāpā*), the performer of the ritual is always a woman, and she must be a wife of the village in which she does the ritual and makes the prestations. A daughter may never perform these actions in her *pīhar*. It is of course the wife, the *bahū,* who is responsible for ensuring the well-being of her conjugal family by making prestations, and it is the married daughter or sister who as *dhiyānī* is often called upon to accept these prestations and thus the inauspiciousness. The performer of these calendrical rituals must fast (that is, observe *vrat*) all day until the time that the *pujāpā* is given. *Dhok mārnā* is performed before a representation of the deity (a pile of straw in the center of the village in the case of Holikā Mātā, and cow-dung outlines on the wall of an inner room in the case of Guggā), special foodstuffs are offered to the deity, and the remainder is given to a particular recipient as the *pujāpā* of that deity.

Table 7 provides details about the major calendrical festivals concerned with such offerings to deities and the giving of *pujāpā*. In all of these, the linguistic contexts and the permutational possibilities are precisely the same as in the rituals of the life course and the harvest rituals. Here too, the *pujāpā* is given to a specific "receptacle" (*pātra*) whose "appropriate obligation" (*pharmāyā*) it is to accept it for the auspiciousness of the donor.

There are several other rituals of the yearly cycle that involve the giving of *caṛhāpā,* though deities are not involved in these rituals. The new-moon day (*amāvas*) is a time of great fluidity of inauspiciousness, and for each of the twelve *amāvas* days of the year there is a specific kind of *dān* that may be made to remove this inauspiciousness, the *doṣ* that may be engendered. The *amāvas* days of the months of Māgh and Kārttik are the most important of these, the ones observed most frequently in Pahansu.

The new-moon day of the month of Māgh is called *maunī amāvas* ("silent new-moon day"). On that day, women bathe and keep a *vrat,* and then grind *sawā ser* of sesame seeds and *sawā ser* of unrefined sugar, and prepare large round sweetmeats (*laḍḍū*s) from this mixture. The sweets are placed on a brass tray and covered with *sawā gaj* (one and one-quarter measures) of cloth. The *laḍḍū*s and the cloth are given in silence (neither the donor nor the recipient should speak) to the family Brahman *purohit* as *pujāpā* or *dān*. This prestation is said to be the *udāpan* of the *amāvas* rites.

Kārttik *amāvas* is said to be the most dangerous new-moon day, for several reasons. Villagers say that "sorrows" (*dukh*) and "afflictions"

TABLE 7

Some Calendrical Rituals and the Giving of Pujāpā

Calendrical Rite (Deity)	Time	Performer	Purpose	Prestation	*Pujāpā* Recipient
Guggā naumī (Guggā)	Ninth day of bright fortnight of the month of Bhādwe	Mothers	Protection of *dūdh, pūt,* and *dehlī:* the milk (of the lineage), sons, and the threshold (of the house)	For each son: small pile of grain, five *puṛā* (fried savory morsels) and four *khīngrī* (small fried breads), and milk	Those who have been possessed by Gugga (in Pahansu, a Potter and two Camars)
Holī (Holikā *mātā*)	Full moon day of the month of Phālgun	Mothers	Protection of sons	Tray of flour and unrefined sugar, a ten-*paisā* coin	Brahman *purohit*/*dhiyānī*
Badhāvā (ancestral deities)	Lunar day of death	Wives of the family	Protection of men of the *kunbā*	A tray of cooked rice and lentils and sugar, a set of cloth	Brahman *purohit*/*dhiyānī*
Badhāvā (*Mātā* village goddess)	Bhādwe, on a Monday or Thursday	Mothers	Protection of sons	For each son: a leaf packet containing *satanajā* and cotton seeds, and five packets of fried savory morsels (*puṛā*)	Sweeper/*dhiyānī*
Badhāvā (Bhūmiyā)	Bhādwe, on a Saturday in the bright fortnight	Wives of the village	Protection of the village and sons	*Mīṭhe chīlṛe* (sweet whole-wheat flour pancakes)	Brahman *purohit*/*dhiyānī*

(*kaṣṭ*) wander about (*ghūmnā*) on this day; again the notion of the fluidity of inauspiciousness is connected with particular lunar days and astrological phenomena. This inauspiciousness may emanate from *bhūt-pret* that are abroad at this time; from *sayānā*s (experts in "spells" and in the control of ghosts), whose work is particularly efficacious at this time, or from the planetary conjunction (the "dwelling together" of the sun and the moon) itself. In order to "make far" (*dūr karnā*) the "sorrows" caused by the planets in this conjunction (*grahõ kā dukh*), the oldest woman of the house disposes of this inauspiciousness at dusk.

In our house, as darkness descended on the day of Kārttik *amāvas,* Asikaur busied herself with the fashioning of a *cūn kā diyā,* a dough lamp with four wicks (also called a *langārī*) exactly like the ones used in the wedding *bān*. Just as it got dark, Asi filled this lamp with mustard oil, lit the four wicks, and placed it in a winnowing basket along with some unrefined sugar. She very quickly performed a *chuwānā* or a *wārpher* over everyone in the house, including me, and then ran out the door without saying a word. Because Kārttik *amāvas* is the night on which *divālī* is celebrated with great pomp in many places and by other castes, particularly by Baniyas, I had expected "wealth" in the form of the goddess Lakṣmi to be welcomed into the house on this night. As it became apparent that this was not the way Kārttik *amāvas* was observed by these Gujar landholders, I ran out the door in pursuit of Asikaur, asking questions and fumbling for my notebook. She looked over her shoulder and shook her head at me, and I realized she wouldn't answer then. So I followed her across the lane to the village pond, where she dumped the contents of the winnowing basket into the water. Relieved of her burden she was free to talk. She had done this, she said, for "the well-being achieved through gift-giving of all the children" (*sab baccõ ke khair-khairāt ke māro*), to "make far the sorrows of the planets" (*grahõ ka dukh dūr karnā*), and if she had spoken at all during the *wārpher*s or before the disposal of the dough lamp, this removal would not have been accomplished.

Sandhārā is the second type of *dān* prestation made in the course of the yearly calendrical festivals. *Sandhārā* is always given to one's married daughters and sisters and to the people of their *sasurāl*s, to the *dhiyānī* of the donor and her conjugal kin. *Sandhārā* is *dān,* villagers say, and it is given regularly, throughout a woman's lifetime, on the occasion of three festivals: *holī, tīj,* and *bhāīyā dauj*.

A typical *holī sandhārā,* sent to Pahansu for the wife of Jaipal, a landholder, consisted of the following sets of cloth:

one *joṛā* for the husband
two sets of cloth for the wife
two sets of cloth, one for each of the husband's younger brothers

one set of cloth for the husband's father's sister
one set of cloth for the husband's sister
one set of cloth for the husband's father
one set of cloth for the husband's mother

Such *sandhārā* prestations are made in addition to the *holī pujāpā* that is given to one's own Brahman *purohit*.

For the festival of *tīj* on the third day of the bright half of the month of Sāvan, *sandhārā* was sent from her natal village for Santroj, a Gujar wife of Pahansu. This *tīj sandhārā* consisted of three sets of cloth:

one for Santroj
one for Rajendar, her husband
one for Asikaur, Rajendar's mother

Both of these sets of prestations, usually brought to the *sasurāl* of the recipient by the donor's Barber, are given, like *pujāpā,* for the auspiciousness of the donor. The meaning of the *sandhārā* prestations may be most easily understood through a discussion of the *bhāīyā dauj* ("brother's second") ritual, performed on the second day of the bright half of the month of Kārttik.

On this day, the buses of northwestern Uttar Pradesh are crowded with brothers journeying to the villages of their married sisters. Married women who have brothers fast on this day, and sometime in the course of the morning they gather together in small groups to hear the story of *bhāīyā dauj*. They sit in an inner room of the house, with turmeric and rice in their right hands, and small "lamps" made from dough in their left hands. After the telling of the story has begun, no one, including the women themselves, should see the dough lamps; they are kept out of sight in the women's *pallā*s, the ends of their shawls. As the story ends, each woman quickly puts her "lamp" into her mouth and swallows it, covering her head with her shawl. If her brother has already arrived in her *sasurāl,* she will then put a *tilak* mark on his forehead with the turmeric and rice from her right hand.

A little later in the day, each sister prepares a tray containing a bit of turmeric and rice and some sweets. The brother is asked to stand on a wooden stool, and the sister places another *tilak* on his forehead and feeds him some of the sweets. He then puts the *sandhārā* he has brought on the tray for her to accept. This *sandhārā* is sometimes given in cash, but more frequently consists of a few sets of cloth and a large quantity of uncooked rice and lentils from which *khicarī* should be prepared in the sister's *sasurāl*. Sukhbir, a Pahansu Gujar man, took the following sets of cloth to his sister's conjugal village on *bhāīyā dauj:*

one set of cloth for his sister
one set of cloth for his sister's husband
two sets of cloth, one for each of Sukhbir's sister's sons
one for the sister's son's son
one for the sister's son's daughter

One further set of prestations may be given in conjunction with the ritual of *bhāīyā dauj,* and this constitutes the *udāpan,* the concluding *dān* of the ritual. A brother may give *udāpan* prestations of this sort several times during his life, for the well-being of himself and his parents. When Ramesh, a Brahman man in Pahansu, made the *udāpan* prestation to his sister who lives in Nainital, he and his wife gave the following items:

a set of cloth for a man (*mardānā joṛā*)
a set of cloth for a woman (*janānā joṛā*)
sawā pā̃c ser (five and one-quarter *ser*) of ingredients for *khicarī* (rice and lentils)
sawā pā̃c ser of *suhālī,* a small sweet made from flour and sugar in the form of a lamp
a small gold pendant in the form of a lamp (*sone kā surak dīyā*)

Before Ramesh gave these things to his sister, he recited a brief Hindi *sankalp* and did *mīnasnā* around them with a handful of water. Santosh, Ramesh's sister, wore the gold *surak dīyā* herself, and gave the sets of cloth, the *suhālī,* and the *sawā pā̃c ser* of lentils and rice onward to her own *dhiyānī* (her husband's sister), for the auspiciousness of her brother and her mother and father.

The wife of Pahel Singh, a Gujar landholder, told me that she and her husband had given such *udāpan* prestations to his father's sister. They gave essentially the same items that Ramesh gave to his sister, but in addition to the gold *surak dīyā* they also gave a silver one (*cāndī kā surak dīyā*). Instead of sending *sawā pā̃c ser* of *suhālī* they sent 360 of the sweets. In these Gujar *bhāīyā dauj udāpan*s, the cloth, the *khicarī,* the *suhālī,* and the silver *surak dīyā* are given to the wife of the family Brahman *purohit* of the sister's (or father's sister's) *sasurāl,* while the sister or father's sister herself wears the gold lamp. It is the *pharmāyā,* villagers say, of the sister to accept these things as *dān* and to give them onward for the auspiciousness and "merit" (*pun*) of her parents. Here again we find the same sequence of prestations—from wife-givers to wife-receivers, and then onward to the wife-receivers or Brahman *purohit* of the first recipient—that characterizes death prestations, the first-tooth prestation given by the mother's brother, the *bhāt,* and so on.

There are actually three instances of the transferral of inauspiciousness in the *bhāīyā dauj* rituals. In the first one, during the telling of the story, the sister holds rice and turmeric in her auspicious right hand, which she later applies to her brother's forehead, and in her inauspicious left hand she holds the *cūn kā dīyā,* the dough lamp that she is to consume quickly at the end of the story. This separation is not unlike those that are iconically represented in other contexts by the pestle and the winnowing basket: there is a separation of auspiciousness and inauspiciousness, and by consuming the dough lamp, so often the receptacle of inauspiciousness, the sister takes upon herself the negative substances and qualities that may be afflicting her brother and that could cause an early death.

The second transferral at *bhāīyā dauj* occurs with the giving of the *sandhārā* as *dān*. And the third is achieved through the giving of the final *udāpan* and the subsequent "giving onward" to one's Brahman *purohit* or *dhiyānī*. The similar nature of all three transferrals is perhaps indicated by the giving of the gold and silver "lamps" in the *udāpan,* which recalls the sister's swallowing of the dough lamp for her brother's auspiciousness that initiates the rituals of *bhāīyā dauj*.

Bayanā is the specific term used in Pahansu for the *caṛhāpā* that is given in the course of two yearly rituals, *hoī* and *kaṛvā cauth*. The word *bayanā* means "to sow," "to transplant," "to apply one thing or substance to another," and the making of these prestations does indeed effect the "transplanting" of inauspiciousness. Indeed, *bayanā* is related to the more common word meaning "to sow," *bonā*. It may be of significance that in the Hindi folktales and dramas collected by Temple in the Panjab and in the western Uttar Pradesh district of Meerut, the giving of *dān* is frequently described as "sowing the *dān*," *dān bonā*. (See particularly Temple 1884–1900, 3 : 140.) Several Pahansu Gujar informants used this image as a simile in their descriptions of the effects of receiving *dān*. Mangal Singh, for example, in discussing the consequences of accepting the *dān* of the planet Śanī—disease (*rog*) and death (*mṛityu*)—commented that negative effects occur just as "fruit" is obtained after seeds have been sown: *jaise kuch bīj boyā jātā hai phīr phal miltā hai*.

The Hoī ritual is performed and the *bayanā* given on the eighth day of the dark half of the month of Kārttik, by women who have sons. The ritual is performed, and the prestation made, for the auspiciousness and the "well-being achieved through gift-giving" of these sons. Women also say that this *vrat* is kept and the prestations made "for [one's] sons and milk [the breast milk of the wives that nourishes the *kunbā*]" (*dūdh-pūt ke lie*). Hoī is the name of a vaguely characterized goddess who is said, in the story told on this day, to alternately inflict misfortunes on one's sons and to protect them. Just how she does this will become clear as the ritual actions of the day unfold.

On the day before the ritual, the mother prepares an image of Hoī on a wall in an inner room of the house or near the family hearth. (A Brahman woman may sometimes do this for a Gujar house, for which service she may receive five *ser* of grain.) The body of the goddess is represented in the drawing by means of an intricately embellished square, to which hands, feet, and legs are attached. As in *payatā* and *godhan,* and in the use of the *ṭakkarpūrat,* whatever is to be "protected" is placed within a bounded square: when the drawing is completed, small stick figures representing all of the sons of the household are drawn within the square body of the goddess.

On the morning of the day on which the ritual is to be performed, the women bathe and keep a *vrat*, which is not to be broken until after the *bayanā* has been given in the early evening. Sometime during the course of the morning, the women of the house, or of several houses, gather in the courtyard for the telling of the Hoī *kahānī,* a story that describes how the anger of the goddess brought about the death of the children of a household, and how the performance of the ritual brought them back to life. During the story, the women hold seven grains of unhusked rice in their hands, and at its conclusion, they tie these grains in a knot in their *pallā*s. Then they massage the legs (*pā̃õ bhī̃cānā*) of any senior women who are present.

In the evening, when the eighth day of the lunar cycle actually commences, the women who are carrying out the ritual place a large earthen pot (*ghaṛā*) filled with water before the drawing of Hoī, and a smaller pot (*kaṛvā*) also filled with water is positioned on top of it. On top of the *kaṛvā* the women place an earthen saucer filled with puffed rice (*khīl*) and sugar wafers (*batāsā*). Protective threads are tied around the neck of each of the pots. Meanwhile the women prepare a sweet pudding (*halawā*), rice, lentils, and fried breads. Each woman prepares a tray of these foods and places one rupee on the tray as *dakṣiṇā,* the "payment" to the recipient for the acceptance of the prestation that is to be made. The sons of each woman are called and seated near the drawing of Hoī, in which they themselves have been represented. Earthen lamps filled with clarified butter are lit, and burning embers are brought from the hearth. Each woman places a full set of cloth over the clay pots, and takes a bit of the food and puts it on the embers. Finally, a *dhok mārnā* is done with the unhusked rice that the women tied in their *pallā*s at the morning activities. Then the women pick up this rice, the tray of food, and the cloth. The set of cloth is first placed on the heads of the sons and then on the head of the recipient, who eats from the food on the tray and receives the grain from the mother's *pallā.*

These prestations are called *bayanā,* and they are given to one's husband's mother (*sās*), or to the wife of one's husband's elder brother (*jiṭhānī*), or more infrequently, to an elder sister of one's husband (*nanad*) or his father's sister (*buā*). (The latter two possible recipients are never referred to as *dhiyānī* in this context, even though referentially they fall into this category.) As the recipient holds the cloth and the tray, the donor massages her legs and receives the blessings of the older woman:

> *Sāī jite raho*
> *bhāī jite raho*
> *beṭā de bhagvān*
>
> May your husband live long,
> may your brothers live long,
> may God give you sons.

Following this, the puffed rice and sugar wafers are given as *prasād* to the sons for whom the ritual has been performed, although this is not nearly as important to the efficacy of the ritual as the giving of the *bayanā*.

The sequence of actions leading up to the acceptance of the *bayanā*, as well as the comments of Pahansu women, indicate that this prestation transfers negative substances from the sons of the performer of the ritual to the recipient, just as *pujāpā* does. But villagers seldom referred to *bayanā* as *pujāpā*, and were agreed that *bayanā* should not be thought of as *dān*, despite the fact that it is given for the same reasons that one gives *dān*, in the context of the same sort of ritual actions.

There are other linguistic usages that bear upon this distinction. When I asked women why this *bayanā* prestation is made to the *sās*, the *jiṭhānī*, older *nanad*, or *phūphas* (husband's father's sister), the reply was always that "it is their appropriate obligation" (*unkā pharmāyā hai*) to accept it. This notion of "obligation" is of course attached to the acceptance of *pujāpā* and *dān* as well. Given the obvious similarities, then, I would go on to ask these informants why *bayanā* is not *pujāpā*, and why it is totally excluded from the category of *dān*. Here again, the answer was always the same. *Bayanā*, the women explained, unlike ordinary *pujāpā* or *dān*, is given to one's seniors in age or genealogical position, to "one's bigger persons" (*bayanā apne baṛe ko de*). This fact is emphasized in the *pāõ bhīcānā* that is performed in the context of the *bayanā* prestation, but never in the context of the giving of *dān* and *pujāpā*, even though the recipients may in some cases (the husband's sister and husband's father's sister) be the same. Such deferential acts as leg massaging or feet touching are never performed in the context of giving *dān* and *pujāpā*. And in the giving of *dān* and *pujāpā*, the recipients are never referred to as *apne baṛe*, "one's seniors."

It is terribly important for the well-being of her sons that each mother be able to give the Hoī *bayanā* to a senior person (almost always a woman) of her *sasurāl*, and elaborate coordination of donors with recipients is sometimes necessary in order to ensure that each woman will be able to make the prestation in the appropriate manner. Several married daughters of the village were in Pahansu at the time I observed this Hoī ritual. It is generally more efficacious if the prestations are made in one's *sasurāl* itself, but should a woman be visiting her *pīhar,* she must nevertheless give the *bayanā* on the eighth day of the dark half of Kārttik. What the daughters of Pahansu did was to locate a woman married into Pahansu who was a "daughter" of the donor's *sasurāl* and who was older than the Pahansu daughter. This woman would be related to the donor in two ways: as *nanad* (husband's sister), from the point of view of her *sasurāl,* but also as *bhābhī* (brother's wife), from the perspective of her *pīhar.* In the context of the *bayanā* prestation, it was the former relationship that was foregrounded and acted upon, although this would in ordinary situations never be the case, because women always say that in the contexts of such double relationships, they normally act upon the relationship "from the direction of the natal village" (*pīhar kī taraf se*).[36]

One very old Gujar woman, a widow in Pahansu known only as *candanpurvālī* ("the one from village Candanpur") was acknowledged, by careful genealogical reckoning, to be the "oldest," the "biggest" woman in Pahansu. Since there was no one "older" than she (*us se baṛī koī nahī̃ hai*), she gave her *bayanā* to a Brahman. A Brahman is "bigger" than a Gujar, just as genealogically senior (though perhaps chronologically younger) women are "older."

What is interesting here is that it is only with reference to the giving of *bayanā* that the linguistic usages, deference behavior, and the intercaste relationship that may be involved, (the *candanpurvālī* gives her *bayanā* to a Brahman precisely because he is "bigger") indicate that hierarchy is an important aspect of one's appropriateness as a *pātra;* the absence of these indications in all of the other *dān, caṛhāpā,* and *pujāpā* prestations is striking.

The ritual of *kaṛvā cauth* is the only other occasion in Pahansu for the giving of *bayanā.* This ritual, also performed in the month of Kārttik, is concerned with the auspiciousness of one's husband, and is therefore performed only by women who have living husbands, that is, women who are *suhāgans.* (*Kaṛvā cauth* is very widely observed in North India, but in Pahansu, Gujars do not observe this *vrat.* What follows is a description of the ritual as it is performed by Pahansu Brahman and Barber women.)

On the morning of *kaṛvā cauth,* the women of a household or neighborhood sit together to hear the story of the efficacy of the ritual. Each woman holds a handful of rice in her hand as she listens to the story and, as in the Hoī ritual, ties it in her *pallā* at the conclusion of the telling. The women keep a fast throughout the day. In the evening, fried breads and a sweet pudding are prepared and placed on a tray, along with one rupee to be given as *dakṣiṇā,* and a set of cloth. A *karvā,* an earthen pot, is filled with water, and the woman who is performing the ritual draws a *sathiyā* design (a swastika) on the pot with a pinch of turmeric. She takes a handful of water from the pot and does a *mīnasnā,* circling in a counterclockwise direction around the tray of food and the set of cloth. Then a bit of food from the tray is placed on some embers and *dhok mārnā* is done to the items on the tray with the grains of rice that have been tied in the *pallā.* Finally, the woman does *nackār* to the tray: she touches the *pallā* of her shawl first to her forehead and then to the tray. Through the *dhok mārnā* and the *nackār,* the inauspiciousness that may be afflicting her husband is transferred to the items to be given as *bayanā.* The *bayanā* prestation is then made to the woman's husband's mother or to his father. Here, too, as in the context of the *hoī bayanā,* the prestation is said to be given to "one's big ones" (*apne baṛe ko*).

The transferral of inauspiciousness effected through the *dhok mārnā* and most particularly through the *nackār* is graphically depicted in the *kaṛvā cauth kahānī* that the Brahman women told in Pahansu.

> There was a king, and he had seven sons and one daughter. These seven brothers had great affection for their sister, and they wouldn't eat their food without their sister.
>
> So that day was *kaṛvā cauth.* They [the seven brothers] came and began saying: "Ma, give food, to us and to our sister." Their mother said: "You eat food, your sister is keeping a fast today. Having seen the moon, then she will eat food." So the brothers said: "We also will eat then." They all spoke in that way.
>
> And then it happened that one of the brothers climbed up into a *pīpal* tree, taking a lamp with him. He showed that lamp [from the tree] and his sister thought that the moon had come out, so that sister poured water out [a reference to the *kaṛvā cauth* ritual action] and ate her food.
>
> And then, just as she was eating food, news came that that sister's husband had died, because she had eaten food [before the moon had really come up]. So her mother said: "Put on white clothes [i.e., clothes of widowhood], and having put on white clothes go off to your *sasurāl.*"
>
> So on the road, she did *nackar* to everything, to the Yamuna River, to trees, to all the men, and in that way she reached her own garden, where her husband was lying. And for the full year, until the next *kaṛvā cauth,* she served (*sevā karnā*) her husband, her dead husband, by massaging his legs and doing other things. So the next *kaṛvā cauth* came. She saw that all the women there were fasting (*vratī thī*) and were taking out the *bayanā* (*bayanā kāṛhnā*). Just then her husband sat up and said: "Since when have I been sleeping?" That girl said: "For a full year I have been serving you." So they went to her *sūsar* [husband's father], to the house of her husband.

> And when she went back [to the house of her brothers], she saw that those trees and plants that she had done *nackār* to, they had dried up, and the men had become sick, from receiving the *nackār* (*nackār milne se*). But when they saw her going back, they became green again.

In the story, the results of receiving the *bayanā* are fairly explicitly compared to the drying up of the plants and the sickening of the men to whom the *nackār* had been directed for the well-being of the woman's husband. When a woman does *nackār* in the course of the *karvā cauth* ritual, she transfers inauspiciousness to the *bayanā* prestations.

But why should it be the case that the prestations of Hoī and *karvā cauth* are given to people of one's household, who are "one's big ones," the older people? I asked this question many times in Pahansu, but was told only that it is the *pharmāyā* of these persons to accept it. But why should it be "appropriately obligatory" in these two cases for *apne baṛe* to accept the *bayanā*, when in all other cases of the giving of such prestations, this dimension of rank or age is not the foregrounded aspect of the social relationship?

It will be remembered that in many ritual contexts, inauspicious substances must be returned to their source in order to remove them from the afflicted person. This is most obvious in the *martak* prestations, and in the *pujāpā* prestations that are offered to a deity before being given onward to an appropriate *pātra*. In these and many other instances, inauspiciousness flows spontaneously in one direction, and then must be turned around and returned to the source before it may successfully be "given onward." It is possible that such a return to the source is relevant to our interpretation of the *bayanā* prestations. There seems to be a general idea in North India that inauspiciousness is very likely to move spontaneously from older people in the family to younger. For example, in the *pair pūjā* (the first ritual action taken to remove the inauspiciousness of death from the dead man's family), the ritual actions and the making of the prestations are done *riśte ke anusār*, "according to relationship": only those women who are junior to the deceased need to make these prestations. This notion is more clearly articulated in *Mamaji*, Ved Mehta's reminiscences of his Panjabi mother. As a child, Mehta caught cerebrospinal meningitis, which left him totally blind. He recounts the circumstances of his illness:

> Mamaji remembers going back and forth between Bhabhiji's bedside and Ved's. Bhabhiji [Ved's father's mother] was sick for only a few days, and then was able to walk around, but Ved was sick for weeks and could scarcely move his head. When Bhabhiji recovered, Mamaji feared all the more for her child's life, because it was said that if a very

old person gets sick and then gets well, the weight of that old person's illness will settle on the shoulders of a small child. She felt resentful, although she often told herself, "As many tongues, so many sayings."

Mamaji remembers that she visited Bhabhiji one day and saw her sitting up and spinning, and then went to the hospital and heard Ved ask, "Is it night or day?"

Mamaji couldn't find her voice to answer. (Mehta 1979, 318)

There are two salient points in this narrative. The first is that this illness, like the inauspicious substances that Pahansu villagers are so often concerned about, cannot simply end or disappear; it must be recycled, and if it leaves one person it must be deposited somewhere else. Second, the spontaneous flow is downward from elder to younger kinsmen. That it is sometimes necessary for such illness, such inauspiciousness, to be taken back by the senior kinsmen was suggested in a story that Telu Ram, my Gujar "brother," told me in the context of a discussion of the *bayanā* prestations.

The emperor Babur's son Humayan was sick. Babur asked a *maulvī* [Muslim healer] how his son could be saved. The *maulvī* told Babur to walk around the son's bed seven times, and in that way Humayan would be saved but Babur would die.

Telu Ram then drew out the parallels between the story and the *bayanā*. In both cases, he said, "sorrows" (*dukh*) and "pain" (*kleś*) are transferred to another, to persons who are older than the person who is to be "saved." It may be that at these two calendrical rituals, it is deemed appropriate that "one's big ones" take back the inauspiciousness that may have flowed from them in the course of the year to their sons and sons' sons. Thus the *bayanā*, "the sowing," is done only in one's own fields.

There is one further peculiarity of *bayanā* as a prestation made to remove inauspiciousness that distinguishes it from all other such prestations. It said that "the *bayanā* is not taken 'empty'" (*rītī nahī̃ lete, bayanā*), that is, the recipient should make a prestation of a set of cloth to the son for whose protection the *bayanā* has been accepted. According to Pahansu women, the Hoī *bayanā*, like *dān* and *pujāpā*, is given "for the well-being achieved through gift-giving of one's children" (*apne baccõ ke khair-khairāt ke māro*). But the prestation made by the *bayanā* recipient to these children is not given for her own well-being but for theirs, the auspiciousness of the sons (*laṛkõ kā śubh*). The older women both accept inauspiciousness and bestow auspiciousness in the form of a set of cloth and with the blessing *sāī jite raho bhāī jite raho beṭā de bhagvān*, which they mutter during the *kaṛvā cauth* and the Hoī leg massages that they receive; recipients of ordinary *dān* and *pujāpā* only remove inauspiciousness.

These rituals of the yearly cycle are performed and the prestations made to remove inauspiciousness and to transfer it to the appropriate recipient. In the case of the *bhāīyā dauj* ritual, a woman performs the ritual actions and accepts a prestation for the well-being and auspiciousness of her brothers. In all other cases, a woman (and sometimes her husband) performs the rituals for her own well-being and that of her husband and sons, and she gives the *dān,* the *pujāpā,* the *caṛhāpā,* or the *bayanā* to remove inauspiciousness. In Pahansu, this giving of *dān* is the most important aspect of these calendrical rituals.

Many of these rituals of the yearly cycle are called *vrat*. This very common North Indian ritual form has been discussed extensively by Wadley (1975, 1976) in particular. Wadley never mentions that prestations are made in the *udāpan,* the conclusion of the *vrat*. She deals almost exclusively with the stories that are associated with these rituals, relying partly on the published Hindi texts of the stories that are available in North Indian bazaars. She attempts to analyze these rituals and stories in terms of hierarchical relations between a woman and her husband, her brothers, and her sons. In these rituals, she argues, the husband, the brother, and the sons are "deities" in relation to the women, "deities whose worship is performed yearly to obtain for women the benefits of their powers" (Wadley 1976, 165). This formulation not only ignores the very different ritual roles of a woman in relation to her brothers and other natal kin on the one hand and to her husband and sons on the other, but it also obscures the most fundamental ritual process in these *vrat*s. What is most crucial in these rituals is not "worship," for as we have seen, identical ritual actions may be performed in the absence of any sort of "deity" at all. What structures all of these ritual sequences is a process of "disarticulation" and "removal" of inauspiciousness from brothers, husbands, and sons—a process we have examined in detail and seen repeated again and again. In Pahansu the culmination of this process is the giving of *dān*.

Getting Sons, Removing *Kaṣṭ:* Discovering Inauspiciousness and the Giving of *Dān*

Vrat and other disarticulative rituals are performed, not only at particular points in the life course and at specified times during the year, but also when a diagnosis has been made, often by an astrologer, that an illness or other distress has been brought about by inauspiciousness that has "come upon" (*caṛhnā*) and "become attached to" (*lagnā*) a person, a household, or a village. We have already seen instances of these rituals: the *kālī kā bhẽṭ* performed in Pahansu after the death of two Camar girls and some of the cases discussed in the final section of chapter 2. In the brief section that follows, I describe other cases in which *dān* was given as an ameliorative technique.

A young Gujar wife in Pahansu had been married for several years and had failed to conceive a son. During a visit to her natal village, she consulted a Brahman whom she characterized, in her description to me, only as a *paṇḍit*. The *paṇḍit*'s diagnosis was that *kaṣṭ* had come upon her husband, and he recommended that she perform a *vrat* for thirty-six *amāvas* (new-moon) days, that is, for three years. The woman fasted on every *amāvas* day, and she told me that she would perform the *udāpan* on the thirty-sixth *amāvas*. The *paṇḍit* had told her to do the *udāpan* in this way: brass pots, *sīdhā khānā* (raw foodstuffs), and sets of cloth were to be given to the family Washerwoman as *caṛhāpā*. As a result of the *vrat* itself, she and her husband's brothers' wives told me, "the *kaṣṭ* comes out" (*kaṣṭ utar jā*) and then, from giving the *udāpan,* "the *kaṣṭ* is made far" (*udāpan karne se kaṣṭ dūr ho jā*). In these statements, the essential structure of the ritual is described just as we have seen it depicted in the *mantra*s recited by the priest at the *mūl śānti:* actions preliminary to the giving of *dān* disarticulate the inauspiciousness from the victim ("the *kaṣṭ* comes out") and the prestation itself removes it ("the *kaṣṭ* is made far").

A family in the village of Landhauri, just to the north of Pahansu, had been experiencing some difficulties; among other things, a member had suffered a serious burn. So the family had decided to consult Buddhu Pandit to find a remedy for the sorrows that had come upon them. Buddhu Pandit determined that it was the Landhauri Bhūmiyā who had visited these afflictions upon them and that the only way to remove the difficulties was to perform a Bhūmiyā *pāṭh* and to make offerings at his shrine that would then be given as *dān*. For five days Buddhu recited *mantra*s at the shrine. On the fifth day, he took me with him to Landhauri for the fire sacrifice that was to be performed, as Buddhu put it, "for the protection of the village" (*gā̃õ kī rakṣā ke lie*). The *havan* was performed, at the end of which Buddhu told the men to circumambulate the Bhūmiyā shrine three times, as he recited the *mantra*s for "the guardian of the space" (*khetrapāl*). As the men circled, these *mantra*s would remove the evil (*pāp*) that had brought about their misfortunes. Offerings of food were then made to Bhūmiyā, which Buddhu received as *caṛhāpā*. Finally, Buddhu instructed the men to "make the *sankalp* and give the *dakṣiṇā*." They did so, and Buddhu received a *dakṣiṇā* of fifty rupees for the recitation of the *mantra*s of the *pāṭh,* and one and one-quarter rupees for conducting the worship of the nine planets that had preceded the *havan*.

While I was in Landhauri with Buddhu, several people came to him asking his advice about various problems. A Water-carrier man told of the difficulties that had been besetting him and asked Buddhu to "look in the almanac" to see what could be done. Using the determinations based on the name *rāśi,* Buddhu determined that the planet Śani was the source of the man's afflictions. Buddhu told the man that exactly at noon on a Saturday, he should cast his reflection (*chāyā*) into an iron vessel filled with oil, into which a copper coin or some other copper thing had been placed, making sure that the copper was in the oil before the reflection was cast. After doing that, the man should "secretly" (*cup-cāp se*) take these things and dump them into a crossroads. This, Buddhu said, would remove and make far the *kaṣṭ* of Śani. When the man left, Buddhu said to me that whenever there is any distress (*āpatti*), *dān* is given. The "remedy" (*upāy*) that he had described to this man is a kind of *dān:* "There is a giver but no special taker" (*dān denevālā hai lekin koī khās lenevālā nahī̃ hai*), but the *kaṣṭ* would nevertheless be removed when the oil and the piece of copper were placed in the crossroads.

Punno, a Gujar man of Pahansu, consulted Buddhu Pandit and his father, Raghu, after two of his water buffaloes died unexpectedly. According to Buddhu Pandit, "the very fierce glance of Śani was upon him" (*uske ūpar bahut krūr driṣṭi hai śani kā*). Buddhu advised Punno to have a Śani *pāṭh* performed in an inner room of his house and then to give the *dān* of Śani.

For nine days, Raghu recited the *mantra*s in an inner room of Punno's house. On the ninth day, as he completed the *mantra*s, he led Punno in the recitation of the *sankalp* for the *dān* that was to be given: Punno of the Barsohe *got,* the resolution said, in the year 2035, in the *uttarāyaṇa* segment of the year, on the tenth day of the bright half of the month of Māgh, was prepared as *jajmān* to give the *dān* of Śani. A *havan* was performed, and the *dān* of Śani—a set of black cloth, ten and one-quarter *ser* of uncooked foodstuffs, and an iron vessel—was given to a Dakaut in order to remove the inauspiciousness that had beset Punno's household because of "the motions of the planets" (*grahacāl*).

That ritual centrality is a particularly emphasized characteristic of Gujars as the dominant caste is underscored in a comparison of Buddhu's advice to the Water-carrier and his consultation with Punno's family. The Water-carrier man was told to dump his iron vessel in the crossroads. When I asked Buddhu about this, he told me that he would seldom give such advice to a Gujar, and in fact I never heard him do so. Gujars expect to be able to give *dān* to a "particular recipient" (*khās pātra*) whose innate disposition befits (*phabnā*) him to accept that particular *dān.* Gujars see this as a more efficacious *dān,* and they also see it as an essential component of their ritual centrality, their position as the preeminent *jajmān*s in relation to the other castes of the village.

On the Appropriateness of *Pātras*

To the extent that *dān* has been considered at all in ethnographic accounts of intercaste and kinship relationships, it has been seen as an inherently hierarchic prestation. As I pointed out in the Introduction, Parry (1980) has argued that *dān* is given to Brahmans (and Brahmans are the only recipients of *dān* that he acknowledges) because they are hierarchically superior to the donor; if they see this as an acceptance of the "evil" of the donor, it is because, according to Parry, the donor is an "inferior" person and the Brahman is accepting "inferior essences" through the gift. Trautmann too interprets the hesitation of the Brahman to accept *dān* as arising from the inferior status of the donor (Trautmann 1981, 287).

In Pahansu and apparently in many other parts of Hindu South Asia, *dān* is given, not only to Brahmans, but also to Barbers, to Sweepers, to Doms and Dakauts, to anyone who happens to pass by a crossroads, to one's married daughters and sisters and their husbands, and to many other recipients. Hierarchically, these recipients of *dān* are extremely heterogeneous, and as all of them acknowledge that they receive the *pāp* and *nāśubh* of the donor, the *jajmān*, this evil and inauspiciousness cannot simply be a matter of relative superiority and inferiority of donor and recipient.

Sanskrit textual traditions concerning sacrifice and the gift also describe the giving of prestations containing evil and sin not just to the Brahman (Gonda 1965, 222) but to an equally heterogeneous list of recipients. In the *rājasūya* sacrifice, for example, the king as sacrificer is circled with a copper razor, which is given to a Barber in order to remove "danger" from the king: "He throws away the evil" as the texts put it (Heesterman 1957, 111–12). At the conclusion of an *aśvamedha* sacrifice, evil is taken away by affinal relatives and by the rival (Heesterman 1985, 135).

That such a diverse list of recipients is necessary to maintain the auspiciousness and well-being of the donor is indicated in Pahansu thought about the sources of evil and inauspiciousness in the world, and the proper disposition of this evil. When I asked villagers why certain kinds of *dān* were given to certain recipients, the answer that almost inevitably followed was *unkā pharmāyā hai,* "it is their appropriate obligation." This comment was sometimes followed by a remark to the effect that those recipients cannot refuse to accept the *dān*. There were a few villagers who were able to discuss the issue at greater length, and their remarks enabled me to discern some of the patterns in the giving of *dān*, *caṛhāpā*, and *pujāpā*.

One important insight came from Mangal Singh, a Gujar man who because of his devotion to the goddess Shakumbhari and her shrine in the Siwalik Hills was perhaps less interested in the village gods, and because

A Gujar neighborhood in Pahansu.

A Camar woman prepares the elaborate *ṭakkarpūrat* for the protection of Gujar cattle, agricultural implements, and the sugarcane harvest at the annual ritual of *godhan*. On the following day, she will accept the *godhan caṛhāpā* from Gujar *jajmāns*.

A Barber woman accepts flour and unrefined sugar as the *caṛhāpā* of the *ṭakkurpūrat* she has drawn on the ground at a Gujar wedding.

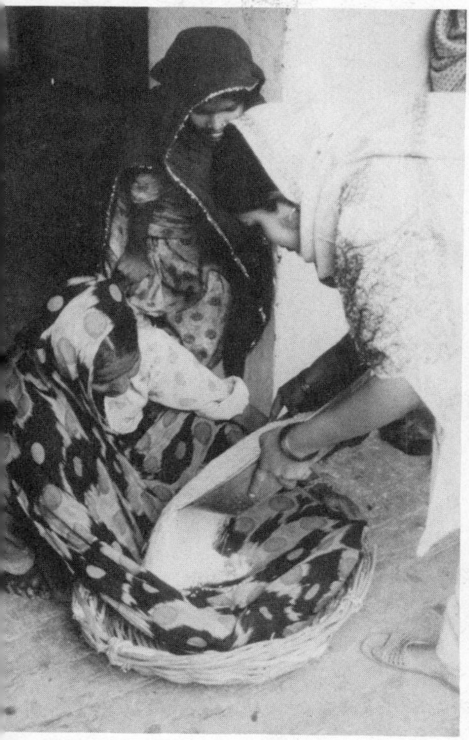

Jholī pasārnā: a Sweeper woman spreads out the end of her shawl to receive flour and salt as the *caṛhāpā* of the "goddess of the village site" (*gām-kheṛī mātā*) from a Gujar woman.

A Brahman *purohit* of Pahansu accepts flour and unrefined sugar as *caṛhāpā* at the festival of *holī*.

Asikaur, a Gujar woman, gives the *caṛhāpā* of Gugga to a man of the Potter caste.

Trays of food and sets of cloth to be given as *dān* for the "well-being achieved through gift-giving" (*khair-khairāt*) of Gujar men at the festival of Hoi.

Gujar women perform the winnowing of the rice during the *halad* segment of the wedding rites. The rice will later be given as *caṛhāpā* to the family's Brahman *purohit*.

Dahej dekhan: women inspect the *joṛās* (sets of cloth) to be given at a Gujar wedding.

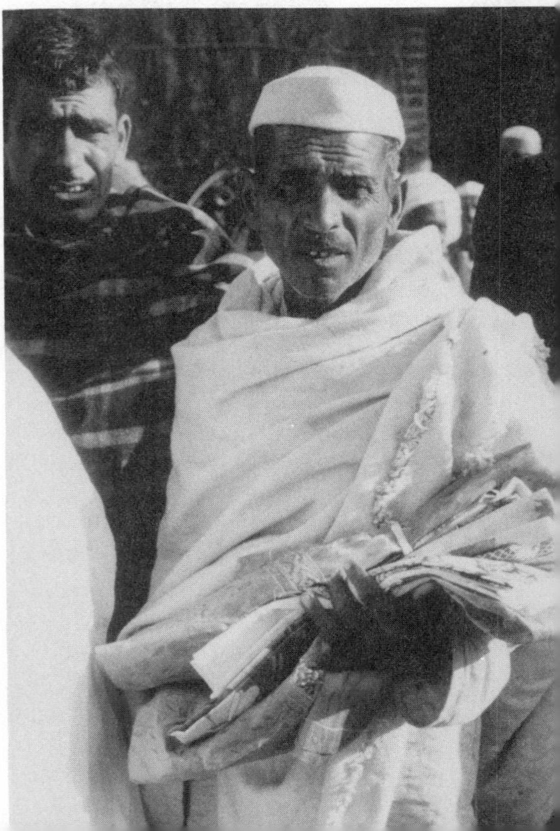

A Gujar man, the *māmā* (mother's brother) of a girl about to be married in Pahansu, comes to the village to give a *telṇ* (full set of cloth) as part of his *bhāt* prestation. For "his own well-being achieved through gift-giving" (*apne khair-khairāt ke māro*), he will place the set of cloth on his sister's head at the threshold of her conjugal house.

Gujar men at the *maṇḍhā* wedding rite.

Jholī pasārnā: a Gujar groom "spreads out the begging bag" as the cash portion of the *dahej* is placed in the outstretched end of his shawl at the *paṭṭā* segment of the wedding rites. Jewelry to be given in the *dahej* lies in a brass tray, and other items to be given—brass vessels, sets of cloth, a bed, and so forth—are arrayed behind the groom.

A heavily veiled Gujar bride arrives at the threshold of her husband's house for the first time, and *wārpher* is performed with pots of water, mango leaves, and the rope from the household churn.

Buddhu Pandit prepares the *vedis* for the ritual of the giving of Rāhu *kā dān*. The nine "planets" are represented in the square to the right.

Buddhu Pandit places black cloth on Arvind's head before it is given as Rāhu *kā dān* to the Dakaut who waits at the left. The other items to be given in *dān* are on the ground. The flat iron vessel at Arvind's feet contains the "bitter oil" into which Arvind's reflection, and the inauspiciousness afflicting him, will be cast.

Two Gujar men of Pahansu.

Ram Swarup Bhāṭ, who before his death in 1978 served as professional genealogist and bard to his Gujar *jajmān*s in Pahansu. He made his home in a Gujar village in Muzaffarnagar District and traveled across several districts to visit his patrons. His *pothī*, the book in which he recorded the births and marriages of the men of the village, is spread out before him.

Gujar women approach the shrine of Bhūmiyā ("the one of the land") to make offerings to him and to give the *caṛhāpā* to the wife of their Brahman *purohit*.

Mangal Singh: "We too are such givers of *dān*, the Khūbaṛs of today."

of his childlessness, less interested in the rituals of the life course that defined and established well-being and auspiciousness for most villagers. Just after I had begun to learn of the importance of giving *pujāpā* to particular recipients at the conclusion of rituals addressed to the gods of the village and the gods of the calendrical cycle, I asked Mangal Singh why there were different *pātras*, different appropriate recipients, for the *pujāpā* of the different gods. My tape recorder was not running at the time, but his remarks, which I recorded in Hindi in my notebooks, filled three and one-half pages.

He began by telling me that Kali is a goddess who "gives the punishment of death" (*mṛityu daṇḍ denevālī hai*) and who has "the form of a demon" (*rākṣas rūp*). She kills men and drinks their blood. Mangal Singh went on to say that among the Sudra castes, Sweepers do the most violence and meat-eating (*śudrā jātõ mẽ bhangī sab se zyādā hinsā karte haĩ*); they raise pigs and offer them to their ancestral deities, and then eat the meat themselves, and that is the reason that it is appropriate to give the *pujāpā* of Kali to Sweepers. One gives *pujāpā* to a recipient who is in some way like the deity or the source of the inauspiciousness that the *dān* is intended to remove. As Mangal Singh put it, "As the nature and the form [of the deity] is, to such a person the *pujāpā* is given" (*jaise svabhāv aur mūrti hai, aise ādmī ko pujāpā dete haĩ*).

Mangal Singh, still in response to my original question, began to tell me of the shrine of a Muslim saint called Sarwar Pir in the nearby village of Baghakheri. *Pūjā* is done there on Thursdays, Mangal said, and women may go there after a water buffalo has given birth. When the first milk comes from which butter can be made (a week or two after the birth), the first *baloā* of butter, the yield of one churning (*bilonā*), is offered at the shrine of this Muslim *pīr*. The butter is then given as *pujāpā* to a man of the Muslim Pharai caste who serves as *pujārī* at the shrine. Mangal Singh told me that the Pharai is the appropriate recipient in this case, just as Water-carriers are the appropriate recipients and *pujārīs* when *pūja* is done near a well.

In the examples that Mangal Singh gave, and in the relationship that he saw between the nature (*svabhāv*) and form (*mūrtī*) of the deity and the nature and form (*ākār*) of the recipient of *pujāpā*, he was very clearly postulating a similarity between the sources of inauspiciousness and the various "receptacles," the recipients. It is a question, Mangal Singh said, of whether the recipients are "fit for the work" (*kām karne yogya*); "purity" (*pavitratā*) and matters of high and low are "different reckonings" (*dūsrā hissāb*) according to him.

The resemblances to the source of inauspiciousness may sometimes involve considerations that are relevant to the hierarchical orderings of castes, but there are many other such considerations that do not seem to implicate hierarchy. The *pujāpā* of Guggā, for example, given at *gūggā naumī* in the month of Bhādwe, is given to a recipient who is appropriate by virtue of the fact that he had once been possessed by Guggā, who had "come into his body" (*śarīr mẽ ānā*). When offerings are made to these recipients, Guggā is said to receive them, while the inauspiciousness of the *bāgharvālā* (Guggā, "the one from Baghar") is assimilated by the *pātra*, the recipient of the *pujāpā*. In Pahansu, this *pujāpā* is given to a Potter and two Camars, and in Landhauri, a village near Pahansu in which there is a Guggā shrine (called a *māṛhī*) a man of the Padha caste receives the *pujāpā*.

In these cases, and in many of the *dān* prestations discussed in this chapter, it is possible to discern correspondences, or more properly, sharing of qualities or substance between the source of inauspiciousness and the appropriate *pātra*. They must "match" or befit one another (*phabnā*), in the words of many Pahansu informants, if the recipient is to "digest" (*pacnā*) and assimilate the inauspiciousness. Each particular *dān* must be given to a "matched" (*phabyā*) recipient, or the transferral of inauspiciousness will not be accomplished. Thus Gujars and other donors in Pahansu do not give *dān, caṛhāpā,* and *pujāpā* to recipients other than Brahmans as a less efficacious, less meritorious alternative; some *dān* and *caṛhāpā* must by its very nature be given to Brahmans, while others must be given to Barbers, to Sweepers, to those into whose body the *bāgharvālā* has come, to *dhiyānī* and *dhiyāne,* and to many other *pātra*s who are the appropriate recipients and whose obligation it is to accept them.

Hierarchy, as an aspect of intercaste relations, is not the foregrounded aspect of the social situation in the context of the giving of *dān*. Further evidence for this assertion is presented in the following chapter, through a detailed discussion of prestations other than *dān,* and of the various ways of construing these prestations that are encountered in everyday life in Pahansu.

CHAPTER FIVE

Prestation Types and Terminological Usages: Shifting Configurations of Castes and Kinsmen in Pahansu

The many forms of *dān* described in chapter 4 are all given, it is said, "for one's own well-being" and "to remove inauspiciousness." A number of general characteristics typify prestations of this sort. First, they are given to kinsmen and to people of various *jāti*s because, in the particular contexts in which the prestations are made, these recipients are conceived of, not as "one's own" (*apnā*), but as "other." Second, it is of the essence of *dān, caṛhāpā,* and *pujāpā* that they not be reciprocated in any way, and that they not be given "in exchange" (*badle mẽ*) for any goods or services. And finally, the giver of *dān* is said to have the "right" (*hak*) to give, while the recipient has the "obligation" (*pharmāyā*) to accept.

Prestations construed in these terms are not the only form of giving and receiving in the village. The Gujars, the Brahmans, the Barbers, and the Sweepers, the givers of *kanyā dān* and their *dhiyānī* and *dhiyāne,* those who have the "right" to give *dān* and those who have the "obligation" to accept it are all involved in the giving and receiving of many other specifically named prestations that are fundamentally different from *dān, caṛhāpā,* and *pujāpā* and, I will argue, that foreground other aspects of kinship and intercaste relationships in Pahansu. In this chapter, I will consider a number of prestations that are said to be given to "one's own" people rather than to those who are "other." These gifts are frequently reciprocated, sometimes with excruciating precision, and it is said that the recipient has a "right" to claim them. I will then consider the multiple and shifting meanings of both sorts of prestations, and finally, their relationship to hierarchically constituted relationships within the village. I will examine the way in which a given relationship may in some instances be characterized by an oriented flow of inauspiciousness, in others by what I will term "mutuality," and in still other contexts by hierarchical distinctions.

There is no one Hindi term that encompasses a category of reciprocal prestations, those that imply a mutuality of services rendered and payments received, and those that are given to "one's own people" (*apne ādmī*) simply because it is appropriate to engage in "giving and receiving" (*len-den*) with them. Nonetheless, I discuss many such prestations together here, and I view them as being culturally constituted in very similar terms, as possessing what Wittgenstein (1958, 17) might call "family resemblances," which emerge from a number of different sources: (1) proverbs and villagers' characterizations of these givings and receivings, (2) terminological usages with respect to donor and recipient that occur when the prestations are made, and (3) the permutational patterns that present themselves when intercaste prestations of this sort become matters of intra-*jāti* kinship gifting. These "family resemblances," and the particular named prestations that may thus be subsumed under the general rubric "mutuality" will be described in detail in the following pages.

At the Threshing Place: *Phaslānā*

Of the fifteen castes that are represented in Pahansu, members of six *jāti*s obtain their livelihood primarily through what has been called the *jajmānī* system. Members of these castes are said to be "attached" (*lage hue*) or "joined" (*joṛe hue*) to their Gujar *jajmān*s; in exchange for their various services, they receive payments of grain called *phaslānā* (from *phasal*, harvest) at the *sāvanī* harvest of rice and the *sāṛhī* harvest of wheat.

The only portion of the harvest that Brahmans receive is the *sāvṛī* prestation, described in the previous chapter, and it is not considered to be *phaslānā* precisely because it is not seen as payment for services rendered. The "shares" (*hissā*) of the harvests given in 1978–79 by Telu Ram, a substantial Gujar landholder, are as follows:

Barber: The Barber's "reckoning" (*hissāb*) is according to the number of men to be shaved in the *jajmān*'s household. For each man, he receives four *dhaṛī* (*kaccā*)—about twenty kilograms—of grain at each harvest. For Telu Ram's household, this amounts to a total of sixteen *dhaṛī* of grain per harvest. The Barber also receives at least three or four *dhaṛī* of unrefined sugar (*śakkar*) at the time it is processed from the *jajmān*'s sugarcane harvest.

Washerman: The Washerman receives eighty kilograms of grain per *chamāī* (six-month period) as well as twenty to thirty kilograms of *śakkar*, specifically for the work of washing clothes in the village pond.

Sweeper: For the Sweeper, the reckoning is according to the number of plows in use by the *jajmān*'s household (according to a presumed connection between the number of bullock-pulled plows and the amount of dung to be collected). Telu Ram uses a tractor now, but prior to this purchase his family had three plows in use, so they use this number for determining the payment to their Sweeper. For each plow, three and one-half *dhaṛī* of grain is given at each harvest. The Sweeper of this family thus receives "three plows of grain" (*tīn halõ kā anāj*), or ten and one-half *dhaṛī* per *chamāī*. Just before the rainy season (usually in May), each Sweeper family also receives one *dhaṛī* of grain for constructing a *biṭauṛā,* a structure for storing cow-dung cakes during the months that follow.

Carpenter: The primary responsibilities of the Carpenter to his *jajmān* involve the maintenance of plows and other agricultural implements. Thus their *phaslānā* is also given according to the number of plows used by the *jajmān*. For each harvest, Telu Ram's Carpenter receives twenty kilograms per plow, and ten to fifteen kilograms of *śakkar* once a year.

Ironsmith: Also compensated according to the "plow-reckoning," (*hal kā hissāb*), the Ironsmith receives twenty kilograms of grain per *chamāī* for each plow.

Several points should be noted concerning this enumeration of the "shares" of the harvest given by the Gujar *jajmān* to those he calls his *gharelū,* those who are "of the house," and who are nourished and sustained by the grain of his fields. First, all the shares are given after the *jajmān* has winnowed, threshed, and weighed the grain, and the shares themselves are carefully weighed. While we must be careful to avoid the suggestion that a rationally accounted system of "wages" is a feature of this exchange system, it is the case that a relationship between services and compensation received is a part of the indigenous conceptual system, evidenced particularly here in the notion of *hal kā hissāb*. Most important, perhaps, it should be emphasized that *phaslānā* "shares" are not given to *kamīn*s for the performance of ritual services at life-cycle and calendrical rites; *phaslānā* is given for the specific services involved in shaving and hair-cutting, laundering, sweeping and collecting cow-dung, carpentry, and ironsmithing. (Payments for specific ritual services are termed *lāg, neg,* or *dakṣiṇā;* they will be discussed in detail below.)

When Gujars give *phaslānā* to their Barbers, Washermen, Sweepers, Carpenters, and Ironsmiths, the notion of "shares" is stressed as strongly as the notion of "payment." Gujar cultivators say that they give *phaslānā* to these castes because they are "sharers" (*hissedār*) and "one's own" (*apnā*) and because they are "of the house" (*gharelū*), "attached to and joined with" (*lage hue, joṛe hue*) the cultivator's household. Such terms, which foreground a "sharing" and a "one's own" relationship, never occur when the giving of *dān* to these same castes is at issue.

Non-*phaslānā* Payments for Caste-specific Goods and Services

The Potter, Merchant, Bangle-seller, and Goldsmith castes in the village still adhere to their traditional craft specialties and occupations, but they are not involved in hereditary relationships with patrons, and they do not receive *phaslānā*.

Potters supply various types of earthen vessels, manufactured in the village, for which they receive amounts of grain commensurate with the size of the vessels provided:

five *ser* (a *ser* is approximately two and one-half kilograms) of grain for a large pot
one and one-half *ser* of grain for a small pot
six *ser* of grain for a large vessel in which butter is churned
one *ser* of grain for two *cillam*s (water-pipe bowls)

In many villages around Pahansu, and in a number of the natal villages of the wives of Pahansu, Potters do receive *phaslānā* and in those cases the twice-yearly grain payments are said to be given *badle mẽ,* in exchange for the pots and other earthen vessels provided for the use of the *jajmān*.

The Muslim Bangle-sellers of Pahansu visit village houses periodically, especially at the time of weddings and particular calendrical festivals when it is deemed to be auspicious for married women to wear new sets of glass bangles. Payment for these bangles is made in grain. A Pahansu Goldsmith is engaged primarily in the repair of silver jewelry; his remuneration may be either in grain or in cash.

Because people of these three castes are not involved in hereditary relationships with Gujar *jajmān*s and because they do not receive *phaslānā,* Gujars say that they do not have "one's own" Potters, Bangle-sellers, and Goldsmiths in the village, though they recognize that in other villages such ties may exist. But there are nevertheless contexts in which the nature of the "taking-and-giving" (*len-den*) foregrounds an "attachment" (*lagnā*) between Gujar *jajmān* and the Potters, Bangle-sellers, and Goldsmiths of the village. At the birth of a son in a Gujar household, for instance, members of these three *jāti*s (as well as the *kamīn*s, the *gharelū*s of the household) visit the Gujar family at the sixth-day ritual (*chaṭṭhī*) and present *dūb* grass to the mother of the child; for this service they receive *lāg* (from *lagnā,* "to be attached" or "to be related") and are thought of as being in some ways and in this limited context "one's own."

This is not the case with the Jain Baniyas in Pahansu. Gujars say quite unequivocally that "they are not attached to us," not "connected" and not "related" (*hamāre gail lage hue nahī̃ haī̃*); Baniyas are "separate" (*alag-alag*). Payments for the small items purchased in their shops (for major purchases villagers generally travel to Rampur or to Saharanpur) are generally made on the spot; cash may occasionally be used but handfuls of grain are more frequently given. Here there is not "mutuality" but only exchange. The relationship of "one's own" between giver and taker that makes exchange a matter of *len-den* and mutuality is absent in the case of the relationship between Baniyas and other villagers. As people in Pahansu say, there is no *len-den* with Baniyas.

Agricultural Labor Arrangements

Because cultivating the soil often requires labor that the individual household is not able to provide (either because of extensive landholdings or because of the intensive labor that is required by almost all landholders at particular times in the growing seasons), there are many varieties of agricultural labor arrangements in Pahansu. Although all of these are conceptualized as arrangements in which remuneration is given in "exchange," these too, like the giving and taking between Gujars and Potters, Bangle-sellers, Goldsmiths, and Baniyas, may be seen as lying along a continuum, to the degree that the parties involved are "one's own" to one another.

For the planting of sugarcane (*īkh boāī*) in the months of March and April, a great deal of additional labor is needed, and it is generally obtained through an arrangement called *badlā* ("exchange," a term implying a reciprocity of giving and receiving) or *ḍangvārā*.[1] Such labor exchanges usually occur among men of one *kunbā*, but men of other Gujar *kunbā*s, and even men of other *jāti*s, may sometimes be involved. A group of men may work in the fields of one landholder for several days, and then move on to the fields of another. The cultivator is expected to provide a noon meal of *kaṛhī* (a soup made from chick-pea flour and buttermilk), rice, and bread made from a mixture of wheat flour and chick-pea flour, called *mīsī roṭī,* which is made only for this occasion and which is said to replace the strength (*tākt*) that the men expend in their arduous task.

The term *ḍangvārā* may also be used to refer to cooperative arrangements for plowing. If a Gujar man has two bullocks and a plow, he may take them to the fields of another Gujar cultivator and help him with the plowing, and the second man will in turn labor in the fields of the first. Other reciprocal arrangements among Gujar cultivators may also be defined as *ḍangvārā*. Sahib Singh, a Gujar resident in Pahansu but of a *got* other than Khūbaṛ (one of the *barsohevāle;* see chap. 1) inherited a small amount of land (fourteen *kaccā bīghā*s) and lives in Pahansu in order to cultivate those fields. He keeps only one water buffalo, and he has no bullock to pull a plow. A Khūbaṛ landholder, who lives in the house next to his, does the plowing for him, in return for which Sahib Singh provides occasional assistance in other agricultural tasks. This arrangement is *ḍangvārā,* the men explained, because the two men are "equal" (*barābar*) within its terms. Of the agricultural labor arrangements found in Pahansu, *ḍangvārā* exhibits the highest degree of mutuality, because of the symmetry in the conception of the relationship, and because of the very close "one's own" relationship between the men involved.

Another category of these labor arrangements involves fairly long-term relationships between landholders and men of the village who own little or no land but who work perhaps a few *bīghā*s of the land of the former in exchange for a percentage of the yield at the harvest. These relationships are called *sājhedārī* ("partnership"), *baṭāīdārī* ("crop-sharing," from the verb *bānṭnā,* "to distribute or divide") or *bohandārī* (from *bohanā* or *bonā,* "to sow"). They are characterized by Pahansu farmers as relationships that are most properly entered into among Gujars (although Gujar landholders do sometimes enter into them with men of other castes, on a limited basis) because of the inherent reciprocity that is involved:

sajjā dhoye khabbe ko
khabbā dhoye sajje ko

The right [hand] washes the left,
the left [hand] washes the right.

This saying (*kahāvat*) was often quoted to me, and it conveys the idea that both partners benefit from such arrangements. In Pahansu, few farmers entered into *baṭāīdārī* arrangements for the cultivation of rice, wheat, or sugarcane crops; they are most commonly employed in the small plots of cotton and vegetables that are grown for household use. (In Pahansu, cotton and vegetable yields are neither divided and apportioned as *phaslānā* nor sold as cash crops by Gujars.) The proportion of the yield that is given to the person who provides the labor varies; if labor only is provided, he receives one-fifth or one-sixth of the total yield. If the man providing the labor also provides one-third of the irrigation and fertilizer costs, and one-third of the land revenue, he receives one-third of the total yield. This sort of arrangement is, however, quite rare in Pahansu. If the "sharer" (*baṭāīdār*) has no bullocks for use in the plowing and other agricultural operations, a quantity of the produce called *hal yog,* about 10 percent of the total yield, is taken out by the landholder prior to the division of the crops. Larger shares may occasionally be given to *baṭāīdār*s working very small plots of land. A Water-carrier agricultural laborer of one Gujar landholder has also entered into a *baṭāīdārī* relationship with his employer; the Water-carrier cultivates vegetables on a two-*bīghā* plot of land and also provides half of the irrigation, seed, and fertilizer costs, for which he receives one-half of the crop yield. Several Water-carriers, including this laborer and his wife, also perform all the work of cultivating a small cotton crop on a few *bīghā*s of the same Gujar's land, for which they receive a share equal to one-third (*tihāī*) of the cotton that is produced.

Members of the Leatherworker, Water-carrier, and Shepherd *jāti*s in Pahansu are no longer engaged in their traditional occupations. (The work of skinning dead cattle and processing the hides is now performed by a Muslim *kasāī* from the nearby town of Rampur; since the introduction of tube wells and hand-pumps in the village, the services of the Water-carrier are no longer required, except on feasting occasions and in the context of the Bhūmiyā rituals; and the Shepherds of Pahansu do not have any particular connection with the care of animals.) Many men of these three *jāti*s, as well as a few Gujars whose landholdings are very small, work as employees (*naukar*s) of Gujar agriculturalists. Many of them are employed year after year by the same household, but either party may terminate the relationship in any year. Each year in the month of Asāṛh arrangements are made for the following year; the employee is expected to work for the entire year, and the agriculturalist is expected to retain him for that period. To ensure that the relationship will in fact continue throughout the year, thus providing a steady supply of labor, the agriculturalist may often give a large advance, without interest, to the *naukar*—perhaps to build or repair a house—which may only be paid back after a long period of service. One prosperous Gujar landholder, for example, gave a landless Gujar (of which there are very few in Pahansu) an advance of Rs. 5,000 to construct a house for himself, his mother, wife, and children; Rs. 2,000 was given to a Leatherworker *naukar;* and a Water-carrier received Rs. 1,300.

Some Gujar agriculturalists employ more than one *naukar*. A *bāldī,* generally an adolescent boy, is responsible for cutting fodder for cattle, feeding them and caring for them, as well as performing any other tasks that the agriculturalist may require of him. For this work he is given grain at the time of the wheat and rice harvests. He also receives twenty kilograms of unrefined sugar per year, and left-over bread (*bāsī roṭī*) and buttermilk each morning. The *bāldī* is expected to appear for work at the house of the agriculturalist each day, but if he misses days (because of sickness or paying visits to relatives, for instance), the amount of grain that he is given is not decreased. Advances are often given to the *bāldī:* in one case, the mother of a Leatherworker *bāldī* received Rs. 700 as an advance that was to be repaid without interest.

Telu Ram gave his *hālī* (the "plowman" who assists in the plowing and other agricultural work) Rs. 150 per month, *bāsī roṭī* each morning, and a share of the harvest at each *chamāī:* eighty kilograms of wheat, eighty kilograms of rice, and sixty kilograms of unrefined sugar.

If the wives or children of any of these *naukar*s work in the fields of the employer (at the harvests, for example), as they often do, they are given a payment called *gaiyarā*, usually consisting of from five to six kilograms of grain.

There are other less permanent arrangements as well. The persons who enter into these arrangements, again, generally with Gujar agriculturalists, are called "laborers" (*mazdūr*) and here as well we find a very meticulous calculation of services and compensation. Most *mazdūrī* work is performed on a day-to-day basis at the time of harvesting, when rice is being transplanted, and when labor is in short supply; people may come from other villages (indeed, even from other districts) to perform these tasks. Such workers may be paid either in cash or in kind.

Chol, the work of stripping sugarcane stalks at the time of the harvest, is generally performed in the fields by casual labor. Women and children, generally of the Leatherworker and Water-carrier castes, do this work. They are not paid, but are permitted to carry the strippings away as fodder for their livestock.

A great many laborers are needed for the work of transplanting rice seedlings (*dhān ropāī*) when the fields are flooded from the irrigation canal. In Pahansu the rate of pay for such work is five kilograms of grain (wheat is given at this time) per *bīghā* of land on which a *mazdūr* completes the transplanting. In some other villages in Saharanpur District, however, a system called *ṭhekā* ("contracting") obtains, in which male workers are paid approximately Rs. 5 per day, and female workers Rs. 3.

Laborers who work at crushing and processing the sugarcane (at one of the three crushers in Pahansu) for a Gujar farmer receive one and one-half *ser* of *śakkar* for each *man* (a unit of forty *ser*s) that is prepared. This payment is termed *mazdūrī,* but in addition to this they are given *sawā ser* (one and one-fourth *ser*) of unrefined sugar (*śakkar*) each day, for the *barkat* ("increase," "auspiciousness") of the processed sugarcane, and this prestation, called *sīrnī,* is definitely not considered as *mazdūrī,* or as any sort of compensation for services rendered. Rather, it is said to be *caṛhāpā,* and as such it transfers to the recipient any inauspiciousness that may be a hindrance to the *barkat* of the sugar. The two prestations, the *mazdūrī* and the *sīrnī,* are strictly separate, both conceptually and in terms of the actual handing over of the quantities of unrefined sugar.

Harvesting the wheat and rice crops requires an enormous amount of labor; Leatherworkers and Water-carriers often work on a short-term basis for Gujars at these two harvests, and workers frequently come from other villages in Muzaffarnagar and Saharanpur districts as well, particularly from areas in which wheat or rice is not extensively cultivated, and in which there is not a heavy local demand for their labor at the time of those harvests. These workers are called *lāvā* workers, a word presumably derived from the verb *lāvnā,* to reap. In Pahansu there are two separate methods for reckoning the payment made for this work. For the rice harvest, the *lāī* system is generally used, and workers receive a daily wage of ten to fifteen kilograms of grain. The average payment in Pahansu appeared to be twelve or thirteen kilograms per day. Informants said that this is quite a high rate. Formerly, when mostly indigenous varieties of wheat were sown, six kilograms per day was the usual payment, but now that the higher-yielding Mexican varieties have been introduced on a large scale in the district, agriculturalists have increased the daily wage paid to the *lāvā* workers.

In the *ujārā* system that is generally used for the wheat harvest, *lāvā* workers are paid according to a different reckoning. At the beginning of the day, the agriculturalist announces the rate that will be given as a proportion of the amount that is cut and bundled by each worker. If a man cuts twenty-five bundles (*pūlī*), he may receive one bundle for himself, and this would be called a *paccīswā* ("twenty-fifth") arrangement; or, the farmer may give one bundle per twenty that are cut, and this would be called a *bīswā* ("twentieth") *ujārā*. Thus when the farmer announces the day's rate, he tells the *lāvā* workers whether it will be a *bīswā* or a *paccīswā ujārā*. In this system, a man may earn as much as twenty kilograms of grain per day. Most agriculturalists say that they prefer the *ujārā* system over the *lāī* system because workers are paid only for the actual amount of work that they do, and also because it is more convenient for them since no weighing of grain is involved.

Threshing operations may be carried out in three ways. The men of a household may do all the work themselves, they may hire workers to do it and give them one kilogram of grain for every twenty that are threshed, or the work may be done cooperatively through a *ḍangvārā* arrangement.

On any day, then, during the harvesting, the winnowing, and the threshing of the wheat and rice crops, and the processing of the sugarcane, many types of prestations are made. *Phaslānā* is given to one's *kamīns*, bundles of wheat stalks are given to *lāvā* workers, meals are brought to the fields for some workers, and so on. In addition to these "payments," the *muṭṭhī* and *sāvṛī* prestations are also made, for the auspiciousness and increase of the wheat and the rice. These *caṛhāpā* prestations are kept distinct, both conceptually and "on the ground," from those that are given in compensation for agricultural services rendered. Of the latter, *phaslānā* shares and *ḍangvārā* arrangements are predicated explicitly on a relationship with "one's own" people. *Phaslānā* is given to one's *kamīns* insofar as they are "one's own" and "of the house" (*gharelū*), and *ḍangvārā* is explicitly connected with the "brotherhood" (*bhāīācārā*) of Gujars residing in the same village. The other agricultural arrangements are rooted in a notion of balanced exchange (*badlā*). But as the degree to which the parties are thought to be "one's own" decreases, such arrangements become, in Pahansu, less a matter of *len-den* and mutuality, and more a matter of isolated transactions like those in the shops of the village Baniyas.

Payments for Ritual Services: *Neg* and *Lāg*

Neg and *lāg*, as "payments" for ritual services performed at life-cycle and calendrical rituals, also stand in contrast to *dān* and *caṛhāpā* in that they are not thought to transfer inauspiciousness. They are characterizable in terms of an indigenously defined mutuality, and they are, without exception, said to be given to "one's own" people just as *dān* is always said to be given to "others," even though in many, if not most cases, the recipients of both sets of prestations are empirically the same persons. These ritual services are performed by (and the *neg* and *lāg* prestations given to) various kinsmen and persons of particular castes, often those who are tied to the household of the donor in hereditary service relationships and are thus "one's own" to them.

Table 8 provides a listing of the various types of *lāg* and *neg* prestations made in Pahansu in 1977–79. Villagers characterize these prestations in a number of ways, all of which emphasize the culturally defined mutuality of recipient and donor. First, informants always stressed the fact that *neg* and *lāg* are forms of payment for work performed (*mazdūrī*), pointing out in particular that the word *neg* means a "share" (*hissā*). Now "shares" of one's wealth and harvest, including *neg*, are given, according to these same informants, to "one's own people" (*apne ādmī*), those who are "attached to us, joined to us" (*jo hamāre sāth lage hue haĩ, joṛe hue haĩ*); they would never be given to those who are "other" (*dūsrā*). Second, this terminological contrast is paralleled by a contrast in the possible permutations in the types of prestations.

I have used "permutation" to refer to the way in which many prestations may be matters of intercaste relations for some castes, and matters of intra-*jāti* kinship relations for others. In the case of *caṛhāpā* prestations given by Brahmans, Barbers, Sweepers, and so forth, married daughters (and wife-taking affines) as "other" become the appropriate recipients, in place of the Brahmans and *kamīns* who stand in hereditary relationships to the Gujar *jajmān* as donor. In the case of *lāg* and *neg* prestations, the same *kamīns* are very often the recipients, yet the way in which this category of prestations is restructured as a matter of kinship relations is entirely different from the *caṛhāpā* case. When Brahmans, Barbers, and Sweepers themselves require the services for which *lāg* and *neg* prestations are given, those who perform them are considered to be "one's own people," rather than *dhiyānī* or in any way "other," *dūsre*. "One's own" here are either the men of one's own *kunbā*, who are "one's own" regardless of context, or they may be one's married daughters or one's *kamīns*, whose characterization as "one's own" or "other" is context dependent.

Thus in the cases where one's married daughters and sisters perform certain services, ritual or otherwise, for which they receive *lāg* or *neg*, they are never referred to as *dhiyānī*; rather, they are called *beṭī* ("daughter"), *bahan* ("sister"), or *hamārī laṛkī* ("our girl").[2] We have already noted that when these women receive *caṛhāpā* prestations, the contextually appropriate terminological usage is *dhiyānī*, and never *beṭī*, *laṛkī*, or *bahan*.[3] A similar terminological distinction occurs with reference to the spouses of these women, who in castes other than Gujar may sometimes be recipients of *lāg* and *neg*, as well as of *dān* and *caṛhāpā*. In the latter instances, they are called *dhiyāne*; but in the contexts in which they are the recipients of *lāg* and *neg*, they are always referred to as *riśtedār* ("relative," "holder of a relation") and *sage sambandhe* ("closely connected," "tied together"). Both *riśtedār* and *sage sambandhe* are reciprocal terms used between families who have given and received a bride; they would be totally inappropriate, and in fact do not occur, in contexts in which the oriented flow of inauspiciousness, in *dān*, from one to the other is at issue. The argument that the term *riśtedār* is related to that aspect of the "affinal" relationship that encompasses *lāg* and *neg* prestations, but not to that aspect that involves the giving of *dān*, *caṛhāpā*, and *pujāpā*, is supported by the fact that *neg kā riśtā* ("relationship of *neg*") is a linguistically acceptable term, while *pujāpe kā riśtā* is not.[4]

This difference between *caṛhāpā* and *lāg* and *neg* is of course obscured if prestations in the village are viewed as two distinct sets, intercaste prestations on the one hand and kinship exchanges on the other. Only through the examination of the way in which the two types of prestations, *lāg* and *neg* on the one hand, and *caṛhāpā* on the other, are handled differently when they become matters of kinship relations rather than intercaste exchanges can the full significance of the differences between them be discerned.

Villagers themselves characterize this difference in permutational patterns in terms of a distinction between *dhiyānī* (or *dhiyāne*) *kā kām* ("the work of *dhiyānī*") and *āpas kā kām* ("mutual or reciprocal work"). The phrase "the work of *dhiyānī*" is always used to refer to the acceptance of the negatively valued *caṛhāpā*, and the phrase *āpas kā kām* is used with

TABLE 8

NEG AND LĀG PRESTATIONS

Name of Prestation (if specified)	Occasion	Service Performed	Donor	Recipient	Usual Prestation
bidāgī	engagement ceremony	delivery of *ciṭṭhī*, other services	groom's family	bride's family Barber	Rs. 25, a quilt, man's shawl, unrefined sugar and grain (one *dhāṛī* each)
- - - -	engagement ceremony	delivery of *ciṭṭhī*	groom's family	bride's family Brahman	set of cloth (a *joṛa*) and Rs. 25
- - - -	*bān*	rubbing of turmeric paste	bride's family	bride's family's Barber's wife	one *dhaṛī* of grain and Rs. 2
- - - -	*paṭṭā*	showing of mirror to groom	groom	bride's family's Barber	Rs. 5
bāhar rukāī	arrival of bride at groom's	"stopping outside" (*bāhar rukāī*), barring the door at the bride's entrance	groom	groom's sister	several rupees
- - - -	day after wedding	reciting of verses (*chan*)	bride's family	groom	several rupees
- - - -	several days after wedding	delivery of packets of sweets (*kothlī*) from bride's house to groom's house	bride's family	bride's family's Barber	Rs. 10 or 20, and a set of cloth
mū̃h dikhāī	after bride's arrival at groom's house	"showing the face" to groom's female relatives	groom's female relatives	bride	Rs. 1 or 2 from each person
- - - -	marriage feast	providing clay drinking vessels	bride's family	bride's family's Potter	several rupees

- - - -	marriage feast	providing leaf plates	bride's family	bride's family's Barber	several rupees
- - - -	marriage feast	providing cloths for seating guests	bride's family	bride's family's Washerman	several rupees
- - - -	marriage feast	removing soiled plates, cleaning the eating area	bride's family	bride's family's Sweeper	several rupees
- - - -	sixth day after birth	performances of sixth-day rituals	family	midwife	several rupees and a *joṛā*
- - - -	day after birth	bathing of mother	family	midwife	Rs. 1 and some grain
- - - -	at birth of a son	playing of drum	family	family's Sweeper	one *dhaṛī* of grain, one *joṛā*
- - - -	at birth of a son	prestation of *dūb* grass	family	Brahman, *kamīn*, Bangle-seller, Dom, etc.	five *ser* of grain
- - - -	ten days after a birth	spreading of cow-dung paste	family	family's Barber's wife	grain, cooked food
- - - -	after a birth	delivery of *kevkā* prestations from wife's family to husband's family	husband's family	wife's family's Barber	one *joṛā* and Rs. 15; for the birth of a son, also unrefined sugar and a quilt
cūcī dhulāī	after a birth	washing of breasts of mother	mother	husband's sister (*nanad*)	Cash (Rs. 25 to 50) and ornaments
gīt gavāī	after a birth of a son, and at a marriage	singing of auspicious songs	family	family's Brahman	grain, unrefined sugar
- - - -	after the birth of a son	providing "protective threads" for the child	family	Brahman and Bangle-seller	grain and/or one *joṛā*

reference to the ritual services and the acceptance of *lāg* and *neg* as matters of intracaste giving and receiving.[5]

Similar terminological distinctions are evident with respect to the people of various castes attached to Gujars in hereditary service relationships. When the acceptance of *dān* and *caṛhāpā* is at issue, these people are always called *kamīn*. Brahmans are, in such contexts, called "our *pūj*" (*hamāre pūj*), *purohit*, or in Sanskrit *mantra*s often used in the accompanying ritual actions, *śarmanne* ("the protecting ones"). In the context of *neg* or *lāg* prestations, however, while *kamīn* sometimes occurs, *pūj* and *śarmanne* never do. In such instances, both *kamīn*s and Brahmans are likely to be referred to by "village kin terms" in which intercaste as well as intracaste relationships are defined by villagewide "genealogical" links (*nātā*). And in such contexts, Gujars refer to Brahmans and *kamīn*s as "tied-together brothers" (*lagū-bandhū bhāī*), or as "sharers" (*hissedār*), since *lāg* and *neg* are conceived of as shares of the wealth of the *jajmān*, shares that the recipient has a "right" to claim. Indeed, the recipient may in some instances demand certain articles, amounts of grain, or cash as *neg*, as the proverb *apne apne neg par sab jhagṛe*, "Everyone fights for their own *neg*," implies.[6] That *lāg*, in addition to being simply a "payment," is also thought of as a "share" in the wealth of the house is indicated by the way in which *lāg* is distributed at the wedding of a son in contrast to the wedding of a daughter. The *lāg* that is given for the ritual services performed by Brahmans, Barbers, Sweepers, and Washermen at the wedding of a son is substantially larger than that given for the same ritual services performed for the marriage of a daughter. Villagers say that this is so because a "dowry" (*dahej*) comes into the house at the marriage of a son, and one's Brahman and those who receive *phaslānā* are "sharers in the dowry" (*dahej mẽ hissedār*) because they are "attached" (*lagnā*) to the household and have a "connection" (*sampark*) with it.

Neg and *lāg* are most frequently given to one's daughters, who in such contexts are said to be "one's own," to one's Brahman, and to the castes in the village who are related as "sharers" and "tied-together brothers" to a particular household. There are certain instances, however, in which *lāg* is also given to the *kamīn*s of the natal villages of the wives of one's sons. I will give three examples.

The first instance involves the prenuptial negotiations of a Gujar landholding family. When the *ciṭṭhī* (betrothal "letter") was sent from the house of Sevaram to the village of the prospective bridegroom, it was taken, as is generally the case, by Sevaram's Barber and Brahman *purohit*. The people of the groom's side, the *laṛkevāle*, then gave *lāg* to Sevaram's Barber:

Rs. 25
one *dhaṛī* of *śakkar*

one *dhaṛī* of rice
one quilt (*razāī*)

Sevaram's Brahman also received *lāg* at the groom's village:

one *joṛā* (including a *dhotī*, a shirt, and a shawl)
Rs. 25

Lāg is also given in this fashion after a birth, as my second example illustrates. A Gujar woman almost always remains in her conjugal village to give birth, only returning to visit her natal village when her child is about three months old. Thus, when *kevkā* (see chap. 4) is to be given, it must be sent to the *sasurāl;* it is usually sent with the Barber of the mother's natal kin. When Santroj (the youngest wife in the Gujar household in which I lived) gave birth to her first child, a daughter, the Barber came from her *pīhar,* her natal village of Manora, to bring the sets of cloth and other items of the *kevkā*. Santroj's husband's mother, Asikaur, then gave *lāg* to the Barber, consisting of one *joṛā* and fifteen rupees. (If the child had been a boy, Asi told me, she would also have given some unrefined sugar and a quilt.)

My third example occurred just after the wedding of Kaushal, the daughter of Illam Nai, a Pahansu Barber. A few days after the men of the groom's party returned to their own village, Illam sent a large quantity of sweets to that village. (This prestation is called *kothlī,* and it is sent after Gujar weddings as well.) The *kothlī* was delivered by Illam's Brahman priest, and the Brahman received *lāg* from the groom's family, in the form of ten rupees and a *joṛā*. It was Illam's idea to send his Brahman in this case; Gujars usually send the *kothlī* with their Barber, or sometimes with the Barber and the Brahman, and it is the usual Barber practice to send a sister's husband or a father's sister's husband to deliver the *kothlī*. (Illam's reasons for wanting to send his Brahman priest rather than his sister's husband will be discussed in a later section of this chapter.)

These sorts of situations—delivery of prestations before and after a wedding, and after a birth—are the only ones in which I observed that *lāg* was given to the *purohit* and the *kamīn*s of one's wife-giving people. As far as I know, *lāg* is never given in the reverse direction to the Brahmans and *kamīn*s of one's wife-taking people, who on a number of occasions are the recipients of *dān* and *caṛhāpā* prestations. This suggests that the Brahman and the *kamīn*s of the household of one's *bahū* may be thought of, in these contexts, somewhat as "one's own," while those of the household of one's married sisters and daughters are most definitely "other." This interpretation appears congruent with the notion that one shares a *śarīr kā sambandh* with one's mother's brother and the people of his house (those who have given a daughter), but not with the people of the *sasurāl* of one's married daughter or sister, one's *dhiyānī*.

There is one other category of prestation that is said to be given in exchange for the performance of ritual services, and this is the prestation termed *dakṣiṇā*. This prestation presents some difficulties, difficulties that have been noted by other analysts as well. *Dakṣiṇā* is a payment given to Brahmans (and by Brahmans to *dhiyāne*) for the performance of particular ritual services (other than those for which compensation is termed *lāg* or *neg*). More important, *dakṣiṇā* is the Brahman's payment when he receives *dān* and *caṛhāpā* from his *jajmān*. Informants in Pahansu always said that *dakṣiṇā* differed from *dān* because it is given in return for the Brahman's ritual services, while *dān* is never given in this way, "in exchange," *badle mẽ*. Even in the cases when both *dakṣiṇā* and *dān* are given to one's Brahman *purohit,* the two prestations are conceptually quite distinct.

This is apparent in the case of two of the *terāhmī* (thirteenth day after death) rituals that I observed in Pahansu. Buddhu Pandit is the most learned Brahman priest in the village, and the most knowledgeable about the proper performance of many types of rituals. Hence he is often asked to officiate at rituals even when he is not the hereditary *purohit* of the family involved. In the case of the *terāhmī* of Amarnath, a Pahansu Brahman, the *terāhmī dān* was given to Amarnath's *dhiyāne,* but twenty-one rupees were given as *dakṣiṇā* to Buddhu Pandit because he officiated at the ritual. In the case of the *terāhmī* for Dattaram, an old Gujar man, the hereditary priest of the family did not know how to perform the complicated ritual, and Buddhu Pandit again was asked to step in. The *dān*—the foodstuffs, the cloth, the brass vessels, and so on—was given to Ramesh, the family *purohit,* and Buddhu received only a few rupees as *dakṣiṇā*.

People say that *dān* is quite different from *dakṣiṇā* in that the latter is given "for doing work" (*kām karne ke lie*). Yet there would appear to be some ambiguity as to whether *dakṣiṇā* can be a vehicle for the transferral of inauspiciousness, in ways that *lāg* and *neg* would never be. When I put this question to several Gujar men, they said that, yes, *dakṣiṇā* is indeed given *badle mẽ,* but that it is also "a kind of *dān*" (*ek kism kā dān*), for inauspiciousness may sometimes be present in the *dakṣiṇā*. It is "a kind of *dān,*" they said, even though it is also "different" (*alag-alag*) from *dān*.

That inauspiciousness may indeed be transferred in the *dakṣiṇā* is also evidenced by the fact that *dakṣiṇā* is sometimes given in the form of one and one-quarter (*sawā*) measures, one and one-quarter rupees, for example, and by the fact that among Brahmans *dakṣiṇā* cannot be given to "one's own people" (*apne ādmī*) or within one's own *got*. (In the example of Amarnath's *terāhmī* given above, Buddhu Pandit could accept the *dakṣiṇā* from his fellow Pahansu Brahmans because they are of different *gots.*) It is also significant that when Brahmans give *dakṣiṇā* to their married daughters and sisters, these recipients are referred to as *dhiyānī,* not *laṛkī* or *beṭī,* as would be the case when they are given *lāg* and *neg. Dakṣiṇā,* then, seems to stand at the intersection of the categories of *dān* and the prestations that are given "in exchange" as "shares" or as payments for ritual services.

This ambiguity concerning the significance of *dakṣinā* may be a widespread phenomenon. Heesterman's discussion of the Brahman's acceptance of the "sins" of the sacrificer in Vedic ritual (see chap. 1) related primarily to the acceptance of *dakṣiṇā;* but as Fuller points out in his discussion of *dakṣiṇā* (1984, 66), Malamoud (1976) has argued that *dakṣiṇā* implies a wage-like element in the relationship between donor and recipient. Nevertheless, it is said that some rituals will be ineffectual if *dakṣiṇā* is not given (Vatuk and Vatuk 1976, 224), which suggests that more than "wages" are involved in the "payment." There are some indications of this belief in Pahansu, though I never heard it explicitly stated. For example, at the conclusion of a *pāṭh* ("reciting") and fire sacrifice that Raghu Pandit performed for the family of Illam Nai (see chap. 2), Illam asked the Brahman to tell him how much *dakṣiṇā* should be given. Raghu indicated that he expected to receive fifty-one rupees, and Illam agreed. Raghu then put some rice into the right hands of Illam and his two brothers and pronounced his acceptance of the *dakṣiṇā* (in Sanskrit) by announcing the astrological coordinates (the *rāśī,* the *tithi,* and the year) of this acceptance, the donors (the *jajmāns*), and the reason that the *pāṭh* had been performed. After the acceptance of the *dakṣiṇā* had been completed, Illam picked up the one and one-fourth rupees and the *joṛā* that had been lying on the ground, and put them on Raghu's head. This was the *dān,* the *caṛhāpā,* given to remove the "suffering" (*dukh*) in Illam's house caused by the presence of the lingering spirit of Illam's dead son.

In this example, the *dakṣiṇā* and the *caṛhāpā* were given separately, yet the *dakṣiṇā* was given in the context of a ritualized acceptance that would never be found in the acceptance of *lāg* and *neg.* In Pahansu, *dān* is by far the most significant vehicle for the transferral of inauspiciousness; *dakṣiṇā* is clearly a "payment" (and one of my informants who knew a few words of English even referred to it as a "wage"), yet it seems to carry with it a penumbra of inauspiciousness that is not associated with *lāg* and *neg.*

"Signs of Brotherhood": *Nyautā, Parosā,* and *Kothlī*

Prestations made as a "sign of brotherhood" (*bhāīācārā kā pratīk*)[7] are exchanged on the basis of a sometimes excruciatingly precise reciprocity; while there is no question here of a "payment" for goods or services, *nyautā, parosā,* and *kothlī* are, like the prestations discussed in the previous sections of this chapter, said to be given to "one's own people" as "shares" and "in exchange."

In Pahansu, *nyautā* (lit., "invitation") refers primarily to sums of cash (and sometimes to cloth and to brass vessels) that are given by members of one's own *kunbā* and people of one's own village, as well as other "relatives," at the time of the marriage of a daughter. While the preliminary wedding rituals are being performed, wedding guests come forward to give *nyautā* and to have their gift recorded in a record book called a *bahī*. The lunar date of the marriage is recorded, and the village to which the *nyautā* (as part of the *kanyā dān* prestations) will be sent, that is, the groom's village, is also noted. The exact amount that is given is recorded, and a note is made as to whether this is a "new *nyautā*" (*nayā nyautā*) or an "old" *nyautā* (*purānā nyautā*), that is, whether this is the first time that *nyautā* has been exchanged between the two parties. In the case of a "new" *nyautā,* one rupee is usually given. Then, when there is a marriage at the house of the donor, this recipient is expected to give one rupee for the "old *nyautā,*" and one additional rupee. These exchanges may continue for many years and over several generations. Telu Ram has in his house a record book in which *nyautā* transactions have been recorded for the past one hundred years, and he said that he had recently burnt records that had gone back many more years. The importance of giving the appropriate amount in *nyautā,* an amount that reflects what one has received, is evident in the following anecdote.

When Telu Ram's sister Santosh was married a number of years ago, Amar Singh's *māmā kā laṛkā* (mother's brother's son) came to the wedding and gave twenty-five rupees in *nyautā,* and this was recorded in the family's *bahī* (see fig. 15). When Santosh's father, Nyadar Singh, later went to the marriage of that man's daughter, he neglected to consult the *bahī* and simply gave eleven rupees in *nyautā*. As Telu Ram tells the story, there was much resentment when the amounts given in *nyautā* were later compared.

The directionality implicit in the giving of other types of prestations at the wedding—prestations that are made to one's *dhiyānī* (the *bhāt,* a type of *dān* given by the bride's or the groom's mother's brother, for example)—and in the corresponding terminological usages, is absent in the context of these *nyautā* prestations. One's mother's brother gives *bhāt,* precisely because he is the *māmā,* but as a *riśtedār* of the family he generally gives some rupees in *nyautā* as well, money that must be reciprocated when the marriage of his own daughter is celebrated. *Dān,* in any form, including *bhāt,* can never be reciprocated, but it is of the essence of *nyautā* that it is given back, with an increment. Both the donors and the recipients of *nyautā* are referred to as *riśtedār,* and the reciprocal nature

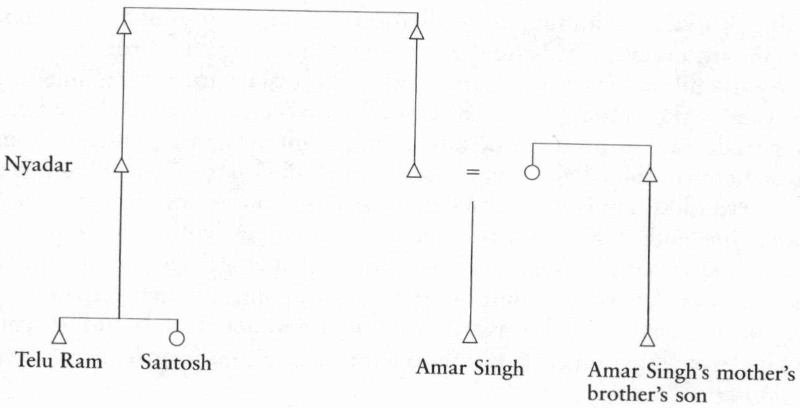

Fig. 15. Nyadar's *nyautā*

of this term foregrounds the reciprocal nature of the prestations, just as in the case of *lāg* and *neg* prestations. Thus the mutuality that is defined by villagers as a "sign of brotherhood" is not only a matter of the *bhāīācārā* community within the village, but extends, in certain contexts, to all of one's *riśtedārs*, whether givers or receivers of brides.

Nyautā is also given to one's *gharelūs*, one's *kamīns*, at the marriages of their daughters. In addition to cash, sets of cloth and brass vessels (*vāsan*) may also be sent. For example, in "my" household Asikaur sent the following items as *nyautā* at the marriage of Kaushal, the daughter of the family's Barber:

one set of cloth for a man
one set of cloth for a woman
two brass vessels
one *dhaṛī* of rice
Rs. 51

At the wedding of the daughter of their Carpenter, Asi sent a *nyautā* consisting of

one set of cloth
one *dhaṛī* of rice
Rs. 5

These are the only cases in which Gujars give *nyautā* but will not accept a reciprocation, because, they say, it is a matter of their prestige (*izzat*) that they not take such prestations from their *kamīns*. Yet even in this case, the giving of *nyautā* is a "sign of brotherhood"; it is given to one's *gharelūs*, people say, precisely because they are one's "tied-together brothers."

Nearly all major life-cycle and calendrical rituals are accompanied by feasting or the preparation of special foods. When such foods have been prepared, trays of food, each constituting a full meal, are sent to various households in the village. These food trays, called *parosā* (from *parasnā*, "to serve food") may be sent to ten to twenty houses "of one's lineage," *kunbe mẽ,* and occasionally to families of other *jāti*s whom one considers as one's *lagū-bandhū bhāī*.[8] The reciprocity that characterizes these prestations is evidenced by a phrase that I heard countless times as women reminded their sons' wives as to whom these trays of food should be sent: "Where one must take, there also one must give" (*jahā̃ se lenā hai vahā̃ denā hai*).

The distribution of *kothlī,* too, is a "sign of brotherhood," a *bhāīācārā kā pratīk. Kothlī* is a quantity of sweets, usually a large basket of *panjīrī,* that is carried by a woman when she travels between her *pīhar* and her *sasurāl.* While Vatuk and Vatuk (1976, 226) imply that among the Gaur Brahmans of western U.P. *kothlī* is given only by the natal kin to the woman's husband's family, Pahansu Gujars send *kothlī* in both directions, and this is emphasized in the use of the term *riśtedār* for both donor and recipient when such prestations are being discussed. But *kothlī* is a *bhāīācārā kā pratīk* inasmuch as it is redistributed within the *kunbā* of the recipient household. It is redistributed, as one Gujar man said to me, because "in happiness and sadness, everyone is united; in sadness and happiness, all of the people of a *khāndān* are sharers" (*khuśī aur dukhī mẽ sab log ikaṭṭhā haĩ, dukh aur sukh mẽ hissedār haĩ sab khāndān ke ādmī*). As in the case of the *nyautā* prestations, here too the *bhāīācārā* includes one's *kamīn*s as well as one's *kunbedār*s, because *kamīn*s also receive a share of the *kothlī* when a large amount of sweets is received.

Gifts of the Meeting, Gifts of the Road: *Milāī* and *Wādā*

Milāī, translated literally, means "meeting," "joining," or "mixing," and is given, it is said, "to increase unity" (*mel baṛhāne ke lie*). It is usually a comparatively small gift of a few rupees or a set of cloth, although there are occasions on which considerably larger prestations are made. The most common situation in which *milāī* is given is when a brother visits the conjugal village of one of his "sisters" (his own *sagī bahan,* "sister of the same womb," a woman of the same *got* as his own, or a woman of any caste from his own village). He is then expected to give her a small gift, usually one or two rupees. If a groom arrives in a village for his wedding, and there are "sisters" already married there, the *milāī* will be considerably larger. Just after the wedding of a Pahansu Gujar girl had taken place, for example, the Barber of her father's household delivered two sets of cloth and five rupees to Santroj, a Pahansu *bahū*, as *milāī* from the groom, sent by him because he was from Manora, the natal village of Santroj.

Milāī is also given by women to their younger sisters, and to the husbands of these sisters. *Milāī* is not given to a woman's elder sister, though it is given to her children. When, for example, Rajavati, her two brothers, her elder sister Jnanavati and Jnanavati's husband and husband's sister (*nanad*) met in Saharanpur for the rite of entry at Jnanavati's new house, *milāī* (one rupee in each case) was given as follows: Rajavati's *bahenoi* (sister's husband) gave *milāī* to her; the two brothers gave *milāī* to each of their sisters, and to Jnanavati's *nanad* and her children; Rajavati gave *milāī* to her sister's children, her sister's *nanad,* and to the latter's children.

It has already been noted that Gujars do not give *caṛhāpā* or *dān* to the husbands of their *dhiyānī* (except in the wedding *dān,* and in the *cālā, kevkā,* and *cūcak* prestations), but these men do receive *milāī* when they visit their wives' natal villages. When Santosh's husband visited Pahansu, for example, Santosh's mother gave him five rupees in *milāī.* Santosh's brothers' wives did not give *milāī* because, they said, they were still living jointly (*ikaṭṭhā*); if the households became separate (*nyāre-nyāre*), then they would give *milāī* separately to their husband's sister's husband. *Milāī* is also given to the brothers of one's daughter's husband. When Santosh's *devar* (husband's younger brother) visited her parents' household, for example, her mother gave him several rupees and a set of cloth. She gave this *milāī,* she said, because her daughter's *devar* is her *samdheṭā,* a term that may be used with reference to both the younger and elder brothers of one's daughter's husband. The husband of one's sister's daughter (*bhaṇan jamāī*) and the husband of one's daughter's daughter (*doth jamāī*) also receive *milāī* if they come for a visit. In such cases, the *milāī* may be as much as ten rupees and several sets of cloth. If a man visits the *sasurāl* of his sister's daughter, he will also give *milāī* there (see fig. 16). When Omi's *māmā* (mother's brother) visited Pahansu, for example, he gave *milāī* in the following amounts:

Rs. 10 to Omi
Rs. 5 to Raj Pal
Rs. 5 to Dharmendra
Rs. 5 to Kavita
Rs. 5 to Asikaur, as his *samdhin*
Rs. 5 to Shanti, as *samdhin*

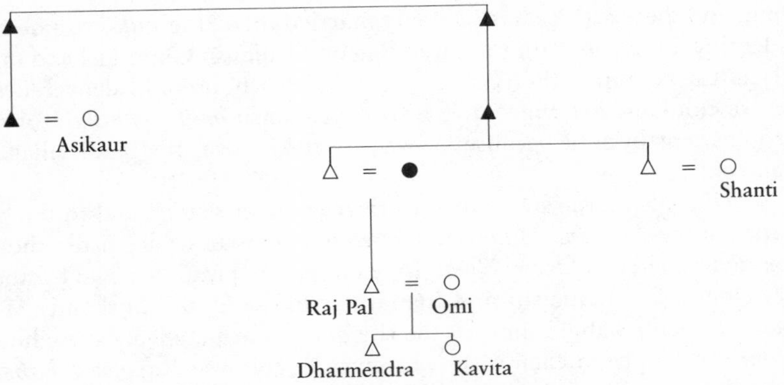

Fig. 16. Omi's *māmā*'s *milāī*

Milāī is also given to a woman by the natal kin of her husband's brothers' wives because the *bahū*s of a house are said to be "like sisters" and therefore a daughter's husband's brother's wife is like a daughter (Vatuk 1975, 183). When I accompanied Rajavati, a *bahū* in the house in which I lived, on a short visit to her own natal village, we stopped at the village of Manora, where Santroj, another *bahū* of the house, was paying an extended visit at her *pīhar*. Rajavati gave the two sons of Santroj's brother two rupees each as *milāī,* and she received *milāī* from Santroj's mother in the form of three sets of cloth for herself, one each for her two sons, and a set of cloth for her sister's son, who had also accompanied us to Manora. Because I was considered the *nanad* (husband's sister) of Rajavati and Santroj, the latter's mother insisted on giving me five rupees in *milāī* as well.

The term *milāī* is used in one further context: at the conclusion of a wedding, the bride's father gives *milāī* (usually one rupee) to each of the men who have come in the groom's party, but excluding the groom himself. *Milāī* is also given at this time to those guests who are related as *phūphā* (father's sister's husband), *bahenoi* (sister's husband), *bhānjā* (sister's son), and *bhaṇan jamāī* (sister's daughter's husband) to the bride's father. It was in discussions of this particular *milāī* that I was most frequently told by villagers that *milāī* is given "to increase unity" (*mel baṛhāne ke lie*), to increase the "mixture" between the kin of the bride and the kin of the groom, the *laṛkīvāle* and the *laṛkevāle*.

What, then, is the meaning of these "gifts of the meeting"? In Vatuk and Vatuk's typology of gift transactions observed in Meerut District, *milāī* is classified with *dān*, which they define as a gift given to a status superior, here one's "daughters" and their husbands (1976, 223), along with *dān-dahej, bhāt, cūcak,* and *pujāpā*. I would like to suggest, however, that *milāī* has a fundamentally different significance for Pahansu Gujars; *milāī* is not *dān,* and it is given for reasons that are quite different from those that prompt the giving of *dān-dahej, bhāt, cūcak* and the other types of *dān* that are given to one's *dhiyānī* and *dhiyāne.*

Dān is always given, villagers say, to those who are "other," and we have seen how the wedding ritual transforms the status of a daughter from "one's own (*apnī*) to "other" (*dūsrī*), and it is precisely as "other" that she becomes an appropriate "receptacle" (*pātra*) for *dān* and *caṛhāpā.* After her wedding, a daughter is no longer "one's own" in her father's house from this perspective, but because of the "new mixture" (*nayā milān*) that is accomplished in the marriage, she becomes a "sharer" in the household of her husband. But from another perspective, Gujars in Pahansu say that *milāī* is given to married "sisters" and "daughters" (though I think there are instances in which *milāī* would be given to one's own daughter) because they are "one's own," just as, we have seen, *lāg* and *neg* are given to those women because they are, in those particular contexts, "one's own." And as in the case of *lāg* and *neg,* the terminological usages that occur in the giving of *milāī* are always *laṛkī* ("girl"), and *bahan* ("sister") rather than *dhiyānī.*

In other ways too, terminological differences are evident with respect to the two types of gifts. In the case of the *milāī* given by Omi's mother's brother (fig. 16), for example, the *milāī* was said to be given to Asikaur and Shanti because they are the *samdhin* (daughter's husband's mother; also son's wife's mother) though here they are not in fact Omi's own husband's mother; Shanti is Omi's *pitasarā* (husband's father's younger brother's wife) and Asikaur is related as her *dādasarā* (husband's father's father's wife). Now, in the only contexts in which these two women could expect to receive *dān* from Omi's natal kin, in the form of sets of cloth designated particularly for them (at Omi's *cālā,* and in her *kevkā* and *cūcak*), they would always be referred to as *aglī,* "the next ones," the ones to whom the *dān* is passed on. This term, *aglī,* is heard constantly as women gather to view the sets of cloth that are being sent in the *dāt* of a *cālā, kevkā,* or *cūcak,* as they comment on the quality of the *joṛā*s that are being sent to the various recipients of the groom's family. *Ye agliõ ke,* "these are the ones for the *aglī,*" they say, to distinguish them from the sets of cloth being sent to the daughter, her husband, and his parents. Just as one's daughters and sisters are "other" as they receive *dān* and "one's own" as they receive *milāī,* these women, Shanti and Asikaur in this example, are *aglī* as they receive sets of cloth as *dān,* and *samdhin* (lit., "joined with") as they receive *milāī.* Similarly, when sets of cloth to be given as *dān*—at the *kanyā dān* itself, at the *cālā,* and in the *kevkā* and *cūcak* prestations—to the parents of one's daughter's husband are exhibited in this way, people say that these sets of cloth are "for the *sās* and *sūsar,*" and the terms *samdhī* and *samdhin* are never used.[9] And finally, when *milāī* is given at a wedding to one's father's sister's husband, sister's husband, sister's daughter's husband, and sister's son, it is always the specific kin terms that are used to describe this event, that is, *phūphā, bahenoi, bhaṇan jamāī,* and *bhānjā,* rather than the term *dhiyānā,* which quite unambiguously indexes the contextually emphasized "otherness" of these men.

If *milāī* is indeed given to those who are in some sense "one's own," or at any rate in order to "increase mixture," it is also the case that *milāī* is not given to one's unmarried sisters, who have yet to "become other" (*begānī ho jānā*) in the wedding ritual. Nor is it given to one's own *kunbedār*s who are unambiguously "one's own people" in all contexts. And while *milāī* is given to one's *phūphā* and *bahenoi* at the wedding of one's daughter, as well as to the men of the groom's party on that occasion, it is not given to one's *māmā* (mother's brother), with whom, it is said, one shares a "bodily connection," *śarīr kā sambandh.*

At least part of the reason that *milāī* may not be given, for example, to the parents of one's son's wife (they too are *samdhī* and *samdhin*) lies in the very general and pervasive feeling that one should never accept hospitality or gifts of any sort from the conjugal household of one's daughters (for discussion of this, see Vatuk 1975, 185–86), that is, from the households to which one has given *dān.* This stricture does not, on the other hand, mean that *milāī* too is *dān* or that it is given for the same reason that *dān* is given. Why, then, is it given to some of those people who have been given *dān* in the past, or have been conduits for the flow of *dān* prestations? Part of the answer to this question can be found in the linguistic usages that are implemented when villagers talk about *dān,* about *nyautā, parosā,* and *kothlī,* and about *milāī.* In the wedding ritual, a daughter becomes, quite explicitly, "other" (*begānī, parāyī,* or *dūsrī*), and it is as such that she becomes an appropriate receptacle for future *dān* prestations. Now the verb form that is most often used when people speak of giving *milāī* is *milāī karnā,* "to do *milāī,*" literally, "to make mixture." One then creates the "unity ," the "mixture" within relationships where previously it has been necessary, for one's own auspiciousness, to create the "otherness." When, on the other hand, villagers speak of *nyautā, parosā,* and *kothlī,* prestations that are given primarily to the people of one's own *kunbā* where the "mixture" is taken-for-granted, they say that these gifts are "signs of brotherhood," *bhāīācārā kā pratīk.* Now what I have translated as "sign" does not have the meaning of "symbol" in our sense, but of *bhāg* ("portion") and *ãś* ("part"). *Nyautā, parosā,* and *kothlī* do not "symbolize" brotherhood, but are "parts" of it; they are metonyms, and stand for "brotherhood" as a part of a whole may stand for the whole in a figure of speech.[10] *Milāī,* in contrast, is not a "sign" of an everyday, taken-for-granted "unity." It stands in the face of a culturally constituted "otherness" and "creates mixture" where there might otherwise be only difference. Despite the fact that she elsewhere classified *milāī* as *dān,* Sylvia Vatuk has recognized the sociological implications of this "mixture," specifically in her discussion of "the cognitive process by which, at each new marriage, all persons allied through former marriages on bride's and groom's 'sides', respectively, are considered joined in opposition to those with whom the new alliance is being forged" (Vatuk 1975, 194). *Milāī* is the cultural expression, or rather, the creation, the "making" (*karnā*) of this joining.

There are other prestations, lacking a specific name, that appear to have a similar set of meanings. Married women, particularly young women, travel frequently between their natal and conjugal villages, and when they do, gifts of cloth and sweets are always taken along. When they go to their *pīhar*s, they do not give gifts to their own parents, but sets of cloth are taken for brothers, brothers' children, and for any of the wives of their brothers who have not yet borne children. When they return to their *sasurāl*s they will bring many *joṛā*s: for themselves and their children, for their husbands and for their husbands' parents, as well as for the brothers and brothers' wives of their husbands. Some of these sets of cloth may have been given to them as *dān,* in the course of rituals in which *pujāpā* had been generated, from the wedding of a brother or brother's son, or from a *cūcak* or *kevkā* of a brother's wife. But most of the sets of cloth that a woman brings from her *pīhar* have been given simply because she has gone there *milne ke lie,* to visit her natal kin, and are not *dān.* The preparations for these comings and goings that take place at both the natal village and the conjugal village—the buying of cloth, the opening up of trunks to select cloth that will be given, the tying of the cloths into sets with protective threads—are called *wādā.* When a wife is preparing for a visit to her *pīhar,* and when a daughter is returning to her *sasurāl,* women say *wādā ho rahā hai,* "the *wādā* is under way."

The two types of *joṛā*s—those given in *dān* and *caṛhāpā* and those of the *wādā,* given because a woman has gone to "meet" (*milnā*) her natal kin—are conceptually distinct, and this distinction is manifested in a very important way. If a woman goes to her *pīhar* to receive *cūcak* gifts, or for the wedding or *cālā* of her brother or brother's son, or to receive some particular *caṛhāpā,* she receives, without any accounting, the number of sets of cloth and other items that are conventionally given in these instances. When she goes *milne ke lie,* to "meet" her natal kin, on the other hand, a number of factors are taken into account when her natal kin—her mother and her brothers' wives in particular—reckon the number of *joṛā*s they should give to her. If, for example, there is an occasion when *caṛhāpā* is to be given to one's *dhiyānī* for one's own auspiciousness, the wives of a group of brothers will always give sets of cloth to their *dhiyānī* (here, their husband's sister) separately; each will give the conventional number of sets of cloth herself, for her own auspiciousness and for that of her husband and sons. But in the case of *wādā* prestations of cloth, there is the sense that it is the collective responsibility of the joint household to provide the daughter with *joṛā*s to take back to her *sasurāl*. While each of a woman's brothers' wives gives sets of cloth of her own to the husband's sister, she does not give separately to the husband's sister's husband or to the husband's sister's husband's father and mother, until the households become separate (*alag-alag*). Until then, sets of cloth are given to these people by the girl's mother, on behalf of the entire household.

For example, when Devi, the eldest daughter of the household in which I lived in the village, went back to her *sasurāl* after a brief stay in Pahansu, she was given the following sets of cloth:

From Asi, her mother:
- two for Devi's husband, one from Asi's own store and one that had come in the *kevkā* of Santroj, Devi's brother's wife
- four for Devi
- one for Devi's son
- one for Devi's daughter

From Rajavati, Devi's brother's wife:
- three for Devi
- one for Devi's son

From Simla, Devi's brother's wife:
- two for Devi
- one for her son

From Santroj, Devi's brother's wife:
- five for Devi (some of which had come in Santroj's *kevkā*)
- one for Devi's daughter

When Premo, a younger daughter of the same household, returned to her *sasurāl* after the *cālā* of her youngest brother, she took with her *joṛā*s of many types:

From Asi, her mother:
- one for Premo's husband's father
- one for her husband's mother
- one for her husband's younger brother
- one for her husband
- one for each of her four children

From Rajavati, Premo's brother's wife:
- three for Premo, including one given as *caṛhāpā* in a *sankrānt udāpan*

From Simla, Premo's brother's wife:
- three for Premo, including one from her *sankrānt udāpan*

from Santroj, Premo's brother's wife:
- four for Premo, including one from Santroj's *kevkā*
- one for Premo's husband, from the *kevkā*

From Sarla, Premo's youngest brother's wife, whose *cālā* had just occurred:
four for Premo, including one from *sandūk khulāī* and one from the *cālā*

In these two examples, only Asi, the daughter's mother, gave sets of cloth to her daughter's husband, to his parents, and to his brothers, except for the sets of cloth from Santroj's *kevkā,* which Santroj gave to Premo's husband as the "next one" of her parents, for her own auspiciousness and that of her parents. And because, in the second example, Premo received so many *joṛā*s from her brother's wives, Asi did not feel that it was necessary to give to her daughter from her own trunk.

Several other sorts of reckonings enter into the calculations of how many *joṛā*s should be given to a visiting daughter or sister of the house. The most important of these are the time that has elapsed since the daughter's previous visit (see Vatuk 1975, 190), the length of her stay, and the number of *joṛā*s she has brought to her natal kin from her *sasurāl.* When Rajavati, a Gujar wife in Pahansu, returned from a very short visit to Titron, her *pīhar,* she brought only a few sets of cloth, and explained to me very carefully that this was because she had just gone to her *pīhar* for a visit several months before. She brought the following sets of cloth from Titron:

one for herself, from her mother
one for herself, from her brother's wife
one set of cloth for her husband
one for each of her two sons
one bed cover
one warm shawl for her husband's mother

(This last gift, the shawl, was one of the very few in which I observed an attempt to give a gift that the recipient actually needed for her own use; see Vatuk and Vatuk 1976, 218.)

Similarly, when Omi, another Gujar wife of the village, went to Hathchoya, her *pīhar,* for a ten-day visit, she returned with nine *joṛā*s, and made it a point to tell me that she had been given so little because, even though she had not visited her natal kin for one and a half years, the visit was not sufficiently long to warrant a gift of many sets of cloth. She brought the following sets of cloth from Hathchoya to Pahansu:

two for herself, from her mother
one for her husband, from her mother
one for her husband, from her brother's wife's mother, because he had stopped at Omi's brother's *sasurāl* (at the time of the brother's *cālā*) while en route to another village

one for her son, from her mother
one for her son, from Omi's father's younger brother's daughter
one for her daughter, from her father's younger brother's daughter

But a careful balance must be maintained if the visit has been a short one, but the time elapsed since the last visit was great; the donor should not give too few, or it will become a matter of gossip and abuse (*gālī*) in the recipient's *sasurāl*. When, for example, a Gujar wife in Pahansu made a four-day visit to her natal village when her step-mother (*mausī*) was ill, the latter sent only six sets of cloth in *wādā* prestations to Pahansu, five for her stepdaughter, and one for her husband; she sent none for the woman's *devar* (husband's younger brother) or her *sās* (husband's mother). Now my notebooks, filled as they were with detailed information on the *len-den,* sets of cloth given and sets of cloth received, were of great interest to Asikaur, my Pahansu mother; after a day of visiting and the recording of such matters, she would ask me for a precise accounting of who had given what to whom. And when I told her that this particular *bahū* had brought back six sets of cloth from her natal village, her reaction was this: "What did she give, that 'second wife-widow' [a terrible abuse], she gave very little, her stepmother. And several months have passed [since her last visit]" (*kyā diyā sauk-rāṇḍ toṛā diyā uskī mausī aur kaī mahine ho gaye*).

The number of sets of cloth that a woman takes to her natal kin from her *sasurāl* is also taken into account when the trunks of her mother and brothers' wives are opened and the *joṛā*s given to her. Kamala and Shanti are two "true sisters," *sagī bahan,* married into different Pahansu households. When their mother was ill, the two made a four-day trip to Titron, their natal village. Kamala brought back seven sets of cloth upon her return to Pahansu:

three for herself
one for each of her three sons
one for her husband

Shanti, however, brought back seventeen sets of cloth:

ten for herself
two for each of her two sons
one for her daughter
two for her husband

Shanti's mother had given two of these sets of cloth, the wife of her brother's son had given five, and the wives of her two brothers had each given five. The rather large difference in the number of *joṛā*s given to the two sisters was due to the fact that in addition to the usual number of *joṛā*s a daughter would take to her natal kin, Shanti had also taken five sets of cloth for the daughter who had just been born to the wife of her brother's son, the woman who gave her five sets of cloth in return. Kamala had not taken *joṛā*s for the child, but planned to take some on her next visit, and this was the reason, according to both Shanti and Kamala, that the latter had received relatively few *joṛā*s from her natal kin. Thus, while it is always the case that one should never accept gifts of any sort from one's own daughter, and one's sisters and husband's sisters should always leave the house with more *joṛā*s than were brought from the *sasurāl,* there is, in a limited way, a sense of reciprocation in these *wādā* prestations that would never enter into the considerations of giving and receiving the sets of cloth that are given in *dān*. Similarly, the length of a woman's stay in her *pīhar* and the time elapsed since her previous visit would never be considered in the giving of *dān* and *caṛhāpā*.

When villagers are asked by the anthropologist why they are giving sets of cloth and other items in *dān* or *caṛhāpā,* the inevitable reply is *apne śubh ke māro,* "for one's own auspiciousness," or perhaps *nāśubh haṭāne ke lie,* "to remove inauspiciousness." When, on the other hand, I asked women why all these sets of cloth are given in the *wādā,* the answer was always that one "should not go empty-handed, should not go 'empty'" (*khālī hāth nahī̃ jātī, rītī nahī̃ jātī*). The answer was the same to questions concerning the sets of cloth taken to the *sasurāl* as for those taken to the *pīhar*. Why, then, should a daughter or a wife of a village not make such a trip empty-handed? The calculations of the number of *joṛā*s a woman brings to her natal kin do, as we have seen, seem to imply that *wādā* prestations are fundamentally different from *dān,* that they are characterized by a sense of mutuality, a balancing of what is given and what is received, though this is of course modulated by the ever-present necessity to give to one's sisters more than one receives. That a balancing, or perhaps even a "repayment," is involved in these prestations is clearly indicated in the meaning of the word *wādā,* which refers to the time of preparing for these trips and these prestations. *Wādā,* in its dictionary definition, means "the time of repaying a debt" (*karj adā karne kā wakt*) (*Bṛhat Hindī Koṣ,* 1025).

When I asked villagers, as I sometimes did, to list the kinds of prestations made to *dhiyānī* and *dhiyāne,* they generally mentioned *dān-dahej, bhāt,* and the various kinds of *caṛhāpā* from life-cycle and calendrical rituals (the latter, of course, differ from caste to caste). No one ever mentioned *milāī* or the sets of cloth given at the time of *wādā*. Though these are in fact given to the same empirical persons, the use of the terms *dhiyānī* and *dhiyāne,* with their pragmatic implications, effectively prevented my informants from including *milāī* and *wādā* prestations in such a listing; these prestations are, as my linguistic evidence demonstrates, given to those who are contextually defined as "one's own" and not "other," to *laṛkī, bahan,* and *beṭī,* and not to *dhiyānī*. In discussing their reasons for giving *milāī* and the sets of cloth at the time of *wādā,* women sometimes offered the saying *dhī-pūt to apnī bahū begānī* ("Daughters and sons are one's own, the son's wife is 'other'") as an explanation of the meaning of these prestations. This "saying" would clearly be inappropriate as a commentary on the aspects of relationships involved in the giving of *dān* and the ensuring of auspiciousness, since in contexts in which that aspect of the relationship is foregrounded the daughter, the *dhiyānī,* is explicitly said to be "other," while the *bahū* performs the rituals and gives *dān* to the *dhiyānī* on behalf of her husband precisely as "one's own" to him.

Prestation Types and Terminological Usages

The types of givings and receivings, the *len-den,* discussed in this chapter appear to belong to a general category of prestations that contrast in many ways with *dān* and *caṛhāpā*. How may we characterize this category of prestations? Wittgenstein's notion that many categories in language are definable, not in terms of a single common element, but in terms of what he calls "family resemblances" may help us in thinking of all of these givings and receivings—*phaslānā, lāg* and *neg, milāī,* the *wādā* prestations, and so forth—as indeed being similar in the indigenous view.

> Consider for example the proceedings that we call "games." I mean board games, card-games, ball-games, Olympic games, and so on. What is common to them all?—Don't say: "There *must* be something common, or they would not be called 'games'"—but *look and see* if there is anything common to all.—For if you look at them you will not see something that is common to *all,* but similarities, relationships, and a whole series of them at that. To repeat: don't think, but look!—Look for example at board games, with their multifarious relationships. Now pass to card-games; here you find many correspondences with the first group, but many common features drop out, and others appear. When we pass next to ball-games, much that is common is retained, but much is lost.—Are they all "amusing"? Compare chess with noughts and crosses. Or is there always winning and losing, or competition between players? Think of patience. In ball games there is winning and losing, but when a child throws his ball at the wall and catches it again, this feature has dropped out. Look at the parts played by skill and luck; and at the difference between skill in chess and skill

in tennis. Think now of games like ring-a-ring-a-roses; here is the element of amusement, but how many characteristic features have disappeared! And we can go through the many, many other groups of games in the same way; can see how similarities crop up and disappear.

And the result of this examination is: we see a complicated network of similarities overlapping and criss-crossing: sometimes overall similarities, sometimes similarities of detail.

I can think of no better expression to characterize these similarities than "family resemblances"; for the various resemblances between members of a family: build, features, colour of eyes, gait, temperament, etc. etc. overlap and criss-cross in the same way.—And I shall say: "games" form a family. (Wittgenstein 1958b, 31–32).

Though the category of prestations I am delineating here is perhaps more amenable to concise definition than our category of "games," I have proceeded to define this set of prestations in much the same way that Wittgenstein suggests: by building up the resemblances among them, resemblances that are sometimes common to most of the members of the category, but that sometimes overlap and criss-cross in complicated ways. The "family resemblances" that are most important in the definition of the prestations that I have suggested might be grounded in "mutuality" are "exchange" (*badlā*), giving to "one's own" rather than "other," the fact that recipients are said to have a "right" (*hak*) to claim the particular prestation, and finally the use of specific terms of reference for the recipients of these prestations, terms that stand in contrast to those used for the same persons when they are the recipients of the prestations—*dān* and *caṛhāpā*—that transfer inauspiciousness. These terminological distinctions are summarized in table 9.

The most fundamental contrast that emerges when these linguistic usages are considered in their social contexts is that between "one's own" people and "others" as recipients of the various named prestations. This contrast is reinforced by the distinction between *āpas kā kām* (the "mutual work" involved in the performance of ritual services and the acceptance of *lāg* and *neg*) and *dhiyānī kā kām* (the "work of *dhiyānī*," that is, the acceptance of *dān*), as well as by the distinction between the differing "rights" and "obligations" in the two sorts of prestations. In all cases of the giving of *dān* to "others," it is said to be the "obligation" (*pharmāyā*) of the recipient to accept it, and the "right" (*hak*) of the donor to give it. In the case of prestations to "one's own," on the other hand, it is the right of the recipient to receive the prestation, and the obligation of the donor to give it.

The contrast between "one's own" people and "others," then, as well as the other sorts of discriminations that follow from it, is not a terminological distinction that is referable to distinct groups or categories of

TABLE 9

PRESTATION TYPES AND CORRESPONDING TERMINOLOGICAL USAGES

Centrality	Mutuality	
dān, caṛhāpā, and *pujāpā*	*phaslānā, lāg,* and *neg* *nyautā, parosā,* and *kothlī* *milāī* and wādā	
dhiyānī (married daughter, sister, father's sister)	*beṭī* ("daughter") *laṛkī* ("girl") *bahan* ("sister")	married daughter, sister, and father's sister
dhiyānā (husband of *dhiyānī*) *pūj* (recipient of *pujāpā*); used by all castes except Gujar	*riśtedār* ("holder of a relationship," a "relative") specific kin terms, e.g. *phūphā* (father's sister's husband), *bahenoi* (sister's husband)	
śarmanne ("protecting"); used only in the context of the *pherā*		spouses of *dhiyānī* and their kin
aglī ("the next ones"); used by Gujars in the context of *cālā, cūcak, kevkā,* and *bhāt*	*samdhin* (here, women of daughter's conjugal family who stand in the relation of daughter's husband's mother)	
[a]"the *sās*" (husband's mother), "the *sūsar*" (husband's father)	*samdhin* (daughter's husband's mother) and *samdhi* (daughter's husband's father)	
[a]*kamīn* *pujārī* (recipient of *pujāpā* when a deity is involved)	*gharelū* ("of the house") *kamīn* *lagū-bandhū bhāī* ("tied-together brother") *dahej mẽ hissedār* ("sharers in the dowry") village kin terms *hamārā* Nai ("our Barber"); used likewise for all *kamīn* castes in these contexts	Barbers, Sweepers, etc., in hereditary service relationships with Gujars
purohit *pūj* (recipient of *pujāpā*) *śarmanne* ("protecting"); used for other Brahman recipients of *dān,* e.g., Dakauts, as well *pujārī* (recipient of *pujāpā*)	*hamārā* Brahman ("our Brahman") village kin terms *lagū-bandhū bhāī* *dahej mẽ hissedār* *gharelū*	Brahmans in hereditary service relationships with Gujars

[a]These terms may occur in many contexts other than the acceptance of *dān;* their significance here is that their referentially equivalent counterparts in the opposite column would never occur in the contexts in which the acceptance of *dān* was at issue. All other terms in the left column are used *only* in the context of the acceptance of *dān, caṛhāpā* or *pujāpā.*

persons or to certain empirical relationships.[11] In other words, these terminological usages not only enter into propositional statements *about* particular persons, categories, or events, but more important, they function as indicators of shifting, contextually appropriate and purposive foregroundings of the aspects of relationships—the oriented transfer of inauspiciousness or "mutuality," "otherness" or "brother-conduct" (*bhāīācārā*)—that may be at issue as relevant social variables of the speech situation. Indeed, the usages summarized in table 8 constitute a set of regular pragmatic indices of the aspects of relationships that are at issue in any given context, make explicit the parameters of the situation at hand, and foreground the cultural constructs in terms of which the event may be understood.[12]

The final section of this chapter will consider the relationship of these two types of prestations and their corresponding terminology to hierarchical orderings within the village. Before proceeding, however, I want to discuss the ritual uses that are made of *mol lānā*, "bringing for a price," and what they tell us about the types of prestations that we have been considering, and then I wish to illustrate some alternative perspectives on these prestations, perspectives that we have not so far examined.

Mol Lānā: The Ritual Uses of "Bringing for a Price"

We have seen that prestations involving *badlā*, "exchange," or any notion of compensation for goods or services rendered are thought to be incapable of transferring inauspiciousness. The contrast between this sort of transaction and those that involve the removal of inauspiciousness is thrown vividly into relief in the ritual, discussed in chapter 4, that is performed when a son is born to a family after three daughters, a situation thought to be productive of great inauspiciousness for the child as well as his family. The child, called a *tīkun*, is placed in a winnowing fan, on top of one and one-fourth *ser* of grain, and given as *dān* to the family's Sweeper, who thereby accepts the afflictions that beset the child because of the circumstances of his birth. Although of course the family wants its son, one may not take back what is given in *dān*, because the inauspiciousness would thus be taken back as well. Hence the family "takes for a price" (*mol lānā*) the child from the Sweeper. They give the Sweeper some money or a quantity of grain in exchange for the child, and one of the names of the child will henceforth be Molhar, "one who has been bought." The contrast between *dān* and reciprocal exchange is thus highlighted in this rather obscure ritual; *dān* effects the transferral of inauspiciousness that is held to be impossible in the subsequent *mol lānā*, "bringing for a price."

The notion of *mol lānā* turns up in another context in which it is contrasted with *dān*. If a Gujar man, for one reason or another (usually having to do with landlessness or advanced age), is unable to be married in the usual way, in a *kanyā dān* wedding, he may go to one of the northern Uttar Pradesh hill districts in order to find a wife or he may obtain a Gujar bride from a very impoverished family. He makes a payment to the woman's parents, and the same term, *mol lānā*, is used for this transaction.[13] In such a *mol lānā* marriage, the bride's parents do not give the girl as a *dān*, and none of the usual wedding prestations (or subsequent prestations to *dhiyānī* and *dhiyānā*) are made; it is said of them that their *pāp* is not removed, and inauspiciousness is not transferred to the groom. In both of these cases, the *mol lānā* of the *tīkun*, and the *mol lānā* marriage, the "exchange" precludes the possibility of the transfer of inauspicious substances. The same is true of the other prestations characterized by mutuality that have been discussed in this chapter.

"You Can't Look a Gift Calf in the Mouth": Another Perspective on *Dān*

While the meanings of the two categories of prestations are conventional, pervasive, and fundamental in the ordering of everyday social life in Pahansu, there is nevertheless often the possibility of multiple interpretations of a prestation or set of prestations.

Gujars value their way of life as cultivators of the soil not only because of the ritual centrality that it affords them, but also because in farming, they say, there is no "bondage" (*bandhan*), no "hindrances" (*rukāvat*), and no "restrictions" (*pratibandh*). It also tests their "courage" (*himmat*), their qualities as Ksatriya "warriors," in that they must wrest their living from the soil through much hard work (*mehannat*) in the face of "the fury of the gods, the fury of fate" (*daiv prakop*), in dust storms and drought, hail storms that ruin their crops, and rain storms during the harvests. Even when we were discussing such everyday matters as rain storms and irrigation problems, the subject of *dān* would arise spontaneously on the part of the Gujar men with whom I talked about the rigors of tilling the soil. Farming is the best occupation, they would insist, because of the "independence" (*āzādī*) it affords, in contrast to the dependency of those whose obligation it is to take *dān*. Many times, in such situations, I heard this saying:

uttam khetī, madhyam bān
nīc cākrī, bhīkh na dān.

Farming is best, next is trade
service is low, but the worst is asking for *dān*.

Now this saying foregrounds not so much the transferral of inauspiciousness in *dān* as the fact that such acceptance implies dependency, a dependency that Gujars, as farmers and givers of *dān,* do not experience. My "brother" and patron, Telu Ram, was fond of the saying *dān kī bachiyā ke dā̃t nahī̃ dekhe jāte* ("You can't look at the teeth of a calf received in *dān,*" or "You can't look a gift calf in the mouth.") Whatever is given in *dān,* he would say, must be taken; if one buys a calf, however, one can decide whether it is good or bad by examining its teeth and looking it over. While one might construe this second *kahāvat* as referring to the inauspiciousness that may be transferred in the *dān,* what Telu Ram meant was that although the actual items received in *dān,* the cloth and the brass vessels, and perhaps even a cow, may not be of good quality, the recipient must accept them anyway. *Būṛhī gāy paṇḍit ke sir:* "Old useless cows fall to the *paṇḍit.*"

These three *kahāvat*s focus, not on the inauspiciousness transferred in *dān,* but rather on the fact that some people actually make their living by accepting *dān,* a situation of dependency. At issue, then, are the items received in *dān,* the grain, the cows, the money, the brass vessels, the cloth, and the meals. The recipients of *dān* do not, in the estimation of Gujars, "work" for these things, as they themselves do as they cultivate the soil. They themselves must labor, carry out the arduous tasks of the *kāśtkār,* the cultivator, in order to be able to give so much in *dān.* This, too, is important in their definition of themselves as Gujars, as givers of *dān.* And because they work to acquire these things, they know that it is not easy to acquire grain and cloth and cash and brass vessels to use and to give. It is their right to give *dān,* and they do it, they say, for their own auspiciousness, yet it is nevertheless difficult to give.

Just after a new bride arrives for the first time at her *sasurāl,* her first gift there is a prestation called *sandūk khulāī,* "opening the trunk," a gift of several sets of cloth for her *nanad,* her husband's sister and now her own *dhiyānī. Sandūk khulāī* is *dān,* and the bride gives it for her own auspiciousness and that of her husband. This first *dān* skims off the top layer, as it were, of the inauspiciousness of the cloth brought in the *dāt* from her *pīhar.* It is her right to give these sets of cloth to her *nanad;* and this is the first of many times that she will "open the trunk" and give from her stock of cloth. She has the right to give and must give, if her own auspiciousness is to be ensured, at very many occasions in the course of her life and in the course of the yearly cycle of calendrical rituals. It is from the stock of cloth in her tin trunk that a woman's own clothes are made, but she will wear only a very small number of the sets of cloth that are in her trunk. Most are destined to be "given onward" as *dān* or in *wādā* gifts to her husband's sisters. The trunk is very precious to a woman, and it is sometimes hard for her to open it up and give away the contents. Once when Rajavati, my *bhābhī* (the wife of Telu Ram), decided that my own *oṛhnā*s (thin shawls used as head-coverings) were much too drab and that I should have a brightly colored flowered one, she opened her trunk and told me to pick one for my own. I had just had a new *salwār-kamīz* (baggy pants fitted at the ankles and a long shirt) sewn for me in the village style by Roshan, the Pahansu tailor, and Rajavati thought that I should pick an *oṛhnā* that would look nice with that particular *salwār-kamīz*. And so I picked one; but even though she had offered the *oṛhnā* to me, I could see that opening the trunk and giving from the contents was not easy for her to do. She admired the *oṛhnā* each time I wore it and always seemed to be just a bit regretful of the loss of it from her own store of cloth. Now this gift was not *dān*, but the reluctance to part with one's cloth may exist even as women say that it is their right to give *joṛā*s as *dān*, and the obligation of the recipient to accept them.

Men too may sometimes balk at the extravagance of *len-den*, though it is true that for the most part they see it as an essential component, not only of their well-being and auspiciousness, but of their "prestige" (*izzat*) as well that they give much in *dān*. Late one morning I was squatting with Asikaur, my "mother," in the closed *dahlīz* (entrance way) of our house, looking over the wares of an itinerant cloth-seller as she prepared to purchase cloth that would be given in an *udāpan* (a *dān* prestation) to two of her daughters, Premo and Santosh. Asi finally made her purchases and took them into the courtyard of the house, where Jabar Singh, her second eldest son, was eating his lunch. An argument instantly broke out between them and lasted nearly an hour, during which time I didn't dare switch on my tape recorder or even take notes, but I did try to remember as much as possible of what they said. Jabar Singh was shouting that all of this *len-den* was a custom of the "old times" (*purāne zamāne*) and should be curtailed. Asi, becoming just as vociferous as Jabar Singh, asserted that "there are four brothers and four sisters [Asi had eight children, by then all married], and so there is the right to take and give" (*cār bhāī haĩ aur cār bahan to lene dene kā hak hai*) and that one "must maintain one's prestige" (*izzat rākhnā paṛegā*) by giving to one's daughters and sisters and to their children. At that, Jabar Singh stood up, threw the remains of his lunch onto the floor and, with all the cadence and magisterium of a man pronouncing a hoary proverb, said:

beṭī nahī̃ hotī to terā mauj;
ham nahī̃ hote to terā nāś.

If it weren't for daughters you would have luxury and enjoyment;
if it weren't for us [the four brothers] you would be destroyed.

And with that he stormed out of the courtyard. Premo, one of the sisters of Jabar Singh to whom the cloth in question was to be given, was also sitting in the courtyard and was by then in tears. Asi too wiped at her eyes as she sat on a cot holding Neelam, her newborn *potī* (son's daughter). But the cloth of course was given. Eight days later Ashok, another of Asi's sons, took five *udāpan joṛās* to Santosh in her *sasurāl,* and two months later, when Premo returned to her conjugal village, she took twenty sets of cloth (see pp. 228–29).

Now telling Jabar Singh that these *udāpan* sets of cloth were being given for the auspiciousness of the four brothers would probably not have made the slightest bit of difference to him, I venture to guess. Indeed, Asikaur did not mention this reason for giving the *joṛās* in her not inconsiderable verbal onslaught against Jabar Singh. The point, of course, is that inauspiciousness can very often be transferred in one set of cloth as easily as in five; what is given in *dān* beyond the one that is necessary for one's auspiciousness is a matter of one's prestige, according to Asikaur. What was at issue in this argument, then, was the quantity and quality of the items to be given in *dān,* the fact that brothers provide most of the cloth that sisters wear and give, just as they provide the grain and cash and cloth and brass vessels for their Brahmans and *kamīns* who are dependent upon them as the tillers of the soil, the *kāśtkārs*.

Centrality, Mutuality, and Hierarchy: Aspects of Relationships in Kinship and Caste

The many types of prestations we have documented and described are given, villagers say, either for one's own auspiciousness or as part of a more or less reciprocally defined relationship among "one's own people." Very little has been said in these chapters about what is generally taken to be the most fundamental and pervasive aspect of village life in Hindu South Asia, namely, hierarchy. Hierarchy, or rank, has been discussed in the ethnographic literature in a number of ways. Hierarchy has sometimes been seen as an attributional ordering of castes based on their inherent purity or impurity, often held to be associated largely with the work involved in their traditional occupations (Blunt 1931; Stevenson 1954; for discussion of these attributional theories of rank, see Marriott 1959; 1968, 133–38). Early theorists attended very little, if at all, to exchanges of food and other items within the village setting; in their view, a hierarchy of castes could be constructed simply in terms of a set of attributes—occupation, diet, marriage patterns, and so forth—which they saw as placing castes in a hierarchical ordering. The importance of exchanges, particularly of food and water, but also of bodily substances such as hair, menstrual blood, feces, and saliva in food leavings, has been extensively discussed by Marriott (1968, 1976; Marriott and Inden 1974, 1977) and Dumont (1970). Both scholars focus on food exchanges in various media—raw foods (*sīdhā*), foods cooked in oil or clarified butter (*pakkā* goods), foods cooked in water or breads cooked without oil or butter (*kaccā* foods), and water—as constituted from (Dumont) or creative of (Marriott) a ranked order of *jāti*s. For Dumont, the exchanges in these media simply reflected the distinction between the pure and the impure, although in his view such exchanges are often refracted through a nonideological empirical residuum, the "power" of the dominant caste.

Marriott's continuing assertion that purity and impurity represent, not the overarching conceptual framework of Indian society, but simply one manifestation of a much more complex and fundamental set of assumptions has raised new questions and admitted a much broader range of ethnographic data as relevant to our understanding of South Asian social life. Despite the deemphasis of purity and impurity, however, a notion of rank, whatever its indigenous conceptualization, has still been seen as the conceptual underpinning for much of everyday life, particularly for the giving and receiving of prestations.

> Transactors and transactions are oriented ultimately neither toward "purity" nor toward "power" as usually understood in social science, but toward a unitary Indian concept of superior value—power understood as vital energy, substance-code of subtle, homogenous quality, and high, consistent transactional status or rank. All of these are regarded as naturally coincidental or synonymous. (Marriott 1976, 137)

It is this orientation toward "superior value" and consistent high rank that is held to structure relationships among kinsmen, marriage patterns, intercaste relationships, and ritual relations between men and gods, at least insofar as transactions of any sort are concerned. While the great value of Marriott's work, particularly the 1976 paper, has been to show that an understanding of the varying "transactional strategies" in fact makes sense of a great deal of variation in South Asian marriage patterns, ritual practices, personal interactional styles, dietary and commensal practices, styles of leadership, and so forth, analyses of prestation patterns remain tied to the assumption that exchanges of all kinds are linked in all contexts to the system of rank.

In everyday village life in Pahansu, there is very little talk about hierarchy in ordinary conversation. When asked by the anthropologist about the giving and receiving of *pakkā* and *kaccā* foods and other media of this type, villagers responded that such considerations indicate "dispositions about high and low" (*ū̃c-nīc kā bhāv*) and "touching and not touching" (*chuāchūt*). In these contexts, the terminology reflects hierarchical distinctions of "high caste" (*ū̃cī jāti*) and "low caste" (*nīcī jāti*), or juxtaposes "big" castes and "little" castes (*baṛī jāti* and *choṭī jāti*); or specific caste names occur (Brahman, Nai, Bhangi, Jhinvar, etc.) but without the use of the possessive "our" (*hamārā*). These terminological usages contrast with those that occur in connection both with the giving of *dān* and *caṛhāpā* and with those implemented in the giving and receiving of the prestations of "mutuality."[14]

The relationships characterized in this manner (high and low, little and big), and in which transactions are construed in terms of the media involved (e.g., *kaccā* and *pakkā* foods) are not in fact those of giving and receiving, properly speaking. And in the terms of village talk, they are not those in which *len-den* is construed. The question "Who did the cooking?" rather than "Who is the donor?" is the more fundamental one here, as Blunt (1931, 89) and Dumont (1970, 142) rightly point out. More generally speaking, a concern with gross bodily substances and their qualities and their mixing with what is given is involved, and such mixing occurs most significantly in the cooking process. That particular relation of donor and recipient, appearing in Pahansu as by far the most significant, remains unexplicated if we focus attention on this issue alone. Further, although as we have seen there are perhaps hundreds of specifically named prestations in Pahansu, there are few situations in which these are made because of a hierarchical relationship between donor and recipient. Hierarchical considerations only partially structure the patterns of giving and receiving in the village; they provide merely a parameter or set of assumptions concerning the media in which the prestations will be made, prestations that are culturally constructed primarily in terms of other concepts and concerns and that foreground aspects of relationships other than hierarchy.

If, for example, a particular prestation needs to be made by a Gujar family to a Brahman, a prestation that involves the giving of a meal, the women of the Gujar household may prepare *pakkā* food, which a Brahman may properly accept from a Gujar cook, or they may present the Brahman with the uncooked ingredients for a *kaccā* meal and ask the Brahman to prepare it himself in their home, since hierarchical considerations generally prevent a Brahman from accepting prepared *kaccā* food from a Gujar cook. (Which of these two options is adopted is generally a matter of complete indifference to Gujar donors.) The hierarchical aspects of the relationship between Gujar and Brahman are thus evidenced in these acts of giving and receiving, but they tell us nothing of why the prestation had to be made to begin with; the donor-recipient relationship and the meaning of the prestation itself remain obscure if we attend only to the relative rank of the persons involved in the transaction, or to the media in which the prestation is made.

In the context of prestations made to remove inauspiciousness, and in the context of those given *badle mẽ*, "in exchange," to "one's own people," hierarchy is not a foregrounded aspect of the social situation. The cultural constructs in terms of which both of these sorts of prestations are understood provide alternative orderings of both kinsmen and people of different castes, orderings that are indexed in the different terminological usages summarized above in table 9. These contextually implemented orderings of kinsmen and castes in Pahansu are diagrammed in figure 17. There are, of course, a number of details of the situation, the ramifications of these different orderings, that are not easily representable. Most important, I have not attempted to diagram here the permutations in these prestation patterns that are evident when castes other than Gujar give either *dān, caṛhāpā,* or *pujāpā,* on the one hand, or the prestations associated with mutuality on the other. I have already discussed how these permutations were of great importance for me in sorting out the varying significances of these two categories of prestations. They are also important to the castes that are involved, the castes that give *dān* to their *dhiyāne* as Gujars give *dān* to them.

Whenever I attempted to question Gujars about the hierarchical considerations involved in giving and receiving, that is, the considerations concerning who can receive *pakkā* and *kaccā* foods from whom, they treated the question as a trivial one, one that concerned, for the most part, hypothetical situations in which they are little interested. Yes, they would say, we suppose we could take *kaccā* food from a Brahman, but we don't take anything from Brahmans at all. They may, of course, eat at a feast cooked by a Brahman (but given by a Gujar), but they never stand in the relationship of recipient of prestations from Brahmans. They always stressed, just when I was trying to elicit hierarchical discriminations in terms of these various media, that they would never, under any circumstances, take anything from a Brahman, and most particularly, they would never take grain from a Brahman. (Grain has generally been seen as a "superior medium" in transactions, a substance that does not so readily transmit the "substance-codes" of the donor and may thus be accepted from most other castes, superior or inferior [Marriott 1968, 143; 1976, 110; see also Dumont 1970, 142].) It is true, as Marriott has pointed out (1965, 53–61), that the elaboration of caste ranking in what he calls the Upper Ganges region of northern India is relatively slight in comparison with other areas of India, particularly in the southern areas of Kerala and the Coromandel plains. That is, the givings and receivings, represented in terms of hierarchical considerations about types of media, do not discriminate as many discrete ranks of castes in the Upper Ganges region as would be the case in these other areas. Therefore, perhaps, one might not expect rank to be such an obvious part of everyday social life here as it might be elsewhere. In Pahansu, for example, Brahmans will accept *pakkā* food from all castes except Sweeper and Leatherworker,

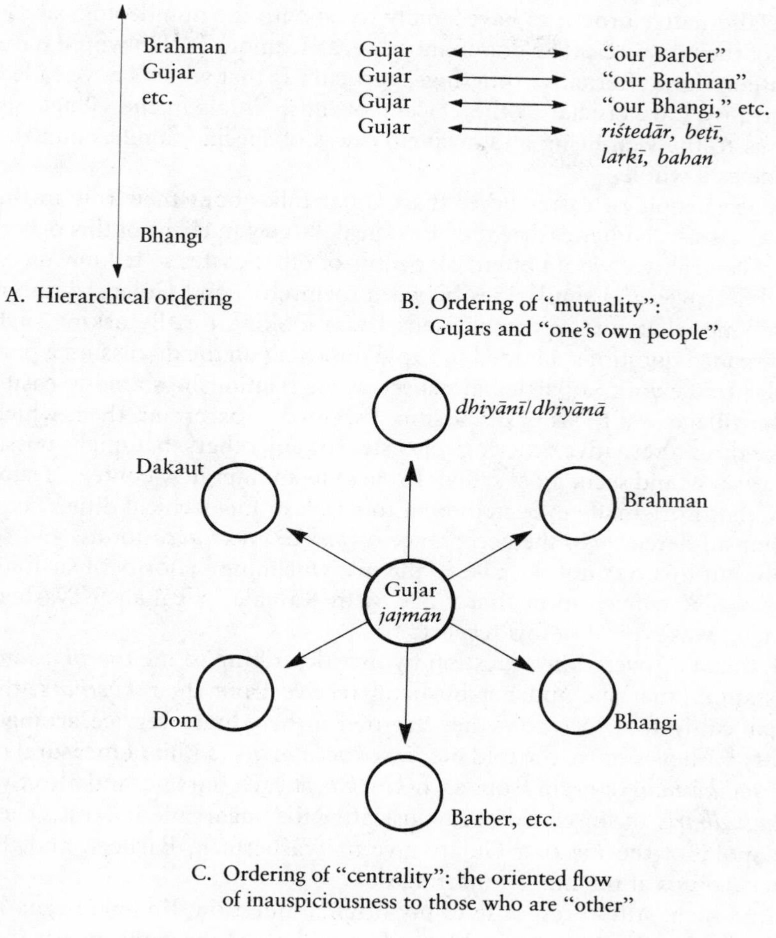

Fig. 17. Orderings of castes and kinsmen in Pahansu

and so the differences among the castes from this perspective are less salient than they might otherwise be.

But, as I say, Gujars are little interested in these matters, precisely because they have little to do with the actual prestations, the nonhypothetical patterns of *len-den,* the giving and receiving of prestations that transfer inauspiciousness and those that are given to "one's own people."[15] For Gujars, as well as for other castes in the village, their position in the local configuration of castes is defined most importantly in terms of the actual prestations that are given, in terms of the orderings summarized in diagrams B and C of figure 17. And it is not the case, as we have seen, that these alternative orderings have simply to do with the nonideological aspect of the "power" of the dominant caste, as Dumont (1970) would have it; rather, these alternative orderings, particularly that which I have called "centrality," are crucial to the efficacy of most rituals in the village, as well as to the well-being and auspiciousness of specific families and the village as a whole.

When people of castes other than Gujar talk about their role in the village vis-à-vis other castes, they too speak largely in terms of this ordering of centrality. I would often ask people of other castes to tell me about the differences and similarities between themselves and Gujars, without specifying what sort of comparisons I was looking for. By asking such open-ended questions, I hoped to avoid imposing on the discussion a particular framework, a particular aspect of the relationships among castes in the village as a focus of discussion. I wanted to ascertain, then, which of the three alternative orderings of castes (or any others that might possibly arise) would seem most salient to them in an interview context. I suppose that I originally expected them to speak of hierarchical differences, perhaps differences in the acceptance of *pakkā* and *kaccā* foods, and so forth. But this was not the case in the overwhelming majority of such interviews. A conversation that I had with Kamala, a Pahansu Washerwoman, was typical in this respect.

Kamala answered my question by first describing to me the *phaslānā* prestations that she and her husband receive from their *kāśtkār*s, the Gujar cultivators to whom they are tied in hereditary service arrangements.[16] They receive, she told me, two *kaccā man*s (a unit of measure) or one *pakkā man* of grain from each *kāśtkār* at each harvest, and also two *pakkā dhaṛī*s of unrefined sugar just after the sugarcane harvest. Then she spoke of the *lāg* that Gujars give to Washermen, Barbers, and the other *kamīn*s at the time of marriages.

And then, still in response to my original question, Kamala began to tell me about Washerman weddings. She told me of the many sweets that are made, the feasts that are given at the time of tying the *manḍhā,* and she told me that she had sent two hundred *parosā*s to her *kāśtkār*s at the time of the wedding of her daughter. There is no difference, she said, in the customs of the Gujars and the Washermen as far as these things are concerned. She told me of the *dahej* she had given in her daughter's wedding: three pieces of jewelry (*ṭūm*)for her daughter, three for the groom, a table and chairs, a bicycle, a tin trunk, and many sets of cloth. Like Gujars, she said, Washermen do much "taking and giving" (*len-den*) at weddings. (She suggested that Barbers do little of this *len-den* at weddings, at least in comparison with Gujars and Washermen.) At the birth of a child, Kamala said, Washermen give the *kevkā* and *cūcak* prestations just as Gujars do.

I must stress here that I was recording all of this without asking further questions; Kamala was perhaps uncharacteristically loquacious that day, but all of her rather lengthy discourse was in response to my initial question. Kamala went on: "Just as Gujars do, we too give grain to our 'workers'" (*gūjarõ ke jaise ham bhī kārīn ko anāj dete haĩ*), to Barbers, to Brahmans, and to Sweepers. She pointed out to me that Washermen give *pujāpā* and *mīnsāī* as *dān* to appropriate recipients, just as Gujars do.

Then Kamala began to talk of the *bhāt* prestation made by the mother's brother of the bride or groom at the time of a wedding. She said that in Washermen weddings, Barbers receive some sweets as *caṛhāpā* at the time of the giving of the *bhāt* just as they do in Gujar weddings. Finally, she spoke of the *bār dwārī* rite that is preliminary to the central marriage ritual of the *pherā*. In the weddings of Brahmans and Leatherworkers and Sweepers, she said, the *sevel* (touching the end of one's shawl to the groom's head and receiving *caṛhāpā*) is done by a *dhiyānā*, but in Washermen weddings, as in Gujar weddings, the Brahman family *purohit* performs the *sevel* and receives the *caṛhāpā*. Here Kamala spoke with obvious pride in the fact that the patterns of giving and receiving at the *bār dwārī* were just like those of Gujars, rather than those of Brahmans, Leatherworkers, and Sweepers. It was the fact that Washermen give these *caṛhāpā* prestations to the same recipients as Gujars do (here the Brahman and the Barber), rather than to *dhiyāne*, that was most important to her in defining the position of her own *jāti* in relation to the others of the village. This is what I meant when I said that the permutation patterns for the various castes, as far as these prestations are concerned, are of great significance to them in regard to their position in the local configuration of castes. For many non-Gujars, the fact that their pattern of giving and receiving approximates, more or less closely, that of the Gujar *jajmān*s is of greater importance than their hierarchical position vis-à-vis other castes in the village.

This is true for Barbers as well as Washermen. Several months after I arrived in Pahansu, I was sitting in the *gher* of Mangal Singh and Sukhbir, Gujar brothers, while their Barber, Illam Singh, was shaving Mangal. I had only recently become aware of the significance of the giving of *dān*, *caṛhāpā*, and *pujāpā* in village life, and I had been asking Mangal and Sukhbir about who takes *pujāpā* and who doesn't, the differences between *prasād* and *pujāpā*, and so forth. Mangal Singh was telling me that Gujars, as Ksatriyas, never accept *pujāpā*, but that Brahmans, Sweepers, Water-carriers, Bangle-sellers, Dakauts, Leatherworkers, and many other *jāti*s do indeed accept particular *pujāpā* prestations. It was perhaps significant that Mangal Singh did not mention that Barbers actually receive many types of *caṛhāpā*, since the Barber Illam had been listening to our conversation as he shaved Mangal. Mangal again emphasized that

Ksatriyas do not accept *pujāpā;* at that point, Illam joined the discussion and said that Barbers likewise do not accept *pujāpā* (*nāī nahī̃ lete,* he said, with some pride in his voice). Mangal answered this assertion, saying, "You take the *pujāpā* of the betrothal" (*āp sagāī kā pujāpā lete haĩ*), but Illam said no, that was not *pujāpā.* Neither Mangal nor Sukhbir contradicted this statement, but in fact prestations that a Barber receives at the betrothal are, in everyone's estimation, *pujāpā,* and Barbers receive many kinds of *pujāpā, caṛhāpā,* and *dān* from Gujars in the rituals of the life course and the harvests. Barbers do not receive any *pujāpā* during the rituals of the calendrical cycle or the *pujāpā* generated in the course of rituals that concern the gods, so perhaps Illam was thinking of this when he made his assertion. In any case, it seems significant that Illam wanted to place his own *jāti* in the caste configuration in terms of its approximation to the pattern of Gujars in the giving and receiving of prestations, just as Kamala the Washerwoman had done.

That Illam did indeed aspire to model his giving and receiving on the pattern set by Gujars became evident much later on the occasion of the marriage of his daughter. As I indicated earlier in this chapter, it is a Gujar practice to send gifts of sweets called *kothlī* to a daughter's conjugal village shortly after her marriage; the *kothlī* is generally sent with the family Barber, or with the Barber and the Brahman, who then receive *lāg* from the girl's conjugal family. Two days after the wedding of Illam's daughter Kaushal, I was sitting in their courtyard watching Illam's wife make *panjīrī* for the *kothlī* that was to be sent the next day. She told me that while Gujars send their Barber to deliver these sweets, as Barbers themselves they would send her *nanadoyyā,* her husband's sister's husband, to take the sweets to the village in Muzaffarnagar District into which her daughter had been married. We talked of the wedding for a while; she told me that she had sent out twenty-five *parosā*s on the day of the wedding, that Rs. 808 had been given in the *kanyā dān,* and she enumerated the many things that had been given in the *bhāt* by her brothers: Rs. 264, nine brass vessels, three pieces of jewelry (*ṭūm*), and fifteen sets of cloth. At that point Illam came into the courtyard and, seeing that the sweets for the *kothlī* were being prepared, announced that he did not intend to send the *kothlī* with his sister's husband in the usual Barber way; instead he would send it with Buddhu Pandit, their Brahman, who would receive a *lāg* of Rs. 10 or 20 and a set of cloth from Kaushal's husband's family. Then both he and his wife complained that Buddhu Pandit had carried out Kaushal's *pherā* very quickly, with an insufficient number of *mantra*s, and in general had not taken the care that he would have taken in a Gujar wedding. Illam's wife went so far as to call him a "bastard" (*harām*), a fairly serious abuse. They even spoke of establishing a relationship with a different Brahman family (*ham dūsrā brahman rākhenge*).

As all of this happened just a few days before I left Pahansu for the last time, I don't know whether or not they really did try to do this. But the point of this story is that just when Illam and his wife had suffered what they thought of as a slight, inasmuch as Buddhu Pandit had, in their estimation, failed to perform their daughter's marriage with the care he would have taken for a Gujar *śādī,* Illam decided to send their Brahman on an errand that, in the usual Barber fashion, his sister's husband would normally carry out. By sending Buddhu Pandit instead, he was attempting to approximate the Gujar model of giving and receiving, in much the same fashion as he had tried to insist, so many months before, that Barbers, like Gujars, do not accept *pujāpā.*

CHAPTER SIX

Conclusions

In Pahansu, intercaste relationships, as they appear most significantly in everyday discourse and in the giving and receiving of prestations, are concerned with promoting auspiciousness, and they implicate the configuration of castes that I have termed centrality. From the cultivator's grain piles and stores of cloth, prestations are made almost daily for the "well-being achieved through gift-giving" of the household and the village as a whole. The cultivator is the *jajmān,* the "sacrificer," and he stands at the conceptual center of village ritual organization; the Barber, the Sweeper, the Brahman, and many other castes of the village carry out virtually identical ritual roles in relation to the *jajmān,* particularly in their acceptance of *dān*. These recipients of *dān* take upon themselves and "digest" the sin, the evil, and the inauspiciousness of the *jajmān,* his household, and the village.

The ritual centrality of the village cultivator, or of the king in Indic textual discourse, has been virtually ignored in anthropological and Indological debate concerning caste and kingship, in favor of a view that founds caste and ritual solely upon considerations of hierarchy or rank. Whatever importance has been granted to the locally dominant landholding caste, to Ksatriyas, or to kings has generally been seen in terms simply of their "temporal power" or a "shame-faced Ksatriya model" (Dumont 1970, 91) devoid of ritual significance.[1]

Such was not always the case. Hocart, in his work on kingship (1970) and caste (1950), originally published in 1936 and 1938, recognized that at the village level the cultivator is analogous in many respects to the king (1950, 68) and that there exists an ordering of castes in which "priest, washerman and drummer are treated alike, for they are all priests" (ibid., 44). Indeed, this ordering is the most important aspect of intercaste relationships. These castes render essential ritual services to the cultivator and the king, services that have primarily to do with the procurement of prosperity, freedom from premature death, and freedom from disease (ibid., 18). The king appears, then, as "the chief actor [of the ritual who] supplies the offerings and bears the expense" (ibid., 35), and the prosperity of his kingdom depends upon his observance of this duty, his *dharma*.

While Hocart does not discuss in detail acceptance of gifts as a component of the ritual services performed by the Brahman, the Potter, and the Washerman, his interpretation of the relationship of the king or the cultivator to these castes is clearly paralleled by Pahansu "centrality." When Brahmans and *kamīns* in Pahansu are given and are obliged to accept *dān, caṛhāpā,* and *pujāpā* they serve, like the Sinhalese castes discussed by Hocart, to promote the "auspiciousness" (*śubh*) and "well-being achieved through gift-giving" (*khair-khairāt*) of the donor and of the village as a whole. Many aspects of these evil-dispelling donative relationships as they are enacted in Pahansu appear in ancient and classical Indic texts, and have been discussed by Mauss in his 1925 work on the gift (1967) and by Trautmann (1981) and Heesterman (1959, 1964, 1985).

In a brief discussion of "the law of the gift" (*dānadharma*) as it appears in the epic traditions and in the texts of the *dharmaśāstras*, Mauss in fact descries several very important aspects of the giving and receiving of *dān*.[2] The first and most obvious is that the obligation to make a return prestation, a major focus of interest in *The Gift,* is conspicuously absent in the case of *dān*. Mauss is unable to offer a convincing reason for this, and does not even make it clear in his text whether the lapse in reciprocation is at the wish of the donor or the recipient of *dān*. Second, Mauss sees that the donor gives, not only the thing given, but a part of himself as well (1967, 57). He notes that the texts are very explicit about the dangers to the Brahman of accepting the king's gifts, as in the *Mahābhārata,* when seven *ṛsis* refuse the gifts of the king, saying that "to receive from kings is honey at first but ends as poison" (ibid., 58). At this Mauss remarks, succinctly, "This is a quaint theory."

> A whole caste which lives by gifts pretends to refuse them, then compromises and accepts only those which are offered spontaneously. Then it draws up long lists of persons from whom, and circumstances in which, one may accept gifts, and of the things which one may accept; and finally admits everything in case of famine—on condition, to be sure, of some slight purification. (Ibid., 58)

Mauss then attempts to interpret this reluctance of the Brahman to accept the gifts of the king:

> The bond that the gift creates between the donor and the recipient is too strong for them [the Brahmans] . . . the one is bound too closely to the other. The recipient is in a state of dependence upon the donor. It is for this reason that the Brahman may not accept and still less solicit

> from the king. Divinity among divinities, he is superior to the king and would lose his superiority if he did other than simply take from him. (Ibid.)

This is a crucial passage. Having seen in the texts that the gift represents a danger to the Brahman, and read through the many warnings and precautions addressed to the Brahman who would accept *dān,* Mauss clearly hesitates, and then interprets all of this in terms of a rather abstract idea of the Brahman's fear of "dependence" upon the Ksatriya, though he cites no explicit textual evidence for such an interpretation. He fails here, as Fuller has noted (1984, 196), to draw together his analysis of the gift with his work on sacrifice (Hubert and Mauss [1898] 1964), even though the earlier work described the sacrificial removal of the evil of the sacrificer, and the fact that the sacrificers

> give their old garments to the priests, thus abandoning their former personality, and by putting on new ones they are acquiring "a new skin like a serpent." "There is now no more sin in them than in a toothless infant." (Hubert and Mauss 1964, 139)

In writing *The Gift,* Mauss must certainly have come upon passages in the epics and *dharmaśāstra*s that describe the transferral of sin from donor to recipient. He refers to such a passage from Manu in a footnote, but dismisses it as an "absurd theological interpretation" (1967, 125). Thus it is the idea of temporal dependency and its avoidance that Mauss stresses most in his interpretation of the Brahman's reluctance to accept the gifts of the king.

Both Trautmann and Heesterman have elaborated on the nature of this dependence, and both have very explicitly relied on Dumont's formulation of the relationship between Brahman and Ksatriya. It is precisely at this point that Trautmann speaks of a "conundrum," and Heesterman of a "contradiction."

In his description of the *kanyā dān* form of marriage, Trautmann discusses the general characteristics of *dān* at some length. He identifies what he refers to as "the central conundrum of Indian social ideology" as the source of the Brahman's reluctance to accept *dān* (1981, 285–88). According to Trautmann, the conundrum implicated in the relation between Brahman and king, between "spiritual authority" and "temporal power," springs from the fact than *dān* prestations are interpretable within two contradictory frameworks. "Religious gifts," Trautmann says, "flow upward to superior beings," while "royal gifts flow down a hierarchy of dependency." Thus, as the Brahman accepts *dān,* he does so at once as a "superior being" and as an inferior, dependent upon the king.

Having interpreted the Brahman's reluctance to accept the gifts of the king in terms of this abstract idea of dependence, just as Mauss had done, Trautmann goes on to say that the texts themselves "speak a more concrete language." The dangers of acceptance, seen by both Mauss and Trautmann in terms of dependency, are described in the texts as substantial, tangible dangers, dangers that Trautmann views as simply those of the "impurity" transferred to the Brahman as he accepts the gifts of the hierarchically inferior Ksatriya king (Trautmann 1981, 287).[3] As I have shown throughout this study, however, the invocation of hierarchy simply does not account for the fact that Brahmans, as well as other lower castes in the village, are reluctant to accept *dān* precisely because of the transferral of inauspiciousness that is involved in these prestations. This inauspiciousness is said by villagers to be quite different from "impurity," it is seen to have different implications for social life in the village, and it is quite clearly transmitted from donor to recipient regardless of their relative hierarchic positions.

In his work on sacrifice and sacrificial gifts, Heesterman (1959, 1964) describes the roles of the Brahman and the sacrificer in Vedic ritual.

> The function of the Brahman officiant is to take over the death impurity of the patron by eating from the offerings and by accepting the *dakṣiṇā*s. By gifts and food evil and impurity are transferred and purity attained, especially if the donee is a Brahman.[4] (Heesterman 1964, 3)

Heesterman also saw that it was because "evil" accompanied the *dakṣiṇā* that the Brahman was reluctant to accept such gifts. He quotes, for example, from the *Taittirīya Saṃhita:*

> "One should not officiate (for a *yajamānā*) at the twelve-day sacrifice so as to avoid evil" (because through accepting the *dakṣiṇā*s one would "eat what falls from the head" of the *yajamāna*). (Heesterman 1964, 17)

Having discerned, in what he terms the "preclassical" texts, these remarkable parallels to the Pahansu transferral of evil and inauspiciousness in *dān,* Heesterman, like Mauss, asserts that such prestations have no place in the subsequent "classical" ritual or in the social relations in which it is embedded. The historical transformation he envisions, a transformation he sometimes calls "the axial breakthrough" (Heesterman 1985, 95–107, 153), changed the ritual, the prestations, and the very nature of the relationship between Brahman and king, Brahman and Ksatriya. Whereas in the "preclassical" ritual the *dakṣiṇā* was a sacrificial gift that passed on evil and death to the recipient, it now became simply a matter of a "salary" or a "fee" (1959, 258; 1985, 155, 212). Indeed, with what he calls the "individualization" of the ritual and the elaboration of the "*karma* doctrine," Heesterman views it as an impossibility that evil and death could be passed on to others. The sacrificer, he says, "must digest it himself" (1964, 15). With this "breakthrough," the relation of the Brahman and the king underwent a fundamental change, a change that Heesterman views as the transition to a "caste society." The interdependence of the sacrificial nexus, in which the king as sacrificer depended upon the Brahman to receive the *dakṣiṇā*s and take away the evil gave way to a situation in which the worlds of the Brahman and the king, the Brahman and the Ksatriya, are definitely split. The old pattern of social life in which royal "power" and Brahmanical "authority" were interwoven came to an end, and the pattern of "caste" came into being, in which power and authority, the king's social and temporal world and the Brahman's ritualistic order came to stand in opposition to one another (Heesterman 1964, 16; 1985, 152–53).

Henceforth, according to Heesterman, the king does not require the Brahman *purohit* to receive the *dakṣiṇā*s and to remove evil and sin, but only to provide the "divine or transcendent authority" that is said to legitimize royal power (1985, 141). The Brahman need not shun the king because of the burden of sin and evil conveyed in the royal gifts, but because in serving the king and the community, the Brahman would "jeopardize his claim to represent ultramundane authority" (ibid., 142), authority that is grounded in the Brahman's "independence" from the social world represented by the king or the dominant caste (ibid., 12–13).

In postulating a radical break between these two "opposite and irreconcilable principles of organization," Heesterman relies heavily on Dumont's formulation of the distinction between priestly hierarchy and temporal power (Dumont 1962, 1970). It is Heesterman's view that the split between the two, and indeed, caste society itself, came about precisely at the point when the Brahman ceased to take upon himself the sin, death, and evil of the king, the sacrificer.

In one isolated passage, Heesterman begins to see, perhaps, that such a transformation may not have occurred as definitively in South Asia as he has suggested. In discussing the old pattern of the distribution of evil at the sacrifice, Heesterman writes:

> This situation still seems to be reflected in the diffusion of priestly functions throughout local communities, where we may see potters, barbers, washermen, and others acting in priestly capacities at particular occasions, while in some cases, members or branches of families function as sacrificial priest for their cognate and affinal relatives. Nor is it

> exceptional to see the king at great state occasions as the chief celebrant and sacrificial patron of festivals on which the general well-being depends. . . . All this, however, is remote from the strict separation of power and authority. . . . In fact, it is its very opposite. (1985, 152)

The pattern to which Heesterman alludes here recalls that traced by Hocart in his analysis of caste, and it also resembles the "centrality" of intercaste relationships I have described in Pahansu. That the existence of such a pattern flies in the face of an analysis that defines the role of the king or the dominant caste simply in terms of "temporal power" is grasped by Heesterman, but he makes nothing of the fact that such a pattern may still be seen in Hindu villages, despite his postulation of an "axial breakthrough" that should have done away with all such interdependencies.

In order, then, to reconcile his own depiction of the ancient role of the Brahman and others as recipients of evil and sin as they accept the gifts of the king with Dumont's position that "caste refers exclusively to the value of purity" (Heesterman 1985, 187) and that the ritual and hierarchical aspects of caste have as their conceptual focus the preeminent position of the Brahman, Heesterman has argued that the patterns of giving and receiving he delineated in his work on sacrifice are no longer to be found in South Asian Hindu society. Dumont too had found it necessary to postulate a historical transformation of Hindu society in order to maintain his position on the absolute distinction between the world of caste and the so-called temporal power of the king or the dominant caste. In a brief discussion of Hocart's work in *Homo Hierarchicus,* Dumont argues that the Hocartian pattern of royal centrality in the ritual was found only in "pre-Aryan India" (1970, 285). Hocart, he says,

> failed to see how the Indian system encompasses this small universe, despoiled of its sacredness, within a larger one, governed not by the king but by the priest. . . . It can be supposed that pre-Aryan India had Hocart-style chiefdoms with "lineages" specialized in the services which the *taboo* person of the chief commanded. The disjunction between status and power . . . led to the transformation of the "Hocartian" system into a caste system. (ibid., 213)[5]

Mauss, Heesterman, and Dumont, then, while seeing textual and indeed some ethnographic evidence of the centralized ritual and prestational pattern that in Pahansu places the Gujars at the center of a configuration of castes for the disposal of inauspiciousness, have postulated the existence of historical transformations destroying such a pattern in order to preserve intact what now seem to be untenable positions on the relationship between Brahman and Ksatriya and the very nature of caste and intercaste relationships in India. In asserting that *dānadharma* came to an end in the third century A.D., that an "axial breakthrough" occurred ending the preclassical ritual interdependency of the Brahman and Ksatriya and the role of the *purohit* in removing the evil of the king, and that a disjunction between hierarchical status and temporal power came to replace the Hocartian system, Mauss, Heesterman, and Dumont have legitimated the neglect by anthropologists of the hundreds of *dān* prestations that are made every day in Hindu villages. By neglecting these prestations, South Asianists have overlooked some of the most fundamental aspects of kinship, caste, and ritual.

In a work that has focused very closely on intercaste and kinship relations within a particular North Indian village, I have hesitated to discuss the major themes of the work, in this concluding chapter, in relation to interpretations of textual materials that may seem remote from the dusty lanes and walled courtyards of such a village. That it has been impossible for me to refer to systematic ethnographic interpretations of *dān* and the social life in which it is contextualized indicates the extent to which the giving and receiving of *dān* has been ignored in anthropological studies of South Asian ritual and society. But it is perhaps the case that those textual discourses are alive and relevant to present-day village life; it may not be the texts that are remote, but the alien interpretations of them.

NOTES

CHAPTER ONE

1. Such a situation is apparently more prevalent in the Upper Doab than in other regions of Uttar Pradesh (Schwartzberg 1968, 103).

2. Saharanpur is one of the leading districts in the state of Uttar Pradesh in terms of the gross value of agricultural output per hectare of cropped area, and in terms of the gross value of agricultural output per cultivator. The average size of agricultural holdings per cultivating household is also quite large in relation to the average holding in Uttar Pradesh (Census of India 1971, *Census Atlas of Uttar Pradesh,* 77–80).

3. Spankie is also remembered by villagers as the British official who ordered the burning of many Gujar villages in retaliation for Gujar uprisings in the district at the time of the Mutiny of 1857. (See Atkinson 1875, 254–57, for a contemporary account from the British perspective.) Gujar communities of Saharanpur District are to this day proud of their resistance to British rule, and it figures prominently in locally written and printed accounts of their own history and identity as Ksatriyas (Varma 1971, 99–109).

4. The very possibility of indebtedness arose in large part as a result of the fact that as land became officially an alienable commodity under British rule, it could be used as security for loans (Kessinger 1974; Darling 1947).

5. Defining these tenurial types—*zamīndārī, bhāīācārā,* and *paṭṭīdārī*—has been notoriously difficult, ever since Baden-Powell (1892) first attempted to describe them. They are very commonly discussed in terms of the manner in which shares of an "estate" are divided. Cohn's definitions are of this type:

> The *pattidari* estate was one in which descendents of a common ancestor had divided the lands of their ancestral patrimony following genealogical principles; usually some lands such as orchards, tanks, and some waste land was held in common. . . . In *bhaiyachara* estates, unlike *pattidari* estates, the land was jointly and commonly held undivided; only the produce was divided according to shares based on principles of genealogical descent. . . . *Zamindari* estates [were those] in which one person or family had established, through a long-standing grant, purchase, or tradition, the right to be recognized as the sole proprietor of an estate. He or his agents collected the revenue from individuals who were in legal fact his tenants. (1969, 101–4)

Cohn also suggests that these three tenurial patterns should not be thought of as fixed types but as phases of a developmental cycle in which an estate, say, of twenty villages with one man as sole *zamīndār* would be subdivided at his death and would then become either a *bhāīācārā* or a *paṭṭīdārī* estate. Fox (1971) has made a similar argument based, like Cohn's, on data from eastern Uttar Pradesh.

Stokes, however, has conceived these distinctions in a different fashion. His characterization of these tenurial patterns involves not simply the manner in which the shares are divided, but a much broader sense of the sociological aspects of the tenures:

> The hallmark of the true *bhaiachara* tenure was, indeed, that it was tribal, that practically all cultivators belonged to a single clan or tribe, that all held at equal rates and almost all shared in the proprietary management. A territory occupied by a small conquering lineage could become *bhaiachara* only if it intermingled with or extirpated the existing inhabitants and only if it depended in no way on a tributary "tenant" class. . . . The real test of approximation to true *bhaiachara* was the extent to which the cultivating and the proprietary body coincided. (1978 : 77)

In Stokes's discussion, the sociological dimensions of *paṭṭīdārī* tenures appear to be of the same type as the *bhāīācārā*, but the revenue was collected from *lambardārs*, the representatives of particular lineage groups within the village, rather than from the proprietary body as a whole.

Stokes's definitions, then, grant a great deal of importance to the local kinship system, the caste homogeneity of village landholders, and the identity of the proprietor and cultivator in setting apart the *bhāīācārā* and the *paṭṭīdārī* types from the *zamīndārī* tenurial pattern. He argues against the notion that these types are simply phases of a developmental cycle; rather, he says, they should be seen as fundamentally different social configurations. And where "cultivating brotherhoods" were the rule, land transfers to outsiders, whether of different clans or different castes, could effectively be prevented in many cases.

6. Many Gujar clan names are said to be derived from the name of the village in which the clan originated (see Crooke 1896b, 2 : 443). The genealogist (*bhāṭ*) who serves the Pahansu Khūbaṛs told me that the Khūbaṛ *got* originated in the village of Khubaru, located in the present Sonepat subdivision of Rohtak District, Haryana.

7. Gujars are the only people in the village who patronize the Bhāṭ genealogists. These professional bards and genealogists have hereditary relationships with their Gujar *jajmāns*; they visit Pahansu every few years to update the genealogies, recording the births and marriages of the sons of the village. Throughout northern India, such genealogists are employed primarily by dominant landholding castes who consider themselves Ksatriyas; they are not patronized by Brahmans and Baniyas (Shah and Shroff 1959). These very deep professionally maintained genealogies that connect the dominant *jajmāns* with royal progenitors are extremely important as markers of their identity as Ksatriyas, in Pahansu as elsewhere in northern India (Hitchcock 1959, 16; Shah and Shroff 1959, 57).

8. Atkinson gives this account: "Islamnagar is said to have been founded by Sardar Abdullah Khan. . . . He quelled a Gujar insurrection in the reign of Aurangzeb, and expelling the inhabitants, changed the name from Gujarwala to Islamnagar" (1875, 292).

9. There is a large mound in the Pahansu habitation site, just to the east of the house of Telu Ram and Jabar Singh (see fig. 5), that is said by villagers to mark the site of an old mud fort constructed in defense against the Marathas. A large part of Saharanpur District was in fact depopulated by Maratha incursions in the 1770s (Siddiqi 1973, 9).

10. The term *lambardār*, according to Cohn, "is derived from the English word 'number' and can be translated as one who has a number in the *jamabandi* or revenue role" (1969, 102).

11. The name of the village, Pahansu, is not a pseudonym. My friends and informants in the village insisted that I use its real name, confident that what I wrote of their way of life would never be used in any way against them. I trust that this confidence was not misplaced.

12. Variants of this story of Harishcandra abound in epic and Puranic literature. The version from the *Mahābhārata,* summarized in Dowson 1972, corresponds fairly closely to the story I recorded in Pahansu. This story has, apparently, a very wide currency in western Uttar Pradesh. Temple (1884–1900, 3:53–88) records a version told by a bard from Meerut District that is virtually identical to that told and sung in Pahansu.

13. Jagdev Singh's story is well-known in North India, and again, a very similar version is recorded by Temple (2:198–203). In Temple's version, the incident that Mangal Singh recounted to me occurs, significantly, at the festival of *salonā* or *rakṣā bandhan* ("tying on protection"), at which time, in many parts of northern India, sisters, *kamīn*s, and Brahman *purohit*s tie protective threads around the wrists of their *jajman*s and are given *dān.* (See, for example, Aggarwal 1971, 166.)

14. Jonathan Parry's discussion of *jajmānī* relationships in a Kangra village (1979, 58–83) is an important exception. He explicates the indigenous distinction between *dān* and *gadi-kalothi* "payments," but he does not discuss the significance of *dān* prestations for the ritual construction of dominance. He does not report any instances of *kamīn*s receiving *dān,* though it is certainly the case in Pahansu as elsewhere in North India that *kamīn*s receive very many and very substantial *dān* prestations. Thus Parry makes the assertion that *dān* is a "charitable donation humbly offered to somebody of superior status" (ibid., 65). Though Parry acknowledges that Brahmans and Barbers both receive prestations bearing the same name at certain life-cycle rituals, he states, "I do not think that the word *dān* would be used . . . for the Barber's perquisites here" (ibid., 72).

15. As I will show in chapter 5, the term *dhiyānī* is used only in the context in which the giving of *dān* to these women is at issue. *Dhiyānī* are those to whom one has the "right" (*hak*) to give *dān;* and because a married couple act conjointly as givers of *dān,* a woman regards as *dhiyānī* the natal kinswomen of her husband. For a full description of the range of kinswomen to whom the term may be applied, see Vatuk 1975, 178–81. The masculine form of the word (*dhiyānā*) refers to the husbands of these women in their capacity as receivers of *dān.*

16. Though he has not described *dān* or the transferral of inauspiciousness in such prestations, Good (1982, 26–27) has also pointed out that intercaste and kinship gift-giving may have overlapping meanings in the South Indian village he studied.

17. M. N. Srinivas introduced the concept of the "dominant caste" into anthropological discourse:

> A caste may be said to be "dominant" when it preponderates numerically over the other castes, and when it also wields preponderant economic and political power. A large and powerful caste group can more easily be dominant if its position in the local caste hierarchy is not too low. (1955, 18)

In this definition and in his later discussion of the phenomenon of dominance (1959), Srinivas suggested that moderately high rank contributed to the dominance of a local caste group and also that local dominance could bolster the status of a caste in the local hierarchy (1955, 25). "Ritual dominance" is understood only in terms of hierarchical position, and not in relation to a ritual or donative role specific to the dominant caste.

18. Hocart does not use the word *jajmānī* to describe the network of relationships that he discusses, but it is clear that it is just this sort of system that he is attempting to characterize.

19. It should be pointed out that for Dumont, Pocock, and Parry, hierarchy and the opposition of the pure and the impure structure only some of the relationships and services within the *jajmānī* system. Caste specialities that are not concerned with the removal of impurities are treated by Pocock in terms of a "religiously neutral" division of labor, and by Dumont in terms of differential functions that are still oriented toward the whole, the hierarchic collectivity (and represented in terms of the "encompassing" religious ideology of hierarchy), even if they have more to do with "temporal power" of the dominant caste *jajmān* than with the pure and the impure (Dumont 1970, 106–8). Parry discusses the system in terms of three categories of caste specialities: *purohits* (Brahmans, Barbers, and Funeral Priests) whose services are essential in life-cycle rituals, *kamīns* whose craft specialities may be religiously significant or religiously neutral, and a small group of castes called "those who beg."

20. In his early work, Srinivas (1952) grasped the significance of the concepts of auspiciousness and inauspiciousness in the ritual life of the Coorg village he studied, but he did not explore their implications for the understanding of prestation patterns and the nature of caste and dominance. Following Srinivas, several anthropologists have recently discussed the way in which certain aspects of Hindu ritual are structured in terms of this set of concepts (Marglin 1985a, 1985b; Madan 1985), but like Srinivas, they have not attempted to analyze intercaste relationships in light of these cultural constructs, and they make no mention of the connection between the giving of *dān* and the removal of inauspiciousness.

21. It is curious that while Fuller argues that gifts are thought to transfer sin and evil only in the North, Pfaffenberger (1982) argues that while the "Gangetic culture" of the North is concerned exclusively with purity and impurity, much of the social and ritual life of the "Dravidian South" is organized around ideas of "order" and "disorder," ideas that appear to be very much like the ideas of auspiciousness and inauspiciousness in Pahansu.

22. Das's contention (1977) that an opposition of life and death, particularly with respect to ritual action, is fundamental in Hindu thought might be compared to Fuller's discussion of the significance of death in North India.

CHAPTER TWO

1. *Śubh* is used both as an adjective and as a noun in Pahansu, and *aśubh* is the adjectival form, "inauspicious;" *nāśubh* and *kuśubh* are used as nouns, "inauspiciousness."

2. Buddhi Prakash Pandit, known in Pahansu and surrounding villages as Buddhu Pandit, is a Gaur Brahman, about thirty-two years old in 1978. He serves as hereditary priest (*purohit*) to many of the Gujar families of Pahansu, but he also serves many more, both in Pahansu and in surrounding villages, when ritual or astrological knowledge beyond the reach of other village Brahmans is required. Buddhu says that he learned his ordinary priestly duties from his father, Raghu Pandit; he studied further at the Sanatan Sanskrit Vidyalaya in Saharanpur, and at the Rishikul Brahmacarya Ashram Vidyapith in Haridwar. He studied Sanskrit at the K. K. Jain Degree College in Saharanpur, and he has had some training in Ayurvedic medicine as well.

3. Of the three humors, "wind" is most frequently cited by villagers as the

cause of illness. The notion that illness may be brought about by an inappropriate matching of bodily constituents and the seasons is a central part of the Ayurvedic conception of the relationship between person and temporal cyclings. See Zimmermann (1980) for an account of such relationships.

While the Sanskritic tradition generally recognizes six seasons, Pahansu informants divided the year into three: *karsā* is the hot season, and comprises the months of Phālgun, Cait, Baisākh, and Jeṭh. The rainy season (*camāsā*) includes the months of Asāṛh, Sāvan, Bhādwe, and Asauj, and the cold season (*jaḍa*) includes the months of Kārttik, Mangsar, Pau, and Māgh.

4. Some of the cultural routines for such diagnoses will be discussed in this chapter; the social contexts in which actual decisions are made will only be touched on here, but variation in diagnoses is evident in indigenous therapeutic practices. For example, in Pahansu, diagnoses concerning astrological influences and other inauspiciousness tended to predominate, perhaps because there was a resident astrological specialist in the village, but no Ayurvedic practitioner. Nichter (1979, 191) also notes that diagnoses in rural South Kanara District tended to be influenced by the types of indigenous practitioners of a specific locality. I do think, however, that the structural position of the Gujar caste in the village and the region is a factor that must be taken into account in this matter. Given the very pronounced emphasis on Gujar "centrality" in Pahansu, that is, their position as *jajmān*s and givers of *dān*, there seems to be a strong propensity for them to accept and act upon diagnoses of inauspiciousness that require the giving of *dān*.

5. These manuals are *Jyotiṣa Sarva Sangrah* by Pandit Ramsvarup Sharma of Meerut District, published by Bhagavat Book Depot in Bulandshahar, and *Lagnacandrika*, published by Govardhana Pustakalaya in Mathura.

6. For an account of South Indian conceptions of the compatibilities and incompatibilities between persons and villages, see Daniel 1984, 81–95.

7. Other uses of astrological determinations based on the "name" (*nām*) are discussed in a later section of this chapter.

8. Lunar asterisms (*nakṣatra*s) figure in two kinds of temporal cycles. *Nakṣatra* months last twelve to thirteen days, and *nakṣatra*s also play a part in the monthly cycle of lunar days. In the latter context, they are called "day *nakṣatra*s" (*din nakṣatra*). See Pugh 1983 for further details on this point.

9. These statements tell us little, however, about the indigenously defined "closeness" of these relationships. See Raheja 1985, chap. 6, for a discussion of this point.

CHAPTER THREE

1. These are the terms used in Pahansu to designate such prestations. While these particular terms seem to occur only in western Uttar Pradesh Hindi dialects, I have found, in a survey of available ethnography, that there are many indications that similar categories exist in practically every region of India, though they have never been systematically described.

2. These two functions of *caṛhāpā* were isolated from Pahansu informants' statements and the analyses of the ritual sequences themselves, but the dictionary definition (*Sankṣipt Hindī Śabd Sāgar*) of *caṛhāvā* (*caṛhāpā*) precisely describes them as well. The definition is as follows:

(1) Those items that are offered to some deity, *pujāpā;*
(2) the items of a magical device (*ṭoṭkā*) that are placed at the crossroads or at a village boundary (*kinārā*) in order to take an illness from one place to another.

The second part of this definition perhaps characterizes the transferral function a bit too narrowly, but the fundamental idea of transferral is the same as that described by people in Pahansu as occurring in the giving of any *dān* or *caṛhāpā*.

3. The term *dān* is occasionally used in a more general sense to include charity, alms, and the like, prestations that are not made in a ritual context and do not transfer inauspiciousness. When villagers say that all *dān* is given to remove inauspiciousness, the contextually delimited meaning of the term is at issue. The distinction is, however, sometimes marked lexically. The former category of *dān* prestations, for example, could never be referred to as *caṛhāpā* or *pujāpā*. Furthermore, in many of the Hindi and Panjabi folktales and dramas collected by Temple (1884–1900) in the general area of my fieldwork, a differentiation of *dān* (also *dān-jahej*) from "alms" (*bhīk* or *bhicchā*) emerges. *Bhīk* and *bhicchā* are used to refer to alms, given in nonritual contexts, to *yogi*s and wandering ascetics, while *dān* and *dān-jahej* are prestations made at the birth of a son and at other ritual occasions to one's daughter's son (*dohtā*), and to Brahmans, Doms, and so forth, in order to assure well-being and auspiciousness. (See particularly "The Legend of Raja Gopichand," "Puran Bhagat," and "The Legend of Niwal Dai" in Temple's collection.)

4. Khare's comment (1976, 103) that *prasād* is a new cultural code that became important with the spread of *bhakti* devotionalism and is therefore not comparable to the sacrificial leftovers of the earlier orthodox ritual systems raises the intriguing question of whether there is in fact an analogue in contemporary Hinduism of these sacrificial remains. This study cannot encompass the textual, philological, and historical studies that would be necessary in order to definitively answer such a question; I would suggest, however, that the prestations called *caṛhāpā* do in fact carry many of the same meanings as those older sacrificial distributions.

5. Items given as *caṛhāpā* are very frequently given in one and one-quarter measures (*sawāī*), and such measures are never involved in other types of prestations. Villagers sometimes referred to a *sawāī* as *kaṛhāī*, a noun formed from the verb *kāṛhnā*, "to take out." A *sawāī* measure, then, is the appropriate vehicle for "taking out" the inauspiciousness.

6. I have translated this *kathā* from the popular text *Saptavār Vrat Kathā* (*Vrat* Stories of the Seven Days) published in Delhi by Anand Prakashan. The Sanskrit versions of this myth of the dispelling of Indra's *pāp* appear in the *Mahābhārata*, in books 5 and 12. (See O'Flaherty 1976 and van Buitenen 1978.)

7. The role of the *purohit* in the acceptance of such prestations in Pahansu is discussed at length in chapters 4 and 5.

8. The word *saubhāgya*, of which *suhāg* is the dialectal variation, means "good fortune."

9. In a myth recounted by Stanley (1978), Hanuman wrestles with Śani and injures him, spattering Śani's blood upon himself, and thus, it is said, Hanuman's image is often red, or reddened with *sindūr*, as is the case with the Hanuman image in the Śakumbhari temple in the Siwaliks. As Stanley goes on to say: "The spattering of Śani's blood seems to be offered as a partial explanation of the dissemination of his *pīḍā* throughout the cosmos." Thus the "blood" on Hanuman's image, the thickly smeared *sindūr* into which, at Śakumbhari, pilgrims often press coins, may be an iconic representation of the *pīḍā*, the inauspiciousness of Śani, that Hanuman takes upon himself.

10. That a turning away from ritual centrality and the giving of *caṛhāpā* is indeed a significant defining feature of *bhakti* cults is suggested in the behavior of

two or three Gujar families in Pahansu who are followers of the Radhaswami devotional cult. These people perform many of the calendrical and domestic rituals of their Gujar neighbors, but in a form that is incomprehensible to the latter: they give no *dān* or *caṛhāpā* at all, and they eliminate this giving explicitly because they have "gone to Byas," that is, they have been initiated into the Radhaswami cult centered in that town.

11. The *Sankṣipt Hindī Śabd Sāgar* dictionary indicates that *wārnā* is the same as the more common Hindi verb *utārnā,* which means "to take or bring down, to remove an attached or clinging object."

12. The pouring out of water as a ritual sign of the donative act is a very ancient practice and is described in the Sanskritic textual traditions (Gonda 1965, 220).

13. There is a great difference between the use of "hot" substances, including foods, to effect a disarticulation of inauspiciousness, and the use of "hot" foods to counterbalance a "cold" disposition or illness in the body. In the latter case, the foods are consumed in order to bring about a balance of hot and cold, or a balance of the three *doṣa* (that is, the three humors) within the body; here, the catalytic agency of heat is not particularly relevant. In the former case, however, it is precisely this catalysis that is at issue, and the "hot" substances would never be consumed by the *jajmān* or subject of the ritual.

14. The word *pacnā* may be used in the context of the acceptance of any *caṛhāpā*. The *caṛhāpā* need not be a food item; gifts of cloth, brass vessels, a bed, and so forth, all must be "digested" by the recipient. It is sometimes, however, regarded as particularly dangerous for the recipient to actually consume anything given in *dān*.

15. Recipients of *dān* may attempt to avoid these negative consequences by giving the *dān* onward (*āge denā*) to yet another recipient. Keeping the inauspiciousness in circulation in this way is a particularly prominent theme in the marriage rituals to be discussed in chapter 4.

16. These are necessary but not sufficient conditions for the appropriateness of a *pātra*. Other conditions for the successful rearticulation of inauspiciousness transferred via *caṛhāpā* will be discussed in chapter 4.

17. According to Brahmans in Pahansu, this is why their early morning hours are spent in the recitation of *mantra*s; they must replenish their store of *śakti* and *tej* before beginning their almost daily acceptance of *dān*. The differences between the early morning activities of Brahmans and Gujars (givers of *dān* par excellence) in Pahansu are striking. Gujars, particularly the women, are frequently engaged in wrapping parcels of cloth that are to be given, preparing the foodstuffs that may later be given as *caṛhāpā,* or haggling with an itinerant cloth merchant over the price of cloth that will be purchased for giving in *dān*. The bustle of the Gujar household is in marked contrast to the relative quiet of Brahman houses where often the most conspicuous noise is the quiet murmur of a Brahman as he chants his *mantra*s. (In all except one of the Pahansu Brahman families, at least one or two of the men serve as *purohit*s to Gujars and others in the village.)

CHAPTER FOUR

1. Brahmans will accept such prestations from all castes in the village except Sweepers and Leatherworkers. Sweepers consistently give these to their *dhiyānī* and *dhiyāne* (the husbands of *dhiyānī*), as do Brahmans. Pahansu Leatherworkers, about whom my data is very incomplete, appear to give some presta-

tions of this sort to their *dhiyānī* while others are given to their own "Barbers" and "Brahmans," many of whom live, apparently, in the town of Saharanpur.

2. Unlike the other ritual roles assigned to *dhiyānī,* that is, the acceptance of *pujāpā* and *caṛhāpā, cūcī dhulāī* may not be performed by all women of the *dhiyānī* category. Women of generations senior to the mother may not perform this service; only those *dhiyānī* who are of the same or a junior generation may carry it out.

3. If *chaṭṭhī* is not performed on the sixth day, it may be done after forty days (*sawa mahīnā*), after six months, or even after six years, though this would be very unusual. *Chaṭṭhī* therefore has no connection with "birth impurity" (*sūtak*), which greatly diminishes on the tenth day and ends completely on the fortieth day after birth. (This forty-day period is termed *jāpā.*)

4. This is the blessing always said in the village by senior women as junior women massage their legs: *sāī jite raho bhāī jite raho tere beṭe ho būṛhī suhāgan raho.*

5. The giving of a complete set of cloth is necessary on a number of ritual occasions involving the transfer of inauspiciousness.

6. The nonspecialist, the average villager, is familiar with the dangers of a birth in the *mūl nakṣatra.* The astrologer, however, recognizes six asterisms that engender the same difficulties: *mūl, jyeṣṭha, śeṣa, revati, māgha,* and *aśvini.*

7. Each *nakṣatra* is divided into time periods of sixty *ghaṛī,* and four *caraṇ.* The *kaṣṭ* and *doṣ* will beset the father, mother, brother, the *kunbā,* the mother's father, the mother's mother, or the mother's brother depending upon the *ghaṛī* and *caraṇ* in which the birth occurs. The time periods during which any of these persons may be afflicted are different for each of the six asterisms.

8. After her marriage, according to people in Pahansu, a *dhiyānī* shares a *riśtā* ("relationship") but not a "bodily connection" and is thus not affected by the *mūl doṣ.*

9. In his discussion of the general class of *śānti* rites as they are described in Sanskrit textual traditions, Kane (1974, vol. 5, pt. 2: 719–814) suggests that the word *śānti* means, in such contexts, "the removal of evil effects." Thus *mūl śānti* is "the removal of the evil effects of the *mūl* asterism."

10. The ritual is begun very early so that the *dān* may be given at the appropriate time. Each planet's and asterism's *dān* must be given at a specified time if the transfer of inauspiciousness is to be effected.

11. It is interesting to note that Śeṣnāg ("the remainder snake") is iconographically represented as holding a plow in one hand and a pestle in the other. Further, Śeṣnāg himself was used as the churning rope when the gods churned the Milky Ocean to produce clarified butter, Soma, prosperity, on the one hand, and poison (*viṣ*) on the other, poison that was removed from the world by Śiva, who held it in his throat. This separation of what we might think of as auspicious and inauspicious substances is what the plow and the pestle effect in the *mūl śānti* ritual. (On the iconography of Śeṣnāg, see Dowson 1972; for a translation of this myth from the *Mahābhārata,* see O'Flaherty 1976, 273–80.)

12. A "bath of disjoining" may sometimes be performed to remove the "faults" (*doṣ*) and "pain" (*pīṛā*) engendered by the nine planets, though this is not a treatment that I ever observed in Pahansu. Buddhu Pandit showed me a page of his almanac that listed the various substances that should be used for bathing (*snān*) the afflicted person. The almanac states, in Sanskrit (most of the almanac is in Hindi) that such baths, when followed by the giving of the appropriate *dān,* "remove the faults deposited by the planets" (*nidhānen graha doṣam praṇaśati*).

13. A square is drawn on the earthen floor of the room with flour and turmeric and variously colored powders, and the emblem of each of the planets is drawn within it. Sometimes these figures are barely discernible, being little more than spots of flour and turmeric on the ground. Buddhu Pandit, however, was known for his detailed renderings of the planetary emblems.

14. Buddhu Pandit told me that he would not accept such planetary *dān,* nor would he allow his sons to do so. He told me a story. Once a Brahman in a nearby village accepted the *dān* of Śani, the planet Saturn, and then gave the things to a Camar, hoping to rid himself of the "faults." The Camar became "mad" (*pāgal*) and remained so for eight years, because of this *dān.*

15. The *Atharva Veda* (Bloomfield 1897, 110) also describes the inauspicious ("fierce") qualities that arise when two upper teeth appear before the lower. Offerings are prescribed in that text to protect the parents of the child by making these qualities "pass away" elsewhere.

16. That this deemphasis of hypergamous ordering among Gujar clans was also evident in the nineteenth century is indicated by observations made by Atkinson (1875, 184) and Elliot (1869, 1: 100) that Gujar clans in Saharanpur District are considered equal and intermarry with one another. Of the nineteenth-century British administrators writing on Gujar social organization, only Crooke has stated that Gujar *gots* in the Upper Doab are formally ranked with respect to marital alliances: "It . . . appears that hypergamy occurs among some of the sections; thus in Saharanpur the Kalsiyān, Khaprāe, Rāthi and Rause hold the highest rank and intermarry, while the Kalsiyān will not give their daughters to the Chhokar, Diveru and Dāpu sections" (1896b, 444). Crooke's information on this point was apparently obtained from the headmaster of the high school in Saharanpur (ibid., 439) and does not appear to be reliable. Indeed, a number of these clans are considered to be in some ways "one *got*" and "of one blood." I was told in Pahansu, for example, that the Dhivre, Dāppe, and Kalśān Gujars do not intermarry; a *riśtā* (affinal relationship) among them is impossible because they are already "one blood," and not because of a hypergamous ordering of clans.

17. The number of days preceding a wedding depends upon the astrological calculations made to determine the number of times *bān* should be done (see table 6).

18. *Bān lagānā* is repeated every day until the wedding, except on Tuesdays and Saturdays (*mangalvār* and *śanivār*), lest the inauspiciousness of those days be applied to the body.

19. These items are frequently used in other rituals and prestations to remove inauspiciousness.

20. The placing of the *teḷṇ* on the head is emphasized in songs (*gīt*) sung by women of the *kunbā* as the *bhāt* is given; and the *teln* is also referred to as "the *teḷṇ* given from the wooden stool" (*cōk par kī teḷṇ*).

21. The translation of these verses is from O'Flaherty 1981, 270. I am indebted to Wendy O'Flaherty for pointing out these Ṛg Vedic parallels to my own data from Pahansu.

22. The connection between the "tying" (*bāndhnā*) of the *kānjol* that unites the bride and groom, and this inauspiciousness is replicated in the Ṛg Vedic Sūryā verses. The bride's own kin prosper, and "her husband is bound in the bonds." The word used here for "bonds" (*bandhan*) has, according to O'Flaherty, a double meaning: it refers at once to the bonds of marriage and to the lines drawn on the marriage gown by the blood of defloration that brings disease and danger to the husband. Further, the fact that the *kānjol* is given onward to the groom's *purohit* is paralleled in the giving of the marriage gown to the priest in the marriage of Sūryā.

23. The preparation of the *bhalle* is itself an iconic representation of the "absorption" (*sokhnā*) of negative qualities. These morsels are fried in oil and then, in nonritual contexts as well, placed in a container and covered with water. The *bhalle* absorb the water and puff up, and when the water is later squeezed out, they are very light. The *bhalle* actually absorb the water, just as in this ritual context, they are made to absorb the *nāśubh* qualities that have been transferred into the water in which they have been soaking.

24. Translated literally, the word *paṭṭā* refers to a document that confers the right to use some particular wealth or property. In Sanskrit, the word referred to a copper plate for inscribing royal grants, generally to Brahmans.

25. The importance of these offerings to the well-being of the bride can be seen in the account of the troubles of Sudesh given in chapter 2.

26. This is the main distinction to be made between Gujar prestations to *dhiyānī,* and Brahman gifts to their *dhiyāne,* but a further difference is that the *caṛhāpā* given by Gujars to their *dhiyānī* carries less inauspiciousness than the very dangerous death prestations and other such *dān* given by Brahmans to their *dhiyāne.*

27. In his chapter on *dān* in the texts of the *dharmaśāstra*s, Kane (1974, 851) reports that according to the *Brahma Purāṇa,* if a person accepts the bed and the clothes of one who is dead he will go to hell.

28. This action is called *mūṭh mārnā.* The dictionary definition of the phrase is "having recited a *mantra,* to throw something in the direction of one's enemy; to perform sorcery (*ṭonā*)."

29. *Dhān boāī* is said by Gujars to be concerned with the increase of the rice in their fields; that it perhaps has a wider meaning is indicated by the fact that both Barbers and Brahmans, who do not cultivate the soil, nevertheless perform a *dhān boāī* in the course of their marriage rituals. But Sweepers do not do the *dhān boāī,* because, they said, "it is a matter of farming," *khetī kī bāt,* so they have no reason to do it.

30. I describe here the sequence for the death of a man who has lived a long life and produced sons, because in such instances all of the major death prestations are made. In particular, there is, as we shall see, one prestation that is made to a widow following the death of her husband that would not be given after a woman's death. Otherwise, the same prestations are made for a woman's death, both from her *pīhar* and from the people of her husband's *kunbā,* as in the event of her husband's death.

Much of this description is based on my observations of the *terāhmī* of Dattaram, a very old Gujar man with five sons and many grandchildren; the *terāhmī* of Amarnath, a middle-aged Brahman man; and the *terāhmī* of Lado, an old Gujar woman, the mother of two sons.

31. Occasionally, if the family's *purohit* is not well-versed in these matters, another more knowledgeable Brahman may conduct the *terāhmī* ritual. In such cases, the latter will receive only a few rupees as *dakṣiṇā,* and all of the *dān* items must still be given to the family *purohit.* I once asked a Brahman who occasionally conducted these rituals as a substitute if it wasn't unfair that he should do all the work and then not receive the five new brass vessels, the sets of cloth, and so forth, that make up the *dān.* He replied that he wouldn't want to accept such an inauspicious *dān* in the first place, unless as *purohit* he simply had to accept it; and second, it was the "fitting obligation" (*pharmāyā*) only of the "*purohit* of the house" (*ghar kā purohit*) to accept this *pujāpā.* It is clear from all of this that the *dān* is not a payment for services rendered at the death ceremonies.

32. Myths of the origin of the Mahabrahman caste are similar to those of the

Dakaut *jāti*. In both cases, the myths are concerned with the acceptance of inauspicious *dān*. (See, for example, Crooke 1896b, 3:402).

33. Das sees a similarity between birth and death only in the fact that both engender "impurity," which she sees as a metaphor for liminality.

34. In a South Indian poem about Kṛṣṇa and the mountain translated by Ramanujan (1981, 13) the rains are said to be "heaven's evils," the evil of the gods visited upon men.

35. Compare the *pancak* ritual of transferral. These regions of the body seem to be appropriate points of entrance and exit of inauspicious substances.

36. This is a very complicated point. See Raheja 1985, 403–22, for a discussion of the manner in which relationships "from the direction of the natal village" are stressed and acted upon in the context of double relationships in which another tie "from the direction of the conjugal village" can also be traced.

CHAPTER FIVE

1. Vatuk and Vatuk (1976) report the occurrence of the term *ḍangvārā* in Meerut District, Uttar Pradesh, where it is said to be an alternative to *bhāīācārā* ("brotherhood"), denoting balanced exchanges among neighbors in a village, or among agnatically related households. They write that it is "a somewhat derogatory extension of meaning from the common transaction in which two farmers, each owning one draft animal, combine forces and complete the work of each other with the resulting team: $A \rightleftarrows B$."

2. As Vatuk points out (1975, 176), the use of the terms *laṛkī* and *beṭī* is not restricted by the relative generation of the two persons in the relationship; for example, "girl" and "daughter" may in some contexts be used with reference to one's father's sister, in which case the two terms stand in contrastive relationship with the term *bahu* ("wife"), which means, in its most usual usage, the wife of a junior male of the *kunbā* or of the village.

3. I was first alerted to this contrast between the terms *dhiyānī* on the one hand, and *laṛkī, beṭī,* and *bahan* on the other, in the course of a conversation with my "brother" Telu Ram and his wife, Rajavati. They had been describing some *caṛhāpā* prestations to me, and said that they are given to one's *dhiyānī*. As I was recording this in my notebook, I said something like *acchā, to apnī laṛkī ko dete haĩ* ("I see, you give it to your *laṛkī*"). At my remark, they both looked quite astonished and said no, of course not, they don't give it to "one's own girl." As I was later able to see, what astonished them was the sudden juxtaposition of *caṛhāpā* and "one's own girl" (*apnī laṛkī*). We hadn't had a referential misunderstanding here, but a pragmatic one. Understanding the referential equivalence of the two terms, I had assumed that they were pragmatically equivalent as well, when in fact they are indices of what are quite distinct aspects of the relationship with the women who are involved.

4. I am grateful to Veena Das for pointing out to me this difference in linguistic appropriateness, between *neg kā riśtā* and *pujāpe kā riśtā*.

5. Purificatory functions—the smearing of cow-dung after a birth or death has occurred, the sprinkling of water, and so forth—are also characterized as *āpās kā kām;* that is, when the *jāti* whose function it is to perform these tasks for Gujars and other castes themselves require such services, members of their own *kunbā*, not *dhiyānī* or *dhiyāne*, do the work.

6. Vatuk (1975, 168) too discusses this aspect of the etiquette of *neg;* in Meerut District, she writes, recipients of *neg* often argue vociferously over the *neg* that is to be given for ritual services.

7. The *Bṛhat Hindī Koṣ* dictionary defines *pratīk* in these terms: *ãg* ("part of the body"); *ãś* ("part, share"); *avayav* ("limb, component"); *bhāg* ("share, portion").

8. The actual situation is more complex than this. For further discussion, see Raheja 1985, 418–19.

9. This discussion is based on my recordings of women's comments to one another as they examined the sets of cloth being exhibited in village courtyards and, to a lesser extent, on their remarks to me as they told me to whom all the different sets of cloth would be given. The limitation on the use of the term *aglī* is quite conscious and explicit. They told me that they only use the term *aglī* with reference to the *cālā, kevkā, cūcak,* and *bhāt* prestations, and these are in fact the only contexts in which I heard the term.

10. See Daniel 1984 for a discussion of the pervasiveness of metonym and synecdoche in South Indian social life.

11. In his discussion of the Benares Mahabrahmans' acceptance of *dān,* Parry mentions that there is a general "reluctance to sustain any long-term relationship with him" (1980, 94, 96). In the Benares case, we find an empirical separation from those to whom one gives *dān,* while in Pahansu we find that there are contextually differentiated ways of construing relationships, so that as one gives *dān,* the recipient is "other," but in other contexts, he may be "one's own."

12. See Silverstein 1976 for a discussion of the pervasiveness of indexicality in language and culture, and for an account of why an adequate theory of meaning must take indexical meaning as well as semantico-referential meaning into account.

13. It should be noted that *mol lānā* marriages are contracted fairly infrequently in the Gujar community. While the offspring from such marriages suffer no definite stigma, a *mol lānā* marriage adversely affects the prestige (*izzat*) of a family and it may be a matter of gossip for many years. Long before my stay in the village, the wife and children of a prosperous Gujar landholder died. Because of the man's age, it was difficult for him to secure another wife; he was forced to resort to a *mol lānā* arrangement with a very poor Gujar family from the village of Barthol. Although I knew the Pahansu family very well, I never heard a word about this *mol lānā* marriage from the wife or anyone in her household, and I heard only scattered whispers about it from other women in the village, from which I pieced together this account. I heard many different stories as to how much money had been given to the woman's parents in the exchange, but it was by all accounts a very large sum. It was definitely a *mol lānā* marriage, given without *dān-dahej,* but because of the position in the village of the husband's family, this fact has been systematically hidden and ignored. The wife's brothers still bring a few sets of cloth to her as *dān* at the appropriate times, but even the woman herself seems to regard this as a more or less meaningless gesture. Once I entered her courtyard just after the *bhāīyyā dauj* festival and saw her looking over a few sets of cloth that were obviously of very poor quality. I asked her who had given them, and with a disdainful flick of her wrist she answered *baṛthol kī dab* ("from the direction of Barthol"). Her brother had brought them from her natal village.

14. This indigenously defined "mutuality" among *jāti*s within a village has generally been ignored in the ethnographic literature. Dumont and Pocock (1957), for example, have argued that "the village as an architectural and demographic fact is secondary to the social facts of kinship" and is not a significant social category in rural India. The referent for the indigenous terms for "village," they say, is not the entire village composed of many caste groups, but the local

caste group of the speaker (see also Pocock 1972). Because of their emphasis on a noncontextualized principle of hierarchy as the only relevant ideology in intercaste relations, these two authors, and others following them, have chosen to ignore the phenomenon of "kinship" relations (*nātā*) among castes of the same village, conceived of as "connections of the village site" (*gām bastī ke nāte*). In such relationships, usually reckoned according to relative age, persons of different castes address each other through the use of kin terms. The Brahman Buddhu Pandit, for example, calls the Barber Illam Nai's mother *tāyī*, "father's elder brother's wife"; and when, as I have already pointed out, men visit villages in which women of their own village have been married, they give *milāī* to those women as their "sisters," despite the fact that the two may be of different castes. In this situation, the hierarchic aspect of intercaste relationships is not the foregrounded aspect of the social situation. That hierarchy may often be deemphasized in intercaste relationships is also indicated by the relationships among women in the village. Junior in-married women, upon meeting a senior in-married woman or a senior married "husband's sister" of the village, always perform a brief ritualized leg massage (*pāõ dabānā*) for her. What is significant here is that *pāõ dabānā* is done, in some contexts, by a woman of higher caste for a woman of a lower caste (e.g., a Gujar or Brahman woman may do *pāõ dabānā* for a senior Carpenter woman). This is fairly infrequent; usually when a woman of a lower caste comes to a Gujar household, for example, she comes to receive *caṛhāpā* or for some other reason that underscores either her position in the "centrality" ordering of castes or in the hierarchical ordering, and the *pāõ dabānā* would be contextually inappropriate then. But I have seen leg massaging for hierarchically lower women done in relatively "neutral" contexts, such as when women of several different castes meet at a courtyard where they have all come to examine sets of cloth that are being sent in a wedding *dahej*.

15. Several Gujar women remarked to me that Brahmans will not normally accept *kaccā* food from Gujar kitchens because, in their words, Brahmans *ū̃c-nīc samajhe,* they "understand things [as] high and low"; they construe relationships according to high and low, so to speak, in ways that Gujars often do not.

One of the few times I ever heard a Gujar talk animatedly about the distinctions of types of media was in an interview in which Mangal Singh expounded on the difference between *pakkā* and *kaccā* foods in a way that was quite different from their hierarchical implications. Mangal Singh said that when a new *bahū* comes to the house, after her *cālā,* and she is invited for a meal at the homes of the people of her husband's *kunbā,* it is necessary that she be given rice, *dāl* (lentil sauce), *būrā* (semirefined sugar) in a mound, to be sprinkled on the rice, and *ghī* (clarified butter) to be poured on the rice. These are, Mangal Singh pointed out, *kaccā* foods. The same menu is standard at the meal given for one's *kundebar*s, one's *kamīn*s, and one's Brahman at the *manḍhā,* one of the preliminary marriage rites. Then he went on to say that at Baniya and Brahman feasts, *pakkā* foods are generally served, foods that, according to Mangal Singh, include many items not grown in one's own village. Mangal Singh made the contrast quite explicit:

> *baniyā aur bahman pakkā khānā acchā mānte haĩ aur ham gūjar log kaccā khānā acchā mānte haĩ; kaccā khānā hamāre yahā̃ paidā hotā hai.*
>
> Baniyas and Brahmans regard *pakkā* foods as good and we Gujar people regard *kaccā* foods as good; *kaccā* foods are produced here in our village [lit., "at our place"].

Mangal Singh and many other Gujars often spoke of the different qualities of the foods grown in different locales, dependent on the quality of the soil, whether it is "sweet" (*mīṭhī*) or "bitter" (*kaṛvī*); and they often said to me that the people in these different locales were different because of the effects of the foods grown in the different kinds of soils. I also heard many stories, both mythological and about their own *riśtedār*s, about the consequences of eating food or even drinking the water in places other than one's own origin place. Many of the differences among men, Gujars would tell me, are due to the effects of varying water and soil, *pānī aur miṭṭī kī bāt,* they would say; in some places, where the soil is "sweet," the hearts of men are gentle (*naram*), but where the soil is "bitter," particularly along the banks of rivers, and most particularly along the banks of the Hindan River that flows to the east of Pahansu, the men are quarrelsome (*laṛakū*) and full of anger (*gussā*). The saying that I heard from Gujars in discussions of these matters was *jaise khāye ann, taise ho jāy man,* "The mind becomes like the grain that is eaten."

The point, then, is that Gujars seemed to me to be more attentive to the appropriateness of the match between the person and the foods that are eaten, in terms of their origin in particular kinds of soil, while Brahmans were more concerned with the hierarchical implications of accepting foods from particular cooks.

16. When *kamīn* castes such as the Washerman speak of Gujars as the givers of *phaslānā,* they very often refer to them as *kāśtkār*s, "cultivators"; but when they speak of them as givers of *dān,* they always refer to them as *jajmān*s, "sacrificers."

CHAPTER SIX

1. Alternative views of the king and the dominant caste, more in accord with the findings of this work, have recently been set forth by Dirks (1976, 1982, 1987), Inden (1978, 1982), Marglin (1985a), Pfaffenberger (1982), and Shulman (1985). Of these, both Dirks and Shulman attempt to relate royal prestations to indigenous conceptions of sovereignty.

2. In 1925 Mauss made the pronouncement that "the law of *dāna,*" *dānadharma,* disappeared in India sometime around the third century A.D. (Mauss 1967, 54).

3. Trautmann's view on this point recalls Dumont's contention that the idea of "danger" at the time of a death or a birth is absent in Hindu society, having been done away with by the opposition between the pure and the impure: "Elsewhere, the dangerous contact [at a death] acts directly on the person involved, affecting his health for example, whereas with the Hindu it is a matter of impurity, that is, of fall in social status or risk of such a fall. This is quite different, although traces of the other conception can be found in India" (Dumont 1970, 49). Thus it is the case that Trautmann and Dumont, as well as Heesterman, fail to perceive the central importance of the ideas of "evil," "danger," or inauspiciousness in the constitution of Hindu social life, and the fact that these ideas are in fact quite distinct from the ideas of purity and impurity.

4. I have already pointed out, in chapter 1, the problematic nature of Heesterman's conflation of evil and "impurity." Though Trautmann, and Heesterman as well, interpret the reluctance of the Brahman to accept these prestations as stemming from the hierarchic inferiority of the donor, here it is implied that other castes too may be the recipients of *dakṣiṇā.* In an earlier paper, Heesterman had mentioned that the *Maitrāyani Saṃhita* and the *Kāṭhaka Saṃhita* refer to the giving of *dakṣiṇā* to recipients other than Brahmans, but he says only that this is "interesting" (Heesterman 1959, 241).

5. Dumont and Pocock, in a review of Hocart's work on caste, criticize the latter for placing the king or the Ksatriya at the center of the ritual organization, and for neglecting to define the relation of the Brahman and the king in terms of a distinction between religion and power, hierarchical status and the material dependence of the Brahman and the Ksatriya (Dumont and Pocock 1958).

REFERENCES

Abbott, John. [1932] 1974. *The keys of power.* New York: Dutton.

Aggarwal, Pratap C. 1971. *Caste, religion, and power.* New Delhi: Shri Ram Centre for Industrial Relations.

Aiyanagar, K. V. Rangaswami. 1941. *Introduction to Bhaṭṭa Lakṣmīdhara's* Kṛtyakalpataru: 5. Dānakāṇḍa. Gaekwad's Oriental Series, vol. 92. Baroda: Oriental Institute.

Appadurai, Arjun, and Carol Breckenridge. 1976. The South Indian temple: Authority, honor, and redistribution. *Contributions to Indian Sociology,* n.s. 10 : 187–209.

Atkinson, Edwin T. 1875. *Statistical, descriptive, and historical account of the Saharanpur District.* Allahabad: North-Western Provinces Government Press.

Babb, L. A. 1975. *The divine hierarchy: Popular Hinduism in Central India.* New York: Columbia University Press.

Baden-Powell, B. H. 1892. *The land systems of British India.* 3 vols. Oxford: Clarendon.

Beck, Brenda E. F. 1972. *Peasant society in Konku: A study of right and left subcastes in South India.* Vancouver: University of British Columbia Press.

Beidelman, Thomas O. 1959. *A comparative analysis of the jajmani system.* Monographs of the Association for Asian Studies, no. 8. New York: J. J. Augustin.

Bloomfield, M., ed. 1897. *The* Atharva-Veda *and the* Gopatha Brāhmaṇa. Strassburg: Karl J. Trubner.

Blunt, E. A. H. 1931. *The caste system of Northern India, with special reference to the United Provinces of Agra and Oudh.* London: Oxford University Press.

Briggs, George W. 1920. *The Chamars.* Calcutta: Association Press.

Carter, Anthony. 1975. Caste "boundaries" and the principle of kinship amity: A Maratha caste purana. *Contributions to Indian Sociology,* n.s. 9 : 123–37.

Census of India 1891. 1895. *District census statistics, North-Western*

Provinces and Oudh: Saharanpur District. Allahabad: North-Western Provinces and Oudh Government Press.

Census of India 1931. 1933. Volume 18, part 1. *United Provinces of Agra and Oudh.* Allahabad: The Superintendent, Printing and Stationery, United Provinces.

Census of India 1971. 1978. *Census Atlas of Uttar Pradesh.*

Cohn, Bernard S. 1969. Structural change in Indian rural society. In *Land control and social structure in Indian history,* ed. Robert Eric Frykenberg, 53–121. Madison: University of Wisconsin Press.

Commander, Simon. 1983. The *jajmani* system in North India: An examination of its logic and status across two centuries. *Modern Asian Studies* 17 : 283–311.

Crooke, William. 1896a. *The popular religion and folklore of Northern India.* 2 vols. Westminster: Archibald Constable.

———. 1896b. *The tribes and castes of the North-Western Provinces and Oudh.* 4 vols. Calcutta: Superintendent of Government Printing.

Daniel, E. V. 1984. *Fluid signs: Being a person the Tamil way.* Berkeley: University of California Press.

Darling, Malcolm. 1947. *The Punjab peasant in prosperity and debt.* 4th ed. Oxford: Oxford University Press.

Das, Veena. 1977. *Structure and cognition: Aspects of Hindu caste and ritual.* New Delhi: Oxford University Press.

Das, Veena, and Jit Singh Uberoi. 1971. The elementary structure of caste. *Contributions to Indian Sociology,* n.s. 5 : 33–43.

David, Kenneth. 1977. Hierarchy and equivalence in Jaffna, North Sri Lanka: Normative codes as mediators. In *The new wind: Changing identities in South Asia,* ed. K. David, 179–226. The Hague: Mouton.

Dirks, Nicholas B. 1976. Political authority and structural change in early South Indian history. *Indian Economic and Social History Review* 13 : 125–57.

———. 1982. The pasts of a *pāḷaiyakārar:* The ethnohistory of a South Indian little king. *Journal of Asian Studies* 41 : 655–83.

———. 1987. *The hollow crown: Ethnohistory of an Indian kingdom.* Cambridge: Cambridge University Press.

Dowson, John. 1972. *A classical dictionary of Hindu mythology and religion, geography, history, and literature.* 12th ed. London: Routledge and Kegan Paul.

Dubois, Abbé J. A. 1906. *Hindu manners, customs, and ceremonies.* 3d ed. Trans. Henry K. Beauchamp. Oxford: Clarendon Press.

Dumont, Louis. 1962. The conception of kingship in ancient India. *Contributions to Indian Sociology* 6 : 48–77.

———. 1964. Marriage in India: The present state of the question. Part 2:

Marriage and status, Nayar and Newar. *Contributions to Indian Sociology* 7:77–98.
———. 1966. Marriage in India: The present state of the question. Part 3: North India in relation to South India. *Contributions to Indian Sociology* 9:90–114.
———. 1970. *Homo hierarchicus: An essay on the caste system*. Trans. Mark Sainsbury. Chicago: University of Chicago Press.
Dumont, Louis, and David Pocock. 1957. Village studies. *Contributions to Indian Sociology* 1:23–41.
———. 1958. A. M. Hocart on caste—Religion and power. *Contributions to Indian Sociology* 2:45–63.
Elliot, Henry M. 1869. *Memoirs on the history, folk-lore, and distribution of the races of the north western provinces of India*, 2 vols, ed. J. Beames. London: Trübner.
Fox, Richard G. 1971. *Kin, clan, raja, and rule*. Berkeley: University of California Press.
Fuller, C. J. 1977. British India or traditional India? An anthropological problem. *Ethnos* 3–4:95–121.
———. 1984. *Servants of the goddess: The priests of a South Indian temple*. Cambridge: Cambridge University Press.
———. N.d. Misconceiving the grain heap: A critique of the Indian jajmani system. Manuscript.
Fürer-Haimendorf, C. von. 1959. Status differences in a high Hindu caste of Nepal. *Eastern Anthropologist* 12:223–33.
Gold, Ann Grodzins. 1984. Life aims and fruitful journeys: The ways of Rajasthani pilgrims. Ph.D. dissertation, University of Chicago.
Gonda, J. 1965. Gifts. In *Change and continuity in Indian religion*, 198–228. The Hague: Mouton.
Good, Anthony. 1982. The actor and the act: Categories of prestation in South India. *Man*, n.s. 17:23–41.
Harper, Edward. 1959. Two systems of economic exchange in village India. *American Anthropologist* 61:760–78.
Heesterman, J. C. 1957. *The ancient Indian royal consecration*. The Hague: Mouton.
———. 1959. Reflections on the significance of the *dakṣiṇā*. *Indo-Iranian Journal* 3:241–58.
———. 1964. Brahmin, ritual, and renouncer. *Wiener Zeitschrift für die Kunde Süd-und Ostasiens* 8:1–31.
———. 1985. *The inner conflict of tradition: Essays in Indian ritual, kingship, and society*. Chicago: University of Chicago Press.
Hiebert, Paul. 1971. *Konduru: Structure and integration in a South Indian village*. Minneapolis: University of Minnesota Press.

Hitchcock, John T. 1959. The idea of the martial Rajput. In *Traditional India: Structure and change,* ed. Milton Singer, 10–17. Philadelphia: American Folklore Society.

Hocart, A. M. [1936] 1950. *Caste: A comparative study.* London: Methuen.

———.[1938] 1970. *Kings and councillors.* Chicago: University of Chicago Press.

Hubert, Henri, and Marcel Mauss. 1964. *Sacrifice: Its nature and function.* Chicago: University of Chicago Press.

Inden, Ronald B. 1976. *Marriage and rank in Bengali culture.* Berkeley: University of California Press.

———. 1978. Ritual, authority, and cyclic time in Hindu kingship. In *Kingship and authority in South Asia,* ed. J. F. Richards, 28–73. South Asian Studies Publication Series. Madison: University of Wisconsin.

———. 1982. Hierarchies of kings in medieval India. In *Way of life: King, householder, renouncer,* ed. T. N. Madan, 99–125. Delhi: Vikas.

Inden, Ronald, and Ralph W. Nicholas. 1977. *Kinship in Bengali culture.* Chicago: University of Chicago Press.

Ishwaran, K. 1966. *Tradition and economy in village India.* London: Routledge and Kegan Paul.

Kane, Pandurang Vaman. 1974. *History of Dharmaśāstra.* 2d ed. Poona: Bhandarkar Oriental Research Institute.

Karve, Irawati, 1968. *Kinship organization in India.* Bombay: Asia Publishing House.

Kaushik, Meena. 1976. The symbolic representation of death. *Contributions to Indian Sociology,* n.s. 10 : 268–92.

Kemper, Steven. 1979. Sinhalese astrology, South Asian caste systems, and the notion of individuality. *Journal of Asian Studies* 38 : 477–97.

Kessinger, Thomas. 1974. *Vilyatpur 1848–1968: Social and economic change in a North Indian village.* Berkeley: University of California Press.

Khare, R. S. 1960. The Kanya-Kubja Brahmans and their caste organization. *Southwestern Journal of Anthropology* 16 : 348–67.

———. 1972. Hierarchy and hypergamy: Some interrelated aspects among the Kanya-Kubja Brahmans. *American Anthropologist* 74 : 611–28.

———. 1976. *Hindu hearth and home.* Delhi: Vikas.

Knipe, David. 1977. *Sapiṇḍikaraṇa:* The Hindu rite of entry into heaven. In *Religious encounters with death,* ed. Frank E. Reynolds and Earle H. Waugh, 11–24. University Park: Pennsylvania State University Press.

Kolenda, Pauline M. 1963. Toward a model of the Hindu *jajmani* system. *Human Organization* 22 : 11–31.

Madan, T. N. 1985. Concerning the categories *śubha* and *śuddha* in

Hindu culture: An exploratory essay. In *Purity and auspiciousness in Indian society,* ed. Frédérique Marglin and John Carman, 11–29. Leiden: E. J. Brill.

Majumdar, D. N. 1958. *Caste and communication in an Indian village.* Bombay: Asia Publishing House.

Malamoud, Charles. 1976. Terminer le sacrifice. In *Le sacrifice dans l'Inde Ancienne,* ed. Madeleine Biardeau and Charles Malamoud, 155–204. Paris: Presses Universitaires de France.

Mandelbaum, David. 1966. Transcendental and pragmatic aspects of religion. *American Anthropologist* 68 : 1174–91.

Manu. [1886] 1969. *The laws of Manu.* Trans. Georg Buhler. Sacred Books of the East 25. New York: Dover Books.

———. 1976. *Manusmṛti* [Sanskrit and Hindi text]. Ed. Caman Lal Gautam. Bareilly, Uttar Pradesh: Lokhit Sansthān.

Marglin, Frédérique Apffel. 1985a. *Wives of the god-king: The rituals of the Devadasis of Puri.* Delhi: Oxford University Press.

———. 1985b. Types of oppositions in Hindu culture. In *Purity and auspiciousness in Indian society,* ed. F. A. Marglin and John Carman, 65–83. Leiden: E. J. Brill.

Marriott, McKim. 1955. Little communities in an indigenous civilization. In *Village India,* ed. McKim Marriott, 171–222. Chicago: University of Chicago Press.

———. 1959. Interactional and attributional theories of caste rank. *Man in India* 39 : 92–107.

———. 1965. *Caste ranking and community structure in five regions of India and Pakistan.* 2d reprint ed. Poona: Deccan College Post-Graduate and Research Institute.

———. 1968. Caste ranking and food transactions: A matrix analysis. In *Structure and change in Indian society,* ed. Milton Singer and Bernard S. Cohn, 133–71. Chicago: Aldine.

———. 1976. Hindu transactions: Diversity without dualism. In *Transaction and meaning,* ed. Bruce Kapferer, 109–42. Philadelphia: Institute for the Study of Human Issues.

———. 1982. Terminating Indian impurity. Manuscript.

Marriott, McKim, and Ronald B. Inden. 1974. Caste systems. Encyclopedia Britannica, 15th ed., 3 : 982–91.

———. 1977. Toward an ethnosociology of South Asian caste systems. In *The new wind,* ed. Kenneth David, 227–38. The Hague: Mouton.

Mauss, Marcel. [1925] 1967. *The gift.* Trans. Ian Cunnison, New York: W. W. Norton and Company.

Mehta, Ved. 1979. *Mamaji.* New York: Oxford University Press.

Moffatt, Michael. 1979. *An Untouchable community in South India: Structure and consensus.* Princeton: Princeton University Press.

Neale, W. C. 1957. Reciprocity and redistribution in the Indian village: A sequel to some notable discussions. In *Trade and market in the early empires,* ed. K. Polanyi, C. M. Arensberg, and H. W. Pearson, 218–36. Glencoe: Free Press.

Nevill, H. R. 1921. *Saharanpur, a gazetteer.* Vol. 2 of *The District Gazetteers of the United Provinces of Agra and Oudh.* Lucknow: Superintendent of the Government Press, United Provinces.

Nichter, Mark. 1979. The language of illness in South Kanara (India). *Anthropos* 74 : 181–201.

O'Flaherty, Wendy Doniger. 1976. *The origins of evil in Hindu mythology.* Berkeley: University of California Press.

———. 1981. *The Rigveda: An anthology.* Harmondsworth: Penguin.

Orenstein, Henry. 1962. Exploitation and function in the interpretation of *jajmani. Southwestern Journal of Anthropology* 18 : 302–15.

Östör, Ákos. 1980. *The play of the gods: Locality, ideology, structure, and time in the festivals of a Bengali town.* Chicago: University of Chicago Press.

Parry, Jonathan P. 1979. *Caste and kinship in Kangra.* London: Routledge and Kegan Paul.

———. 1980. Ghosts, greed, and sin: The occupational identity of the Benares funeral priests. *Man,* n.s. 15 : 88–111.

Pfaffenberger, Bryan. 1982. *Caste in Tamil culture: The religious foundations of Sudra domination in Tamil Sri Lanka.* Foreign and Comparative Studies, South Asian Series 7. Syracuse: Maxwell School of Citizenship and Public Affairs, Syracuse University.

Pocock, David F. 1962. Notes on *jajmani* relationships. *Contributions to Indian Sociology* 6 : 78–95.

———. 1972. *Kanbi and Patidar: A study of the Patidar community of Gujarat.* London: Oxford University Press.

Prasad, Kalika, Rajvallabh Sahay, and Mukundilal Srivastav, eds. N.d. *Bṛhat Hindī Koṣ.* Varanasi: Jnanamandal Limited.

Pugh, Judy. 1983. Into the almanac: Time, meaning, and action in North Indian society. *Contributions to Indian Sociology,* n.s. 17 : 27–49.

Raheja, Gloria G. 1976. Transformational processes in Hindu ritual: Concepts of "person" and "action" in the performance of a *vrat.* A. M. thesis, University of Chicago.

———. 1985. Kinship, caste, and auspiciousness in Pahansu. Ph.D. dissertation, Department of Anthropology, University of Chicago.

Ramanujan, A. K., trans. 1981. *Hymns for the drowning: Poems for Viṣṇu by Nammālvār.* Princeton: Princeton University Press.

Report of the settlement of Saharunpore. 1870. Allahabad: North-West Provinces Government Press.

Reynolds, Holly Baker. 1980. The auspicious married woman. In *The powers of Tamil women,* ed. Susan S. Wadley, 35–60. Foreign and Comparative Studies, South Asian Series 6. Syracuse: Maxwell School of Citizenship and Public Affairs, Syracuse University.

Schwartzberg, Joseph E. 1968. Caste regions of the North Indian plain. In *Structure and change in Indian society,* ed. Milton Singer and Bernard S. Cohn, 81–113. Philadelphia: American Folklore Society.

Shah, A. M., and R. G. Shroff. 1959. The Vahīvancā Bārots of Gujarat: A caste of genealogists. In *Traditional India: Structure and change,* ed. Milton Singer, 40–70. Philadelphia: American Folklore Society.

Shulman, David. 1985. Kingship and prestation in South Indian myth and epic. *Asian and African Studies* 19 : 93–117.

Siddiqi, Asiya. 1973. *Agrarian change in a Northern Indian state: Uttar Pradesh, 1819–1833.* London: Oxford University Press.

Silverstein, Michael. 1976. Shifters, linguistic categories, and cultural description. In *Meaning in anthropology,* ed. Keith H. Basso and Henry A. Selby, 11–55. Albuquerque: University of New Mexico Press.

Srinivas, M. N. 1952. *Religion and society among the Coorgs of South India.* Oxford: Clarendon.

———. 1955. The social system of a Mysore village. In *Village India,* ed. McKim Marriott, 1–35. Chicago: University of Chicago Press.

———. 1959. The dominant caste in Rampura. *American Anthropologist* 61 : 1–16.

Stanley, John M. 1977. Special time, special power: The fluidity of power in a popular Hindu festival. *Journal of Asian Studies* 37 : 27–43.

———. 1978. Hanuman wrestles on Saturday: An examination of the conceptualization of the special power of certain days. Paper presented at the Eightieth Annual Meeting of the American Anthropological Association, Los Angeles.

Stern, Henri. 1977. Power in traditional India: Territory, caste, and kinship in Rajasthan. In *Realm and region in traditional India,* ed. Richard G. Fox, 52–78. Delhi: Vikas.

Stevenson, H. N. C. 1954. Status evaluation in the Hindu caste system. *Journal of the Royal Anthropological Institute* 84 : 45–65.

Stokes, Eric. 1978. *The peasant and the Raj: Studies in agrarian society and peasant rebellion in colonial India.* Cambridge: Cambridge University Press.

Stone, Ian. 1984. *Canal irrigation in British India: Perspectives on technological change in a peasant economy.* Cambridge: Cambridge University Press.

Tambiah, S. J. 1973. Dowry and bridewealth and the property rights of women in South Asia. In *Bridewealth and dowry,* Jack Goody and S. J. Tambiah, 59–169. Cambridge Papers in Social Anthropology 7. Cambridge: Cambridge University Press.

Temple, R. C. 1884–1900. *Legends of the Panjab.* 3 vols. Bombay: Education Society Press.

Trautmann, Thomas R. 1981. *Dravidian kinship.* Cambridge: Cambridge University Press.

van Buitenen, J. A. B., trans. 1978. *The Mahābhārata.* Vol. 3. Chicago: University of Chicago Press.

Varma, Ramacandra. 1971. *Sankṣipt Hindī Śabdsāgar.* Kashi: Nagari Pracarini Sabha.

Varma, Ratanlal. 1971. *Gūjar Vīr-Gāthā* [The saga of the heroic deeds of Gujars]. Delhi: Akhil Bhāratīya Gūjar Samāj Sudhār Sabhā.

Vatuk, Sylvia J. 1969. A structural analysis of the Hindi kinship terminology. *Contributions to Indian Sociology,* n.s. 3 : 94–115.

———. 1971. Trends in North Indian urban kinship: The "matrilateral asymmetry" hypothesis. *Southwestern Journal of Anthropology* 27 : 287–307.

———. 1975. Gifts and affines in North India. *Contributions to Indian Sociology,* n.s. 9 : 155–96.

Vatuk, Ved Prakash, and Sylvia Vatuk. 1976. The social context of gift exchange in North India. In *Family and social change in modern India,* ed. Giriraj Gupta, 207–32. Main Currents in Indian Sociology, vol. 2. Delhi: Vikas.

Wadley, Susan S. 1975. *Shakti: Power in the conceptual structure of Karimpur religion.* Chicago: University of Chicago Studies in Anthropology, Series in Social, Cultural, and Linguistic Anthropology 2.

———. 1976. Brothers, husbands, and sometimes sons: Kinsmen in North Indian ritual. *Eastern Anthropologist* 29 : 149–70.

Whitcombe, Elizabeth. 1972. *Agrarian conditions in Northern India. 1: The United Provinces under British rule, 1860–1900.* Berkeley: University of California Press.

Whitehead, Henry. 1921. *The village gods of South India.* Calcutta: Association Press.

Wiser, William. 1936. *The Hindu jajmani system.* Lucknow: Lucknow Publishing House.

Wittgenstein, Ludwig. 1958a. *The blue and the brown books.* New York: Harper and Row.

———. 1958b. *Philosophical investigations.* 3d ed. Trans. G. E. M. Anscombe. New York: Macmillan.

Zimmermann, Francis. 1980. *Ṛtu-sātmya:* The seasonal cycle and the principle of appropriateness. *Social Science and Medicine* 14B:99–106.

INDEX

Abbott, J., 33
Abuse for niggardly gift-giving, 230
Affinal prestations. See *Dhiyānī / dhiyānā,* acceptance of *dān* by; Marriage ritual; *Martak*
Aggarwal, P. C., 257 n.13
Agriculture: crops in, 17, 18, 34; Gujar valuation of, 23–37; irrigation in, 3–4, 14, 16; labor arrangements in, 18, 204–12, 265 n.1. *See also* Landholding, tenurial patterns of
Ain-i-Akbari, 1
Amāvas, and the giving of *dān,* 49, 173–74
Ancestral deities (*dev-pitars*), 101–2, 117, 124, 126, 127–28, 138, 141–42, 147, 156–62, 165–66
Appadurai, A., 68
Astrology: auspicious and inauspicious times in, 38–42; horoscopic calculations in, 50–52, 58, 66, 102, 108–9, 125–26, 187; housebuilding and, 54–56, 169–70; planets in, 50–52, 65–67, 72, 80–82, 125, 187, 260 n.9, 262 nn.10,12, 263 nn.13,14; place in, 52–56. See also *Dān,* planets in; *Diśaśūl; Mūl śānti, Pancak;* Planets, *varṇa* classification of
Āṭā-sāṭā (reversal of directionality in marriage), 120
Atharva Veda, 263 n.15
Atkinson, E. T., 3, 255 n.3, 256 n.8, 263 n.16
Auspiciousness and inauspiciousness, linguistic usages, 37–38, 42–45, 47, 52, 258 n.1. *See also* Inauspiciousness
Ayurvedic medicine. *See* Humoral theory

Babb, L. A., 68, 71
Baden-Powell, B. H., 255 n.5
Badhāvā ritual, 117–18, 174
Bāhar rukāī, 214
Bān ritual, 124–25, 127–28, 263 nn.17,18
Bangle-seller caste, 19, 206, 215
Baniya (merchant) caste, 3, 5, 12, 17, 206–7, 256 n.7
Bār dwārī, 132–33, 152
Barāt lena (reception of groom at wedding ritual), 132
Barber caste, acceptance of *dān* by, 28, 30, 91–92, 121, 202, 245, 248, 252, 257 n.14; at death rituals, 148, 156; at harvests, 164–65; at *mūl śānti* ritual, 106; and reluctance to accept, 245–46; in Sanscrit texts, 188; at weddings, 122–23, 124–30, 133–34, 138, 144, 146, 147
Barber caste, ritual services of, 30; at Bhūmiyā ritual, 20; at birth, 214; at *mūl śanti* ritual, 105; at death ritual, 149–50, 156; at wedding ritual, 121–23, 124–30
Barī-mātā (smallpox goddess), 116
Barsī ritual, 156–57
Bayanā prestation, 172, 178–85
Beck, B. E. F., 45
Beidelman, T. O., 24–25
Bemātā goddess, 96–97
Ghaīacārā land tenure. *See* Landholding, tenurial patterns of
Bhāīyā dauj ritual, 175–78, 185
Bhakti, 83–84, 260 n.4, 261–62 n.10

Bhalwāī kā din, 125–26, 138–39, 264 n.23
Bhāṭ (genealogist), 8, 22–23, 256 nn.6,7
Bhāt (prestation made by mother's brother at wedding), 129–31, 144, 156, 245, 263 n.20
Bhūmiyā (protector deity of the village site), 20, 22, 96, 117, 166, 174, 186–87
Bhūt-pret (ghost), ritual for, 59–64, 127, 146, 147, 150, 159–62
Bidā (departure of bride for husband's village), 145–46, 158
Bidāgī prestation, 214
Birth impurity (*sūtak*), 94, 262 n.3. *See also* Purity and impurity
Birth ritual (*chaṭṭhī*), 21, 96–99, 206, 262 n.3
Bloomfield, M., 263 n.15
Blunt, E. A. H., 119, 239, 241
Brahman caste
—acceptance of *dān* by, 20, 21, 22, 28, 32, 34–36, 84, 91, 118, 188, 248–254, 257 n.14, 261 n.17; at *badhāvā* ritual, 174; at *bhāīyā dauj* ritual, 177–78; at Bhūmiyā ritual, 20, 174, 186; at birth ritual, 94, 100; at death rituals, 151–155, 158, 160, 218, 264 n.31; at harvest ritual, 19–20, 162–66; at Hoi ritual, 181; at *holī* ritual, 174; at marriage ritual, 123–24, 126, 128, 133, 134, 136–39, 142, 147; at *mūl śanti* ritual, 105–7; at *pāṭh* ritual, 219; at planetary ritual, 110, 112; at protective ritual for smallpox goddess, 116; at *rakṣā bandhan* ritual, 257 n.13; in *vrat* ritual, 72, 75
—distinctive ritual practices of, 143–45, 154, 166–67, 256 n.7, 261 n.17
—equivalent to *Kamīn* castes as recipient of *dān,* 32, 34, 118, 121, 138, 147, 153–54, 165–66, 188, 202, 248, 252–53
—internal organization of, 119–120
—landholding by, 3, 17, 28–29, 164
—ritual services of, 25, 29, 248–54, 258 n.2; at Bhūmiyā ritual, 20; at death rituals, 149, 151–56, 159–60, 218, 264 n.31; at marriage ritual, 85, 121–22, 124, 126, 127, 132–33, 136–37, 143, 217, 245, 246–47; at *mūl śānti* ritual, 103–7; at *pāṭh* ritual, 63–64, 186–87, 219; at planetary ritual, 111–13
Breckenridge, C., 68
Bṛhaspati *vrat,* 72–75
Briggs, G., 33

Cālā, 100, 139–43
Calendrical cycle, 56–58, 172–85
Camār (leather worker) caste, ritual services of and acceptance of *dān* by, 167, 174
Candan chaṭh vrat, 75–82
Cāng lagānā (ritual for harvest prestations), 163–64
Caṛhāpā, ritual functions of, 69–70, 83–84, 161, 259–60 n.2, 260 nn.3, 4, 5, 261 n.10
Carpenter caste, 19, 205
Carter, A., 31
Caste
—attributional theories of, 239
—central-peripheral configurations of, xi, 25, 28–33, 121, 146, 147, 187, 233–35, 242–47, 248–49, 253–54, 267 n.14, 269 n.5; in relation to landholding, 5, 12–14, 28–29
—hierarchical configurations of, xi, 26–35, 45, 69, 147, 188, 239–43, 245, 250–51, 258 n.19, 266–67 n.14, 267–68 n.15, 268 n.4, 269 n.5; regional variation in, 242–43
—kinship and, 29–31, 121, 212–13, 216, 234, 243, 257 n.16. *See also* Gujar caste, hierarchy in affinal relations; Marriage and hierarchy
—mutuality in, xi, 203–204, 207, 212, 233–35, 243, 266–67 n.14
—sacrificial basis of, 25, 248–54
—terminological usages in, 216, 233–35, 240–41, 243
Chāyā kā dān ("*dān* of the reflection"), 90–91, 112–14, 138
Chetri caste, 153
Churning (as ritual procedure), 87, 146, 262 n.11

Mantras (Sanskrit verses used in ritual), 59, 105–6, 111, 136–37, 138, 154, 157, 186, 187
Manu, Laws of, xi, xii, 250
Marglin, F. A., 258 n.20, 268 n.1
Marriage: and astrological considerations, 40–41, 122; and hierarchy, 118–21, 152–55 (*see also* Caste, and kinship; Gujar caste, hierarchy and affinal relations in); as *kanyā dān,* 119, 120, 121, 134–35; *mol lānā* form of, 120, 235–36, 266 n.13; reversal of directionality in, 120
Marriage ritual, 118–47; and inauspiciousness, 58, 263 n.22
Marriott, McKim, xi, 27, 28–29, 30, 45, 46, 68, 84, 120, 239–42
Martak (*dān* given at death), 151–56
Mātā (goddess). *See Baṛī-mātā; Gāmkheṛī mātā* goddess
Mauss, M., 249–51, 253–54, 268 n.2
Media of transactions, 45, 239–43, 267–68 n.15
Mehta, V., 183–84
Milāī, 222–27, 267 n.14
Mīnasnā, 88, 151, 157, 159, 261 n.12
Moffatt, M., 31
Mol lānā ("taking for a price"): as form of marriage, 120, 235–36, 266 n.13; in *tīkun* ritual, 102, 235
Mother's brother (as giver of *dān*), 115, 129–31, 155–56
Mūl śānti ritual, 102–7, 113–14, 125, 149, 262 nn.6,7,9
Mūñh dikhāī prestation, 214
Mutiny of 1857, Gujar role in, 225 n.3
Mutuality. *See* Caste, mutuality in; Kinship, mutuality in

Nackār (ritual procedure), 88–89, 182–83
Naurātrī, 57
Neale, W., 13
Neg (payment for ritual services), 95, 146, 212–18, 221, 265 n.6
Nepal, marriage in, 153
Nevill, H. R., 3, 4
Nicholas, R., 30, 31, 118, 161
Nichter, M., 259 n.4
Nyautā prestation, 219–22, 226

O'Flaherty, W., 33, 57, 260 n.6, 262 n.11, 263 nn.21,22
Oil-presser (Telī) caste, 19
Orenstein, H., 24–25
Östör, A., 69

Padha caste, 202
Pahansu: distinctive demographic structure of, 5, 28–29; history of, 8–9; landholding in, 17, 28–29; land transferrals in, 5, 11–13; occupations in, 18–19; physical description of, 14–17; population of, 17–19
Pair pūjā ritual, 148, 183
Pakkā foods. *See* Media of transactions
Pancak: inauspiciousness of, 39–40, 107; ritual at death, 149, 265 n.35
Pancāyat (village council), 11, 12
Parosā prestation, 222, 226
Parry, J., 26, 31, 34, 35, 188, 257 n.14, 258 n.19, 266 n.11
Pāṭh ritual, 63–64, 186–87, 219
Paṭṭā (ritual for bestowal of *dahej* at wedding ritual), 139–41, 143–44, 264,n.24
Paṭṭdārī tenure. *See* Landholding, tenurial patterns of
Pāyatā ritual, 166–67, 179
Pfaffenberger, B., 36, 258 n.21, 268 n.1
Pharai caste, 201
Phaslānā. See Harvest prestations, *phaslānā*
Pherā (central rite of wedding), 58–59, 121, 135–39
Planets, *varṇā* classification of, 108–9. *See also* Astrology, planets in; *Dān,* and planets
Pocock, D., 26, 163, 258 n.19, 266–67 n.14, 269 n.5
Potter (Kumhār) caste, 19, 204; acceptance of *dān* by, 174, 252–53; ritual services of, 20, 214
Prasād, 28, 68–70, 84, 180, 260 n.4
Pregnancy, rituals during, 93–94
Pugh, J., 57, 259 n.8
Pūj, 130, 133, 152–54, 158
Pūjā, 68–69
Pujāpā: in calendrical festivals, 172–74; ritual functions of, 69–70